W. S. Ford.

9/26/24.

See Dewey - How we think
Chapt. VI.

Willard S Ford.

SOURCE BOOK IN THE
PHILOSOPHY OF EDUCATION

TEXT-BOOK SERIES

Edited by PAUL MONROE, Ph.D.

TEXT-BOOK IN THE HISTORY OF EDUCATION.
By Paul Monroe, Ph.D., Professor of History of Education, Teachers College, Columbia University.

SOURCE BOOK IN THE HISTORY OF EDUCATION.
For the Greek and Roman Period.
By Paul Monroe, Ph.D.

PRINCIPLES OF SECONDARY EDUCATION.
By Paul Monroe, Ph.D.

TEXT-BOOK IN THE PRINCIPLES OF EDUCATION.
By Ernest R. Henderson, Ph.D., Professor of Education and and Philosophy, Adelphi College.

DEMOCRACY AND EDUCATION. An Introduction to the Philosophy of Education.
By John Dewey, Ph.D., Professor of Philosophy, Columbia University.

STATE AND COUNTY SCHOOL ADMINISTRATION.
Source Book.
By Ellwood P. Cubberley, Ph.D., Professor of Education, Stanford University, and Edward C. Elliott, Ph.D., Professor of Education, University of Wisconsin.

STATE AND COUNTY EDUCATIONAL REORGANIZATION.
By Ellwood P. Cubberley, Ph.D.

THE PRINCIPLES OF SCIENCE TEACHING.
By George R. Twiss, B.Sc., Professor of the Principles and Practice of Education, Ohio State University.

THE PRUSSIAN ELEMENTARY SCHOOLS.
By Thomas Alexander, Ph.D., Professor of Elementary Education, George Peabody College for Teachers.

HOW TO MEASURE IN EDUCATION.
By William A. McCall, Ph.D., Assistant Professor of Education, Teachers College, Columbia University.

A HISTORY OF THE FAMILY AS A SOCIAL AND EDUCATIONAL INSTITUTION.
By Willystine Goodsell, Ph.D., Assistant Professor of Education, Teachers College, Columbia University.

THE EDUCATION OF WOMEN.
By Willystine Goodsell, Ph.D.

STATISTICAL METHOD.
By Truman L. Kelley, Ph.D., Professor of Education, Stanford University.

SOURCE BOOK IN THE PHILOSOPHY OF EDUCATION.
By William H. Kilpatrick, Ph.D., Professor of Education, Teachers College, Columbia University.

A HISTORY OF EDUCATION IN THE UNITED STATES.
By Paul Monroe, Ph.D. *In preparation.*

SOURCE BOOK IN THE PHILOSOPHY OF EDUCATION

BY
WILLIAM HEARD KILPATRICK
PROFESSOR OF EDUCATION, TEACHERS COLLEGE
COLUMBIA UNIVERSITY

New York
THE MACMILLAN COMPANY
1924

All rights reserved

PRINTED IN THE UNITED STATES OF AMERICA

COPYRIGHT, 1923,
BY THE MACMILLAN COMPANY.

Set up and electrotyped. Published September, 1923.

Reprinted .... January, 1924

Press of
J. J. Little & Ives Company
New York, U. S. A.

PREFACE

THIS book has grown up in connection with the compiler's classes, especially with his principal course in the philosophy of education. With this origin its chief function has been to supplement otherwise available reading resources, especially by rendering many short and inaccessible references easy of access. While many topics have thus been treated with perhaps satisfactory fullness, others will call for additional reading in the easily accessible books treating of educational and social theory. The author's Syllabus in the Philosophy of Education (Teachers College Bureau of Publications) will furnish specific references to such additional material as is used by the author with his classes.

As is to be expected from a book so made, the quotations here presented furnish definite material in the philosophy of education for studying the topics discussed in the author's classes especially from the point of view held by the author. But the selection of quotations is by no means limited to this point of view. On the contrary care has been taken to present all sorts of opposed views and positions, the chief criteria for inclusion being pertinence and clearness with brevity of statement. The beginner in the subject is accordingly warned to be on his guard and think before he accepts. Indeed a primary intent has been that the student be forced to think in order to accept.

For courteous permission to use material the compiler hereby expresses his grateful appreciation not only to the several owners of the copyrights giving such permission, but also to many others of whom it was not legally necessary to get this permission. The chief indebtedness here is to Professor John Dewey. The asterisk (*) found in the body of the work in connection with the source of any selection is used to indicate copyright material for which the owner of the copyright has given permission of reproduction. Specific reference to author and publisher is given not only in connection with each selection quoted, but also in an author index of sources to be found at the close of the book (pp. 341-349).

Pains have been taken to refer every quotation to its original source and to locate it there precisely either by edition and page or otherwise as is expected in such matters. In a few instances the effort to do this has failed. For any help that the reader may give either in locating sources or by indicating any sort of errors, the author will be grateful.

For most valuable assistance especially in the arduous tasks of locating references and otherwise preparing the manuscript for the press the author is deeply indebted to his very capable assistant, Miss Marion Y. Ostrander.

W. H. K.

August, 1923.

CONTENTS

CHAPTER		PAGE
I	THE MEANING AND BEARING OF THE PHILOSOPHY OF EDUCATION	1
II	THE CONCEPT OF EXPERIENCE	19
III	THE SOCIAL INHERITANCE	31
IV	THE NATURE OF SOCIETY	37
V	SOCIALIZATION	46
VI	THE NATURE OF THE INDIVIDUAL	54
VII	ACTIVITY LEADING TO FURTHER ACTIVITY	74
VIII	WHAT CONSTITUTES THE GOOD LIFE	84
IX	THE INDIVIDUAL AND SOCIETY	99
X	DEMOCRACY	113
XI	DEMOCRACY AND EDUCATION	137
XII	SOCIAL CONTROL	174
XIII	THE MOBILIZATION OF THOUGHT POWER	185
XIV	PROGRESS	209
XV	EDUCATION AND SOCIAL PROGRESS	233
XVI	SOCIAL STABILITY IN A DYNAMIC SOCIETY	244
XVII	THE STATE AND EDUCATION	260
XVIII	HOW SHALL WE CONCEIVE EDUCATION	270
XIX	THE EDUCATIVE PROCESS: SUBJECT MATTER AND THE CURRICULUM	279
XX	THE EDUCATIVE PROCESS: THE PROBLEM OF METHOD	298

CHAPTER		PAGE
XXI	THINKING	322
XXII	MORAL EDUCATION	329
INDEX OF SOURCES		341
INDEX OF SUBJECTS		351

SOURCE BOOK IN THE
PHILOSOPHY OF EDUCATION

SOURCE BOOK IN THE PHILOSOPHY OF EDUCATION

CHAPTER I

THE MEANING AND BEARING OF THE PHILOSOPHY OF EDUCATION

1. Dewey on the Meaning of Philosophy

"What philosophy has been unconsciously, without knowing it or intending it, and, so to speak, under cover, it must henceforth be openly and deliberately. When it is acknowledged that under disguise of dealing with ultimate reality, philosophy has been occupied with the precious values embedded in social traditions, that it has sprung from a clash of social ends and from a conflict of inherited institutions with incompatible contemporary tendencies, it will be seen that the task of future philosophy is to clarify men's ideas as to the social and moral strifes of their own day. Its aim is to become so far as is humanly possible an organ for dealing with these conflicts. That which may be pretentiously unreal when it is formulated in metaphysical distinctions becomes intensely significant when connected with the drama of the struggle of social beliefs and ideals. Philosophy which surrenders its somewhat barren monopoly of dealings with Ultimate and Absolute Reality will find a compensation in enlightening the moral forces which move mankind and in contributing to the aspirations of men to attain to a more ordered and intelligent happiness."

Dewey, *Reconstruction in Philosophy* * (New York, Holt, 1920), p. 26 f.

2. James on the Meaning of Philosophy

"In the preface to that admirable collection of essays of his called 'Heretics,' Mr. Chesterton writes these words: 'There are some people—and I am one of them—who think that the most practical and important thing about a man is still his view of the universe. We think that for a landlady considering a lodger it is important to know his income, but still more important to know his philosophy. We think that for a general about to fight an enemy it is important to know the enemy's numbers, but still more important to know the enemy's philosophy. We think the question is not whether the theory of the cosmos affects matters, but whether in the long run anything else affects them.'

"I think with Mr. Chesterton in this matter. I know that you, ladies and gentlemen, have a philosophy, each and all of you, and that the most interesting and important thing about you is the way in which it determines the perspective in your several worlds. You know the same of me. . . . The philosophy which is so important in each of us is not a technical matter; it is our more or less dumb sense of what life honestly and deeply means. It is only partly got from books; it is our individual way of just seeing and feeling the total push and pressure of the cosmos."

James, *Pragmatism* * (New York, Longmans, 1907), p. 3 f.

3. PAULSEN ON THE MEANING OF PHILOSOPHY

"The intellectual life of man is distinguished from that of the brute by his capacity to theorize and his ability to see things in their relation to the whole. The lower animal sees and hears, and, most likely, has ideas and recollections, but it does not reflect in them. They come and go as isolated facts in the natural course of events. They are significant only as motives for the will. In man, intellectual activity emancipates itself from necessity. Theoretical interest is aroused. He gathers and examines the elements supplied by perception; he does not rest until he has combined them into a systematic conception of the whole. Practice and technics are satisfied with a knowledge of details; theoretical interest is directed towards the whole. In this way philosophy arises. In the most general sense of the term, philosophy is simply the continually-repeated attempt to arrive at a comprehensive and systematic knowledge of the form and connection, the meaning and import of all things.

"It is apparent that in this sense every nation and every man, at least every normally-developed man, has a philosophy. The plain man of the people, too, has a philosophy. His catechism may have supplied him with the fundamental ideas of the same. He gives an answer to the questions regarding the origin and destiny of the world and man. In this sense peoples living in a state of nature have their philosophy also. Thus the Indian and the New Zealander formed a conception of the universe and its spatial structure. They had an answer to the question concerning the Whence and the Whither of things, and saw a rational connection between cosmic occurrences and human life. In this interpretation, therefore, philosophy is a universal human function. Philosophy is coextensive with mental life."

Paulsen, *Introduction to Philosophy* * (Trans. by Thilly. New York, Holt, 1895), p. 2 f.

4. Dewey on the Meaning of Truth

"If ideas, meanings, conceptions, notions, theories, systems are instrumental to an active reorganization of the given environment, to a removal of some specific trouble and perplexity, then the test of their validity and value lies in accomplishing this work. If they succeed in their office, they are reliable, sound, valid, good, true. If they fail to clear up confusion, to eliminate defects, if they increase confusion, uncertainty and evil when they are acted upon, then are they false. Confirmation, corroboration, verification lie in works, consequences. Handsome is that handsome does. By their fruits shall ye *know* them. That which guides us truly is true—demonstrated capacity for such guidance is precisely what is meant by truth. The adverb 'truly' is more fundamental than either the adjective, true, or the noun, truth. An adverb expresses a way, a mode of acting. Now an idea or conception is a claim or injunction or plan to *act* in a certain way as the way to arrive at the clearing up of a specific situation. When the claim or pretension or plan is acted upon *it guides us truly or falsely;* it leads us to our end or away from it. Its active, dynamic function is the all-important thing about it, and in the quality of activity induced by it lies all its truth and falsity. The hypothesis that works is the *true* one; and *truth* is an abstract noun applied to the collection of cases, actual, foreseen and desired, that receive confirmation in their works and consequences. . . .

"A society that chiefly esteems order, that finds growth painful and change disturbing, inevitably seeks for a fixed body of superior truths upon which it may depend. It looks backward, to something already in existence, for the source and sanction of truth. It falls back upon what is antecedent, prior, original, *a priori,* for assurance. The thought of looking ahead, toward the eventual, toward consequences, creates uneasiness and fear. It disturbs the sense of rest that is attached to the ideas of fixed Truth already in existence. It puts a heavy burden of responsibility upon us for search, unremitting observation, scrupulous development of hypotheses and thoroughgoing testing. . . . To generalize the recognition that the true means the verified and means nothing else places upon men the responsibility for surrendering political and moral dogmas, and subjecting to the test of consequences their most cherished prejudices. Such a change involves a great change in the seat of authority and the methods of decision in society."

Dewey, *Reconstruction in Philosophy* * (New York, Holt, 1920), pp. 156-7, 159 f.

5. Dewey on the Power of the School

"To an extent characteristic of no other institution, save that of the state itself, the school has power to modify the social order."

Dewey, *Moral Principles in Education* * (Boston, Houghton Mifflin, 1909), p. v.

6. Erasmus on the Power of Education

"Give me for a few years the direction of education and I agree to transform the world."

Morgan, *Educational Mosaics* (Boston, Silver Rogers, 1887), p. 152.

7. Bismarck on the Significance of Training

"The German child when handed over to the teacher is like a blank sheet of paper, and all that is written upon a child during the course of elementary education is written with indelible ink and will last through life. The soul of a child is like wax. Therefore he who directs the school directs the country's future."

8. A Former Religious Attitude Toward Play

". . . All in our College [Cokesbury (M. E.) College, founded 1788] . . . [shall] be kept at the utmost distance as from vice in general, so in particular from softness and effeminacy of manners.

"We shall therefore inflexibly insist on their rising early in the morning . . . this is of vast importance both to body and mind . . .

"On the same principle we prohibit *play* in the strongest terms . . .

"The students shall rise at five o'clock . . . summer and winter. . . . Their recreation shall be gardening, walking, riding, and bathing, without doors, and the carpenter's, joiner's, cabinetmaker's or turner's business within doors. . . . A person skilled in gardening shall be appointed to overlook the students . . . in this recreation. . . . A master . . . shall always be present at the time of bathing. Only one shall bathe at a time; and no one shall remain in the water above a minute. No student shall be allowed to bathe in the river. A *Taberna Lignaria* [carpenter's shop] shall be provided . . . with all proper instruments and materials, and a skillful person . . . to overlook the students at this recreation. . . . The students shall be indulged with nothing which the world calls *play*. Let this rule be observed with the strictest nicety; for those who play when they are young, will play when they are old."

Discipline of the M. E. Church, 1792.

9. VOLTAIRE

"Voltaire (1694-1778) poet, philosopher, historian, critic, was perhaps the most puissant man of letters that ever lived." "When the right sense of historical proportion is more fully developed in men's minds, the name of Voltaire will stand out like the names of the great decisive movements in the European advance, like the Revival of Learning, or the Reformation. The existence, character, and career of this extraordinary person constituted in themselves a new and prodigious era. The peculiarities of his individual genius changed the mind and spiritual conformation of France, and in a less degree of the whole of the West, with as far-spreading and invincible an effect as if the work had been wholly done, as it was actually aided, by the sweep of deep-lying collective forces. A new type of belief, and of its shadow, disbelief, was stamped by the impression of his character and work into the intelligence and feeling of his own and the following times. We may think of Voltairism in France somewhat as we think of Catholicism or the Renaissance or Calvinism. It was one of the cardinal liberations of the growing race, one of the emphatic manifestations of some portion of the minds of men, which an immediately foregoing system and creed had either ignored or outraged. . . .

"The sentimentalist has proclaimed him a mere mocker. To the critic of the schools, ever ready with compendious label, he is the revolutionary destructive. To each alike of the countless orthodox sects his name is the symbol for the prevailing of the gates of hell. Erudition figures him as shallow and a trifler; culture condemns him for pushing his hatred of spiritual falsehood much too seriously; Christian charity feels constrained to unmask a demon from the depths of the pit. . . .

"Yet Voltaire was the very eye of eighteenth-century illumination. It was he who conveyed to his generation in a multitude of forms the consciousness at once of the power and the rights of human intelligence. Another might well have said of him what he magnanimously said of his famous contemporary, Montesquieu, that humanity had lost its title-deeds, and he had recovered them. . . .

"Voltaire was a stupendous power, not only because his expression was incomparably lucid, or even because his sight was exquisitely keen and clear, but because he saw many new things, after which the spirits of others were unconsciously groping and dumbly yearning. Nor was this all. . . . Voltaire was ever in the front and centre of the fight. His life was not a mere chapter in a history of literature. He never counted truth a treasure to be discreetly hidden in a napkin. He made it a perpetual war-cry and emblazoned it on a banner that was many a time rent, but was never out of the field. . . .

"The old-fashioned nomenclature puts him down among sceptics, because those who had the official right to affix these labels could think of no more contemptuous name, and could not suppose the most audacious soul capable of advancing even under the leadership of Satan himself beyond a stray doubt or so." . . . But Voltaire had less of the sceptic in his constitution than some of his most conspicuous opponents. Rather did his strength and power lie just opposite. "Voltaire boldly put the great question, and he boldly answered it. He asked whether the sacred records were historically true, the Christian doctrine divinely inspired and spiritually exhaustive, and the Christian church a holy and beneficent organization. He answered these questions for himself and for others beyond possibility of misconception. The records were saturated with fable and absurdity, the doctrine imperfect at its best, and a dark and tyrannical superstition at its worst, and the church was the arch-curse and infamy. Say what we will of these answers, they were free from any taint of scepticism. . . .

"To Voltaire . . . an irrational prejudice was not the object of a polite coldness, but a real evil to be combated and overthrown at every hazard. Cruelty was not to him as a disagreeable dream of the imagination, from thought of which he could save himself by arousing to sense of his own comfort, but a vivid flame burning into his thoughts and destroying peace. Wrong-doing and injustice were not simple words on his lips; they went as knives to the heart; he suffered with the victim, and consumed with an active rage against the oppressor.

"Nor was the coarse cruelty of the inquisitor or the politician, who wrought iniquity by aid of the arm of flesh, the only kind of injury to the world which stirred his passion. He had imagination enough and intelligence enough to perceive that they are the most pestilent of all the enemies of mankind . . . who take away the keys of knowledge, thrusting truth down to the second place, and discrowning sovereign reason to be the serving drudge of superstition or social usage. . . . To check the energetic discovery and wide propagation of scientific truth, he rightly held to be at least as destructive in the long run to the common weal, as the unjust extermination of human life; for it is the possession of ever more and more truth that makes life ever better worth having and better worth preserving. . . .

"France had outgrown the system that had brought her through the middle ages. The further development of her national life was fatally hindered by the tight bonds of an old order, which clung with the hardy tenacity of a thriving parasite, diverting from the roots all their sustenance, eating into the tissue, and feeding on the juices of the living tree. . . . The whole power and ordering of the nation were with the sworn and chartered foes of light, who had every interest that a desire to cling to authority and wealth can give, in keeping the understanding subject. . . .

"Voltaire's task was . . . preparatory. It was to make popular the genius and authority of reason. The foundations of the social fabric were in such a condition that the touch of reason was fatal to the whole structure, which instantly began to crumble. . . . After the death of Louis XIV, not only the grace and pomp, but also the social utility of spiritual and political absolutism passed obviously away. Spiritual absolutism was unable to maintain even a decent semblance of unity and theological order. Political absolutism by its material costliness, its augmenting tendency to repress the application of individual energy and thought to public concerns, and its pursuit of a policy in Europe which was futile and essentially meaningless as to its ends, and disastrous and incapable in its choice of means, was rapidly exhausting the resources of national well-being and viciously severing the very tap-root of national life. To bring reason into an atmosphere so charged, was, as the old figure goes, to admit air to the chamber of the mummy. And reason was exactly what Voltaire brought; too narrow, if we will, too contentious, too derisive, too unmitigatedly reasonable, but still reason. . . .

"We may well deplore that Voltaire's attack, and every other attack of the same sort, did not take the fair shape prescribed by the apostle to the servant of the Lord, of gentleness, patience, and the instruction of a sweet and firm example. But the partisans of the creed in whose name more human blood has been violently shed than in any other cause whatever, these, I say, can hardly find much ground of serious reproach in a few score epigrams. Voltaire had no calm breadth of wisdom. It may be so. There are moments which need not this calm breadth of wisdom, but a two-edged sword, and when the deliverers of mankind are they who 'come to send fire on the earth.'"

Morley, *Voltaire* * (London, Macmillan, 1906[1]), pp. 1-43 (with slight adaptations).

10. Napoleon on Education

(a) *The Purpose of his Educational System.* "My principal aim in the establishment of a teaching body is to have a means for directing political and moral opinions."
Paroles de Napoléon I au Conseil d'Etat.

(b) *The Control of Education.* "It is impossible, indeed, to remain long in the present state of things, since everyone may now set up a shop for education as he would for broadcloth . . . I feel called upon to organize a system of education for the new generation, such that both political and moral opinions may be duly regulated thereby."
Ross, *Social Control* * (New York, Macmillan, 1915), p. 174.

(c) *Education as a Means of Social Solidarity.* "Of all political questions this [of education] is perhaps of the highest impor-

[1] 1st ed., 1885.

tance. There will be no fixed political State if there is no teaching corps with fixed principles. As long as one will not learn from childhood on if one must be a republican or a monarchist, a Catholic or an atheist, the State will not form a nation."
Correspondance de Napoléon I, No. 8.328.

(d) *On the Press.* "The printing office is an arsenal which must not be within the reach of everybody. It is very important for me that only those be allowed to print, who have the confidence of the government. A man who addresses the public in print, is like a man who speaks in an assembly and certainly no one can dispute the sovereign's right to prevent the first comer from haranguing the public."
Napoleon, cited by Taine, *Modern Régime,* Vol. II, p. 200.

(e) *Military Character of Napoleon's Schools.* "It was impossible for the essentially military character of Napoleon not to be marked in his work. The University, in fact, was organized like a regiment. The discipline was severe; the teachers as well as the pupils were subjected to it. Punishments were not for pupils only; they struck the teachers as well. When a teacher had committed some infraction against a rule and had merited some censure, he was put under arrest. There was a uniform for all the members of the university; it was a black coat with blue palms. The college was in a small way the image of the army. Each establishment was divided into companies, with its sergeants and its corporals. Everything was done to the beating of the drum. They wished to turn out soldiers, not men" (p. 335).

"What Napoleon was interested in, was the training of the possible officers of his army. That this was one of his aims in education can be seen in the rigid military discipline under which the whole educational system was conducted. Everything was done in military fashion. The schools were conducted to the beating of the drum. Military law was observed in the schools. Classes were organized into companies with their captains, lieutenants, sergeants and corporals. A martial spirit pervaded every nook of the school. Military science formed a most important part of the curriculum. In the students of the lycées Napoleon saw the future officers of his army. It was then one of the functions of the lycées to turn out fit officers" (p. 35).

Compayré, *Histoire critique des doctrines de l'éducation en France,* Vol. 2.

(f) *Prescription of Courses.* "It [the government of Napoleon] regulated everything; even to the most minute details; for example, going as far as to prescribe to the professors of law to divide their lessons into dictations and oral explanations, according to an invariable proportion."

Liard, *L'enseignement supérieur en France,* V. 2, p. 40.

(g) *Education of Girls.* "Religion is an important matter in a public institution of girls. It is, whatever one may say about it, the surest guarantee for the mothers and for the husbands. Bring up women who believe and not women who reason. The weakness of women's minds, the fickleness of their ideas, their destination in the social order, the necessity for a constant and perpetual resignation and for a sort of indulgent and ready charitableness, all this can be obtained only through religion, through a charitable and gentle religion."

Correspondance de Napoléon I, No. 12.585.

11. Napoleon's Catechism

"*Question.* What are the duties of Christians toward those who govern them, and what in particular are our duties towards Napoleon I, our emperor?

"*Answer.* Christians owe to the princes who govern them, and we in particular owe to Napoleon I, our emperor, love, respect, obedience, fidelity, military service, and the taxes levied for the preservation and defense of the empire and of his throne. We also owe him fervent prayers for his safety and for the spiritual and temporal prosperity of the state.

"*Question.* Why are we subject to all these duties toward our emperor?

"*Answer.* First, because God, who has created empires and distributed them according to His will, has, by loading our emperor with gifts both in peace and in war, established him as our sovereign and made him the agent of His power and His image upon earth. To honor and serve our emperor is, therefore, to honor and serve God himself. Secondly, because our Lord Jesus Christ Himself, both by His teaching and His example, has taught us what we owe to our sovereign. Even at His very birth He obeyed the edict of Cæsar Augustus; He paid the established tax and while He commanded us to render to God those things which belong to God, He also commanded us to render unto Cæsar those things which are Cæsar's.

"Question. What must we think of those who are wanting in their duties toward our emperor?

"Answer. According to the Apostle Paul, they are resisting the order established by God Himself, and render themselves worthy of eternal damnation."

Hayes, *History of Modern Europe* * (New York, Macmillan, 1916), Vol. I, p. 535.

12. NAPOLEON'S PRESS CENSORSHIP

"What adverse criticism Frenchmen might have directed against the [Napoleonic] empire was stifled by the activity of a splendidly organized secret police and by a rigorous censorship of the press. So complete was Napoleon's control of the state that the decisive naval defeat of Trafalgar [Oct. 21, 1805] was not mentioned by a single French newspaper until after the fall of the empire [Mar. 31, 1814]."

Hayes, *History of Modern Europe* * (New York, Macmillan, 1916), Vol. I, p. 534 f.

13. JEFFERSON ON ELEMENTARY EDUCATION

"Were it necessary to give up either the Primaries or the University, I would rather abandon the last, because it is safer to have a whole people respectably enlightened, than a few in a high state of science, and the many in ignorance. This last is the most dangerous state in which a nation can be. The nations and governments of Europe are so many proofs of it."

Letter to J. C. Cabell, Jan. 13, 1823 (Jefferson and Cabell, *Early History of the University of Virginia, Richmond,* Randolph, 1856, p. 267 f.).

14. JEFFERSON'S PLAN FOR EDUCATION IN VIRGINIA

(Presented to the Legislature in 1779 but never adopted.)

"This bill proposes to lay off every county into small districts of five or six miles square, called hundreds, and in each of them to establish a school for teaching reading, writing, and arithmetic. The tutor to be supported by the hundred, and every person in it entitled to send their children three years gratis, and as much longer as they please, paying for it. These schools to be under a visitor, who is annually to chuse the boy, of best genius in the school, of those whose parents are too poor to give them further education, and to send him forward to one of the grammar schools, of which twenty are proposed to be erected in different parts of the country, for teaching Greek, Latin, geography, and the higher branches of numerical arithmetic. Of the boys thus sent in any one year, trial is to be made at the grammar schools one or two years, and the best genius of the whole selected, and continued six years, and the residue dismissed. By this means twenty of the best geniuses will be raked from the rubbish annually, and be instructed, at the public expense, so far as the grammar schools go. At the end of six years' instruction, one half are to be discontinued (from among whom the grammar schools will probably be supplied with future masters); and the other half, who are to be chosen for the superiority of their parts and disposition, are to be sent and continued three years in the study of such sciences as they shall chuse, at William and Mary college, the plan of which is proposed to be enlarged, . . . and extended to all the useful sciences. The ultimate result of the whole scheme of education would be the teaching of all the children of the state reading, writing, and common arithmetic: turning out ten annually of superior genius, well taught in Greek, Latin, geography, and the higher branches of arithmetic: turning out ten others annually, of still superior parts, who, to those branches of learning, shall have added such of the sciences as their genius shall have led them to: the furnishing to the wealthier part of the people convenient schools, at which their children may be educated, at their own expense. . . . Of all the views of this law none is more important, none more legitimate, than that of rendering the people safe, as they are the ultimate guardians of their own liberty. For this purpose the reading in the first stage, where they will receive their whole education, is proposed, as has been said, to be chiefly historical. History by apprising them of the past will enable them to judge of the future."

The Writings of Thomas Jefferson (Ford, editor. New York, Putnam, 1894), Vol. III, p. 251-4.

15. JEFFERSON ON LOCAL CONTROL OF EDUCATION

"If it is believed that these elementary schools will be better managed by the Governor and Council, the Commissioners of the Literary Fund, or any other general authority of the Government, than by the parents within each ward, it is a belief against all experience. Try the principle one step further, and amend the bill so as to commit to the Governor and Council the management of all our farms, our mills, and merchants' stores. No, my friend, the way to have good and safe government, is not to trust it all to one; but to divide it among the many, distributing to every one exactly the functions he is competent to. Let the National Government be entrusted with the defence of the nation, and its foreign and federal relations; the State Governments with the civil rights, laws, police and administration of what concerns the State generally; the counties with the local concerns of the counties, and each ward direct the interests within itself. It is by dividing and subdividing these republics from the great national one down through all its subordinations, until it ends in the administration of every man's farm and affairs by himself; by placing under every one what his own eye may superintend, that all will be done for the best. What has destroyed liberty and the rights of man in every Government which has ever existed under the sun? The generalizing and concentrating all cares and powers into one body, no matter whether of the autocrats of Russia or France, or of the aristocrats of a Venetian Senate. And I do believe, that if the Almighty has not decreed that man shall never be free, (and it is blasphemy to believe it,) that the secret will be found to be in the making himself the depository of the powers respecting himself, so far as he is competent to them, and delegating only what is beyond his competence by a synthetical process, to higher and higher orders of functionaries, so as to trust fewer and fewer powers, in proportion as the trustees become more and more oligarchal. The elementary republics of the wards, the county republics, the State republics, and the republic of the Union, would form a gradation of authorities, standing each on the basis of law, holding every one its delegated share of powers, and constituting truly a system of fundamental balances and checks for the government. Where every man is a sharer in the direction of his ward republic, or of some of the higher ones, and feels that he is a participator in the government of affairs, not merely at an election, one day in the year, but every day; when there shall not be a man in the State who will not be a member of some one of its councils great or small, he will let the heart be torn out of his body, sooner than his power be wrested from him by a Cæsar or a Bonaparte."

Letter to J. C. Cabell, Feb. 2, 1816 (Jefferson and Cabell, *Early History of the University of Virginia,* Richmond, Randolph, 1856, pp. 54-5).

16. EDUCATION FOR A CASTE SYSTEM (RUSSIA, 1828)

"A public system of education should aim at securing for the children of each class such a training as would fit them to be useful and contented in that rank of life to which it had pleased a most high Providence to call them at their birth."

Darlington, *Education in Russia* (Special Report on Educational Subjects, Vol. 24, London, H. M. Stationery Office, 1909), p. 67.

17. EDUCATION IN AN AUTOCRACY

The Russian Minister of Education in 1824 said: "Learning . . . is useful only when like salt, it is used and taught in due measure, having regard to the position in life of its recipient and the necessities of his particular vocation. A superfluity of learning is as much opposed to real enlightenment as a deficiency of it. To teach the whole people or a disproportionate number of them to read and write would do more harm than good. To instruct a farmer's son in rhetoric would be to make of him a bad and worthless, if not a positively dangerous, citizen."

Darlington, *Education in Russia* (Special Report on Educational Subjects, Vol. 24, London, H. M. Stationery Office, 1909), p. 63.

18. ORTHODOXY, AUTOCRACY, AND NATIONALISM

"I firmly believe we shall be able to avoid these mistakes [i. e., the pernicious influence of Western European ideas], and shall succeed in gradually capturing the minds of the youth and bringing them to that point where there must merge together— a regulated, fundamental education with a deep conviction and warm belief in the true Russian conservative principles of Orthodoxy, Autocracy, and Nationalism, which present the last anchor of our salvation and the surest pledge of the strength and majesty of our country."—The Russian minister of education (about 1833).

Quoted in Leary, *Education and Autocracy in Russia* (Buffalo, University of Buffalo, 1919), p. 63.

19. KAISER WILLIAM II'S ORDER TO THE SCHOOLS (1889)

"For a long time I have been considering ways and means of making the schools in their various grades more useful in combating the spread of socialistic and communistic ideas. In the first place the school will have to lay a foundation for a sound understanding of civil and social relationships through the cultivation of a fear of God and a love of country. But I cannot rid myself of the idea that in a time when Social-Democratic errors and misrepresentations are being spread abroad with increased zeal, the school should make more vigorous efforts to further a knowledge of what is true and real and practically possible. It must make a special effort to furnish even the youth with the conviction that not only are the teachings of Social-Democracy contrary to the commandments of God and to Christian morals, but also impracticable of realization and dangerous to the individual and to society at large. More than has formerly been the case, the school must include in the course of study modern, even contemporary history and give proof that state authority alone can protect for the individual his family, his freedom, and his rights. It must make the youth conscious of how the kings of Prussia have labored to improve the living conditions of the workingman in a progressive evolution, beginning with the legislative reforms of Frederick the Great and the abolition of serfdom down to the present day. Further, through the use of statistics it must show how essentially and how constantly during the present century the wages and living conditions of the working class have improved under the guiding care of the Prussian kings. . . .

"The history of our country will have to treat with special emphasis of the history of our social and economic development and legislation from the beginning of the nineteenth century up to current socio-political legislation, in order to show how the Prussian kings have always regarded it as their special mission to confer upon that portion of the population which is destined to labor with its hands a protection that was consistent with the title 'father of the country,' and to increase its physical and spiritual well-being, and how in the future as well the workingman can look forward to just and secure pursuit of his calling only under the protection and the solicitous care of the king at the head of a well-ordered state. Especially important will it be from the standpoint of practical utility to have it made clear to the youth through the use of striking concrete examples that a well-ordered political economy under firm monarchical guidance is the indispensable condition of the security and prosperity of the individual in his legal and economic life, and that, on the contrary, the teachings of Social-Democracy are impracticable of realization, and, if they were practicable, would subject the individual even in his domestic and private life to an unbearable constraint."

Reisner, *Nationalism and Education since 1870* * (New York, Macmillan, 1922), pp. 194-5.

20. A Caste System of Education

"In a free nation where slaves are not allowed of, the surest wealth consists in a multitude of laborious poor; for, besides that they are the never-failing nursery of fleets and armies, without them there could be no enjoyment, and no product of any country could be valuable. To make the society happy, and people easy under the meanest circumstances, it is requisite that great numbers of them should be ignorant as well as poor. Knowledge both enlarges and multiplies our desires, and the fewer things a man wishes for, the more easily his necessities may be supplied.

"The welfare and felicity therefore of every state and kingdom, require that the knowledge of the working poor should be confined within the verge of their occupations, and never extended (as to things visible) beyond what relates to their calling. The more a shepherd, a plowman, or any other peasant, knows of the world, and the things that are foreign to his labour or employment, the less fit he will be to go through the fatigues and hardships of it with cheerfulness and content.

"Reading, writing, and arithmetic, are very necessary to those whose business require such qualifications; but where people's livelihood has no dependence on these arts, they are very pernicious to the poor, who are forced to get their daily bread by their daily labour. Few children make any progress at school, but at the same time they are capable of being employed in some business or other, so that every hour those of poor people spend at their book is so much time lost to the society. Going to school, in comparison to working, is idleness; and the longer boys continue in this easy sort of life, the more unfit they will be, when grown up, for downright labour, both as to strength and inclination. Men who are to remain and end their days in a laborious, tiresome, and painful station of life, the sooner they are put upon it at first the more patiently they will submit to it for ever after."

Manderville, *An Essay on Charity and Charity Schools* (c. 1722. Bound with *The Fable of the Bees*, Edinburgh, 1772, Vol II, p. 215 f.).

21. Epicurus on Philosophy

"Let no one delay to study philosophy while he is young, and when he is old let him not become weary of the study; for no man can ever find the time unsuitable or too late to study the health of his soul. And he who asserts either that it is not yet time to philosophize, or that the hour is passed, is like a man who should say that the time is not yet come to be happy, or that it is too late. So that both young and old should study philosophy, the one in order that, when he is old, he may be young in good things through the pleasing recollection of the past, and the other in order that he may be at the same time both young and old, in consequence of his absence of fear for the future."

Bakewell, *Source Book in Ancient Philosophy* * (New York, Scribners, 1907), p. 296.

22. Plato on the Service of Philosophy

"When . . . the spirits arrived, . . . first of all there came a prophet who arranged them in order; then he took from the knees of Lachesis lots and samples of lives, and having mounted a high pulpit, spoke as follows: 'Hear the word of Lachesis, the daughter of Necessity. Mortal souls, behold a new cycle of life and mortality. . . . Let him who draws the first lot have the first choice, and the life which he chooses shall be his destiny. Virtue is free, and as a man honours or dishonours her he will have more or less of her; the responsibility is with the chooser— God is justified.' . . . Then the Interpreter placed on the ground before them the samples of lives; and there were many more lives than the souls present, and they were of all sorts. There were lives of every animal and of man in every condition. . . .

"And . . . the prophet said . . . 'Even for the last comer, if he chooses wisely and will live diligently, there is appointed a happy and not undesirable existence. Let not him who chooses first be careless, and let not the last despair.' And when he had spoken, he who had the first choice came forward and in a moment chose the greatest tyranny; his mind having been darkened by folly and sensuality, he had not thought out the whole matter before he chose. . . . But when he had time to reflect, and saw what was in the lot, he began to beat his breast and lament over his choice, forgetting the proclamation of the prophet; for, instead of throwing the blame of his misfortune on himself, he accused chance and the gods, and everything rather than himself. Now he was one of those who . . . in a former life had dwelt in a well-ordered State, but his virtue was a matter of habit only, and he had no philosophy. . . . For if a man had always on his arrival in this world dedicated himself from the first to sound philosophy, and had been moderately fortunate in the number of the lot, he might, as the messenger reported, be happy here . . . Most curious, he said, was the spectacle—sad and laughable and strange; for the choice of the souls was in most cases based on their experience of a previous life. . . . "

Plato, *Republic* * (Trans. by Jowett. Oxford, Clarendon Press, 1888), X, 617-619.

CHAPTER II

THE CONCEPT OF EXPERIENCE

23. Experience

"Experience is the ultimate universe of discourse."
Adapted from Bush, in *Journal of Philosophy*, 6:175-6 (April 1, 1909).

24. Experience the Basis of Everything

"Man has nothing at all but experience, and everything he comes to, he comes to only through experience. All his thinking, be it loose or scientific, common or transcendental, starts from experience ultimately in view. Nothing has unconditional value and significance except life. All other thinking, conception, knowledge has value only in so far as in some way or other it refers to the fact of life, starts from it, and has in view a subsequent return to it."
Fichte, *Werke*, Vol. II, p. 333.

25. Men Masters of Their Fate

"Men at some time are masters of their fates."
Shakespeare, *Julius Cæsar*, Act i, sc. 2.

26. The Struggle Element in Life

"A life absolutely free from pain and fear would, so long as we are what we are, soon become insipid and intolerable. For if the causes of pain were eliminated, life would be devoid of all danger, conflict, and failure, exertion and struggle, the love of adventure, the longing for battle, the triumph of victory, all would be gone. Life would be pure satisfaction without obstacles, success without resistance. We should grow as tired of all this as we do of a game which we know we are going to win. What chess player would be willing to play with an opponent whom he knows he will beat? What hunter would enjoy a chase in which he had a chance to shoot at every step he took, and every shot was bound to hit? Uncertainty, difficulty, and failure are as necessary in a game, if it is to interest and satisfy us, as good luck and victory."

Paulsen, *System of Ethics* * (Trans. by Thilly. New York, Scribners, 1899), p. 260.

27. AIMS

"Ends are ends-in-view or aims. They arise out of natural effects or consequences which in the beginning are hit upon, stumbled upon so far as any purpose is concerned. Men *like* some of the consequences and *dislike* others. Henceforth (or till attraction and repulsion alter) attaining or averting similar consequences are aims or ends. These consequences constitute the meaning and value of an activity as it comes under deliberation. Meantime of course imagination is busy. Old consequences are enhanced, recombined, modified in imagination. Invention operates. Actual consequences, that is effects which have happened in the past, become possible future consequences of acts still to be performed. This operation of imaginative thought complicates the relation of ends to activity, but it does not alter the substantial fact: Ends are foreseen consequences which arise in the course of activity, and which are employed to give activity added meaning and to direct its further course. . . .

"Roughly speaking, the course of forming aims is as follows. The beginning is with a wish, an emotional reaction against the present state of things and a hope for something different. Action fails to connect satisfactorily with surrounding conditions. Thrown back upon itself, it projects itself in an imagination of a scene which if it were present would afford satisfaction. This picture is often called an aim, more often an ideal. But in itself it is a fancy which may be only a phantasy, a dream, a castle in the air. In itself it is a romantic embellishment of the present; at its best it is material for poetry or the novel. Its natural home is not in the future but in the dim past or in some distant and supposedly better part of the present world. Every such idealized object is suggested by something actually experienced, as the flight of birds suggests the liberation of human beings from the restrictions of slow locomotion on dull earth. It becomes an aim or end only when it is worked out in terms of concrete conditions available for its realization, that is in terms of 'means.'

"This transformation depends upon study of the conditions which generate or make possible the fact observed to exist already. The fancy of the delight of moving at will through the air became an actuality only after men carefully studied the way in which a bird although heavier than air actually sustains itself in air. A fancy becomes an aim, in short, when some past sequence of known cause-and-effect is projected into the future, and when by assembling its causal conditions we strive to generate a like result. We have to fall back upon what has already happened naturally without design, and study it to see *how* it happened, which is what is meant by causation."

Dewey, *Human Nature and Conduct* * (New York, Holt, 1922), pp. 225, 234-5.

28. MAN'S RESOURCES

"Man's resources are the causalities inherent in things. When anything whatever is to be accomplished, causalities have to be invoked that make no concession to vision. That is only to say that they can be depended upon. To put into operation causalities that will generate specific results is the aim both of the man who plants a potato and of the man who seeks to reform the state. Causality will operate in any case, and intelligence will see to it that, as far as possible, the causalities that operate are the causalities of its choice. Only then can there be a technique for generating a chosen future out of a given present."

Bush, in *Journal of Philosophy*,* 8: 178 (Mar. 30, 1911).

29. THE USE OF IDEAS

"Some very important consequences concerning the nature of ideas, meanings, conceptions, . . . Because they are suggestions of something that may happen or eventuate, they are . . . platforms of response to what is going on. The man who detects that the cause of his difficulty is an automobile bearing down upon him is not guaranteed safety; he may have made his observation-forecast too late. But if his anticipation-perception comes in season, he has the basis for doing something which will avert threatening disaster. Because he foresees an impending result, he may do something that will lead to the situation eventuating in some other way. All intelligent thinking means an increment of freedom in action—an emancipation from chance and fatality."

Dewey, *Reconstruction in Philosophy* * (New York, Holt, 1920), p. 144.

30. THE CONCEPT OF EXPERIENCE

"Experience is primarily a process of undergoing: a process of standing something; of suffering and passion, of affection, in the literal sense of these words. The organism has to endure, to undergo, the consequences of its own actions. . . . Undergoing, however, is never mere passivity. The most patient patient is more than a receptor. He is also an agent—a reactor, one trying experiments, one concerned with undergoing in a way which may influence what is still to happen. Sheer endurance, side-stepping evasions, are, after all, ways of treating the environment with a view to what such treatment will accomplish. Even if we shut ourselves up in the most clam-like fashion, we are doing something; our passivity is an active attitude, not an extinction of response. Just as there is no assertive action, no aggressive attack upon things as they are, which is all action, so there is no undergoing which is not on our part also a going on and a going through.

"Experience, in other words, is a matter of *simultaneous* doings and sufferings. Our undergoings are experiments in varying the course of events; our active tryings are trials and tests of ourselves. This duplicity of experience shows itself in our happiness and misery, our successes and failures. Triumphs are dangerous when dwelt upon or lived off from; successes use themselves up. Any achieved equilibrium of adjustment with the environment is precarious because we cannot evenly keep pace with changes in the environment. These are so opposed in direction that we must choose. We must take the risk of casting in our lot with one movement or the other. Nothing can eliminate all risk, all adventure; the one thing doomed to failure is to try to keep even with the whole environment at once—that is to say, to maintain the happy moment when all things go our way.

"The obstacles which confront us are stimuli to variation, to novel response, and hence are occasions of progress. If a favor done by the environment conceals a threat, so its disfavor is a potential means of hitherto unexperienced modes of success. . . . The progress of the race has been stimulated by ills undergone, and . . . men have been moved by what they suffer to search out new and better courses of action . . .

"The preoccupation of experience with things which are coming (are now coming, not just to come) is obvious . . . Since we live forward, since we live in a world where changes are going on whose issue means our weal or woe: since every act of ours modifies these changes and then is fraught with promise, or charged with hostile energies—what should experience be but a future implicated in a present! Adjustment is no timeless state; it is a continuing process. . . . Every step in the process is conditioned by reference to further changes which it effects. What is going on in the environment is the concern of the organism; not what is already 'there' in accomplished and finished form. In so far as the issue of what is going on may be affected by intervention of the organism, the moving event is a challenge which stretches the agent-patient to meet what is coming. Experiencing exhibits things in their unterminated aspect moving toward determinate conclusions. The finished and done with is of import as affecting the future, not on its own account: in short, because it is not, really, done with.

"Anticipation is therefore more primary than recollection; projection than summoning of the past; the prospective than the retrospective. Given a world like that in which we live, a world in which environing changes are partly favorable and partly callously indifferent, and experience is bound to be prospective in import; for any control attainable by the living creature depends upon what is done to alter the state of things. Success and failure are the primary 'categories' of life; achieving of good and averting of ill are its supreme interests; hope and anxiety (which are not self-enclosed states of feeling, but active attitudes of welcome and wariness) are dominant qualities of experience. Imaginative forecast of the future is this forerunning quality of behavior rendered available for guidance in the present. . . . Imaginative recovery of the bygone is indispensable to successful invasion of the future, but its status is that of an instrument. To ignore its import is the sign of an undisciplined agent; but to isolate the past, dwelling upon it for its own sake and giving it the eulogistic name of knowledge, is to substitute the reminiscence of old-age for effective intelligence. The movement of the agent-patient to meet the future is partial and passionate; yet detached and impartial study of the past is the only alternative to luck in assuring success to passion. . . .

"Experience, to return to our positive conception, is primarily what is undergone in connexion with activities whose import lies in their objective consequences—their bearing upon future experiences. Organic functions deal with things as things in course, in operation, in a state of affairs, not yet given or completed. What is done with, what is just 'there,' is of concern only in the potentialities which it may indicate. As ended, as wholly given, it is of no account. But as a sign of what may come, it becomes an indispensable factor in behavior dealing with changes, the outcome of which is not yet determined.

"The only power the organism possesses to control its own future depends upon the way its present responses modify changes which are taking place in its medium. A living being may be comparatively impotent, or comparatively free. It is all a matter of the way in which its present reactions to things influence the future reactions of things upon it. Without regard to its wish or intent every act it performs makes some difference in the environment. The change may be trivial as respects its own career and fortune. But it may also be of incalculable importance; it may import harm, destruction, or it may procure well-being.

"Is it possible for a living being to increase its control of welfare and success? Can it manage, in any degree, to assure its future? Or does the amount of security depend wholly upon the accidents of the situation? Can it learn? Can it gain ability to assure its future in the present? These questions center attention upon the significance of reflective intelligence in the process of experience. The extent of an agent's capacity for inference, its power to use a given fact as a sign of something not yet given, measures the extent of its ability systematically to enlarge its control of the future.

"A being which can use given and finished facts as signs of things to come; which can take given things as evidences of absent things, can, in that degree, forecast the future; it can form reasonable expectations. It is capable of achieving ideas; it is possessed of intelligence. For use of the given or finished to anticipate the consequence of processes going on is precisely what is meant by 'ideas,' by 'intelligence.'

"As we have already noted, the environment is rarely all of a kind in its bearing upon organic welfare; its most whole-hearted support of life-activities is precarious and contemporary. Some environmental changes are auspicious; others are menacing. The secret of success—that is, of the greatest attainable success—is for the organic response to cast in its lot with present auspicious changes to strengthen them and thus to avert the consequences flowing from occurrences of ill-omen. Any reaction is a venture; it involves risk. We always build better or worse than we can foretell. But the organism's fateful intervention in the course of events is blind, its choice is random, except as it can employ what happens to it as a basis of inferring what is likely to happen later. In the degree in which it can read future results in present on-goings, its responsive choice, its partiality to this condition or that, become intelligent. Its bias grows reasonable. It can deliberately, intentionally, participate in the direction of the course of affairs. Its foresight of different futures which result according as this or that present factor predominates in the shaping of affairs permits it to partake intelligently instead of blindly and fatally in the consequences its reactions give rise to. Participate it must, and to its own weal or woe. Inference, the use of what happens, to anticipate what will—or at least may—happen, makes the difference between directed and undirected participation. And this capacity for inferring is precisely the same as that use of natural occurrences for the discovery and determination of consequences—the formation of new dynamic connexions—which constitutes knowledge."

Dewey, in *Creative Intelligence* * (New York, Holt, 1917), pp. 10-23.

31. Laws of Nature do not Govern

"Elsewhere lurks the apprehension that the progress of scientific method will deliver the purposive freedom of man bound hand and foot to the fatal decrees of iron necessity, called natural law. The notion that laws govern and forces rule is an animistic survival. It is a product of reading nature in terms of politics in order to turn around and then read politics in the light of supposed sanctions of nature. This idea passed from medieval theology into the science of Newton, to whom the universe was the dominion of a sovereign whose laws were the laws of nature. From Newton it passed into the deism of the eighteenth century, whence it migrated into the philosophy of the Enlightenment, to make its last stand in Spencer's philosophy of the fixed environment and the static goal.

"No, nature is not an unchangeable order, unwinding itself majestically from the reel of law under the control of deified forces. It is an indefinite congeries of changes. Laws are not governmental regulations which limit change, but are convenient formulations of selected portions of change followed through a longer or shorter period of time, and then registered in statistical forms that are amenable to mathematical manipulation. . . . Savage and child delight in creating bogeys from which, their origin and structure being conveniently concealed, interesting thrills and shudders may be had. Civilized man in the nineteenth century outdid these bugaboos in his image of a fixed universe hung on a cast-iron framework of fixed, necessary, and universal laws. Knowledge of nature does not mean subjection to predestination, but insight into courses of change; an insight which is formulated in 'laws,' that is, methods of subsequent procedure."

Dewey, *Influence of Darwin on Philosophy and Other Essays* * (New York, Holt, 1910), pp. 72-3.

32. SIGNS, SUPERSTITIONS, MAGIC, AND SCIENCE

"Coming events cast their shadows before them." In two quite different senses has this old adage been taken. First as in ordinary affairs: From a high hill we see a dark cloud driving towards us. Below it are the lines that we recognize as distant rain. These signs portend a storm and we hurry to shelter. Two things characterize this kind of sign: the portent connection is founded on actual verifiable experience and the connection itself is inherent. The rain we now see is the same rain that will soon be falling about us. So says common sense, and science after some refinements of statements agrees. But for some among us there is still extant a quite different kind of sign. In certain remote regions for a dove to alight about a house of illness portends the death of the one who is ill. Here even for those who accept the omen there is no inherent "natural" or "causal" connection between the bird's coming and the threatened death. Sign and thing signified are disparate, and stand in disparate lines of "natural" "causal" eventuation. Clearly this sign is essentially different from that seen in the driving raincloud. The sign of the raincloud belongs to a group that the modern world calls "natural" or common sense or, if seen only through carefully studied steps, scientific. The sign of the dove and such like we who reject them call superstitions. And they are in fact "left overs," as the word itself implies, remnants from a past type of thinking.

So far attention has not been directed to the factor of control. To know what is portended often gives us the opportunity to avert it. So science sets out to join "causally" the varied phenomena of experience especially that we may the better control affairs to our liking. When we saw the rain storm hurrying upon us, we hastened to shelter. When we fear typhoid we may take a serum injection to avert it; because science has established a "causal" connection between the two. In like manner may "superstitious" signs be used for control. If thirteen are about to sit down together at table, the "bad luck" may be averted, so those who fear it say, by increasing the number to fourteen. So also with a journeying on Friday, walking under a ladder, breaking a mirror and the like. Closely connected with this is "knocking on wood" to avert this or that minor bad luck. In all these cases of both kinds man seeks by "manipulating" the present to control the future.

With the foregoing the distinction between magic and science has already been implicitly made. Both seek to control our future affairs. Both do this by changing the present. In each case some matter at hand which we can change is assumed to bring or avert some as yet distant event. So far magic and science agree. Wherein then do they differ? Exactly in the *kind* of *connection* which each respectively assumes to exist between the present thing which we change and the future event which we seek to avert or bring. Science holds that the connection between the two is inherent and observable to proper scrutiny. In the case of magic the connection is utterly mysterious. No scrutiny can find how it comes about. For those who accept it, it just is and must be so accepted. No other explanation is possible or needed. *How* Friday or the 13th day should bring bad luck or *how* "knocking on wood" can avert bad luck is thus a useless question to those who believe such things. But ask the scientist how the *bacillus typhosus* "causes" typhoid, and he is ready to tell you by tracing the bacillus from some outside source through some means of ingress into the human body and showing there its almost countless multiplication with certain characteristic effects on the human organism which we call typhoid.

The difference then between science and magic is in the last analysis one of attitude and consequent endeavor. The scientist assumes that the connection between the present thing which we can change and the distant event which we thereby bring or avert is "inherent" and that the intervening steps are observable if only proper means of scrutiny be applied, and he ever seeks to find such connections. Magic is quite content to accept and—supposedly—use connections that are forever "mysterious," where in fact there are no intermediate connections of the kind that science assumes. It is perhaps not too much to say the history of science is exactly the history of the progressive banishment of magic in all its forms from the minds of men.

33. Fundamental Priority of Movement and Action

"It may at first sight seem strange that so significant and all-important an organ as the brain should have been evolved secondarily in relation to sense organs, but such seems to be the case and we are justified, I believe, in stating that animals possess a brain in consequence of their having previously had sense organs, not that they possess sense organs because they have a brain. . . .

"It . . . seems quite certain that we have . . . primitive animals possessed of muscle but devoid of nerve even in the form of sense organs, and that we may therefore conclude that, between muscle and sense organs, the muscle is of more ancient origin and marks the beginnings of that series of functionally related parts that culminates in the central nervous systems of the higher animals. . . .

"If this outline of the sources of our nervous activity is true, it follows that any conception of the nervous system that assumes sensation as a basal phenomenon is most assuredly to be abandoned. Sensations are associated with only the later phases of nervous development. The feature that has been present throughout the whole period of this evolution is muscular activity. In fact, as I have already stated, we have reason to believe that muscular activity preceded nervous origins and that nervous tissue appeared in consequence of the presence of muscles. Our own sensations, then, are not our most fundamental and primitive nervous processes, but behind these and of much more ancient lineage are our impulses to action, our wishes, our desires, and the whole vague body of nervous states that drive us to do things. These are the most ancient and deeply seated of our nervous propensities, and immeasurably antedate in point of origin, our sensations with all that supergrowth that constitutes the fabric of our mental life. We do well to warn ourselves to think before we act. Action is the oldest and most ingrained of our nervous functions, thinking the newest."

Parker, in *Science* n. s.,* 45:622, 623, 625. (June 22, 1917.)

34. Relativity of Order and Reason

"Order and reason, beauty and benevolence, are characteristics and conceptions which we find solely associated with the mind of man."

Pearson, *Grammar of Science* * (Macmillan, London, 1911), p. 108.

35. Means, End, End-in-Itself

When one takes steps to secure or attain anything, the thing sought we call the *end* [1] of desire or endeavor, the steps taken we call the *means* to this end. Sometimes we restrict the term *means* rather to the mere tools or other instrumentalities used in the pursuit of the end and not to the steps taken. Oftentimes an end is sought in order that when attained it may then be used as a means to some further end. So most people seek money not because they wish the money for its own sake but that they may use it for other and further ends. Money is thus an end while it is being sought, but it is a means while it is being spent. It may, however, happen that the end sought is desired for its own sake and not that it may be used as a means to any further end. We say that such an end is an *end-in-itself*. The miser thus seeks to possess money for the mere pleasure of owning it. To him the possession of money is an end-in-itself. It may further happen that one and the same thing may be sought from more than one motive, from one motive that it may later be used as a means, from another motive that it may be enjoyed for its own sake. The impecunious bachelor who says it is just as easy to love a rich girl as a poor one tells himself that he can contemplate marriage both as an end-in-itself and as a means to an end.

36. Disadvantages of *a Priori* Categories

"There are certain disadvantages attached to *a priori* categories. They have a certain rigidity, appalling to those who have not learned to identify stiffness with force. Empirical matters are subject to revision. The strongest belief that claims the support of experience is subject to modification when experience testifies against it. But an *a priori* conception is not open to adverse evidence. There is no court having jurisdiction. If, then, an unfortunate mortal should happen to be imposed upon so that he was led to regard a prejudice or a predilection as an *a priori* truth, contrary experience would have a tendency to make him the more obstinate in his belief. History proves what a danger-

---

[1] The term end is also used at times to denote an unsought result, as "The end of those things is death" (Romans vi, 21).

ous thing it has been for men, when they try to impose their will upon other men, to think of themselves as special instruments and organs of Deity. The danger is equally great when an *a priori* Reason is substituted for a Divine Providence. Empirically grounded truths do not have a wide scope; they do not inspire such violent loyalty to themselves as ideas supposed to proceed directly from reason itself. But they are discussable; they have a humane and social quality, while truths of pure reason have a paradoxical way, in the end, of escaping from the arbitrament of reasoning. They evade the logic of experience, only to become, in the phrase of a recent writer, the spoil of a 'logic of fanaticism.' Weapons forged in the smithy of the Absolute become brutal and cruel when confronted by merely human resistance."

Dewey, *German Philosophy and Politics* * (New York, Holt, 1915), p. 42 f.

CHAPTER III

THE SOCIAL INHERITANCE

37. Dewey on the Social Inheritance

"It is of grace not of ourselves that we lead civilized lives. . . . Loyalty to whatever in the established environment makes a life of excellence possible is the beginning of all progress. The best we can accomplish for posterity is to transmit unimpaired and with some increment of meaning the environment that makes it possible to maintain the habits of decent and refined life. Our individual habits are links in forming the endless chain of humanity. Their significance depends upon the environment inherited from our forerunners, and it is enhanced as we foresee the fruits of our labors in the world in which our successors live."

Dewey, *Human Nature and Conduct* * (New York, Holt, 1922), p. 21.

38. Bury on the Relative Importance of the Social Inheritance

"The social inheritance of ideas and emotions to which the individual is submitted from infancy is more important than the tendencies physically transmitted from parent to child. The power of education and government in moulding the members of a society has recently been illustrated on a large scale in the psychological transformation of the German people in the life of a generation. . . .

"Some [thinkers] are coming round to the opinion that enormous differences in capacity which seem fundamental are a result of the differences in social inheritance, and that these are again due to a long sequence of historical circumstances; and consequently that there is no people in the world doomed by nature to perpetual inferiority or irrevocably disqualified by race from playing a useful part in the future of civilisation."

Bury, *The Idea of Progress* * (London, Macmillan, 1920), pp. 166-7.

39. Social Heredity

"Several things may then be said about Social Heredity.

"(1) The first thing is that it is analogous to physical heredity. The child, apart from the defective in mind or body, learns to speak, write, read, play, combine forces with others, build structures, do book-keeping, shoot firearms, address meetings, teach classes, conduct business, practice law and medicine—or whatever his line of further development may be away from the three 'r's' of usual attainment—just as well as if he had received an instinct for that activity at birth from his father and mother. His father or mother may have the accomplishment in question; and he may learn it from him or her. But then both the father and mother may not have it, and he then learns it from someone else. It is inheritance; for it shows the attainments of the fathers handed on to the children; but it is not physical heredity, since it is not transmitted physically at birth.

"(2) It is hereditary in that the child cannot escape it. It is as inexorably his as the colour of his eyes and the shape of his nose. He is born into a system of social relationships just as he is born into a certain quality of air. As he grows in body by breathing the one, so he grows in mind by absorbing the other. The influence is as real and as tangible; and the only reason that it is variable in its results upon different individuals is that each individual has his physical heredity besides, and the outcome is always the outcome of the two factors,—natural temperament and social heredity. The limits of the relative influence of these two factors I shall speak of again; here it is enough to say that the development of the natural disposition is always directed more or less into the channels opened up by the social forces of the environment. The union of these two factors leads us, however, to observe a further point.

"(3) The influence of social heredity is, in a large sense, inversely as the amount and definiteness of natural heredity. By this is meant that the more a person or an animal is destined to learn in his lifetime, the less fully equipped with instincts and special organic adaptations must he be at birth. This has been made so clear by recent biological discussion that I need do no more than refer to it. The interpretation of a creature's infancy turns upon the question how much the exigencies of future life are to call upon him to learn. If a great deal, then we find him born practically helpless and requiring artificial support and attention during a long infancy period. If the young creature is to have a life of relatively unchanging activities with little need for the acquisition of functions not already possessed by the species as instincts, then he comes into the world with ready-made instinctive activities, and can take care of himself independently very early, or even at birth."

Baldwin, *Social and Ethical Interpretations* * (New York, Macmillan, 1906), pp. 69-71.

40. THE INDIVIDUAL AND THE SOCIAL INHERITANCE

"The greater part of each man's personal experience is made up out of his interaction with others in the multifarious relations of life, and these relations, from the earliest known phases of human society, are controlled by customs which arise out of the needs of social life and are maintained by the social tradition. Through this tradition society exerts a continuous control over the individual, of which avowed and obvious coercion is the least important element. The vital factor is that from infancy upwards the social milieu into which he is born interpenetrates his thought and will, and turns his individuality into a creation of the time and place of his life."

Hobhouse, *Social Evolution and Political Theory* * (New York, Columbia University, 1911), p. 94.

41. VALUE OF THE SOCIAL CONTRIBUTION

"Those means of knowledge and of power are the *capital* of community, capital which is taken over by each successive generation and increased in the measure of the wisdom of each—a true inheritance. This capital is the apparatus, the property of community, external to it as an individual's property is external to himself. It is none the less of incalculable significance. Without it our history would be an endless succession of futile beginnings. This has been well emphasised by an American sociologist: 'Our prehistoric ancestors of the stone age, and of still earlier times, dragged out their miserable lives with little or no capital of any kind. And what should we of western civilisation do, if, at birth, we were thrust into the midst of the primitive struggle for existence? What would distinguish us from our prehistoric ancestors? Nothing of moment. Prehistoric men could not invent the telegraph, discover the differential calculus, build a sky-scraper, nor construct a steam-engine: and we, if removed at birth from all contact with civilisation, with its accumulated capital of all kinds, could not surpass the achievements of our primitive ancestors. We too, growing up from birth wholly outside the influences of civilisation, should live the life of primeval men.' (Wallis, *Examination of Society*, p. 273.) Our native 'inheritance,' that self-hood which we are or will attain, would be a frustrated and unavailing potentiality in the absence of those *means* to knowledge and to power which are in all literalness our social inheritance."

MacIver, *Community* * (London, Macmillan, 1917), p. 85 f.

42. THE POWER OF THE MORES

"The most important fact about the mores is their dominion over the individual. Arising he knows not whence or how, they meet his opening mind in earliest childhood, give him his outfit of ideas, faiths, and tastes, and lead him into prescribed mental processes. They bring to him codes of action, standards, and rules of ethics. They have a model of the man-as-he-should-be to which they mold him, in spite of himself and without his knowledge. If he submits and consents, he is taken up and may attain great social success. If he resists and dissents, he is thrown out and may be trodden under foot. (p. 173 f.) . . . It is in vain to imagine that a 'scientific man' can divest himself of prejudice or previous opinion, and put himself in an attitude of neutral independence toward the mores. He might as well try to get out of gravity or the pressure of the atmosphere. The most learned scholar reveals all the philistinism and prejudice of the man-on-the-curbstone when mores are in discussion. The most elaborate discussion only consists in revolving on one's own axis. (p. 98) . . . When . . . the statesmen and social philosophers stand ready to undertake any manipulation of institutions and mores, and proceed on the assumption that they can obtain data upon which to proceed with confidence in that undertaking, as an architect or engineer would obtain data and apply his devices to a task in his art, a fallacy is included which is radical and mischievous beyond measure." (p. 97.)

Sumner, *Folkways* * (Boston, Ginn, 1913).

43. RELATIONSHIP OF THE INDIVIDUAL WITH SOCIETY

"Whether the individual be conscious or unconscious of the purposes he shares in common with his fellows, his life is so dependent upon society that his social relationships should be regarded, not as an addendum to his personality, but as an integral part of it—not as something he can assume or discard at will, but as an essential part of himself and the very condition of his being. 'He is,' as Mr. Bradley expresses it, 'penetrated, infected, characterised by his relations with his fellows. . . . The soul within him is saturated, is filled up, is qualified by, it has assimilated, has built itself up from, it *is* one and the same life with, the universal life; and if he turns against this, he turns against himself; if he thrusts it from him, he tears his own vitals; if he attacks it, he sets the weapon against his own heart.' . . .

"In the first place, man's life to-day, his thought, his ideals, his actions, are conditioned by the nature of a common inheritance which he owes to those who have gone before him. Does he enjoy freedom of thought and speech? Has he free political institutions? Is the world of Art, of Music, of Painting, of Sculpture, of Architecture, of Literature, in some measure open to him? Has he a State? A City? Laws? Schools? Homes? All these he owes to the thought and efforts of bygone generations. . . . Of all the generations . . . none is so great a debtor as our own. . . . The magic music of Chopin and of Wagner could never have taken form in the minds of those great artists but for the slow perfecting of musical instruments by generations of toilers whose names have long been forgotten. From whatever point of view we regard the matter, the past is not dead, but lives in us. The individual may protest against this or that institution or idea; but the contribution of the most gifted mind sinks to insignificance in comparison with the riches that he has received and that make his own achievement possible.

"In the second place, man is dependent, not only upon a structure of inherited ideas and institutions, but also upon the active and hourly co-operation of those by whose aid this structure is maintained. . . . 'If,' wrote Sir Leslie Stephen, 'I can devote myself to write an ethical treatise, it is because thousands of people all over the world are working to provide me with food and clothes, and a variety of intellectual and material products. If another man lives by putting one brick on another, it is because he can trust the discharge of other essential functions to the numerous classes who are contributing more or less directly to his support, protection, and instruction.' (*Science of Ethics*, p. 109).''

Brown, *Underlying Principles of Modern Legislation* (New York, Dutton, 1915), pp. 111-112.

44. Automatic Inheritance of Allegiance

"It is chiefly competition that keeps institutions adapted to the conditions they face and the people they serve. Without this spur the institution stands still or even degenerates. . . .

"An institution that has the children of its members for nothing need not cater to them, and if it will content itself with such following, it may petrify in its tracks. It is not good, therefore, that the sons should inherit creed, party allegiance, college allegiance, local allegiance from their fathers; they should choose in freedom. The parent that fastens unescapable bonds upon the child before it has reached the age of choice confiscates the child's personality.

"If, instead of inheriting their adherents, organizations had to win them, they would accommodate themselves to to-day. The contrasts between organizations would connect less with differences of origin and history and more with the actual contrasts of type in contemporary society."

Ross, *Principles of Sociology* * (New York, Century, 1921), p. 220.

45. Definitions of Education

(1) "Speaking generally, education signifies the sum total of processes by which a community or social group, whether small or large, transmits its acquired power and aims with a view to securing its own continued existence and growth." (p. 398.)

(2) "Education may be defined as a process of the continuous reconstruction of experience with the purpose of widening and deepening its social content, while at the same time the individual gains control of the methods involved." (p. 400.)

Dewey, article on Education, in Monroe, *Cyclopedia of Education* * (New York, Macmillan, 1911).

CHAPTER IV

THE NATURE OF SOCIETY

46. Association

"An association is an organisation of social beings . . . for the pursuit of some common interest or interests. It is a determinate social unity built upon common purpose. Every end which men seek is more easily attained for all when all whom it concerns unite to seek it, when all co-operate in seeking it. Thus you may have an association corresponding to every possible interest of social beings. Community bubbles into associations permanent and transient, and no student of the actual social life of the present can help being struck by the enormous number of associations of every kind, political, economic, religious, educational, scientific, artistic, literary, recreative, which to-day more than ever before enrich communal life."

MacIver, *Community* * (London, Macmillan, 1917), p. 23 f.

47. Effectiveness of the Wolf Pack

"The wolf pack forms an organism, it is interesting to note, stronger than the lion or the tiger; capable of compensating for the loss of members; inexhaustible in pursuit, and therefore capable by sheer strength of hunting down without wile or artifice the fleetest animals; capable finally of consuming all the food it kills, and thus possessing another considerable advantage over the large solitary carnivora in not tending uselessly to exhaust its food supply. The advantages of the social habit in carnivora is well shown by the survival of wolves in civilized countries even today."

Trotter, *Instincts of the Herd in Peace and War* * (New York, Macmillan, 1917), p. 29 n.

48. Individual and Society

"Now this is the Law of the Jungle—as old and as true as the sky;

And the Wolf that shall keep it may prosper, but the Wolf that
   shall break it must die.
As the creeper that girdles the tree-trunk the Law runneth forward
   and back—
For the strength of the Pack is the Wolf, and the strength of
   the Wolf is the Pack."

Kipling, The Law of the Jungle in *The Second Jungle Book* * (Garden City, Doubleday Page, 1922), p. 29.

49. CIVILIZATION GREW OUT OF COÖPERATION

"Man, being the strongest of all animals, differs from the rest; he was obliged to be his own domesticator; he had to tame himself. And the way in which it happened was, that the most obedient, the tamest tribes are, at the first stage in the real struggle of life, the strongest and the conquerors. All are very wild then; the animal vigour, the savage virtue of the race has died out in none, and all have enough of it. But what makes one tribe—one incipient tribe, one bit of a tribe—to differ from another is their relative faculty of coherence. The slightest symptom of legal development, the least indication of a military bond, is then enough to turn the scale. The compact tribes win, and the compact tribes are the tamest. Civilisation begins, because the beginning of civilisation is a military advantage."

Bagehot, *Physics and Politics* (New York, Appleton, 1887), p. 51 f.

50. MEANING OF THE TERM "GROUP"

"The term 'group' serves as a convenient sociological designation for any number of people, larger or smaller, between whom such relations are discovered that they must be thought of together. The 'group' is the most general and colorless term used in sociology for combinations of persons. A family, a mob, a picnic party, a trade union, a city precinct, a corporation, a state, a nation, the civilized or the uncivilized population of the world, may be treated as a group. Thus a 'group' for sociology is a number of persons whose relations to each other are sufficiently impressive to demand attention. The term is merely a commonplace tool. It contains no mystery. It is only a handle with which to grasp the innumerable varieties of arrangements into which people are drawn by their variations of interest."

Small, *General Sociology* * (Chicago, Univ. of Chicago, 1905), p. 495.

51. Nature of Society

"Just as 'individual' is not one thing, but is a blanket term for the immense variety of specific reactions, habits, dispositions and powers of human nature that are evoked, and confirmed under the influences of associated life, so with the term 'social.' Society is one word, but infinitely many things. It covers all the ways in which by associating together men share their experiences, and build up common interests and aims; street gangs, schools for burglary, clans, social cliques, trades unions, joint stock corporations, villages and international alliances."

Dewey, *Reconstruction in Philosophy* * (New York, Holt, 1920), p. 199 f.

52. The Nature of Society

"Society, and particularly civilized society, is a very complex structure. We have not to do with one society,—the political community standing over against a number of individuals who are its component members. Each individual is a member of many societies. He is one of a family; he belongs to a church, to a corporation, to a trade union, to a political party. He is also a citizen of his state, and his state has a place in the commonwealth of states. In so far as the world becomes one, that is to say, as social relations arise which interconnect human beings all the world over, Humanity becomes the supreme society, and all smaller social groupings may be conceived as constituent elements of this supreme whole."

Hobhouse, *Social Evolution and Political Theory* * (New York, Columbia University, 1911), p. 88.

53. Ties that Bind in Society

"A society consists of beings *related* to one another in various ways, some superficial, some deep and vital. Into social relations men are born, in them they live and develop. None lives or dies to himself, and all are bound up in one unity by reason of their social relationships. It is when men reflect on this essential fact that they fall, so often, into . . . delusion. They come to think of these social relations as literally *ties* between man and man, somehow outside the beings they bind together,

as railway-couplings are outside the carriage they connect. . . .
We speak of the *ties* of friendship, but the ties are the reciprocal
sentiments felt by each toward the other of the beings so related.
The ties exist *in* the personality of each, and there alone. . . .
Social relations, in a word, are simply those elements and functions of personality in each which are dependent on the elements
and functions of personality in others. Society is therefore not
relations, but beings in their relationships. It follows that there
is no social function which is outside of the functions of personalities. Society is in us, in each of us, in some degree in all,
in the highest degree in the greatest of us."

MacIver, *Community* * (London, Macmillan, 1917), p. 69 f.

54. Social Psychology

"There is no problem in all history so artificial as that of
how 'individuals' manage to form 'society' . . . .

"The problem of social psychology is not how either individual
or collective mind forms social groups and customs, but how
different customs, established interacting arrangements, form and
nurture different minds."

Dewey, *Human Nature and Conduct* * (New York, Holt,
1922), pp. 59, 63.

55. "Man Unsocial by Nature"

"Man is not naturally a social being; human society is purely
a product of his reason and arose by insensible degrees, *pari
passu* with the development of his brain. In other words, human
association is the result of the perceived advantage which it
yields, and came into existence only in proportion as that advantage was perceived by the only faculty capable of perceiving
it, the intellect."

Dealey and Ward, *Textbook of Sociology* * (New York, Macmillan, 1907), p. 1.

56. Society, the Individual, and Institutions

"Society is the *process* of associating in such ways that experiences, ideas, emotions, values are transmitted and made
common. To this active process, both the individual and the
institutionally organized may truly be said to be subordinate.
The individual is subordinate because except in and through com-

THE NATURE OF SOCIETY 41

munication of experience from and to others, he remains dumb, merely sentient, a brute animal. Only in association with fellows does he become a conscious centre of experience. Organization, which is what traditional theory has generally meant by the term Society or State, is also subordinate because it becomes static, rigid, institutionalized whenever it is not employed to facilitate and enrich the contacts of human beings with one another."

Dewey, *Reconstruction in Philosophy* * (New York, Holt, 1920), p. 207.

57. EXCHANGE THE FUNDAMENTAL PHENOMENON OF ASSOCIATION

"Exchange is the essential phenomenon of association. This is a truth that appears very commonplace, a mere trifle, and yet at present it is greatly misunderstood by a majority of the people. Some believe that we can have association without exchange; others think that we can have exchange without association. The social bond is created by exchange. If that is absent we have no association. A bank of oysters does not make a society, because there is no exchange between the individuals composing it, though they are packed close together. (p. 292.) . . .

"The sum of exchanges both material and intellectual arising from the exchange of commodities, of industrial products, of men and ideas, we shall call vital circulation. Admitting that society is really nothing but a group of individuals who practice exchange, then the boundaries of society coincide with those of the vital circulation. Should a vital communication exist between A and Z, the two, from the sociological standpoint, would form a single society. They would be two different societies if no such communication existed between them. (p. 300 f.) . . .

"Societies being agglomerations of units, each possessing considerable power of locomotion, constitute organisms the mobility of which is greater than we might possibly suspect.

"We see, therefore, the utter impossibility of fixing the exact limits of human associations. There is constantly an interpenetration between societies due to migration and to transportation of products. But, as we may well imagine, this vital traffic varies from the highest degree to complete absence of all relationship. . . . If there is no relationship, then completely independent centers of civilization are formed which develop solely through their own resources. Such has been the case with the culture of the Aztecs and the Incas. (p. 301 f.) . . .

"On the other hand, that which promises to be some day a federation of all Europe is in the making now as a result of innumerable exchanges which escape our observation because of their frequency and multiplicity. Every business transaction between individuals of different countries is, so to speak, a microscopic event to which nobody pays any attention. It simply escapes our consciousness. But millions and millions of small sales of that nature, repeated uninterruptedly for years, weave the cloth of European federation, as Gladstone has so happily said. First, because exchange brings about division of labor. The Germans have specialized in industry, the Russians in agriculture. Here we have the old specialization between the country and the town, only repeated on an infinitely greater scale. And just as the town cannot exist without the food that comes from the country, so it is that Germany cannot live without the agricultural products of Russia. It is said that the German soil can support only forty-two million people. But Germany (1910) has a population of sixty-five millions. Therefore twenty-three millions of Germans must starve unless they receive food from Russia and other countries.

"The exchanges which have become indispensable between European nations have given rise to a system of various juridical institutions, such as consular agreements, laws regulating international transportation, post-offices, telegraphs, etc. It would take pages just to enumerate them. That system of juridical institutions forms at all times the legislation of the European federation. We see repeated on a larger scale what happened when the colonists, having settled a new country, instituted certain laws to meet the demand of their economic life. As a result of some mental aberrations coming from sources of which I shall speak later the Europeans are still hostile to one another. But sociology, which must study the facts objectively, is obliged to show that in reality Europe already constitutes a single economic unit, and that consequently its political unification, in the domain of civil law, is also in a very advanced stage. (p. 307.) . . .

"To sum up, exchange is the main factor in human association. Association is impossible without it, and the boundaries of human groups coincide, in fact, with the limits within which exchange operates." (p. 310.)

Novicow. in *American Journal of Sociology*,* 23:292 ff. (Nov., 1917.)

58. THE SOCIAL MIND

"It is . . . easy to understand that though there is no thought except in the mind of an individual thinker, yet the thought of any generation is a social product. But we must go further than this. The sum of thought in existence at any time is something more than any thought that exists in the head of any individual; it is something to which many minds contribute, and which yet may be for many purposes a real unity. Consider an advanced complex science. No one thinks the whole of such a science at any moment. Perhaps no one lives who is master of it all. Yet the whole range of truth that the science has elaborated is available for social or individual uses. It is recorded in books. It is, so to say, incorporated in instruments and laboratories, whereby the results worked out by one man for one purpose are available by another man for another purpose. The science is more than the living knowledge of any individual. It is the social knowledge or social thought, not in the sense that it exists in the mind of a mystical social unit, nor in the sense that it is the common property of all men, which it certainly is not, but in the sense that it is the product of many minds working in conscious or unconscious coöperation, that it forms a part of the permanent social tradition going constantly to shape the thought and direct the efforts of fresh generations of learners,—that, in a word, it has all the permanency and potency which the individual has not. . . .

"As the function of the individual mind is to organize the life of the individual, so the function of the social mind is to organize the life of society, to control the physical environment, and to regulate the relations of members of the community to one another and of the community as a whole to other communities. This function is of course more adequately performed in proportion as the social mind develops. Now the development of mind in general consists partly in increase of width or scope. The developed mind has a wider reach. Its grasp extends further over the future and the past. Its insight into reality probes deeper, and in consequence its practical control of life is greater. Secondly, the development of mind lies in increased clearness, articulateness, connectedness of perception and of thought. It takes a more penetrating and concrete view. Lastly, and this has special application to the social mind, the more developed mind is more completely and consciously a unity. In the case of the individual, indeed, a unity may always be predicated by another person, even if it be not conscious. An animal or a child may, for all we know, have no thought of yesterday or to-morrow, but we onlookers are aware that it is one and the same being throughout. In the case of the social mind, on the other hand, the consciousness of unity profoundly affects the unity itself. One is tempted to say that it actually brings it to birth. This, however, would not be true in all cases, for the minds of men who are brought into contact affect one another, and may give to any society a certain oneness, marking it out from others, without perhaps any consciousness of the relation. Moreover, when a new and wider unity is recognized, it is recognized as something already existing, as a relation which was present and was operative somehow while yet unknown. But however this be, any developed unity in the social mind rests on a consciousness, first of some special relation of each individual constituting it to his fellow members, and secondly of the group, society, institution itself as a whole."

Hobhouse, *Social Evolution and Political Theory* * (New York, Columbia University, 1911), pp. 94, 98-9.

59. Disraeli on Institutions

"The rights and liberties of a nation can only be preserved by institutions. It is not the spread of knowledge or the march of intellect that will be found sufficient sureties for the public welfare in the crisis of a country's freedom."

Monypenny, *Life of Disraeli* * (London, Macmillan, 1910), Vol. I, p. 324.

60. Institutions vs. Customs

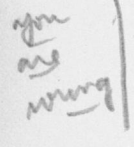

"It appears then that institutions are forms of order established within social life by some common will. The qualifying phrase, "established by some common will," enables us to distinguish these from customs, which are also permanent ways in which men relate themselves to one another. It may be only a question of degree, but institution implies a more definite recognition, a more determinate will. Customs are but the habits of a community. As one man falls imperceptibly into a habit so do many men, the members of a group, form imperceptibly common habits, that is, customs. These customs may come to be recognised and instituted, they may come to be honoured, or perhaps to be condemned as a burden and restriction—or they may be as little felt by those who share them, as little known to them, as is the weight of the atmosphere. Our whole lives are threaded by unfelt, unrecognised customs, of which we can make ourselves aware only by an effort of reflection. These latter can scarcely be called institutions. They are but the raw material of institutions, and common will is for ever taking customs as they emerge into common consciousness, and *instituting* them."

MacIver, *Community* * (London, Macmillan, 1917), p. 150 f.

CHAPTER V

SOCIALIZATION

61. Morality the Socialization of Self

"Our final word about the place of the self in the moral life is, then, that the problem of morality is the formation, out of the body of original instinctive impulses which compose the natural self, of a voluntary self in which socialized desires and affections are dominant, and in which the last and controlling principle of deliberation is the love of the objects which will make this transformation possible."

Dewey and Tufts, *Ethics* * (New York, Holt, 1908), p. 397.

62. Disintegration of Society

"The danger that, above all others, a democratic nation must avoid is the disintegration of society into units with no immediate concern but self-interest, into individuals to whom social duties and bonds are gradually ceasing to appeal."

Fouillée, *Education from a National Standpoint* * (New York, Appleton, 1892), p. 4.

63. Social Solidarity

"Social structure is an important factor. Where men are divided by language, or by religion, or by caste distinctions grounded on race or on occupation, there are grounds for mutual distrust and animosity which make it hard for them to act together or for each section to recognize equal rights in the other. Homogeneity, though it may not avert class wars, helps each class of the community to understand the mind of the others, and can create a general opinion in a nation. A population of a bold and self-reliant character is more fitted to work free institutions than is one long accustomed to passive and unreasoning obedience. Men cool of temper, slow and solid in their way of thinking, are better than those who are hasty, impressionable, passionate; for the habit of resorting to violence is one of the prime difficulties in the orderly working of political institutions, as any one will admit who recalls the sanguine expectations entertained half a century ago, and compares them with the facts of to-day in nearly every free country. Swift wits and a lively imagination are not necessarily an advantage in this sphere. Education, that is to say the education given by schools and books, signifies less than we like to think. Native shrewdness and the willingness to make a compromise instead of yielding to impulses and pushing claims of right to extremes are more profitable. The glib talk, common in our time, which suggests that education will solve the problems of China and Russia, of Mexico and Persia misleads us by its overestimate of the value of reading and writing for the purposes of politics."

Bryce, *Modern Democracies* * (New York, Macmillan, 1921), vol. II, p. 502 f.

64. ORIGINAL NATURE

"I find many of the tendencies born in man to be archaic, useless, immoral adaptations to such a life as man lived in the woods a hundred thousand years ago—when affection had not spread beyond the family or justice beyond the tribe or science beyond the needs of to-morrow, when truth was only the undisputed and goodness only the unrebuked."

Thorndike, in *Educational Review*,* 48:496-7 (Dec., 1914).

65. SOCIAL RELATIONSHIPS DEPENDENT ON COMMUNICATION

"All political and social institutions, all matters of human relationship, are dependent upon the means by which mind reacts upon mind and life upon life, that is to say, upon the intensity, rapidity and reach of mental and physical communication."

Wells (and others), in *Atlantic Monthly*,* 123:108 (Jan. 1919).

66. THE DESTRUCTION OF COMMUNICATION IN AUGUST, 1914

"Of the [German] censorship Dr. Liebknecht said: 'You Americans cannot imagine the awful power of the military. In one day, in one hour, we were cut off. Every man became like a separate cell in the body politic. Every man was isolated with his own thoughts or else he was drowned in the flooding ideas of the war. From the moment the censorship shut down there was no more exchange of ideas. Every thinking man in Germany became a mental prisoner.'"

Evening Post (New York), Dec. 23, 1916.

67. The Individual and Society

"Society exists in individuals. When all the generations through which its unity subsists are counted in, its life is their life, and nothing outside their life. The individuals themselves, indeed, are profoundly modified by the fact that they form a society, for it is through the social relation that they realize the greater part of their own achievements. Each man is, so to say, the meeting point of a great number of social relations. Each such relation depends on him, on his qualities, on his actions, and also affects him and modifies his qualities and his actions. The whole complex of such relations constitutes the life of society. It follows that social development is also in the end personal or individual development. If society develops in any given direction, the persons constituting it develop accordingly, and if development as such means a movement towards a fuller and more complete life, then social development means a movement towards a fuller and more complete life for the persons of whom society consists."

Hobhouse, *Social Evolution and Political Theory* * (New York, Columbia University, 1911), p. 85.

68. A New Era in Human Relationships

"Yesterday, and ever since history began, men were related to one another as individuals. To be sure there were the family, the Church, and the State, institutions which associated men in certain wide circles of relationship. But in the ordinary concerns of life, in the ordinary work, in the daily round, men dealt freely and directly with one another. Today, the everyday relationships of men are largely with great impersonal concerns, with organizations, not with other individual men. . . .

"Now this is nothing short of a new social age, a new era of human relationships, a new stage-setting for the drama of life."

Wilson, *The New Freedom* * (Garden City, Doubleday Page, 1914), p. 6 f.

69. The Great Society

"During the last hundred years the external conditions of civilized life have been transformed by a series of inventions which have abolished the old limits to the creation of mechanical force, the carriage of men and goods, and communication by written and spoken words. One effect of this transformation is a general change of social scale. Men find themselves working and thinking and feeling in relation to an environment, which, both in its world-wide extension and its intimate connection with all sides of human existence, is without precedent in the history of the world.

"Economists have invented the term The Great Industry for the special aspect of this change which is dealt with by their science, and sociologists may conveniently call the whole result The Great Society. In those countries where the transformation first began a majority of the inhabitants already live either in huge commercial cities, or in closely populated industrial districts threaded by systems of mechanical traction and covering hundreds of square miles. Cities and districts are only parts of highly organized national states, each with fifty or a hundred million inhabitants; and these states are themselves every year drawn more effectively into a general system of international relationships.

"Every member of the Great Society, whether he be stupid or clever, whether he have the wide curiosity of the born politician and trader, or the concentration on what he can see and touch of the born craftsman, is affected by this ever-extending and ever-tightening nexus. A sudden decision by some financier whose name he has never heard may, at any moment, close the office or mine or factory in which he is employed, and he may either be left without a livelihood or be forced to move with his family to a new centre."

Wallas, *The Great Society* * (New York, Macmillan, 1914), p. 3 f.

70. INCREASING SOCIAL INTEGRATION INEVITABLE

"I would have our teachers understand the inevitably continuing character of social integration. The industrial revolution began on a new scale the bringing together of people in larger and larger aggregates. As the home and work shop gave way to the factory, so this, in turn, is being joined with others in greater combinations. These enlarging agencies of production sell over wider and wider areas to ever larger and larger numbers. An increasing stream of inventions brings to consciousness an ever increasing number of wants. Means of communication and transportation keep pace so that the morning's paper gives us the news from all quarters of the globe, while the daily life is increasingly dependent on distant parts of the earth for the products that are to sustain it. Men are thus brought together in ever greater and greater aggregates by a process which at the same time increases the number of respects in which each is dependent upon others for the satisfaction of constantly increasing wants. Integration and aggregation go hand in hand. And the tendency is ever growing. Unless civilization goes to pieces, we face an inevitable and unending process of integration. As the seven little kingdoms of earlier Britain had to unite in time into the Heptarchy; as Scotland must in time unite her warring clans into one harmonious whole; as increased travel and exchange of goods and means of communication must make one nation of the thirteen struggling suspicious colonies; so we may say with certainty that the round world is bound in time to return upon itself. Let the integration continue, and sooner or later the ties that bind will outgrow the forces that separate; and the separate nations of the earth will realize that the united welfare of all demands the united action of all. The beginnings of formal joint action may be small; but the beginning is the most difficult. Continuing inevitable integration will at length see one joint compact strong enough to ensure order even in the face of sporadic and local selfish antagonisms."

Kilpatrick, in *Educational Review,* 61:206 f. (March, 1921.)

71. Herd Conduct

"The cardinal quality of the herd is homogeneity. It is clear that the great advantage of the social habit is to enable large numbers to act as one, whereby in the case of the hunting gregarious animal strength in pursuit and attack is at once increased to beyond that of the creatures preyed upon, and in protective socialism the sensitiveness of the new unit to alarms is greatly in excess of that of the individual member of the flock.

"To secure these advantages of homogeneity, it is evident that the members of the herd must possess sensitiveness to the behavior of their fellows. The individual isolated will be of no meaning, the individual as part of the herd will be capable of transmitting the most potent impulses. Each member of the flock tending to follow its neighbor and in turn to be followed, each is in some sense capable of leadership; but no lead will be followed that departs widely from normal behaviour. A lead will be followed only from its resemblance to the normal. If the leader go so far ahead as definitely to cease to be in the herd, he will necessarily be ignored.

"The original in conduct, that is to say resistiveness to the voice of the herd, will be suppressed by natural selection; the wolf which does not follow the impulses of the herd will be starved; the sheep which does not respond to the flock will be eaten.

"Again, not only will the individual be responsive to impulses coming from the herd, but he will treat the herd as his normal environment. The impulse to be in and always to remain with the herd will have the strongest instinctive weight. Anything which tends to separate him from his fellows, as soon as it becomes perceptible as such, will be strongly resisted."

Trotter, *Instincts of the Herd in Peace and War* * (New York, Macmillan, 1917), pp. 29-30.

72. AMERICA OVER-STANDARDIZED

"I know that many discerning Americans are very dubious about the freedom of the individual man in their country, and for my own part I am convinced that the development of one's own unique powers is much freer in England than it is in America. I remember saying to a group of business men in New York just before I sailed for home that if it were not for Russia under Lenine and Trotzky, I should say that America was the only autocracy left in the world. . . .

"But when I deny that there is much scope for the development of individuality in America, I am not thinking entirely in a political sense. The general social theory of America seems to me to have a maleficent effect on the individual man. A man is more definitely a member of a crowd in the United States than he is in any other country with which I am acquainted. I think an American is more definitely a member of a crowd than even a German before the war. . . . The method of conducting the [political] convention, whether it is Republican or Democratic, is identical. It is done by exploitation of mass feeling. The very applause with which the names of candidates are announced is organized and regulated, and robbed of all spontaneity. . . .

"No one on this earth can provoke spontaneous cheers, the only cheers that are worth consideration, from an audience for half an hour. When I hear an orator utter a sentiment of which

I heartily approve, my instinct is to give vent to a loud approving shout or to clap my hands noisily together. I cannot continue to cheer or to beat my hands in applause for more than a few minutes. . . . Applause in America is nearly always organized. The American, in my experience, is not a man who is naturally demonstrative. . . . Left to himself, he would probably cheer a nominee at a convention in a courteous and quiet fashion.

"But he is not left to himself. The organizers of conventions do not believe in leaving him to himself. And so we get regulated enthusiasm, which is a contradiction in terms. I have seen the same sort of thing at a game of basket-ball played in a girl's college. Each side had its official encourager who organized and directed the cheers of the spectators. The result is the appearance of enthusiasm without the reality of it, a sort of clock-work applause which does not carry conviction and is no more than an irrelevant prolonged noise. One feels on such occasions that if a man were to develop a real enthusiasm for anything and were to cheer out of his turn, he would shock his neighbors, disconcert the hero of the occasion, and seriously annoy the leader of the applause. . . .

"Is America, in short, a country in which uniformity or diversity is most commonly practised? Does an American do a thing because he wants to do it or because his next-door neighbor does it? Is life in America dominated by the myriad impulses of a highly diversified population or by the desires of a few persons imposed upon that population? I do not think there is the slightest doubt of the fact that America is essentially a country in which men are governed by the imitative faculty and by the imposition of opinion. The tendency is to make things alike rather than to make them dissimilar. In England every village is different from all other villages, but in America one village is almost an exact replica of another village. . . .

"When you have a people who are governed in such a way that law falls into disrepute, then inevitably freedom of thought and movement become contracted. The mass of the people will accept things that they ought not to accept up to the point at which endurance breaks, and then they fly to violent remedies, and we get lynch-law, which is not law at all, but the denial of it. And when people cannot depend upon the laws of their country for protection, they develop timidity of spirit, the majority of them, or violence of spirit, the minority of them. The majority suppress their individuality, and the minority exaggerate it. On the one hand, we have the majority seeking for protection by doing exactly what every one else is doing; and on the other hand, a minority, seeking through violence, eccentricity, and destructiveness to obtain an outlet for his energy.

"America suffers enormously from standardized thought. . . . It is an old charge against America that the standardization of things has been carried to excess, and probably Americans, aware of the very considerable advantages of a high degree of standardization in material things, are tired of listening to the charge; but it is not one which they should lightly dismiss. . . . One finds this effort to reduce individuality to a piece of well-oiled machinery all over America. Young men in the street seem ambitious to wear exactly the same sort of overcoat that other young men are wearing. The dominant desire is not to differentiate oneself from other people, but to make oneself as like the crowd as possible.

"Now, a great literature cannot flourish in an atmosphere of imitation and suppressed personality, and unless America can somehow solve this problem, of making a man's individuality grow and become vivid, there is slight likelihood of her making credit for herself with an art or a literature to which the world will yield respect."

Ervine, in *Century Magazine,** 101:576-581. (March, 1921.)

CHAPTER VI

THE NATURE OF THE INDIVIDUAL

73. How Man Differs from the Lower Animals

Man differs from the lower animals because he preserves his past experiences. What happened in the past is lived again in memory. About what goes on today hangs a cloud of thoughts concerning similar things undergone in bygone days. With the animals, an experience perishes as it happens, and each new doing or suffering stands alone. But man lives in a world where each occurrence is charged with echoes and reminiscences of what has gone before, where each event is a reminder of other things. Hence he lives not, like the beasts of the field, in a world of merely physical things but in a world of signs and symbols. A stone is not merely hard, a thing into which one bumps; but it is a monument of a deceased ancestor. A flame is not merely something which warms or burns, but it is a symbol of the enduring life of the household, of the abiding source of cheer, nourishment and shelter to which man returns from his casual wanderings. Instead of being a quick fork of fire which may sting and hurt, it is the hearth at which one worships and for which one fights. And all this which marks the difference between bestiality and humanity, between culture and merely physical nature, is because man remembers, preserving and recording his experiences.

Dewey, *Reconstruction in Philosophy* * (New York, Holt, 1920), p. 1 ff.

74. Different Possible Selves

"I am often confronted by the necessity of standing by one of my empirical selves and relinquishing the rest. Not that I would not, if I could, be both handsome and fat and well dressed, and a great athlete, and make a million a year, be a wit, a *bon-vivant*, and a lady-killer, as well as a philosopher; a philanthropist, statesman, warrior, and African explorer, as well as a 'tone-poet' and saint. But the thing is simply impossible. The millionaire's work would run counter to the saint's; the *bonvivant* and the philanthropist would trip each other up; the philosopher and the lady-killer could not well keep house in the same tenement of clay. Such different characters may conceivably at the outset of life be alike *possible* to a man. But to make any one of them actual, the rest must more or less be suppressed. So the seeker of his truest, strongest, deepest self must review the list carefully, and pick out the one on which to stake his salvation."

James, *Principles of Psychology* * (New York, Holt, 1890), Vol. I, pp. 309-10.

75. DOUBLE PERSONALITY

William James tells of a case of double personality that came under his own observation. The Rev. Ansel Bourne of Greene, R. I., had been brought up to the trade of carpenter. He was subject to headaches, depression of spirit, and occasional fits of unconsciousness lasting an hour or so. In consequence of a peculiar experience in which he suffered sudden temporary loss of sight and hearing he was converted from atheism to Christianity and became an itinerant minister. In this capacity he established an unquestioned character for uprightness in his community.

One day he drew $551 from the bank and boarded a horse car to buy a certain lot of land. From that moment he disappeared and was sought for in vain. Two months later a certain "A. J. Brown," who had six weeks before stocked and opened a small candy shop in Norristown, Pa., waked in a fright and demanded to know where he was, declared that he was Ansel Bourne, a minister in Greene, R. I.; that he knew nothing of A. J. Brown, or of Norristown, or of any candy-shop; that the day before he had drawn money from the bank in Providence. The fact that he should have set up a candy shop was mysteriously unconnected with any of his past life; and the missing two weeks between disappearing from Providence and appearing in Norristown remained unexplained as Bourne could not recall any of the acts of Brown.

Three years later James himself hypnotized Bourne to see if the Brown personality would return; and it did. The whole interval was recalled and described, including the missing two weeks; but "Brown" could not tell how he came to be on the horse car or how he left the candy-shop. These events belonged to Bourne. It seemed undoubted that "Mr. Bourne's skull today (1890) still covers two distinct personal selves."

Adapted from James, *Principles of Psychology* (New York, Holt, 1890), Vol. I, p. 390 ff.

76. INDIVIDUALITY

"When we speak of individuality we mean that quality and power of self-determination and self-expression which is as necessary to the growth of personality as is the social environment. Individuality does not therefore mean mere indifference, still less mere eccentricity. Certain philosophies have spurned individuality because they have conceived it in this abstract and unreal form, but that self-determination which is the core of individuality need not and perhaps should not be based on the difference of man from man. Personality is the substantial reality and end which individuality and sociality together determine, and any doctrine which exalts either of these aspects at the expense of the other, or either of them at the expense of their unity in personality, is partial and untrue to the facts of life. To understand how individuality and sociality have revealed their consentaneous growth in the concrete personalities of men, as these have emerged out of the meagre group-controlled uniformities of primitive life into the richer and more autonomous natures which even the most ordinary members of our own civilization possess, that is the key to the understanding of the whole process of communal development."

MacIver, *Community* * (London, Macmillan, 1917), p. 216.

77. HABITS AND SELF AND WILL

"It is a significant fact that in order to appreciate the peculiar place of habit in activity we have to betake ourselves to bad habits, foolish idling, gambling, addiction to liquor and drugs. When we think of such habits, the union of habit with desire and with propulsive power is forced upon us. When we think of habits in terms of walking, playing a musical instrument, typewriting, we are much given to thinking of habits as technical abilities existing apart from our likings and as lacking in urgent impulsion. We think of them as passive tools waiting to be called into action from without. A bad habit suggests an inherent tendency to action and also a hold, command over us. It makes us do things we are ashamed of, things which we tell ourselves we prefer not to do. . . .

"These traits of a bad habit are precisely the things which are most instructive about all habits and about ourselves. They teach us that all habits are affections, that all have projectile power, and that a predisposition formed by a number of specific acts is an immensely more intimate and fundamental part of ourselves than are vague, general, conscious choices. All habits are demands for certain kinds of activity; and they constitute the self. In any intelligible sense of the word will, they *are* will. They form our effective desires and they furnish us with our working capacities."

Dewey, *Human Nature and Conduct* * (New York, Holt, 1922), p. 24-5.

78. The Nature of the Ethical Self

(a) "In the idea of a spiritual, as distinguished from a merely natural being, is involved the notion not only of self-consciousness but of self-determination. Not what I am or find myself to be by nature, not what I am made to be by any foreign or external power, constitutes my spiritual life, but that which, by conscious activity and will, I make myself to be. This does not imply that a spiritual nature is one which is absolutely self-created, or that the spiritual life of the individual has no limits or conditions imposed upon it from without. But it does imply that, so long as there is anything within or without—any element of my inner life which is simply and immediately given, and not taken up, transformed, and, so to speak, re-created by the free self-assertion of the rational will, any outward conditions which constitute a limit to my nature, and which have not become the means of its self-development and self-realisation—so long and to that extent I have not attained to the true life of spirit." (p. 247 f.)

(b) "That I am capable of a universal life, a life transcending the limits of my own individuality, I learn practically in my relations to other human beings, when I find it possible so to identify myself with them as to make their life my own." (p. 263.) . . . "Apart from them I have no real self, or only the false self of a fragment taking itself for a whole. It is when the moral life of society flows into me that my nature reaches a fuller development; and then only are my social duties adequately fulfilled when they cease to have the aspect of an outward law and pass, in love and self-devotion, into the spontaneity of a second nature. For one who felt thus, selfish indulgence at the expense of others would be a greater self-denial, a thing fraught with a keener pain than any private suffering; it would be an injury done to a dearer self for the sake of a self he has ceased to care for, nay, which in one sense has ceased to exist. For social morality reaches its ideal purity only then when the individual not merely loves others as himself, but can scarcely be said to have any other or exclusive self to love. Few indeed are they who have realised this absolute merging of the individual in the universal life, but for the nobler spirits who have nearly approximated to it, pain and pleasure are words which almost cease to have any private or personal significance. It is no longer any pleasure to do what they please, and pain and sacrifice have become touched with a new sense of sweetness. There have been times when, by such men, their country's humiliation and loss have been felt with a far keener pang than personal suffering, and for them the offering up of life itself has had a strange sweetness in it, if the sacrifice could avert or retrieve her ruin. Finally, the capacity of a universal life finds its highest realization when the individual rises above even the organic life of the community or state, to identify himself with the moral life of the race." (p. 265 f.)

Caird, *Philosophy of Religion* * (Glasgow, Maclehose, 1901).

79. KANT ON THE POWER OF EDUCATION

"Man can become man through education only."
Buchner, *Kant's Educational Theory* * (Philadelphia, Lippincott, 1904), p. 107.

80. THE OBJECT OF EDUCATION

"The object of the education . . . is to assist human beings to become themselves. They cannot become themselves without an effort of mind and will, and the discipline by which that effort is stimulated and guided is education. Because they cannot become themselves in isolation from their fellows, education is a social thing. Because their fundamental human affinities are more important than their individual differences, education is the witness to equality. Because their complete development involves not blind or unreasoning obedience, but their intelligent coöperation in purposes which they themselves approve as good, education is the foundation of democracy. Education is, in short, the organised aid to the development of human beings in a society."

Report of the Archbishop's Fifth Committee (London, 1918), p. 110.

81. KANT'S "MAN AS AN END IN HIMSELF"

"Man and generally any rational being exists as an end in himself, not merely as a means to be arbitrarily used by this or that will, but in all his actions, whether they concern himself or other rational beings, must be always regarded at the same time as an end." (p. 55.)

"Accordingly the practical imperative will be as follows: So act as to treat humanity, whether in thine own person or in that of any other, in every case as an end withal, never as means only." (p. 56.)

"As regards necessary duties, or those of strict obligation, towards others; he who is thinking of making a lying promise to others will see at once that he would be using another man merely as a mean, without the latter containing at the same time the end in himself. For he whom I propose by such a promise to use for my own purposes cannot possibly assent to my mode of acting towards him, and therefore cannot himself contain the end of this action. This violation of the principle of humanity in other men is more obvious if we take in examples of attacks on the freedom and property of others. For then it is clear that he who transgresses the rights of men intends to use the person of others merely as means, without considering that as rational beings they ought always to be esteemed also as ends, that is, as beings who must be capable of containing in themselves the end of the very same action." (p. 57.)

Kant, *Fundamental Principles of the Metaphysic of Ethics* (Trans. by Abbot. London; Longmans, 1895).

82. A MEANS TO AN END

"If a woman becomes weary or at last dead from [child] bearing, that matters not; let her only die from bearing. She is there to do it."

Martin Luther.

83. "GOOD" CHILDREN

"Everybody knows that good children are those who make as little trouble as possible for their elders."

Dewey, *Human Nature and Conduct* * (New York, Holt, 1922), p. 2.

84. WORKINGMEN IN MODERN INDUSTRY

"Large numbers of working people are at the present time employed on terms which suggest that they are means to the production of wealth rather than themselves the human end for whom wealth is produced. They too often have cause to feel that they are directed by an industrial autocracy, which is sometimes, indeed, both kindly and capable, but which is repugnant to them precisely because it is an autocracy, and because, in so far as it controls their means of livelihood, it also, not the less certainly because often unconsciously, controls their lives. The conditions of their work may be determined not by them, but for them . . . The worker's pride in his craft is often destroyed by its subdivision into simple and monotonous processes, and his human interest in his work destroyed by his absence of responsibility for its permanent results. He may be employed on processes injurious to his health, or on work of a kind which is degrading because adulterated or dishonest."

Report of the Archbishop's Fifth Committee (London, 1918), p. 55.

85. ROOSEVELT ON THE NEW ERA

" 'Hands' must hereafter be treated as hands with brains and heart, with dignity and vision back of them. Hereafter workingmen must in a very real sense be treated as partners. They must have their seats at the council board . . . a square deal for every man . . . an eight-hour law should be the general rule . . . condescension and patronage by the capitalist must yield to comradeship and partnership. . . ."

Theodore Roosevelt, in *New York Tribune*, March 29, 1918.

86. MODERN INDUSTRY AND THE SANCTITY OF PERSONALITY

"If it is true—and who can doubt it?—that the sanctity of personality is a fundamental idea of Christian teaching, it is evident that Christians are bound to judge their industrial organization by that principle and to ask whether in modern industry human beings are regarded always as ends and never as means. We do not venture to give a dogmatic answer to that question. But we submit that the criticism which the thoughtful workman passes upon the economic system is that it often treats him and his class as instruments of production, and that this criticism is a very weighty one, because it cuts to the root both of modern industrial relationships and of modern social ethics. . . .

"While there are, no doubt, aspects of modern industry which such an indictment omits or misrepresents, there are others to which it must be reluctantly admitted to be applicable, and we think it has too much substance to be lightly dismissed by the conscience of Christians. Workmen are often engaged when there is work and dismissed when there is not. They are employed casually, if casual employment is economically convenient. Unless protected by law or by trade unionism, they are liable to be worked inhuman hours, to be paid the lowest wage which they can be forced by fear of unemployment to accept, and to be bound by regulations which they have no voice in making. That such conditions must produce poverty is obvious, for they leave the weaker members of the community without protection against the downward thrust of economic pressure. But that is not the gravest stricture to be passed upon them. The fundamental objection to them is that they tend to result in men and women being treated as instruments of production, and that to treat human beings as instruments of production is morally wrong."
Report of the Archbishop's Fifth Committee (London, 1918), pp. 14-15.

87. POPE ON TEACHING ADULTS

"Men must be taught as if you taught them not,
And things unknown propos'd as things forgot."
Pope, *Essay on Criticism,* Pt. iii, lines 15-16.

88. INDIVIDUAL GUILT AND SOCIAL RESPONSIBILITY

"No amount of guilt on the part of the evil-doer absolves us from responsibility for the consequences upon him and others of our way of treating him, or from our continuing responsibility for the conditions under which persons develop perverse habits. . . .

"The moral issue concerns the future. It is prospective. To content ourselves with pronouncing judgments of merit and demerit without reference to the fact that our judgments are themselves facts which have consequences and that their value depends upon *their* consequences, is complacently to dodge the moral issue, perhaps even to indulge ourselves in pleasurable passion just as the person we condemn once indulged himself. The moral problem is that of modifying the factors which now influence future results. To change the working character or will of another we have to alter objective conditions which enter into his habits. Our own scheme of judgment, of assigning blame and praise, of awarding punishment and honor, are part of these conditions."

Dewey, *Human Nature and Conduct* * (New York, Holt, 1922), p. 18 f.

89. Freedom

"We must understand that, philosophically, freedom means self-determination, but that self-determination is characterized not only by the absence of outer determining factors, but by the harmonization of all the inner energies. A man is not free in a moral sense, when he is a slave of his passions and lower instincts, when he is unable to control his impulses by his higher ideas."

Münsterberg, *American Traits* * (Boston, Houghton Mifflin, 1901), p. 199.

90. Freedom

"Freedom consists in achievement along lines that seem to the individual worth while."

Henderson, *Principles of Education* * (New York, Macmillan, 1910), p. 498.

91. Spinoza's Definition of Freedom

"That thing is said to be free which exists from the sole necessity of its own nature and is determined to act by itself alone."

Ethics, Book I, Def. 7.

92. Freedom

"The man who is not under restraint is free . . . but who is free from restraint? He who desires nothing that is in the power of others." (p. 313-4.)

"Freedom is acquired not by the full possession of the things which are desired but by removing the desire." (p. 322.)

Epictetus, *Discourses,* Book IV, ch. i. (Bohn ed.).

93. CHARACTER

"Character consists in a man steadily pursuing the things of which he feels himself capable."
Goethe.

94. SUPPRESSION *vs.* EXPRESSION

"The studies of psychiatrists have made clear that impulses driven into pockets distil poison and produce festering sores. An organization of impulse into a working habit forms an interest. A surreptitious furtive organization which does not articulate in avowed expression forms a 'complex.' . . .

"Every impulse is, as far as it goes, force, urgency. It must either be used in some function, direct or sublimated, or be driven into a concealed, hidden activity. It has long been asserted on empirical grounds that repression and enslavement result in corruption and perversion. We have at last discovered the reason for this fact. The wholesome and saving force of intellectual freedom, open confrontation, publicity, now has the stamp of scientific sanction. The evil of checking impulses is not that they are checked. Without inhibition there is no instigation of imagination, no redirection into more discriminated and comprehensive activities. The evil resides in a refusal of direct attention which forces the impulse into disguise and concealment, until it enacts its own unavowed uneasy private life subject to no inspection and no control."

Dewey, *Human Nature and Conduct* * (New York, Holt, 1922), p. 164-6.

95. SUPPRESSION OF IMPULSES

"In the career of any impulse activity there are speaking generally three possibilities. It may find a surging, explosive discharge—blind, unintelligent. It may be sublimated—that is, become a factor coördinated intelligently with others in a continuing course of action. . . . Or again a released impulsive activity may be neither immediately expressed in isolated spasmodic action, nor indirectly employed in an enduring interest. It may be 'suppressed.'

"Suppression is not annihilation. 'Psychic' energy is no more capable of being abolished than the forms we recognize as physical. If it is neither exploded nor converted, it is turned inwards, to lead a surreptitious, subterranean life. An isolated or spasmodic manifestation is a sign of immaturity, crudity, savagery; a suppressed activity is the cause of all kinds of intellectual and moral pathology. One form of the resulting pathology constitutes 'reaction' in the sense in which the historian speaks of reactions. A conventionally familiar instance is Stuart license after Puritan restraint. A striking modern instance is the orgy of extravagance following upon the enforced economies and hardships of war, the moral let-down after its high strung exalted idealisms, the deliberate carelessness after an attention too intense and too narrow. Outward manifestation of many normal activities had been suppressed. But activities were not suppressed. They were merely damned up awaiting their chance.

"Now such 'reactions' are simultaneous as well as successive. Resort to artificial stimulation, to alcoholic excess, sexual debauchery, opium and narcotics are examples. Impulses and interests that are not manifested in the regular course of serviceable activity or in recreation demand and secure a special manifestation. And it is interesting to note that there are two opposite forms. Some phenomena are characteristic of persons engaged in a routine monotonous life of toil attended with fatigue and hardship. And others are found in persons who are intellectual and executive, men whose activities are anything but monotonous, but are narrowed through over-specialization. Such men think too much, that is, too much along a *particular* line. They carry too heavy responsibilities; that is, their offices of service are not adequately shared with others. They seek relief by escape into a more sociable and easy-going world. The imperative demand for companionship not satisfied in ordinary activity is met by convivial indulgence. The other class has recourse to excess because its members have in ordinary occupations next to no opportunity for imagination. They make a foray into a more highly colored world as a substitute for a normal exercise of invention, planning and judgment. Having no regular responsibilities, they seek to recover an illusion of potency and of social recognition by an artificial exaltation of their submerged and humiliated selves.

"Hence the love of pleasure against which moralists issue so many warnings. Not that love of pleasures is in itself in any way demoralizing. Love of the pleasures of cheerfulness, of companionship is one of the steadying influences in conduct. But pleasure has often become identified with special thrills, excitations, ticklings of sense, stirrings of appetite for the express purpose of enjoying the immediate stimulation irrespective of results.

Such pleasures are signs of dissipation, dissoluteness, in the literal sense. An activity which is deprived of regular stimulation and normal function is piqued into isolated activity, and the result is division, disassociation. A life of routine and of over-specialization in non-routine lines seek occasions in which to arouse by abnormal means a *feeling* of satisfaction without any accompanying objective fulfilment. Hence, as moralists have pointed out, the insatiable character of such appetites. Activities are not really satisfied, that is fulfilled in objects. They continue to seek for gratification in more intensified stimulations. Orgies of pleasure-seeking, varying from saturnalia to mild sprees, result."

Dewey, *Human Nature and Conduct* * (New York, Holt, 1922), p. 156-9.

96. Individualization and Socialization

"The individual's normal growth lands him in essential solidarity with his fellows, while on the other hand the exercise of his social duties and privileges advances his highest and purest individuality."

Baldwin, *Individual and Society* * (Boston, Badger, 1911), p. 16.

97. Socialization and Individualization

"The first and greatest of all the laws of community . . . *Socialisation and individualisation are the two sides of a single process.*

"In this brief statement we have used two terms which require careful definition. When we say that a being has become more individualised, we mean that he has become more an autonomous being, more a distinct personality self-directed and self-determining, recognising and recognised as having in himself a worth or value of his own. When again we speak of socialisation we mean the process in which a being strikes deeper root in society, in which his social relations grow more complex and more extensive, in which he finds the fulfilment of his life in and through the increase and development of his relations with his fellows. We can thus express the law as follows: *Sociality and individuality develop pari passu,* sociality and individuality being the qualities corresponding to the processes of socialisation and individualisation."

MacIver, *Community* * (London, Macmillan, 1917), p. 214 f.

98. SOCIAL NATURE OF MAN

"As the State was formed to make life possible, so it exists to make life good. . . .

"Thus we see that the State is a natural institution, that Man is naturally a political animal and that one who is not a citizen of any State, if the cause of his isolation be natural and not accidental, is either a superhuman being or low [in the scale of civilization] . . .

"We see then that the State is a natural institution, and also that it is prior to the individual. For if the individual as a separate unit is not dependent, he must be a part and must bear the same relation to the State as other parts to their wholes; and one who is incapable of association with others or is independent and has no need of such association is no member of a State, in other words he is either a brute or a God. Now the impulse to political association is innate in all men. Nevertheless the author of the first combination whoever he was was a great benefactor of human kind. For man, as in his condition of complete development [i. e., in the State], he is the noblest of all animals, so apart from law and justice he is the vilest of all."

Aristotle, *Politics* * (Trans. by Welldon. London, Macmillan, 1908). Book I, Ch. ii.

99. SOCIUS RATHER THAN INDIVIDUAL

Albion W. Small, the sociologist, "suggests that the category 'individual' is inaccurate as an expression of reality. It is not a tool of precision . . . there is no separate individual as implied in the older sense of the term. The term is used uncritically in popular speech and usually carried the meaning of a separate, discrete, unrelated entity. Such a view is tending to disappear in social science. . . . Sociology and psychology . . . stress the group as the reality and the individual, in the older sense, appears as a fiction. This does not mean, of course, that sociology does not recognize the force of personality in social relations. A personalized factor in the social whole is a reality. Persons are real though socially created; they are more important and powerful than in the older view which made them separate entities. One of the distinct contributions of modern sociology is to aid in clearing the term 'individual' of the confusion with which it has been surrounded. It is because of these confusions that Small suggests the value of a substitute category for the term individual. Among the possible substitutes he suggests the term *socius*. The advantages and significance of this term he sets forth in the following language: 'The socius is that literal factor within the human whole which we now find in the place occupied by that discredited hypothesis the individual. It is the sociological conception of the term individual, freed from former misconceptions.'"

Bodenhafer, in *American Journal of Sociology*,* 26:596 f. (March, 1921).

100. How Self and "Socius" Each Mutually Build Each Other [1]

The conception which I have of myself and the conception which I have of you have both been socially built. In fact the two conceptions grow up together, and each mutually helps the other into being. Much that I now see in myself I first saw in others. Much that I now attribute to you and to others I first saw in myself, and only gradually learned to attribute to you. Each conception—that of self as well as that of other—is thus a compound of elements derived from both subjective and objective sources. The essential factor in the process is that what I know subjectively of myself enables me to understand you, and what I see and understand objectively in you and others enables me to see and understand myself. This "dialectic of personal growth," as Baldwin calls it, is a further and very important respect in which the individual is essentially social. In fact the individual can have no full real existence apart from the company and contribution of others. The steps in this process of growth and reciprocal genesis are not difficult to trace.

Man possessing the kind of mind he has and living in our kind of world inevitably organizes certain groups of related experiences into "things." An "apple" is thus for me a construction of a certain group of related experiences. In what sense there is or is not back of this construction some physical or metaphysical entity is an old bone of contention that need not now delay us. We face a practical matter. This group of related experiences in time builds into my nervous system an organization of learnings which abides as an aggregate of meanings and expectations so joined and interrelated that the presence to experience

[1] For the definition of socius see the preceding extract.

—whether of sense or thought—of a sufficient number of the component elements will tend to bring to use and mind the other elements. Suppose I "like" apples. If I "see an apple," a particularly large, round, luscious-looking apple, I shall quite possibly wish to eat it, and shall with pleasure imagine how it will taste. Here sight stirs desire to eat and brings up imagined taste. I could if occasion demanded also foretell, within certain limits of accuracy, its weight, smell, resistance to pressure, measured shape, inner consistency, etc. Now, whatever else may be true about it, this much is quite certain, that I had to learn to expect these experiences. In Thorndike's terminology, my past experiences of this thing have built for me a group of interrelated S → R reaction connections whereby certain experiences present as stimuli will cause me to respond appropriately to certain other related and expected experiences. This particular organized aggregate of related meanings and expectations is for each one who has built it the thing we call an apple. It is our task now to apply this inevitable thing-making tendency of man to the problem at hand.

The child, as James has well said, first finds the world a "big buzzing blooming confusion." By virtue of his ability to learn, he begins to make over his experiences into expectations. This thing which I have previously experienced is not simply this thing, it means something else; it points to another impending experience. Who has not heard the baby's pleased chuckle as it sees the filled milk bottle approaching? The seeing experience in this case is transformed into an expectation which in interest far eclipses any mere satisfaction of exercising eye muscles or sight. This learning of meanings is the essence of the thing-making tendency of the preceding paragraph. The child then soon begins—not with any conscious intent, to be sure, —to sort out and group his manifold experiences and to organize these as we saw into things.

Among the things that the child is thus in process of constructing there early appears an important division. Some will "stay put," while others move. The moving ones—later to be persons for him—almost from the first exercise peculiar influences over the child's fortune. The gratification of his most insistent wants is in some mysterious way associated with these important moving objects. Is the child cold and does crying seem at length about to fail, suddenly there appears somehow from infinity one of these moving things. Something happens and soon all is warm. If a pin pricks, the child's vehement cry brings even quicker response. Something happens almost at once and now the pain is gone. We must be very careful not to read our definiteness of thought into the child's mind. But the germs of later definiteness are certainly present in these experiences; and among the external things now taking shape these moving objects are indeed unique, in the function they perform and in the interest and attention they receive.

Concomitantly with this external thing-making process and its special emphasis on these all powerful moving things, there has all the while been going on another even subtler kind of thing-making. Out of his wants and their denials and gratifications, the child has begun to build a subjective self. The process is slow, but much hastened, we may believe, when he begins to associate effort with gratification. Want, effort, success or failure —these many times repeated build up in time an inner aggregate of most intimate experiences. The blanket weighs too heavily upon the child, he finds himself struggling against it. Again our words are too definite, but in this struggle the inner self is being born. The child is perchance cold, and he cries. At first this is a pure reflex. Out of the infinite again comes help. Many times repeated the child learns to cry intentionally for help. If more in earnest, he learns to cry harder, and even in conscious anger. The inner self is fast being built.

Still following Baldwin, we may call these two simultaneous processes, the objective and subjective phases of our self conception making. But as yet the two processes are separate. The subjective is as yet all there is to me of myself, as the objective is all there is to me of you. But at length begins a process of mutual interpretation. The beginning of the process is, like many true beginnings, obscure. A bit finger may start it. Thus far a finger has for the child's consciousness existed mainly as something seen, a part of the external objective world. He knows by now what it is to bite down on things he puts in his mouth. To-day he bites on his own finger, and simultaneously he gets two reports of what happened, a tame one through the mouth nerves, another and livelier one through the finger nerves. In time, if not at first, he learns that the finger, long part of the outside world, is now also part of the inside world, of himself, of that inner self of wants and pains and satisfactions. And likewise with his foot. When he grasps it, he gets the same two reports. It too belongs both to the inside and to the outside world. These two worlds are no longer entirely disparate. They have begun to coalesce.

The process may be helped along by another baby. Who has not observed the interest that babies of a certain age take in each other. This other interesting thing is treated just as he is treated. So far as appears the two belong on equal terms to the external world (what dreadful thoughts to ascribe even in germ to innocent babes, yet in the name of science we must go forward!). And now the other baby cries, the same sound that our child knows so well as belonging to himself. The other baby has bumped his head in a fall. "I too have had my falls and bumped my head. Then he feels inside as I do when I fall and bump my head." The 'dialectic' is now under way. Mutual understandings enlighten both. As I am inside, so is he. As he is outside, so am I. And this is true not only of babies. Older children are to our child part babies and part grown. They cry over their pains as do babies, but they also stand with lessened power in the class of the infinities, with mamma and nurse and daddy and the others. These children, if they cry, feel inside as I do; but they look outside somewhat like the other baby and so like me, but also like those older ones. It must be so. We are all people together. But cats are not quite so; they are treated differently. I do not understand. My doll stays put, yet she looks so like to one of us. I somehow think she knows, but mamma does not really care whether dolly has anything to eat. And dolly never cries. I do not know about cats and dogs and dolls; but people, they're different. We are all people together.

The process, thus begun, never ends. Each of us can recall at some tender age dipping into this poem or that passage in the New Testament, only to find it unutterably dull and incomprehensible. But later, after expanding experience had brought insight, the poem and the passage are crowded with meaning. Some sayings in the poem bring to first consciousness stirrings within. Other personal experiences are here for the first time now related, and the poem itself has now even greater meaning than yesterday. And the passage from Paul, I wake almost with a start, "I see it means me. Paul knew what I have felt." And then I look within more closely and find there for the first time some things I had but just the moment before seen first in Paul. And so it is in life. Only those who have sorrowed deeply know what sorrow is. After that the warm hand grasp of sympathy conveys an understanding, back and forth, that beforetimes was impossible. The process never ends. Continually does experience disclose within me what hitherto I had observed unfeelingly in others. Now I know, and if I am a true man I judge less harshly. And more and more I find that feelings I had somehow supposed peculiar to me do in fact belong also to others, only there they take on a different form of outward show. In this continued process my concepts of myself and of others are continually compounded each of self and other. I can neither be nor think myself, if I do not have the help of you and of others. Nor could I know you, if I did not have myself to add its informing quota. The self and its comrade, the 'socius,' each works with the other to form each and the other. This is the ever continuing "dialectic of personal growth."

Adapted with additions from Baldwin, *Social and Ethical Interpretations* (New York, Macmillian, 1902), p. 13.

101. MEN INFINITE ISOLATIONS

"Ah, sir, a distinct universe walks about under your hat and under mine—all things in nature are different to each—the woman we look at has not the same feature, the dish we eat has not the same taste, to the one and to the other; you and I are but a pair of infinite isolations, with some fellow islands a little more or less near us."

Thackeray, *Pendennis*.

102. SOCIAL PARADOXES

"We are now ready to understand the famous paradox: 'Society existed before the individual.' Before there could be individualities like our own there must first be evolved the various activities which we inherit from a long social past and which no isolated human being could have originated, and also the elaborate opportunities for communication through diverse social contacts.

"Another terse embodiment of the same truth is the saying that 'One man is no man'; it may have been originated by someone who had in mind the power of organization and the comparative impotence of isolated and unorganized endeavor, but it is literally true as a fact of social evolution. One man alone could never become a man corresponding to our conception of man, but such an isolated creature lacking all the activities that compose our lives would be nearer to the other animals than to us. Would he speak the English language? No, for even here and now those born deaf are also dumb since language is not a gift of nature but a social product. Would he have heard of Christ or have discovered for himself His message? No, he would be more destitute of religion than any known heathen. Would he despise deceit and indecency and theft? No, he would have no conscience for no one is born with a conscience and conscience is the product of social experience. Would he have clothing of cloth woven from spun yarn? No; these require the previous accumulation of many inventions which no one of us alone would have made. An isolated individual of the genus homo would be a naked savage and a dumb brute. 'The individual man,' says Bastian, 'is nothing, at best an idiot.'

"Whether the first man was as gifted as Aristotle or possessed an intelligence scarcely superior to that of a chimpanzee would have made very little difference. In either case he would have had no language and very little to say if he had possessed one. His content of consciousness would have been mainly confined to the ideas directly presented by sense-perception. He would have been aware of external objects of sense-perception. He would have been conscious of hunger, pain, and instinctive promptings. But *self*-consciousness, according to the elaborate study of Professor Baldwin, is developed only in association. The possession of great capacities or small would mean but little to any descendant of Adam who was obliged to live in absolute isolation from his kind. Society, as Professor Ellwood and others have remarked, produces its individual personalities as truly as an organism produces its cells. It produces their tastes, sentiments, opinions, and arts. We do not inherit a single idea but only the capacities for ideas and activities. If these capacities should not be awakened by social contacts and enriched by the results of social evolution they would be like seeds in bottles.

"With all our education not even the greatest man originates a contribution to the social heritage of ideas, sentiments, and practices that is large when compared to the whole vast store of that heritage to which the humble and common individual is an heir. And the rare contributions that are of greatest moment would be impossible without the previous possession of the common store. We originate a little because we inherit much; we inherit enough to make us men and women because the common store has been produced by ages of social evolution; that which a single life deprived from birth of all association would develop, is as nothing.

" 'The individual is an abstraction' is another paradoxical expression which has become common among sociologists. McDougal writes: 'The strictly individual human mind, with which the older introspective and descriptive psychology contented itself, is an abstraction merely, and has no real existence.' An abstraction is that which can be thought of by itself but which cannot exist by itself. We can think of the individual apart from society but that which we know as individual life is in and of the larger life of society. When once produced it might for a time continue in isolation but it could never have been produced in isolation, and cannot be understood if thought of only by itself. Says Professor Cooley: 'Self and society are twin born, the notion of a separate and independent ego is an illusion.' Possibly Professor Cooley's discussion in his 'Human Nature and the Social Order' may seem a little extreme to some readers: for example, in his italicized statement: 'Self and other do not exist as mutually exclusive social facts.' But the thought of self includes thoughts of social relationship. John thinks of himself as Thomas' son, as Charles' partner and as Mary's husband; the content of John's consciousness, the very substance of his life, is socially derived and self-consciousness develops on a background of other consciousness. In the language of Professor Baldwin: 'Both ego and alter are essentially social.'"

Hayes, *Introduction to the Study of Sociology* * (New York, Appleton, 1915), pp. 441-444.

103. Man's Unsocial Sociableness

"Man cannot get on with his fellows and he cannot do without them."
Kant.

104. The Herd Theory of Conscience

"Conscience, then, and the feelings of guilt and of duty are the peculiar possessions of the gregarious animal. A dog and a cat caught in the commission of an offence will both recognize that punishment is coming; but the dog, moreover, knows that he has done *wrong*, and he will come to be punished, unwillingly it is true, and as if dragged along by some power outside him, while the cat's sole impulse is to escape. The rational recognition of the sequence of act and punishment is equally clear to the gregarious and to the solitary animal, but it is the former only who understands that he has committed a *crime*, who has, in fact, the *sense of sin*."

Trotter, *Instincts of the Herd in Peace and War* * (New York, Macmillan, 1917), pp. 40-1.

CHAPTER VII

ACTIVITY LEADING TO FURTHER ACTIVITY

105. Joy of Chase

"All things that are,
Are with more spirit chased than enjoy'd."
Merchant of Venice, Act ii, Sc. 6.

106. Happiness

"The emotional accompaniment of the progressive growth of a course of action, a continual movement of expansion and achievement, is happiness."
Dewey, *Interest and Effort* * (Boston, Houghton Mifflin, 1913), p. 35.

107. Choice of Playthings

"Give no plaything whose end is only to be looked at; but let every one be such as to lead to work."
Richter, *Levana* (1807 Bohn ed.), p. 156.

108. Lessing on the Search for Truth

"If God were to hold in his right hand all Truth, and in his left the single ever-active impulse to seek after Truth, even though with the condition that I must eternally remain in error, and say to me, 'Choose!' I would with humility fall before his left hand and say, 'Father, give! for Pure Truth belongs to Thee alone.'"
Lessing, *The Laocoon* (Rönnfeldt, editor. London, Scott, no date), p. xvi.

109. Activity Leading to Further Activity

"The human being has an environment of tremendous complexity to which he must adjust himself, and he never can acquire all the adjustments necessary and bring them under automatic control. If his life is reduced largely to habit, it means that he has arbitrarily limited the environment to which he is to react, and, therefore, has shut out the possibility of further development. He has become, as James expresses it, an 'old fogy.' In this sense habit deadens and reduces the life of the individual to the level of non-voluntary activity. These considerations do not mean that the individual should not acquire a large number of habits, but they do mean that also there should be beyond the sphere of habitual activity an unlimited place for the further development of habits. *The difference between the person who continues to make progress all through his life, and the one whose real life is ended in his early manhood is that the former always possesses an open mind and the attitude of finding in his environment further possibilities of adjustment.* It has sometimes been said that most school teachers end their effective period of usefulness in the early years of their professional careers. If this were true, it would be because they originally approached their profession with mind open, and because they found in their school environment new situations to be solved. Those who after a brief period of teaching have become dead are those who have been satisfied in limiting their activities to the things which they have learned in the first years of their professional work. The environment presented by the school may be regarded as a relatively simple one that can be readily comprehended, and the reactions to which can easily be mechanized, or it may be regarded as perhaps the most complex of all environments, in which the possibilities of new adjustments are practically limitless. It is the teacher who regards the school in this latter way who never ceases to grow."

Colvin, *The Learning Process* * (New York, Macmillan, 1911), p. 52-3.

110. Secondary Neurone Connections

(a) "Merely to have sensations is, other things being equal, satisfying to man. Mental emptiness is one of his great annoyers. We may justly picture the brain of man as containing many neurones, in connection with the sensory neurones, which crave stimulation—are in 'readiness to conduct'—though no immediate gratification of any more practical want follows their action. Man wants sense impressions for sensation's sake. Novel experiences are to him their own sufficient reward. It is because they satisfy this want as well as because of their intrinsic satisfyingness, that visual exploration and manipulation are the almost incessant occupations of our waking infancy." ...

(b) "There are not only neurones ready to be set in action by direct stimuli from the sense-organs, but also neurones ready to be set in action by more remote or secondary connections. For example, a baby likes not only to see a pile of blocks tumble or a wheel go around, but also to find the blocks tumbling *when he hits them*, or the wheel revolving *when he pushes* a spring. Satisfactions of the second sort are, indeed, if anything the more potent. Merely hearing the toot of a horn is a feeble joy compared to blowing it. Now 'tumbling when I hit them,' 'whirling when I push,' and 'tooting when I blow' are samples of *secondary* connections, a step removed from mere sensations. They represent the action of the neurones concerned in the child's manipulations, those concerned in his sensations and *those concerned in connecting the latter with the former*." ...

(c) "The tendencies to make and enjoy making secondary connections," which join together existing S→R bonds in some new fashion are very important in the life of men. "These tendencies to secondary, or so-called 'higher,' connections may rise free from the appetites of the single creature who exercises them and deal with the world in the interest of all men. Work and play with *'ideas'* of apples, blows, headaches, friendship, war, marriage, child-birth and family can be impersonal and ideal to an extent and a degree that would never be attained by direct responses to the concrete situations themselves. So, by his peculiar tendencies to go beyond these and to enjoy mental activity in general, man is becoming able to guide the mêlée of personal loves, hates, jealousies, rivalries, seizings, holdings, fightings, masterings and submittings by that impartial judgment of their effects which makes truth and that impartial judgment of their worth which makes justice." ...

(d) We may conclude then that man, in addition to the satisfyingness of sensations which he shares with the lower animals, has the capacity and inclination to engage in the most varied mental activity. Activity of some kind he will have. The most significant characteristic of such varied mental activity is found in the fact of secondary connections, "doing something and having something happen" in novel ways. This tendency to join old ways of doing and thinking in new ways forms thus a principal basis for growth and progress.

Adapted from Thorndike, *Educational Psychology* (New York, Teachers College, 1913), Vol. I, pp. 141, 307-8.

ACTIVITY LEADING TO FURTHER ACTIVITY 77

111. Effect of Age on Learning

"The animals (rats) were divided into four groups: a twenty-five day old group, which is the age at which they become independent of the mother; a sixty-five day old group, or the age of sexual maturity; a two hundred day old group, which might represent the middle of adult life; and a three hundred day old group, to represent the beginning of old age. The twenty-five day old rats and the sixty-five day old rats, which represent our most youthful groups, learned the maze in approximately thirty trials; whereas the two hundred and three hundred day old animals required nearly a third more trials—about forty-two. The young animals required about six seconds for their finally perfected runs; the old groups required about ten seconds. These experiments show clearly two things: first, that, as everyone has hitherto suspected, the young animals do learn faster than the old ones; but in the second place, that the old animals can learn very fast indeed, all things considered. We have continued these experiments with a few very old animals and we find that animals even five and six hundred days old still have the ability to learn this complicated maze. . . . I think these experiments should give those of us who have passed the first bloom of youth a good deal of hope. Many of us in that too often unfortunate condition say that we do not know how to dance, to skate, and to play games because we did not learn such things when we were young; but this excuse is no longer valid. We now have experimental evidence to show that the contention of William James concerning the non-plasticity that is supposed to go with old age, which has been so universally accepted, is completely unfounded. Any one of us who cares to put on the highly skillful acts needed in either work or play can do so provided he is willing to spend approximately a third more time than a youth would have to spend in acquiring the same acts. . . . There is hardly any line of activity which will not yield to 'middle-aged' effort."

Watson, in *Suggestions of Modern Science concerning Education* * (New York, Macmillan, 1917), p. 91 ff.

112. A Broader Problem

"The problem of instruction in reading is not to teach people how to read but to read."

Moore, *What is Education* * (Boston, Ginn, 1915), p. 147.

113. Peter Bell

"A primrose by a river's brim
A yellow primrose was to him,
And it was nothing more."

Wordsworth, *Peter Bell*, Pt. I, st. 12.

114. Indulgence

"Any power, whether of child or adult, is indulged when it is taken on its given and present level in consciousness. Its genuine meaning is in the propulsion it affords toward a higher level. It is just something to do with. Appealing to the interest upon the present plane means excitation; it means playing with a power so as continually to stir it up without directing it toward definite achievement."

Dewey, *The Child and Curriculum* * (Chicago, Univ. of Chicago, 1902), p. 21.

115. When Interests are Vital

"Interests are specific and dynamic; they are the natural terms of any concrete social thinking. But they are damned beyond recovery when they are identified with the things of a petty selfishness. They can be employed as vital terms only when the self is seen to be in process, and interest to be a name for whatever is concerned in furthering its movement."

Dewey, *Reconstruction in Philosophy* * (New York, Holt, 1920), p. 195.

116. When Interest is Proper

"Interest is normal and reliance upon it educationally legitimate in the degree in which the activity in question involves growth or development. Interest is illegitimately used in the degree in which it is either a symptom or a cause of arrested development in an activity. . . .

"When interest is objected to as merely amusement or fooling or a temporary excitation (or when in educational practice it does mean simply such things), it will be found that the interest in question is something which attaches merely to a momentary activity apart from its place in an enduring activity—an activity that develops through a period of time. When this happens, the object that arouses (what is called) interest is esteemed just on the basis of the momentary reaction it calls out, the immediate pleasure it excites. 'Interest' so created is abnormal, for it is a sign of the dissipation of energy; it is a symptom that life is being cut up into a series of disconnected reactions, each one of which is esteemed by itself apart from what it does in carrying forward (or developing) a consecutive activity. As we have already seen, it is one thing to make, say, number interesting by merely attaching to it other things that happen to call out a pleasurable reaction; it is a radically different sort of thing to make it interesting by introducing it so that it functions as a genuine means of carrying on a more inclusive activity."

Dewey, *Interest and Effort* * (Boston, Houghton Mifflin, 1913), pp. 41-3.

117. BASIS FOR JUDGING

"No individual or group will be judged by whether they come up to or fall short of some fixed result, but by the direction in which they are moving. The bad man is the man who no matter how good *has* been is beginning to deteriorate, to grow less good. The good man is the man who no matter how morally unworthy he *has* been is moving to become better. Such a conception makes one severe in judging himself and humane in judging others."

Dewey, *Reconstruction in Philosophy* * (New York, Holt, 1920), p. 176.

118. REPEATED GOODNESS NOT GOOD

"The good man who merely repeats his goodness of the day before is not a good man, but a bad man."

Quoted by Moore, in *What is Education* (Boston, Ginn, 1915), p. 141.

119. THE PROBLEM OF ETHICS

"The problem of ethics consists . . . in showing how life, human-mental life, is preserved and promoted by virtuous deeds, but impeded and destroyed by vice. Honesty is good; theft in every shape and form is bad, for theft injures first the life of the aggrieved person then also that of the thief; it deprives him of the blessings of labor, for thieves do not work. Finally, it destroys the security of property and hence the desire to acquire it; for nations whose property rights are insecure become impoverished. Property, however, is the fundamental condition of all higher development in human-mental life. Thus veracity is good and falsehood bad, because in addition to the disturbances which it produces within the narrowest circles, the deception of the offended person, the isolation of the liar, it has the secondary effect of destroying the confidence of men in general. Confidence, however, is the fundamental condition of human social life, and without society there can be no real human life. Similarly, adultery and licentiousness are reprehensible, because they ruin individuals and tend to destroy healthy family life, the root of all healthy human life; and, conversely, to live a pure and chaste life in word and in deed is good, because it preserves life in the physical and spiritual sense. And so it is everywhere: certain modes of conduct are good in so far as they have the tendency to preserve and to augment human goods, others are reprehensible and bad, because they tend to destroy the conditions of a wholesome, beautiful, and spiritual human life. In so far now as welfare is accompanied by feelings of satisfaction, decline and ruin by feelings of pain, we may also say: Virtue is the road to happiness, vice to unhappiness."

Paulsen, *Introduction to Philosophy* * (Trans. by Thilly. New York, Holt, 1895), p. 426.

120. Growing is Moral Progress

"The heart of the sociality of man is in education. The idea of education as preparation and of adulthood as a fixed limit of growth are two sides of the same obnoxious untruth. If the moral business of the adult as well as the young is a growing and developing experience, then the instruction that comes from social dependencies and interdependencies are as important for the adult as for the child. Moral independence for the adult means arrest of growth, isolation means induration. We exaggerate the intellectual dependence of childhood so that children are too much kept in leading strings, and then we exaggerate the independence of adult life from intimacy of contacts and communication with others. When the identity of the moral process with the processes of specific growth is realized, the more conscious and formal education of childhood will be seen to be the most economical and efficient means of social advance and reorganization, and it will also be evident that the test of all the institutions of adult life is their effect in furthering continued education. Government, business, art, religion, all social

ACTIVITY LEADING TO FURTHER ACTIVITY

institutions have a meaning, a purpose. That purpose is to set free and to develop the capacities of human individuals without respect to race, sex, class or economic status. And this is all one with saying that the test of their value is the extent to which they educate every individual into the full stature of his possibility. Democracy has many meanings, but if it has a moral meaning, it is found in resolving that the supreme test of all political institutions and industrial arrangements shall be the contribution they make to the all-around growth of every member of society."

Dewey, *Reconstruction in Philosophy* * (New York, Holt, 1920), pp. 185-186.

121. THE MEANING OF DUTY

Duty is best understood in relation to a growing character.—"Duty is what is owed by a partial isolated self embodied in established, facile, and urgent tendencies, to that ideal self which is presented in aspirations which, since they are not yet formed into habits, have no organized hold upon the self and which can get organized into habitual tendencies and interests only by a more or less painful and difficult reconstruction of the habitual self. . . . The consciousness of duty grows out of the complex character of the self; the fact that at any given time, it has tendencies relatively set, ingrained, and embodied in fixed habits, while it also has tendencies in process of making, looking to the future, taking account of unachieved possibilities. The former give the solid relatively formed elements of character; the latter, its ideal or unrealized possibilities." . . .

"The conflict of duty and desire is thus an accompaniment of a *growing* self. Spencer's complete disappearance of obligation would mean an exhausted and fossilized self; wherever there is progress, tension arises between what is already accomplished and what is possible. In a being whose "reach should exceed his grasp," a conflict within the self making for the readjustment of the direction of powers must always be found. The value of continually *having to meet the expectations and requirements of others is in keeping the agent from resting on his oars, from falling back on habits already formed as if they were final*. The phenomena of duty in all their forms are thus phenomena attendant upon the expansion of ends and the reconstruction of character." (p. 362 f.)

Dewey and Tufts, *Ethics* * (New York, Holt, 1908).

122. The Creative Impulse and the Joy of Life

"The most important purpose that political institutions can achieve is to keep alive in individuals creativeness, vigor, vitality, and the joy of life. These things existed, for example, in Elizabethan England in a way in which they do not exist now. They stimulated adventure, poetry, music, fine architecture, and set going the whole movement out of which England's greatness has sprung in every direction in which England has been great. These things coexisted with injustice, but outweighed it, and made a national life more admirable than any that is likely to exist under socialism.

"What is wanted in order to keep men full of vitality is opportunity, not security. Security is merely a refuge from fear; opportunity is the source of hope. The chief test of an economic system is not whether it makes men prosperous, or whether it secures distributive justice (though these are both very desirable), but whether it leaves men's instinctive growth unimpeded. To achieve this purpose, there are two main conditions which it should fulfil: it should not cramp men's private affections, and it should give the greatest possible outlet to the impulse of creation. There is in most men, until it becomes atrophied by disuse, an instinct of constructiveness, a wish to make something. The men who achieve most are, as a rule, those in whom this instinct is strongest; such men become artists, men of science, statesmen, empire-builders, or captains of industry, according to the accidents of temperament and opportunity. The most beneficent and the most harmful careers are inspired by this impulse. Without it, the world would sink to the level of Tibet: it would subsist, as it is always prone to do, on the wisdom of its ancestors, and each generation would sink more deeply into a lifeless traditionalism.

"But it is not only the remarkable men who have the instinct of constructiveness, though it is they who have it most strongly. It is almost universal in boys, and in men it usually survives in a greater or less degree, according to the greater or less outlet which it is able to find. Work inspired by this instinct is satisfying, even when it is irksome and difficult, because every effort is as natural as the effort of a dog pursuing a hare. The chief defect of the present capitalistic system is that work done for wages seldom affords any outlet for the creative impulse. The man who works for wages has no choice as to what he shall make: the whole creativeness of the processes concentrates in the employer who orders the work to be done. For this reason the work becomes a merely external means to a certain result, the earning of wages. Employers grow indignant about the trade union rules for limitation of output, but they have no right to be indignant, since they do not permit the men whom they employ to have any share in the purpose for which the work is undertaken. And so the process of production, which should form one instinctive cycle, becomes divided into separate purposes, which can no longer provide any satisfaction of instinct for those who do the work."

Russell, *Why Men Fight* * (New York, Century, 1917), pp. 143-146.

CHAPTER VIII

WHAT CONSTITUTES THE GOOD LIFE

123. Ruskin on the Good

"There is no wealth but life."

John Ruskin.

124. Nirvana: the Way of Holiness

"Sit straight and motionless, never inclining to the left hand nor to the right, never bowing forward nor turning backward. The ears should be in the same plane with the shoulders, and nose and navel in the same straight line. The tongue should stick to the upper jaw, while lip meets lip and teeth with teeth. Open the eyes not too widely yet not too slightly, and keep breathing through the nose. After composing mind and body in this way, you may take a long deep breath. Thus sitting motionless you may think of not thinking. Can you think of not thinking? This is thinking of nothing . . . it is the only way to great calm joy. This is unpolluted practice, and this is enlightenment."

Harada, *The Faith of Japan* * (New York, Macmillan, 1914), p. 89.

125. Compte on the Good

"The inventor of a new spinning-machine was a greater benefactor to humanity than Homer and all his poetry."

Quoted.

126. Gandhi's Idea of the Good Life

"India's salvation consists in unlearning what she has learned during the past fifty years. The railways, telegraphs, hospitals, lawyers, doctors and such like have all to go and the so-called upper classes have to learn to live religiously and deliberately the simple peasant life, knowing it to be a life giving true happiness.

"There was true wisdom in the sages of old having so regulated society as to limit the material condition of the people. . . . Therein lies salvation. People live long under such conditions, in comparative peace, much greater than Europe has enjoyed after having taken up modern activity."

Gandhi, quoted in *Current History Magazine*, 16:1067 (Sept., 1922).

127. A Static Life Intolerable

"Desire, activity, purpose, are essential to a tolerable life, and a millennium, tho it may be a joy in prospect, would be intolerable if it were actually achieved."

Russell, *Why Men Fight* * (New York, Century, 1917), p. 138.

128. A Satisfying Civilization

"What human nature . . . demands in civilization, if it is to stand as a high end and satisfying civilization, is best described by the word *interesting*. Here is the extraordinary charm of the old Greek civilization: that it is so *interesting*."

Matthew Arnold, *Civilization in the United States* * (Boston, DeWolfe Fiske, 1888), p. 170.

129. Socrates on the Good

"You, Antipho, seem to think that happiness consists in luxury and extravagance; but I think that to want nothing is to resemble the gods, and that to want as little as possible is to make the nearest approach to the gods; that the Divine nature is perfection, and that to be nearest to the Divine nature is to be nearest to perfection."

Xenophon, *Memorabilia*, I, vi, 10.

130. Highest Happiness

"We can only have the highest happiness, such as goes with being a great man, by having wide thoughts, and much feeling for the rest of the world as well as ourselves; and this sort of happiness often brings so much pain with it that we can only tell it from pain by its being what we would choose before everything else, because our souls see it is good."

George Eliot, *Romola* (Garden City, Doubleday Page, 1901), p. 209.

131. Omar Khayyám on Life

"Waste not your Hour, nor in the vain pursuit
Of This and That endeavor and dispute:
   Better be jocund with the fruitful Grape
Than sadden after none, or bitter, Fruit. (LIV)

"Ah, my Beloved, fill the cup that clears
To-day of past Regret and future Fears:
   To-morrow!—Why, To-morrow I may be
Myself with Yesterday's Sev'n thousand Years. (XXI)

"A Book of Verses underneath the Bough,
A Jug of Wine, a Loaf of Bread—and Thou
   Beside me singing in the Wilderness—
Oh, Wilderness were Paradise enow!" (XII)

Rubáiyát (Trans. by Fitzgerald. Third edition, London, Quaritch, 1872).

132. Life Active not Passive

"Man is not a consumer of pleasures. He is a creator of life."
Quoted by Tufts, in *Creative Intelligence* (New York, Holt, 1917), p. 374.

133. The Highest Good

"The goal at which the will of every living creature aims, is *the normal exercise of the vital functions which constitute its nature*. Every animal desires to live the life for which it is predisposed. Its natural disposition manifests itself in impulses, and determines its activity. The formula may also be applied to man. He desires to live a *human* life and all that is implied in it; that is, a *mental, historical life, in which there is room for the exercise of all human, mental powers and virtues*. He desires to play and to learn, to work and to acquire wealth, to possess and to enjoy, to form and to create; he desires to love and to admire, to obey and to rule, to fight and to win, to make poetry and to dream, to think and to investigate. And he desires to do all these things in their natural order of development, as life provides them. He desires to experience the relations of the child to its parents, of the pupil to his teacher, of the apprentice to the master; and his will, for the time being, finds the highest satisfaction in such a life. He desires to live as a brother among brothers, as a friend among friends, as a companion among companions, as a citizen among citizens, and also to prove himself an enemy against enemies. Finally, he desires to experience what the lover, husband, and father experience—he desires to rear and educate children who shall preserve and transmit the contents of his own life."

Paulsen, *System of Ethics* * (Trans. by Thilly. New York, Scribners, 1899), p. 270.

134. THE CYNIC IDEA OF THE GOOD

"The Cynics were for doing away with the whole system of logic and natural philosophy . . . and held that one should devote one's self solely to the study of ethics. . . . They would discard all liberal studies. . . . Their doctrine is that the chief good of man consists in living according to virtue. . . . They also teach that men ought to lead the simple life, eating only plain food, and that in moderation, wearing nothing but a cloak, and showing contempt for wealth and fame and noble birth.

"Diogenes used to say that there are two kinds of training, that of the mind and that of the body . . . and that neither is complete without the other. And he said that training gives power to overcome every obstacle, and that everywhere in life training is the condition of success. . . . He held that those who gave up useless labor and confined themselves to the tasks that nature enjoined, could not fail to live happily. It is our folly alone that makes us unhappy. For the very contempt of pleasure, when one has grown accustomed to it, is itself a source of great pleasure. And just as those who are accustomed to a life of luxury are brought very unwillingly to adopt the simple life, so those who have been trained in the latter take pleasure in their very scorn of pleasure."

Diogenes Laertius in Bakewell, *Source Book in Ancient Philosophy* * (New York, Scribners, 1907), p. 147.

135. EPICURUS ON THE GOOD LIFE

"It is right then for a man to consider the things which produce happiness, since, if happiness is present, we have everything, and when it is absent, we do everything with a view to possess it. Now, what I have constantly recommended to you, these things I would have you do and practise, considering them to be the elements of living well. . . .

"We must consider that some of the passions are natural, and some empty; and of the natural ones some are necessary, and some merely natural. And of the necessary ones some are necessary to happiness, others are necessary that the body may be exempt from trouble, and others, again, merely in order that life itself may be; for a correct theory, with regard to these things, can refer all choice and avoidance to the health of the body and the imperturbability of the soul, since this is the end of living happily. For it is for the sake of this that we do everything, wishing to avoid grief and fear; and when once this is the case, with respect to us, then the storm of the soul is, as I may say, put an end to. . . .

"Pleasure is the beginning and end of living happily; for we have recognized this as the first good, being connate with us; and it is with reference to it that we begin every choice and avoidance; and to this we come as if we judged of all good by passion as the standard; and, since this is the first good and connate with us, on this account we do not choose every pleasure, but at times we pass over many pleasures when any difficulty is likely to ensue from them; and we think many pains better than pleasures, when a greater pleasure follows them, if we endure the pain for a time.

"Every pleasure is therefore a good on account of its own nature, but it does not follow that every pleasure is worthy of being chosen; just as every pain is an evil, and yet every pain must not be avoided; but it is right to estimate all these things by the measurement and view of what is suitable and unsuitable; for at times we may feel the good as an evil, and at times, on the contrary, we may feel the evil as good. And we think contentment a great good, not in order that we may never have but a little, but in order that, if we have not much, we may make use of a little, being genuinely persuaded that those men enjoy luxury most completely who are the best able to do without it; and that everything which is natural is easily provided; and what is useless is not easily procured. And simple flavors give as much pleasure as costly fare, when everything that can give pain, and every feeling of want, is removed; and corn and water give the most extreme pleasure when any in need eats them. To accustom one's self, therefore, to simple and inexpensive habits is a great ingredient in the perfecting of health, and makes a man free from hesitation with respect to the necessary uses of life. And when we, on certain occasions, fall in with more sumptuous fare, it makes us in a better disposition toward it, and renders us fearless with respect to fortune. When, therefore, we say that pleasure is a chief good, we are not speaking of the pleasures of the debauched man, or those which lie in sensual enjoyment, as some think who are ignorant, and who do not entertain our opinions, or else interpret them perversely; but we mean the freedom of the body from pain, and of the soul from confusion."

Bakewell, *Source Book in Ancient Philosophy* * (New York, Scribners, 1907), pp. 296-300.

136. ASCETICISM

"A clean body and a clean dress mean an unclean soul." (p. 206.)

"To induce you to take baths they will speak of dirt with disgust." (p. 218.)

"It is usual in the monasteries of Egypt . . . for virgins and widows . . . to cut their hair . . . It is designed to save those who take no baths and whose heads and faces are strangers to all unguents from all accumulated dirt, and from the tiny creatures which are sometimes generated about the roots of the hair." (p. 292.)

St. Jerome's Letters and Select Works (New York, Scribners, 1912).

137. SAINT DOUCELINE, A MEDIEVAL ASCETIC

"Even while she was yet in the world she wore in secret a shirt of pigskin, hard and rough, which galled her to the quick, so that she was oftentimes unable to remove it; and when it was taken off it left her body all torn and covered with sores. It befell one day that this shirt was so ingrown into her flesh as to defy all her efforts to tear it away; whereupon she was fain to call her handmaid, in whom she put her trust, and who drew off the shirt by main force, tearing her flesh with the hide. She was wont to gird her waist so straitly with a knotted cord, that worms would oftentimes breed where the knots entered into her flesh. Moreover, she wore an iron hoop night and day . . . over which she showed fair and choice garments, as though she loved gay stuffs. She lay, for penance' sake, on a little straw in the corner of her room; and lest she should rest in sleep, she bound a cord above her bed with one end, and with the other round her own waist; so that, whensoever she stirred, the cord would drag and wake her. Then would she rise forthwith to say her matins with all devotion, and to read. . . . Such then was her life so long as she lived in the world."

Coulton, *A Medieval Garner* (London, Constable, 1910), p. 320 f.

138. Zeno the Stoic on the Good

"This very thing is the virtue of the happy man and the perfect happiness of life: when everything is done according to a harmony with the genius of each individual with reference to the will of the universal Governor and Manager of all things. . . .

"For our individual natures are all parts of universal nature; on which account the chief good is to live in a manner corresponding to nature, and that means corresponding to one's own nature and to universal nature; doing none of these things which the common law of mankind is in the habit of forbidding, and that common law is identical with that right reason which pervades everything, being the same with Jupiter, who is the regulater and chief manager of all existing things."

Diogenes Laertius (Bohn ed.), Book VII, ch. liii.

139. Epictetus on the Good

"Men are disturbed not by things, but by the views which they take of things. Thus death is nothing terrible, else it would have appeared so to Socrates. But the terror consists in our notion of death, that it is terrible. When, therefore, we are hindered, or disturbed, or grieved let us never impute it to others, but to ourselves; that is, to our own views. It is the action of an uninstructed person to reproach others for his own misfortunes; of one entering upon instruction, to reproach himself; and of one perfectly instructed, to reproach neither others nor himself.

"Demand not that events should happen as you wish; but wish them to happen as they do happen, and you will go on well."

Bakewell, *Source Book in Ancient Philosophy* * (New York, Scribners, 1907), pp. 317-8.

140. The Good Life One of Speculative Activity

"That perfect happiness is a species of speculative activity will appear from the following consideration among others. Our conception of the Gods is that they are preëminently happy and fortunate. But what kind of actions do we properly attribute to them? Are they just actions? But it would make the Gods ridiculous to suppose that they form contracts, restore deposits, and so on. Are they then courageous actions? Do the Gods endure dangers and alarms for the sake of honour? Or liberal actions? But to whom should they give money? It would be absurd to suppose that they have a currency or anything of the kind. Again, what will be the nature of their temperate actions? Surely to praise the gods for temperance is to degrade them; they are exempt from low desires. We may go through the whole category of virtues, and it will appear that whatever relates to moral action is petty and unworthy of the Gods.

"Yet the Gods are universally conceived as living and therefore as displaying activity; they are certainly not conceived as sleeping like Endymion. If then action and still more production is denied to one who is alive, what is left but speculation? It follows that the activity of God being preëminently blissful will be speculative, and if so then the human activity which is most nearly related to it will be most capable of happiness."

Aristotle, *Nicomachean Ethics* * (Trans. by Welldon. London, Macmillan, 1906), Book X, ch. viii.

141. HAPPINESS AND MONEY

"The man who worships money has ceased to hope for happiness through his own efforts or in his own activities: he looks upon happiness as a passive enjoyment of pleasures derived from the outside world. The artist or the lover does not worship money in his moments of ardor, because his desires are specific and directed towards objects which only he can create. And, conversely, the worshipper of money can never achieve greatness as an artist or lover."

Russell, *Why Men Fight* * (New York, Century, 1917), p. 118.

142. HAPPINESS

Happiness is "the unfettered development of all the instincts that build up life and fill it with mental delights" . . .

Russell, quoted in *Atlantic Monthly*, 124:619 (Nov., 1919).

143. HAPPINESS

"Happiness signifies a gratified state of all the faculties. The gratification of a faculty is produced by its exercise. To be agreeable that exercise must be proportionate to the power of the faculty; if it is insufficient discontent arises, and its excess produces weariness. Hence, to have complete felicity is to have all the faculties exerted in the ratio of their several developments; and an ideal arrangement of circumstances calculated to secure this constitutes the standard of 'greatest happiness.'"

Spencer, *Social Statics* (New York, Appleton, 1878[1]), p. 15.

144. HUMAN NATURE

"We understand our original sin to be the innate corruption of man which has passed from our first parents to us; through which, being sunk in depraved desires, averse to good, inclined to every evil, full of every wickedness, of contempt and hatred of God, we are unable to do or even think any good whatever."

The Second Helvetic Confession (1566), Ch. 8.

145. A MODERN IDEA OF THE GOOD

(Regarding the utilization of water power) "The false question of preserving natural scenery has obliterated the real problem in the public mind. I will not take a second seat from anybody in my enjoyment of natural scenery, but that cannot be allowed to interfere with the advancing interests of civilization."

A former Railroad Commissioner of Massachusetts, in the *New York Times Magazine*, Dec. 23, 1917.

146. MATTHEW ARNOLD ON THE GOOD

"Culture says: 'Consider these people [the Philistines, the merely rich], then, their ways of life, their habits, their manners, the very tones of their voice; look at them attentively; observe the literature they read, the things which give them pleasure, the words which come forth out of their mouths, the thoughts which make the furniture of their minds; would any amount of wealth be worth having with the condition that one was to become just like these people by having it?'"

[1] 1st ed., 1850.

WHAT CONSTITUTES THE GOOD LIFE

Arnold, *Culture and Anarchy* * (New York, Macmillan, 1912), p. 16.

147. MATTHEW ARNOLD ON CULTURE

"The pursuit of perfection then is the pursuit of sweetness and light. He who works for sweetness and light, works to make reason and the will of God prevail. He who works for machinery, he who works for hatred, works only for confusion. Culture looks beyond machinery, culture hates hatred; culture has one great passion, the passion for sweetness and light. It has one even yet greater—the passion for making them *prevail*. It is not satisfied till we *all* come to a perfect man; for it knows that the sweetness and light of the few must be imperfect until the raw and unkindled masses of humanity are touched with sweetness and light."

Arnold, *Culture and Anarchy* * (New York, Macmillan, 1912), p. 37.

148. MAN'S PURSUIT OF HAPPINESS

(a) "On the occasion of every act he exercises every human being is led to pursue that line of conduct which, according to his view of the case, taken by him at the moment, will be in the highest degree contributory to his own greatest happiness. (ix 5.)

(b) "Man, from the very constitution of his nature, prefers his own happiness to that of all other sensitive beings put together." (x 80.)

Bentham (1882), *Works*.

149. THE GOOD MORAL CHARACTER

(a) "The genuinely moral person is one, then, in whom the habit of regarding all capacities and habits of self from the social standpoint is formed and active. Such an one forms his plans, regulates his desires, and hence performs his acts with reference to the effect they have upon the social groups of which he is a part. He is one whose dominant attitudes and interests are bound up with associated activities. Accordingly he will find his happiness or satisfaction in the promotion of these activities irrespective of the particular pains and pleasures that accrue." (p. 298.)

(b) "To one in whom these interests live (and they live to

some extent in every individual not completely pathological) their exercise brings happiness because it fulfills his life. To those in whom it is the supreme interest it brings supreme or final happiness. It is not preferred because it is the greater happiness, but in being preferred as expressing the only kind of self which the agent fundamentally wishes himself to be, it constitutes a kind of happiness with which others cannot be compared. It is unique, final, invaluable." (p. 301.)

Dewey and Tufts, *Ethics* * (New York, Holt, 1908).

150. DEMOCRITUS ON THE GOOD LIFE

"Men achieve tranquillity through moderation in pleasure and through the symmetry of life. Want and superfluity are apt to upset them and to cause great perturbations in the soul. The souls that are rent by violent conflicts are neither stable nor tranquil. One should therefore set his mind upon the things that are within his power, and be content with his opportunities, nor let his memory dwell very long on the envied and admired of men, nor idly sit and dream of them. Rather, he should contemplate the lives of those who suffer hardship, and vividly bring to mind their sufferings, so that your own present situation may appear to you important and to be envied, and so that it may no longer be your portion to suffer torture in your soul by your longing for more. . . . And therefore one ought not to desire other men's blessings, and one ought not to envy those who have more, but rather, comparing his life with that of those who fare worse, and laying to heart their sufferings, deem himself blest of fortune in that he lives and fares so much better than they. Holding fast to this saying you will pass your life in greater tranquillity and will avert not a few of the plagues of life—envy and jealousy and bitterness of mind.

"All who delight in the pleasures of the belly, exceeding all measure in eating and drinking and love, find that the pleasures are brief and last but a short while—only so long as they are eating and drinking—but the pains that come after are many and endure. The longing for the same things keeps ever returning, and whenever the objects of one's desire are realized forthwith the pleasure vanishes, and one has no further use for them. The pleasure is brief, and once more the need for the same things returns."

Bakewell, *Source Book in Ancient Philosophy* * (New York, Scribners, 1907), pp. 63-65.

151. ASSUMPTIONS OF A SOCIAL PHILOSOPHY

"You . . . must allow me to make certain initial assumptions. I will be as modest as possible. I will not assume that life is something intrinsically good, but I must assume that the good for man is to be found in some kind of life, not in the negation of life. I will not assume that fullness of vitality is as such desirable, but I must assume that, other things equal, the fuller life is on the whole more desirable. I will not assume that happiness, however attained, is good, but I must assume that there is some form of happiness which is good, or, at lowest, that misery is an evil. I will not assume that the full realization of the capacities of mind defines the end of life, but I must assume that some form of such realization is an integral element in a desirable life. Finally, I will not assume that all social life is good, still less that social growth is necessarily a change for the better, but I must assume that a life which is completely social—which fully realizes the social capacities of man—is good, and that if we use the phrase 'social development' in a precise sense as a short expression for the accomplishment of such a life, social development is good."

Hobhouse, *Social Evolution and Political Theory* * (New York, Columbia University, 1911), p. 83.

152. PLATO'S IDEA OF THE GOOD

"He who would proceed aright in this matter should begin in youth to visit beautiful forms; and first, if he be guided by his instructor aright, to love one such form only—out of that he should create fair thoughts; and soon he will of himself perceive that the beauty of one form is akin to the beauty of another; and then if beauty of form in general is his pursuit, how foolish would he be not to recognize that the beauty in every form is one and the same! And when he perceived this he will abate his violent love of the one, which he will despise and deem a small thing, and will become a lover of all beautiful forms; in the next stage he will consider that the beauty of the mind is more honorable than the beauty of the outward form. So that if a virtuous soul have but a little comeliness, he will be content to love and tend him, and will search out and bring to the birth thoughts which may improve the young, until he is compelled to contemplate and see the beauty of institutions and laws, and to understand that the beauty of them all is of one family, and that personal beauty is a trifle; and after laws and institutions he will go on to the sciences, that he may see their beauty, being not like a servant in love with the beauty of one youth or man or institution, himself a slave mean and narrow-minded, but drawing toward and contemplating the vast sea of beauty, he will create many fair and noble thoughts and notions in boundless love of wisdom; until on that shore he grows and waxes strong, and at last the vision is revealed to him of a single science, which is the science of beauty everywhere. . . .

"He who has been instructed thus far in the things of love, and who has learned to see the beautiful in due order and succession, when he comes toward the end will suddenly perceive a nature of wondrous beauty . . . a nature which in the first place is everlasting, not growing and decaying, or waxing and waning; secondly, not fair in one point of view and foul in another, or at one time or in one relation or at one place fair, at another time or in another relation or at another place foul, as if fair to some and foul to others, or in the likeness of a face or hands or any other part of the bodily frame, or in any form of speech or knowledge, or existing in any other being, as for example, in an animal, or in heaven, or in earth, or in any other place; but beauty absolute, separate, simple, and everlasting, which without diminution and without increase, or any change, is imparted to the ever-growing and perishing beauties of all other things. He who from these ascending under the influence of true love, begins to perceive that beauty, is not far from the end. And the true order of going, or being led by another, to the things of love, is to begin from the beauties of earth and mount upward for the sake of that other beauty, using these as steps only, and from one going on to two, and from two to all fair forms, and from fair forms to fair practices, and from fair practices to fair notions, until from fair notions he arrives at the notion of absolute beauty, and at last knows what the essence of beauty is. This . . . is that life above all others which man should live, in the contemplation of beauty absolute; a beauty which if you once beheld, you would see not to be after the measure of gold, and garments, and fair boys and youths, whose presence now entrances you; and you and many a one would be content to live seeing them only and conversing with them without meat or drink, if that were possible—you only want to look at them and to be with them. But what if man had eyes to see the true beauty—the divine beauty, I mean, pure and clear and unalloyed, not clogged with the pollutions of mortality and all the colors and vanities of human life—thither looking, and holding converse with the true beauty simple and divine? Remember how in that communion only, beholding beauty with the eye of the mind, he will be enabled to bring forth, not images of beauty, but realities (for he has hold not of an image, but of a reality), and bringing forth and nourishing true virtue to become the friend of God and be immortal, if mortal man may."

Plato, *Symposium* (Trans. by Jowett. 2d ed., Oxford, Clarendon Press, 1875), p. 210-212.

153. The Stoics on the Good Life

"Cleanthes . . . asserts that virtue is a disposition of the mind always consistent and harmonious; that one ought to seek it out for its own sake, without being influenced by fear or hope of any external influence. Moreover, that it is in it that happiness consists, as producing in the soul the harmony of a life always consistent with itself, and that if a rational animal goes the wrong way, it is because it allows itself to be misled by the deceitful appearances of exterior things, or perhaps by the instigation of those who surround it; for nature herself never gives us any but good inclinations. . . .

"They say also that the wise man is free from perturbations because he has no strong propensities. But that this freedom from propensities also exists in the bad man, being, however, then quite another thing, inasmuch as it proceeds in him only from hardness and unimpressibility of his nature. They also pronounce the wise man free from vanity, since he regards with equal eye what is glorious and what is inglorious. At the same time, they admit that there is another character devoid of vanity, who, however, is reckoned one of the rash men, being in fact the bad man. They also say that all the virtuous men are austere, because they do never speak with reference to pleasure, nor do they listen to what is said by others with reference to pleasure. At the same time, they call another man austere too, using the term in nearly the same sense as they do when they speak of austere wine, which is used in compounding medicines, but not for drinking.

"They also pronounce the wise to be honest-hearted men, anxiously attending to those matters which may make them better, by means of some principle which conceals what is bad, and brings to light what is good. Nor is there any hypocrisy about them; for they cut off all pretense in their voice and appearance. They also keep aloof from business; for they guard carefully against doing anything contrary to their duty. They drink wine, but they do not get drunk; and they never yield to frenzy. Occasionally, extraordinary imaginations may obtain a momentary power over them, owing to some melancholy or trifling, arising not according to the principle of what is desirable, but contrary to nature. Nor, again, will the wise man feel grief; because grief is an irrational contraction of the soul."

Diogenes Laertius in Bakewell, *Source Book in Ancient Philosophy* * (New York, Scribners, 1907); pp. 274-6.

CHAPTER IX

THE INDIVIDUAL AND SOCIETY

154. Herbart's Definition of the Good Character

"Man ... capable of becoming, as you will, a wild animal or personified reason, ... needs an art which shall build him up and construct him in order that he may receive the form that is right. And the form that is right is that which in the future, when he shall comprehend himself, will please him; which, when others contemplate him, gains their assent; and which, when with them he is to constitute a social whole, enables him to join with them with accuracy and effect."
Herbart, *A B C of Sense Perception* * (Trans. by Eckoff. New York, Appleton, 1903), p. 59.

155. Nature of Institutions

"The sabbath was made for man and not man for the sabbath."
Jesus (Mark 2:27).

156. Institutions and Men

"Social arrangements, laws, institutions are made for man, rather than that man is made for them; that they are means and agencies of human welfare and progress. But they are not means for obtaining something for individuals, not even happiness. They are means of *creating* individuals. Only in the physical sense of physical bodies that to the senses are separate is individuality an original datum. Individuality in a social and moral sense is something to be wrought out. It means initiative, inventiveness, varied resourcefulness, assumption of responsibility in choice of belief and conduct. These are not gifts, but achievements."
Dewey, *Reconstruction in Philosophy* * (New York, Holt, 1920), p. 194.

157. SAVAGES BOUND BY CUSTOM

"It is difficult to exhaust the customs and small ceremonials of a savage people. Custom regulates the whole of a man's actions—his bathing, washing, cutting his hair, eating, drinking, and fasting. From his cradle to his grave he is the slave of ancient usage. In his life there is nothing free, nothing original, nothing spontaneous, no progress towards a higher and better life, and no attempt to improve his condition, mentally, morally, or spiritually."

Macdonald, quoted in Todd, *Theories of Social Progress* (New York, Macmillan, 1918), p. 87.

158. SAVAGES NOT FREE

"No savage is free. All over the world his daily life is regulated by a complicated and apparently most inconvenient set of customs (as forcible as laws) of quaint prohibitions and privileges."

Lubbock, *Origin of Civilization and Primitive Condition of Man* * (New York, Appleton, 1882), p. 445.

159. SAVAGE LIFE

"Dryden had a dream of an early age, 'when wild in woods the noble savage ran"; but 'when lone in woods the cringing savage crept' would have been more like all we know of that early, bare, painful period. Not only had they no comfort, no convenience, not the very beginnings of an epicurean life, but their mind within was as painful to them as the world without. It was full of fear. So far as the vestiges inform us, they were afraid of everything; they were afraid of animals, of certain attacks by near tribes, and of possible inroads from far tribes. But, above all things, they were frightened of 'the world'; the spectacle of nature filled them with awe and dread. They fancied there were powers behind it which must be pleased, soothed, flattered, and this very often in a number of hideous ways."

Bagehot, *Physics and Politics* (New York, Appleton, 1887), p. 55.

160. SOCIAL STATE UNNATURAL

"Forced to combat either nature or society you must make your choice between the man and the citizen, you cannot train both."

Rousseau, *Emile* * (Trans. by Foxley. New York, Dutton, no date), Book I, p. 7.

161. Rousseau on Man and Society

"In human society all the wise man can do is to withdraw himself from the world as much as possible, and remain where chance has placed him, satisfied that by doing nothing he avoids running into harm and falling into new errors."

Boyd, *The Educational Theory of J. J. Rousseau* (London, Longmans, 1911), p. 70 n.

162. The Development of Each in Relation to All

"It is not any and every development of the individual which is socially desirable, or even socially possible. For if one man's personality gains till he bestrides the narrow world like a Colossus, then it remains for the rest to peep in and out and find themselves dishonored graves. His overgrown development means for the mass not development but extinction; and in lesser degree a similar discord results from every development of the individual which is not in accordance with the conditions of social harmony. Social development, then, involves the harmonious development of the constituent members of society."

Hobhouse, *Social Evolution and Political Theory* * (New York, Columbia University, 1911), pp. 86-7.

163. Individual Energies Freed by Institutions

"Breadth in extent of community life goes hand in hand with multiplication of the stimuli which call out an individual's powers. Diversification of social activities increases opportunities for his initiative and endeavor. Narrow and meager social life means limitation of the scope of activities in which its members may engage. It means little occasion for the exercise of deliberation and choice, without which character is both immature and fossilized; it means, in short, restricted personality. But a rich and varied society, one which liberates powers otherwise torpid and latent, also exacts that they be employed in ways consistent with its own interests. A society which is extensive and complex would dissolve in anarchy and confusion were not the activities of its various members upon the whole mutually congruent. The world of action is a world of which the individual is one limit, and humanity the other; between them lie all sorts of associative arrangements of lesser and larger scope, families, friendships, schools, clubs, organizations for making or distributing goods, for gathering and supplying commodities; activities politically organized by parishes, wards, villages, cities, countries, states, nations. Every maladjustment in relations among these institutions and associated activities means loss and friction in the relations between individuals; and thereby introduces defect, division and restriction into the various powers which constitute an individual. All harmonious coöperation among them means a fuller life and greater freedom of thought and action for the individual person." (p. 430.)

"The moral criterion by which to try social institutions and political measures may be summed up as follows: The test is whether a given custom or law sets free individual capacities in such a way as to make them available for the development of the general happiness or the common good. This formula states the test with the emphasis falling upon the side of the individual. It may be stated from the side of associated life as follows: The test is whether the general, the public, organization and order are promoted in such a way as to equalize opportunity for all." (p. 482 f.)

Dewey and Tufts, *Ethics* * (New York, Holt, 1908).

164. INDIVIDUAL AND SOCIETY

"The interests of the social organism and those of the individuals comprising it at any one time are actually antagonistic; they can never be reconciled; they are inherently and essentially irreconcilable."

Kidd, *Social Evolution* * (New York, Macmillan, 1894), p. 85.

165. THE INDIVIDUAL AND SOCIETY

"Thus the old puzzle whether society exists for the good of the individual, or the individual for the good of society, is seen not to be a fair dilemma. If society is essentially group activity, the organization of society has as its object the furtherance of group activity. The value of society to the individual is not a derivative from other values, but arises directly from his capacity for social behavior and his strong drive towards social behavior."

Woodworth, *Dynamic Psychology* * (New York, Columbia University, 1918), p. 206.

166. No Limitations upon Property

"Is it not lawful for me to do what I will with mine own?" Common saying in biblical times (Matthew 20:15).

167. The Sacredness of Office

"A ruler who appoints any man to an office, when there is in his dominions another man better qualified for it, sins against God and against the State."
Koran.

168. Do We Seek Pleasure?

James Mill taught that all desires actually aim not at the thing or action, but at pleasure. For him desire is solely another name for the idea of pleasure. To say that one desires water to drink is, strictly speaking, a figure of speech. Properly speaking, it is not the water we desire, but the pleasure which comes from the drinking. The illusion that we desire to drink is merely the result of a very close association.

This reminds Paulsen of a story in a comic paper. An Englishman is seated on the bank of a lake, fishing. A native approaches him and informs him that there are no fishes in the lake. Whereupon the Englishman stolidly replies that he is not fishing for fish, he is fishing for pleasure.

Adapted from Paulsen, *System of Ethics* * (Trans. by Thilly. New York, Scribners, 1899), p. 254 f.

169. The End of Desire

"We sit down at a table hungry. Is pleasure our end, and is eating related to it as an absolutely indifferent means . . . ? The lover of music goes to a concert. Is pleasure his end, and music the means? . . . No, impulses and powers slumbered in him which craved for exercise and development, just like the forces dwelling in the seed of a plant. And when these powers were exercised and unfolded, pleasure ensued, but this pleasure did not pre-exist in consciousness as an end of which the other things were the means. *The impulse and the craving for activity preceded all consciousness of pleasure*. The consciousness of pleasure did not exist before the impulse, and produce or arouse it. Only the blasé and worn-out idler first experiences a desire for pleasure, and then looks about him for some means of procuring it. Healthy men do not act that way."

Paulsen, *System of Ethics* * (Trans by Thilly. New York, Scribners, 1899), p. 254.

170. RIGHT

"Because right is right, to follow right
Were wisdom in the scorn of consequence."
Tennyson, *Œnone*.

171. RIGHT AND WRONG

"Right and wrong are in the nature of things. They are not [mere] words and phrases. They are in the nature of things, and if you transgress the laws laid down, imposed by the nature of things, depend upon it you will pay the penalty."
John Morley.

172. OBJECTIVE STUDY OF MORALS

"Honesty, chastity, malice, peevishness, courage, triviality, industry, irresponsibility are not private possessions of a person. They are working adaptations of personal capacities with environing forces. All virtues and vices are habits which incorporate objective forces. They are interactions of elements contributed by the make-up of an individual with elements supplied by the out-door world. They can be studied as objectively as physiological functions, and they can be modified by change of either personal or social elements."

Dewey, *Human Nature and Conduct* * (New York, Holt, 1922), p. 16.

173. MORALS BASED ON A STUDY OF HUMAN NATURE

"Morals based upon concern with facts and deriving guidance from knowledge of them would at least locate the points of effective endeavor and would focus available resources upon them. It would put an end to the impossible attempt to live in two unrelated worlds. It would destroy fixed distinction between the human and the physical, as well as that between the moral and the industrial and political. A morals based on study of human nature instead of upon disregard for it would find the facts of man continuous with those of the rest of nature and would thereby ally ethics with physics and biology. It would find the nature and activities of one person coterminous with those of other human beings, and therefore link ethics with the study of history, sociology, law and economics.

"Such a morals would not automatically solve moral problems, nor resolve perplexities. But it would enable us to state problems in such forms that action could be courageously and intelligently directed to their solution. It would not assure us against failure, but it would render failure a source of instruction. It would not protect us against the future emergence of equally serious moral difficulties, but it would enable us to approach the always recurring troubles with a fund of growing knowledge which would add significant values to our conduct even when we overtly failed—as we should continue to do. Until the integrity of morals with human nature and of both with the environment is recognized, we shall be deprived of the aid of past experience to cope with the most acute and deep problems of life. . . . The intelligent acknowledgment of the continuity of nature, man and society will alone secure a growth of morals which will be serious without being fanatical, aspiring without sentimentality, adapted to reality without conventionality, sensible without taking the form of calculation of profits, idealistic without being romantic."

Dewey, *Human Nature and Conduct* * (New York, Holt, 1922), pp. 12-13.

174. NO MUNDANE BASIS OF MORALITY

"Were there no future life morality would cease. Man's only destiny would be to procure for himself the enjoyments of this life, irrespective of the means applied. . . . Moreover . . . there would be no reason why man should be harassed by conscience. His only rational endeavor would be to avoid detection and escape the punishment established by law. . . .

"Were there no future life, no motive whatever would induce us to practice virtue. The only restraint imposed on vice and crime would be the fear of temporal loss or punishment."

Jouin, S. J., *Logic and Metaphysics* (New York, St. John's College, no date), p. 204-5.

175. A CRITERION OF CONDUCT

"That action is best which secures the greatest happiness for the greatest numbers."

Hutcheson, *Inquiry: Concerning Moral Good and Evil* (1720), Sec. 3.

176. CONCEPTIONS OF THE MORAL LAW

"The earliest form in which the idea of law presents itself is that of the law of the tribe, or of the chief of the tribe. But . . . the reflecting consciousness demands something more. . . . At the best it furnishes a *must*, rather than an *ought;* and the free man soon rebels against such government from without. . . .

"It is a stage higher when the moral law is distinguished from the law of the land, and regarded as a principle which owes its authority, not to any man or body of men, but to God or the Gods. . . . But . . . the moral consciousness soon begins to ask on what authority the divine law rests. If it rest merely on the command of powerful supernatural beings, it is still only a *must*, not an *ought*. If God is not Himself righteous, His law cannot be morally binding merely on account of His superior power. But to ask whether God is righteous is to ask for a law above that of God Himself, and by which God may be judged. Hence the law of God cannot be accepted as final."

Mackenzie, *Manual of Ethics* * (New York, Hinds and Noble, 1901), pp. 173-4.

177. FUNDAMENTAL PRINCIPLES OF SOCIAL WELFARE AND PROGRESS

"The sacredness of each human life, the rightfulness of claims for liberty of development and for equality of opportunity and consideration, the duty of mutual help and corporate service— these are the indispensable and sovereign things."

Report of the Archbishop's Fifth Committee (London, 1918), p. 22.

178. BASIS OF THE VIRTUES

"In examining principles, the word *just* is misleading. All the virtues are based on experience, physiological or social, and justice is no exception. *Just* designates a class of rules or principles of which the social utility has been found by experience to be paramount and which are recognized to be so important as to override all considerations of immediate expediency."

Bury, *History of Freedom of Thought* * (New York,[1] Holt, 1913), p. 236.

[1] Originally published in England.

179. THE BASIS OF THE MORAL ORDER

"The claims of morality to our allegiance, so far as its precepts are solidly established, rest on the same positive base as our faith in the truth of physical laws. Moral principles, when they are true, are at bottom only registered generalisations from experience. They record certain uniformities of antecedence and consequence in the region of human conduct. Want of faith in the persistency of these uniformities is only a little less fatuous in the moral order than a corresponding want of faith would instantly disclose itself to be in the purely physical order. In both orders alike there is only too much of this kind of fatuousness, this readiness to believe that for once in our favour the stream shall flow up hill, that we may live in miasmatic air unpoisoned, that a government may depress the energy, the self-reliance, the public spirit of its citizens, and yet be able to count on these qualities whenever the government itself may have broken down, and left the country to make the best of such resources as are left after so severe and prolonged a drain. This is the sense in which morality is the nature of things."

Morley, *On Compromise* * (London, Macmillan, 1910[1]), p. 26-7.

180. INSTITUTIONS IN RELATION TO SOCIETY

"The ideal development of society . . . consists rather in the discovery of the lines upon which these manifold forms of human association (e.g. family, church, corporation, etc.) can be brought each to its fullest pitch of efficiency as a part of a wider organization . . . without cramping the development of personality on the one side or impeding the development of collective responsibility on the other."

Hobhouse, *Social Evolution and Political Theory* * (New York, Columbia University, 1911), p. 89.

181. A PRIORI JUSTICE

"When justice is considered as a mere means of securing man's welfare, and is treated accordingly—whether it be the welfare of individuals or of society as a whole makes no essential difference—it loses all its characteristic features. No longer can it compel us to see life from its own standpoint; no longer can

---
[1] 1st ed., 1886.

it sway our hearts with the force of a primitive passion, and oppose to all consideration of consequences an irresistible spiritual compulsion. It degenerates rather into the complaisant servant of utility; it adapts herself to her demands, and in so doing suffers inward annihilation. It can maintain itself only when it comes as a unique revelation of the Spiritual Life within our human world, as a lofty Presence transcending all considerations of expediency."

Eucken, *The Meaning and Value of Life* (Trans. by Gibson. London, Black, 1910), p. 104.

182. KANT ON CONSCIENCE

"Conscience is not an acquisition, and there is no obligation to acquire it; but every man, as an ethical being, has it originally in himself. To be bound in duty to conscience is as much as saying, to have the duty to recognize duties. Conscience . . . is an unfailing fact, not an obligation and duty. . . . A lack of conscientiousness is not lack of conscience, but an inclination not to respect its judgments."

Buchner, *Kant's Educational Theory* * (Philadelphia, Lippincott, 1904), p. 288 f.

183. KANT ON DUTY

"Duty! Thou sublime great name, thou that does embrace nothing popular which bears insinuation with it, but does demand submission, yet without threats which excite natural aversion in the mind, or arouse fear in order to move the will, but that dost merely set up a law which of itself finds entrance into the mind, and yet wins for itself reluctant esteem (if not always adherence), before which all inclinations are silent, even though they secretly work against it—what is the origin worthy of thee, and where shall one find the roots of thy noble descent, which proudly rejects all relationship with natural inclinations; a root to spring from which is the indispensable condition of that worth which men alone can give themselves?

"Two things fill the mind with ever new and increasing admiration and awe the oftener and more steadily I think about them: *the starry heaven above me and the moral law within me.*"

Buchner, *Kant's Educational Theory* * (Philadelphia, Lippincott, 1904), p. 187 n.

184. Burke on Individual Selfishness and the Common Good

"The benign and wise Disposer of all things obliges men, whether they will or not, in pursuing their own selfish interests, to connect the general good with their own individual success."
Quoted in *Report of the Archbishop's Fifth Committee* (London, 1918), p. 44.

185. Self-Interest Not Sufficient

Certain eighteenth century writers were of the opinion that "each man had only to follow his own apparent interest, and the best possible social results would ensue. Life unfortunately is not so simple. The operation of enlightened self-interest leading each man along the path of least resistance to the goal of greatest desire does not produce social peace or social progress."
Hobhouse, *Social Evolution and Political Theory* * (New York, Columbia University, 1911), p. 86.

186. Communism vs. Private Property

"If . . . the choice were to be made between communism with all its chances, and the present state of society with all its sufferings and injustices; if the institution of private property necessarily carried with it, as a consequence, that the produce of labor should be apportioned as we now see it, almost in an inverse ratio to the labor,—the largest portions to those who have not worked at all, the next largest to those whose work is almost nominal, and so in descending scale, the remuneration dwindling as the work grows harder and more disagreeable, until the most fatiguing and exhausting bodily labor cannot count with certainty on being able to earn even the necessaries of life,—if this, or communism, were the alternative, all the difficulties, great or small, of communism would be but as dust in the balance. But to make the comparison applicable, we must compare communism at its best with the régime of individual property, not as it is, but as it might be made. The principle of private property has never yet had a fair trial in any country."
Mill, *Principles of Political Economy* (New York, Appleton, 1890 [1]), Bk. II, Ch. 1, p. 267.

[1] 1st ed., 1848.

187. Business and City Politics

A New York business man is quoted as saying:

"We have thought this thing over, and we find that it pays better to neglect our city affairs than to attend to them; that we can make more money in the time required for the full discharge of our political duties than the politicians can steal from us on account of our not discharging them."

Anonymous.

188. Selfishness

"It is not necessary to go very far into that form of hair-splitting analysis which considers whether benevolence is not merely another form of selfishness. It is sometimes argued by a certain kind of sophist that the benevolent person is benevolent because he gets pleasure from being benevolent. Since it gives him pleasure, it is only a form of self-gratification; and since it is only a form of self-gratification, it is only another form of selfishness. It may be true, from a certain point of view, that a man may get more pleasure from the taste of food upon the palates of his children than upon his own. A sophist might say that he was as truly selfish as a man who got no pleasure whatever from the taste of food upon any palate but his own. However, no sensible person would remain long in doubt as to which would make the better father. There is no doubt that the man who takes some delight in the welfare of his neighbors and fellow citizens is a better neighbor and citizen than a man who takes no pleasure whatever in such things."

Carver, *Principles of Political Economy* * (Boston, Ginn, 1919), p. 23.

189. "Serial Transfer"

"Original nature, careless of equity, provides no filial instinct of return devotion. . . . One must be a mother for motherhood's sake."

Thorndike, *Educational Psychology* * (New York, Teachers College, 1913), Vol. I, p. 85.

190. Pass it Along

"Kindness received is a good thing; pass it along."
Common Saying.

THE INDIVIDUAL AND SOCIETY

191. Moral Character

"The pleasure or pain which follows upon actions may be regarded as a test of a person's moral state. He who abstains from physical pleasures and feels delight in so doing is temperate; but he who feels pain at so doing is licentious. He who faces danger with pleasure, or at least without pain, is courageous, but he who feels pain at facing them is a coward. . . . Hence the importance of having had a certain training from very early days, as Plato says, such a training as produces pleasure and pain at the right objects; for this is the true education."

Aristotle, *Nicomachean Ethics* * (Trans. by Welldon. London, Macmillan, 1906), Book II, Ch. ii.

192. The Good of Life in Fulfilling Social Demands

"It is the business of men to develop such capacities and desires, such selves as render them capable of finding their own satisfaction, their invaluable value, in fulfilling the demands which grow out of their associated life. Such happiness may be short in duration and slight in bulk; but that it outweighs in quality all accompanying discomforts as well as all enjoyments which may have been missed by not doing something else, is attested by the simple fact that men do consciously choose it."

Dewey and Tufts, *Ethics* * (New York, Holt, 1908), p. 396.

193. Hegel: Individual and Institutions

"What a man ought to do, or what duties he should fulfill in order to be virtuous, is in an ethical community not hard to say. He has to do nothing except what is presented, expressed, and recognized in his established relations." "The individual has his truth, real existence, and ethical status only in being a member of the State. His particular satisfactions, activities, and way of life have in this authenticated, substantive principle, their origin and result." And in another connection: "The striving for a morality of one's own is futile and by its very nature impossible of attainment. In respect to morality the saying of one of the wisest men of antiquity is the true one. To be moral is to live in accord with the moral tradition of one's country."

Dewey and Tufts, *Ethics* * (New York, Holt, 1908), p. 225 f.

194. A Basis for the Criticism of Institutions

When self-hood is perceived to be an active process it is also seen that social modifications are the only means of the creation of changed personalities. Institutions are viewed in their educative effect:—with reference to the types of individuals they foster. The interest in individual moral improvement and the social interest in objective reform of economic and political conditions are identified. And inquiry into the meaning of social arrangements gets definite point and direction. We are led to ask what the specific stimulating, fostering and nurturing power of each specific social arrangement may be. . . . Just what response does *this* social arrangement, political or economic, evoke, and what effect does it have upon the disposition of those who engage in it? Does it release capacity? If so, how widely? Among a few, with a corresponding depression in others, or in an extensive and equitable way? Is the capacity which is set free also directed in some coherent way, so that it becomes a power, or its manifestation spasmodic and capricious?

"Since responses are of an indefinite diversity of kind, these inquiries have to be detailed and specific. Are man's senses rendered more delicately sensitive and appreciative, or are they blunted and dulled by this and that form of social organization? Are their minds trained so that the hands are more deft and cunning? Is curiosity awakened or blunted? What is its quality: is it merely esthetic, dwelling on the forms and surfaces of things or is it also an intellectual searching into their meaning? Such questions as these (as well as the more obvious ones about the qualities conventionally labelled moral), become the starting-points of inquiries about every institution of the community when it is recognized that individuality is not originally given but is created under the influences of associated life."

Dewey, *Reconstruction in Philosophy* * (New York, Holt, 1920), pp. 196-8.

CHAPTER X

DEMOCRACY

195. DEMOCRACY

"Democracy is that order in the state which permits each individual to put forth his utmost effort."
Pasteur.

196. FREEDOM

"It is better for a man to go wrong in freedom than to go right in chains."
Huxley.

197. ONE CONCEPTION OF LIBERTY

"Liberty . . . is for the French, as Baron Jounnes has remarked: The right of each man to do what he likes and to prevent other men from doing what they like."
Faguet, *Cult of Incompetence* (Trans. by Barstow. London, Murray, 1911), p. 68 f.

198. THE "GLOOMY DEAN" ON DEMOCRACY

"Democracy . . . disintegrates society into individuals and only collects them again into mobs."
Dean Inge, in *Atlantic Monthly*,* 129:290 (Mar. 1922).

199. DEMOCRACY

"It is better that the body of the people, with all its faults, should act for itself and control its own affairs, than that it should be set aside as ignorant and incapable, and have its affairs managed for it by a so-called superior class, possessing property and intelligence."
Matthew Arnold, Discourses in America * (London, Macmillan, 1912), p. 7.

200. Hegel on Public Opinion

"Public opinion always contains some truth, but truth falsely expressed. To find the truth is the work of the great political thinkers. We must not ask the people what they think; we must tell the people what they think."

201. Ancient Prayer

"God bless the squire and his relations
And keep us in our proper stations."

Quoted in Brown, *Underlying Principles of Modern Legislation* (New York, Dutton, 1915), p. 184.

202. Extreme Toryism

"The Order of the White Rose . . . holds that sovereign authority is of divine sanction and that the execution of Charles I and the revolution of 1688 were national crimes; it exists . . . to oppose all democratic tendencies, and in general to maintain the theory that kingship is independent of all parliamentary authority and popular approval."
Encyclopædia Britannica (11th edition),* 15:120.

203. Expected Outcome of the Great War

This war, so says an English Tory paper, will "once for all put an end to the poisonous doctrines of internationalism, pacificism, free trade, socialism, and democracy."
Quoted in *New Republic*, 12:347 f. (Oct. 27, 1917).

204. Status Characteristic of Primitive Life

"In modern days, in civilised days, men's choice determines nearly all they do. But in early times that choice determined scarcely anything. The guiding rule was the law of *status*. Everybody was born to a place in the community: in that place he had to stay: in that place he found certain duties which he had to fulfil, and which were all he needed to think of. The net of custom caught men in distincts spots, and kept each where he stood."
Bagehot, *Physics and Politics* (New York, Appleton, 1887), p. 29.

DEMOCRACY

205. THE VISION OF AN IDEAL DEMOCRACY

"The Vision, the picture of an Ideal Democracy, a government upright and wise, beneficent and stable, as no government save that of the people for the people can be, has had greater power than the abstract doctrines, mighty as was their explosive force when they were first proclaimed. It is the conception of a happier life for all, coupled with a mystic faith in the People, that great multitude through whom speaks the Voice of the Almighty Power that makes for righteousness—it is this that constitutes the vital impulse of democracy. The country where the ideal democracy exists has not yet been discovered, but the faith in its existence has survived many disappointments, many disillusionments. Many more will follow, but them also the faith will survive. From time to time hope is revived by the appearance of a group of disinterested reformers, whose zeal rouses a nation to sweep away abuses and leaves things better than it found them. It is only sloth and torpor and the acquiescence in things known to be evil that are deadly. So we may hope that the Ideal will never cease to exert its power, but continue to stand as a beacon tower to one generation after another."

Bryce, *Modern Democracies* * (New York, Macmillan, 1921), Vol. I, p. 50.

206. SOCIAL STRATIFICATION

"Modern society—from top to bottom, is a descending hierarchy of oligarchic groups, each with its own peculiar privileges, for which it fights and by which it lives. I imagine society as a pyramid, broadening down from its apex in a series of steps, each cut off from the one above, not indeed by an impassable barrier, but by a height which it requires a considerable degree of athleticism to scale; and on each step, crowded together, a fighting, trampling mob of desperate men, bent, every one, on enlarging his own space and making room for his children, under penalty, if he fails, that he or they will be thrust down to the step below and perhaps, through all the degrees, to the very bottom . . ."

Dickenson, *Justice and Liberty* * (Garden City, Doubleday Page, 1909), p. 29 f.

207. ONE CONCEPTION OF DEMOCRACY

"We often ask why politeness is out of date, and everyone replies with a smile: 'This is democratic.' So it is, but why should it be? . . . There is no doubt that civility and politeness are a delicate means of showing respect to our fellow-men, and of communicating a wish to be respected in turn. . . . Politeness is a mark of respect and a promise of devotion.

"All this is anti-democratic, because democracy does not recognise any superiority, and therefore has no sympathy with respect and personal devotion. Respect to others involves a recognition from us that we are of less importance than they, and politeness to an equal requires from us a courteous affectation that we consider him as our superior. This is entirely contrary to the democratic ideal, which asserts that there is no superiority anywhere. As for pretending to treat your equal as though he were your superior, that involves a double hypocrisy on the part of your neighbor. You praise his wit, only in order that he may return the compliment.

"Without, however, insisting on this point, democracy will argue that politeness is to be deprecated, because it not only recognises but actually creates superiority. It treats an equal as a superior, as though there were not enough discrepancies already without inventing any more."

Faguet, *The Cult of Incompetence* (Trans. by Barstow. London, Murray, 1912), pp. 156-159.

208. HEGEL ON THE STATE

" 'The State is the rational in itself and for itself. Its substantial unity is an absolute end in itself. To it belongs supreme right in respect to individuals whose first duty is—just to be members of the State'. . . . The State 'is the absolute reality and the individual himself has objective existence, truth and morality only in his capacity as a member of the State.' It is a commonplace of idealistic theism that nature is a manifestation of God. But Hegel says that nature is only an externalized, unconscious and so incomplete expression. The State has more, not less, objective reality than physical nature, for it is a realization of Absolute spirit in the realm of consciousness. The doctrine presents an extreme form of the idea, not of the divine right of kings, but of the divine right of States. 'The march of God in history is the cause of the existence of states; their foundation is the power of reason realizing itself as will. Every state, whatever it be, participates in the divine essence. The State is not the work of human art; only Reason could produce it.' The State is God on earth."

Dewey, *German Philosophy and Politics* * (New York, Holt, 1915), p. 110 f.

209. EQUALITY OF OPPORTUNITY (1850)

"The majority of laborers have as little choice of opportunity as could exist in any system short of actual slavery."
John Stuart Mill.

210. DEMOCRACY AND DISCRIMINATION

"The principle of equal rights . . . is not sufficient. . . . The democratic principle requires an equal start in the race, while expecting at the same time an unequal finish. (p. 181) . . . Whenever the attempt to discriminate in favor of the average or indiscriminate individual has succeeded, it has succeeded at the expense of individual liberty, efficiency, and distinction. . . . Whenever the exceptional individual has been given any genuine liberty he has inevitably conquered." (p. 189)

"The arduous and responsible political task which a nation in its collective capacity must seek to perform is that of selecting among the various prevailing ways of exercising individual rights those which contribute to national perpetuity and integrity. (p. 190) . . . The clew to the best available solution of the problem is supplied by a consideration of the precise manner in which the advantages derived from the efficient exercise of liberties becomes inimical to a wholesome social condition. The hostility depends, not upon the existence of such advantageous discriminations for a time, but upon their persistence for too long a time. When, either from natural or artificial causes, they are properly selected, they contribute at the time of their selection both to individual and to social efficiency. They have been earned, and it is both just and edifying that, in so far as they have been earned, they should be freely enjoyed. On the other hand, they should not, so far as possible, be allowed to outlast their own utility. They must continue to be earned. It is power and opportunity enjoyed without being earned which help to damage the individual—both the individuals who benefit and the individuals who consent—and which tend to loosen the ultimate social bond. A democracy, no less than a monarchy or an aristocracy, must recognize political, economic, and social discriminations, but it must also manage to withdraw its consent whenever these discriminations show any tendency to excessive endurance. The essential wholeness of the community depends absolutely on the ceaseless creation of a political, economic, and social aristocracy and their equally incessant replacement." (p. 195 f.)

Croly, *The Promise of American Life* * (New York, Macmillan, 1914).

211. SMITH ON NATURAL ARISTOCRACY

"Upon the power which the leading men, the natural aristocracy of every country, have of preserving or defending their respective importance depends the stability and duration of every system of free government."

Smith, *Wealth of Nations* (Oxford, Clarendon Press, 1869 [1]), Bk. iv, ch. 7, p. 204.

212. WHAT SHALL WE DO WITH THE FEEBLE-MINDED?

"May it not be possible that we shall find use for all these people of moderate intelligence, and that the production of so many high grade feeble-minded is only the production of so many more people who are able and willing to do much of the drudgery of the world, which other people will not do?"

Goddard, *Feeblemindedness* * (New York, Macmillan, 1914), p. 588.

213. WHO SHALL GOVERN?

"One of the great divisions of politics in our day is coming to be whether, at the last resort, the world should be governed by its ignorance or by its intelligence. According to the one party, the preponderating power should be with education and property. According to the other, the ultimate source of power, the supreme right of appeal and of control, belongs legitimately to the majority of the nation told by the head—or, in other words, to the poorest, the most ignorant, the most incapable, who are necessarily the most numerous."

Lecky, *Democracy and Liberty* * (New York, Longmans, 1896), Vol. I, p. 25 f.

214. SOCIAL SERVICE AND REWARD

"The central point of Liberal economics, then, is the equation of social service and reward. This is the principle that every

[1] First edition, 1776.

function of social value requires such remuneration as serves to stimulate and maintain its effective performance; that every one who performs such a function has the right, in the strict ethical sense of that term, to such remuneration and to no more; that the residue of existing wealth should be at the disposal of the community for social purposes."

Hobhouse, *Liberalism* (New York, Holt, no date), p. 209.

215. FREEDOM

"How much better it is to be under a good master than to live in poverty and be free."

Menander.

216. GOVERNMENT NOT YET SUCCESSFUL

"The history of institutions is the most pathetic of all records. Man has conquered the wild beasts; he has conquered his fellow men; he has conquered nature; but, collectively, he has never succeeded in governing himself. A good government remains the greatest of human blessings, and no nation has ever enjoyed it. There is no ruler, says Plato, who would be unjustly condemned by his subjects. The world swings backward and forward between the ideals of Order and of Liberty; not because anyone thinks it possible or desirable to enjoy either of these boons without the other, but because, after a brief experience of a government ostensibly based on one of them, no price seems too high to pay for being delivered from it. So the pendulum swings, now violently, now slowly; and every institution not only carries within it the seeds of its own dissolution, but prepares the way for its most hated rival."

Dean Inge, in *Atlantic Monthly,** 129:289 (Mar. 1922).

217. ARGUMENTS ADVANCED IN BEHALF OF A DEMOCRACY

"Liberty is a good thing, because it develops the character of the individual, and conduces to the welfare of the community. When one man, or a few men, rule over others, some of the subjects are sure to resent control and rebel against it, troubling the general peace. No one is good enough to be trusted with unlimited power. Unless he be a saint—perhaps even if he be a saint—he is sure to abuse it.

"Every man is the best judge of his own interest, and therefore best knows what sort of government and what laws will promote that interest. Hence those laws and that government will presumably be the best for a community as a whole which are desired by the largest number of its members.

"Two men are presumably better able than one to judge what is for the common good. Three men are wiser still, and so on. Hence the larger the number of members of the community who have a right to give their opinion, the more likely to be correct (other things being equal) is the decision reached by the community.

"Individual men may have selfish aims, possibly injurious to the community, but these will be restrained by the other members of the community whose personal aims will be different. Thus the self-regarding purposes of individuals will be eliminated, and the common aims which the bulk of the community desires to pursue will prevail.

"As every man has some interest in the well-being of the community, a part at least of his own personal interest being bound up with it, every man will have a motive for bearing his share in its government, and he will seek to bear it, so far as his personal motives do not collide therewith.

"Inequality, by arousing jealousy and envy, provokes discontent. Discontent disturbs the harmony of a community and induces strife. Hence equality in political rights, while it benefits the community by opening to talent the opportunity of rendering good service, tends also to peace and good order.

"To sum up, government by the whole people best secures the two main objects of all Governments—Justice and Happiness, Justice, because no man or class or group will be strong enough to wrong others; Happiness, because each man, judging best what is for his own good, will have every chance of pursuing it. The principles of liberty and equality are justified by the results they yield.

"From these propositions it follows that the admission on equal terms of the largest possible number of members of a community to share in its government on equal terms best promotes the satisfaction of all the members as individuals, and also the welfare of the community as a whole; and these being the chief ends for which government exists, a government of the people by themselves is commended by the experience of mankind."

Bryce, *Modern Democracies* * (New York, Macmillan, 1921), Vol. I, p. 44 f.

218. A Conservative View

"Horrid principles and practices of this [the French] Republic: That all men are *equal* by nature; that the free will or liberty of man is unrestrained by any law human or divine; that human nature possesses endless perfectibility."

Guardian of Education (London, 1802), 1:84.

219. Democracy in City and Country

"Some of the deepest students of political and social tendencies have come to doubt whether democracy can ever develop to a high stage of efficiency except among people who are in the main self-employed. It is true that modern democracy arose first in the cities and towns, but it is likewise true that at that time the cities and towns were the homes of self-employed men. Before the rise of the factory system such manufacturing as was done was carried on in small shops by craftsmen who were in the majority of cases self-employed. The rural districts, however, were under the feudal system. Conditions are exactly reversed at the present time. Under the factory system the great majority of people in the indoor industries work under bosses. Since the break-up of the feudal system and the rise of the one-family farm, which is the characteristic farm in this country, the average dweller in the country is his own boss. This may have something to do with the fact that city politics is run by bosses and country politics is not."

Carver, *Principles of Political Economy* * (Boston, Ginn, 1919), p. 217.

220. Bigness of Organization and the Freedom of the Individual

"There is a sense in which the vastest problem by which we are faced is the very scale of the life we are attempting to live. Its bigness tends to obscure the merits of real freedom. And, indeed, there is industrially abroad a certain suspicion of liberty against which safeguards must be erected. The individual suffers absorption by the immensity of the forces with which he is in contact. . . . There are few signs of that energy of the soul which Aristotle thought the secret of happiness. There is little work that offers the opportunity of conscious and systematic thought. Responsibility tends to coagulate at a few centers of social life; so that the work of most is the simple commission of orders it is rarely their business to reflect upon. We are clearly tending to be overawed by our institutions; and we can perceive . . . a genuine danger lest we lose hold of that chiefest source of happiness. Clerks and teachers and tenders of machines, for each of whom there is prescribed a routine that fills the most eager hours of life, dare not be asked for the effort upon which new thought is founded. An expert in the science of factory management has even assumed that for the purpose of productivity a man 'who more nearly resembles in his mental make-up the ox than any other type' is desirable. Happiness in work, which can alone be fruitful of advance in thought, is, as Mr. Wallas has noted, a phrase for most practically without meaning. The problem to-day, as the problem at the time of the French Revolution, is the restoration of man to his place at the center of social life. That is, indeed, the real significance of freedom. It alone enables the individuality of men to become manifest."

Laski, *Authority in the Modern State* * (New Haven, Yale University, 1919), p. 89 f.

221. WORKINGMEN AS "HANDS"

"We would call . . . attention, in the first place, to the peculiar and, as we think, unjustifiable position of subordination in which many wage-earners are placed by the organization of modern industry, except in so far as it has been modified by law or by voluntary combination. We do not allude, of course, to the mere submission of the individual to the general rules and regulations, which is necessary in any common undertaking, and which is not merely compatible with liberty but is one of its indispensable conditions. What we have in mind is the position of economic inferiority in which, unless he has emancipated himself from it by concerted action with his fellows, the worker is liable to be placed by his dependence for his livelihood upon an undertaking whose general policy and organisation he is powerless, as an individual, to control, or sometimes even to influence. . . . The common description of workers as 'hands' summarises aptly an aspect of their economic position which is not the less degrading because it has hitherto met with too general acquiescence. The suggestion is that the worker is an accessory to industry rather than a partner in it; that his physical strength and manual dexterity are required to perform its operations, but that he neither has a mind which requires to be consulted as

to its policy nor a personality which demands consideration; that he is a hired servant whose duty ends with implicit obedience, not a citizen of industry whose virtue is in initiative and intelligence."
Report of the Archbishop's Fifth Committee (London, 1918), pp. 53-54.

222. THE ECONOMIC MAN A FALSE ABSTRACTION

"Political Economy . . . has abandoned the false abstraction of the economic man moved only by motives of acquisition."
Report of the Archbishop's Fifth Committee (London, 1918), p. ix.

223. MORAL LIMITATION TO PROFITS

"There is no moral justification for profits which exceed the amount needed to pay for adequate salaries to the management, a fair rate of interest on the capital invested, and such reserves as are needed to ensure and maintain the highest efficiency of production and the development and growth of the industry."
Report of the Archbishop's Fifth Committee (London, 1918), p. 95.

224. A LIVING WAGE AND ADEQUATE LEISURE

"It is the duty of the nation to take without delay such steps as may be necessary in order to secure a full living wage and reasonable hours of labour to all workers in industry, and . . . it is the duty of Christian men and women to press for the establishment of such conditions by all means in their power. By a living wage we mean not merely a wage which is sufficient for physical existence, but a wage adequate to maintain the worker, his wife and family in health and honour, and to enable him to dispense with the subsidiary earnings of his children up to the age of sixteen years. By reasonable hours we mean hours sufficiently short not merely to leave him unexhausted, but to allow him sufficient leisure and energy for home life, for recreation, for the development through study of his mind and spirit, and for participation in the affairs of the community. We hold that the payment of such a wage in return for such hours of work ought to be the first charge upon every industry."
Report of the Archbishop's Fifth Committee (London, 1918), p. 75.

225. Exploitation

"The will to exploit lasts as long as the power to exploit. Exploiters never tire of exploitation. A kept class never loses its taste for consuming the fruits of other men's toil, nor does it ever give up exploiting out of conviction of sin. Its manner of life becomes completely adjusted to its parasitism and it never fails to develop moral standards, theories and ideals which chime with the economic basis of its life."

Ross, *Principles of Sociology* * (New York, Century, 1921), p. 152.

226. A Definition of Americanism

"You cannot be against the capitalistic system and stand for America; you cannot apologize for that system or feel ashamed of it and still be a good American. You can indeed be a good American, in the sense of being loyal to American traditions, unless you are proud of the capitalistic system."

Quoted from the editor of *The Metropolitan* by Hobson in *The Nation* (London), 26:700 (Feb. 21, 1920).

227. One Attitude Towards Labor

"An ideal location (for a silk mill) would be one in which labor is abundant, intelligent, skilled, and cheap; where there were no labor unions and strikes; where the laws of the state made no restrictions as to the hours of work or age of workers; where people were accustomed to mill life; and where there were no other textile mills in the vicinity to share in the labor and bid up its price . . ."

An editorial in the silk manufacturer's official journal, quoted in the *American Journal of Sociology*, 22:169 (Sept., 1916).

228. Management and Labor

"When you [employes of the Yonkers Street Railway] ask me in case of differences between any of you and the superintendent, to go to arbitration, it seems very much like my going to my cook and saying, 'I want beefsteak for dinner.' She says, 'You will get lamb chops.' I say, 'That won't do.' She says, 'We will arbitrate.' . . .

"As a general principle I think arbitration is one of the greatest things in the world. I am heartily in favor of it. Arbitration between my servants and me is impossible. . . . If there is anything I can do to promote your welfare I will cheerfully do it, but I am manager of this company and you are my servants as I am servant of the company.'

Owner of the Yonkers Street Railway to a committee of employes, quoted in *The Survey*, 36:623 (Sept. 23, 1916).

229. Two Conceptions of Management

"Broadly speaking, there are two schools of opinion, or two tendencies, on the subject of management. There is the tendency of those who would improve efficiency by concentrating knowledge and responsibility for workmanship in the hands of expert directors, and the policy of those who believe rather in the diffusion of responsibility among the workers. The first tendency is represented by the advocates, who propose, in Mr. Taylor's words, that 'the management must take over and perform much of the work which is now left to the men,' and desire 'that there shall be a far more equal division of the responsibility between the management and the workman than exists under any of the ordinary types of management.' If you read Mr. Taylor's book you will find that what he means by 'a more equal division of the responsibility' is that the management is to do all the thinking and the workman all the toiling; that the scientific manager is to use his head and the workmen merely their arms and legs. This is autocratic rule with a vengeance; it takes one back to the days of slavery and of the Pyramids, or of those Assyrian reliefs in the British Museum where you may see scores of laborers harnessed like animals toiling for the Great King. To use the workman's arms and legs, to ignore that he has a brain is to ruin him as a craftsman and to degrade him as a man. . . . Scientific management breaks down, then, . . . because of the system of management with which it is associated.

"Mr. Taylor and his associates may be perfectly right when they are talking of improved tools; it is when they are discussing the government of men that they are at fault. We in this country, if we believe in democracy, are compelled to look for the solution of the problem of management in the opposite direction—not in the management encroaching on the brainwork of the men, but in the men being more closely associated with the management, understanding its difficulties, discussing its problems, and sharing its responsibilities. Our policy must be, not to make output mechanically perfect by turning the workman himself into a mere machine, but to make our organization scientific in the widest sense by the voluntary and harmonious coöperation of all the human factors concerned. It is along this road, and no other that we shall reach the industrial democracy of the future."

Zimmern, *Nationality and Government* * (New York, Macbride, 1919 [1]), p. 264 f.

230. DEMOCRACY IN INDUSTRY (AMERICAN FEDERATION OF LABOR, 1918)

"Two codes of rules and regulations affect the workers: The law upon the statute books and the rules within industry.

"The first determines their relationship as citizens to all other citizens and to property.

"The second largely determines the relationship of employer and employee, the terms of employment, the conditions of labor, and the rules and regulations affecting the workers as employees. The first is secured through the application of the methods of democracy in the enactment of legislation, and is based upon the principle that the laws which govern a free people should exist only with their consent.

"The second, except where effective trade-unionism exists, is established by the arbitrary or autocratic whim, desire, or opinion of the employer and is based upon the principle that industry and commerce can not be successfully conducted unless the employer exercises the unquestioned right to establish such rules, regulations, and provisions affecting the employes as self-interest prompts.

"Both forms of law vitally affect the workers' opportunities in life and determine their standard of living. The rules, regulations, and conditions within industry in many instances affect them more than legislative enactments. It is, therefore, essential that the workers should have a voice in determining the laws within industry and commerce which affect them, equivalent to the voice which they have as citizens in determining the legislative enactments which shall govern them.

"It is as inconceivable that the workers as free citizens should remain under autocratically made laws within industry and commerce as it is that the nation could remain a democracy while certain individuals or groups exercise autocratic powers."

Monthly Labor Review, 8:679 f. (March, 1919).

[1] London, 1918.

231. Democracy in Industry

"Both industry and politics are faced by what in politics is called the constitutional problem and in industry the problem of management—that is, the question of who is to be ultimately responsible for the conduct of the work, and how that responsibility is to be exercised. In politics, so far as this and most Western countries are concerned, this problem of management has been decided in favor of democracy. The people as a whole have taken into their hands the ultimate responsibility for the conduct of public business, and entrust its direction to ministers or servants, who are responsible to the people for their acts and policy. In industry, however, the problem of management is still unsolved, or rather it has hitherto been decided in a direction averse to democracy. The manager in industry is not like the minister in politics; he is not chosen by or responsible to the workers in the industry, but chosen by or responsible to partners or directors or some other autocratic authority. Instead of the manager being the minister or servant and the men the ultimate masters, the men are the servants and the manager and the external power behind him the master. Thus, while our governmental organization is democratic in theory, and by the extension of education is continually becoming more so in practice, our industrial organization is built upon a different basis. It is an autocracy, but not an untempered autocracy. . . .

"To say that industry is carried on by methods of autocracy is not necessarily to impute the blame to those who are responsible for the system. It has yet to be proved that it can be carried on in any other way. Nay, more; it has yet to be shown that those who live under the system desire that it should be carried on differently. But the contrast between political democracy and industrial autocracy—between the workman as a free citizen and the workman as a wage-earner—is so glaring that it has become obvious that it cannot indefinitely continue in its present form. Men who have tasted what freedom and responsibility mean in one department of life are not likely to acquiesce in remaining mere irresponsible instruments of production in the industrial sphere. The problem of management, what I would call the constitutional problem in industry, the question as to how the industrial process shall be controlled, is already, and is likely to continue, the burning issue in industrial policy."

Zimmern, *Nationality and Government* * (New York, Macbride, 1919 [1]), p. 262 f.

232. SELF-EXPRESSION IN INDUSTRY

"I have been in the paper industry twenty-three years. Starting after graduation from college as a workman—not just as a 'looker-on'—I learned the workman's point of view. Later, being promoted from foreman to superintendent, to manager, I learned the manager's point of view. Of course all through my early work in the paper industry I had definitely in mind that I would some day become a manufacturer. This I have been for the last few years. . . .

"When we operate our industries upon the unselfish lines . . . laid out for manufacturers to follow—lines which respect the individual—there is not going to be very much difference of opinion between the employer and the employee. . . .

"Democracy has been defined as 'the organization of society based upon respect for the individual,' and I will show you this afternoon how an industrial organization can be created which will give the maximum amount of opportunity for self-expression of the individual.

"I am going to talk to you about what we have learned to recognize as creative work, which brings forth the intelligent thinking power of the human mind. I believe I will convince you that any type of organization that disregards the right of every individual to think and to plan in the day's work is violating a great fundamental universal law. I hope to show you that these forces which are working destructively in society today have been called into existence primarily because we as manufacturers have been so engrossed in the building up of an organization to express our own individuality that we have forgotten that in doing it we have denied the workman the right to express his individuality also. Please bear in mind I am talking as a manufacturer not as a 'social scientist' or political economist.

"A man in order to work willingly must work because he desires to work from within, not because he is forced through economic pressure to carry out orders given by others. I believe it to be absolutely essential that as manufacturers we use the same degree of intelligence in obtaining a working knowledge of the principles of human nature that we do in the working out of the scientific principles of the manufacturing process. The need is even greater—for civilization itself will be destroyed if humanity's efforts are not constructively directed. . . .

"We have had ample demonstration that the lack of interest

[1] London, 1918.

and present disinclination upon the part of the workers to produce cannot be cured by more wages or shorter hours. . . . The big problem is how to create an environment in our factories that men will become so interested in their work that their main thought is not going to be for quitting time and pay day.

"What are the forces that are making industry so repulsive to the worker? Today the average employee has no love for his job, he cannot have. . . .

"The organization plan which we developed was not a theory worked out and put into practice, but resulted from studying a highly successful plant in operation, in order to explain its remarkable individuality and *esprit de corps*. The conclusion we arrived at is that the problem of individuality is the keynote upon which this whole industrial problem rests. When we began to understand it we ceased repressing the individuality of the workman, and instead encouraged the individual initiative, not only in the human unit, but also in the group, in the department and in each separate plant. . . .

"This is no unpractical theory, for over and over again I have seen men change from indifferent workmen into men who really cared. It is not the irresponsible 'outside' agitator who is to blame for our labor unrest. The whole trouble is entirely because we do not give men an opportunity for constructive self-expression. . . .

"I went into an industrial plant that was making, at the time I went there, the poorest quality of fibre perhaps that was made anywhere. . . .

"Our customers kept very quiet about the fact that they had our pulp in their paper, because they were afraid that their customers would find it out, but in later years it was the boast of the manufacturer who made high-grade papers that our pulp was in his paper.

"We increased the production of that plant from 42,000 tons a year to 111,000 tons, with the same number of digesters for cooking the pulp, and the same number of wet machines for handling the finished product. . . . The thing that I did was to interpret the forces and to give the men a chance to coördinate and work . . . to obtain results.

"I posted the records. . . .

"Instantly I got a response.

"The records at first were quantity records. We posted the production per machine, for instance, putting the highest man at the top and the lowest man at the bottom. No one likes to be the low man, and everybody likes to be the high man, so gradually we got a spirit of emulation started throughout the entire organization.

"An unexpected and unwelcome development occurred, due to the workman's desire to get a good record regardless of the effect on the quality of the pulp. . . .

"We now began to post records that had to do with the quality basis. . . .

"As we changed from a quantity to a quality basis, the rivalry which tended to make hard feeling among the men disappeared, and the men began to work together much more harmoniously. We added later cost records, which gave information of progress where we could not directly measure skill without resorting to some sort of an inspection system or time study method. The result of giving a man knowledge of performance, so that he knows the effect of his actions on the raw materials, then measuring his own accomplishment for his benefit, is to stimulate his desire to do better work." . . .

"Our manufacturing plants are destined to become a continuation of the educational system of the country. . . .The schools, however, must not be used as they have been in Germany for industry, but both schools and industry must become the servants of humanity. . . .

"Three distinct fields of operation . . . the field of the raw materials, the field that has to do with the action of the chemical and mechanical laws inherent in the raw materials. This is the real field for science. . . .

"We also had a distinctly separate field of operation and that is the field we call, for lack of a better name, 'the will of man.' Now, this has to do with that free, volatile, indefinable, but very tangible force which we have all encountered. When, for instance, we lay out a certain method of procedure which seems to us to be exactly right—only the workmen won't do it our way—we usually attribute it to some kind of perverse streak in human nature. Without knowing what we were doing we had in our organization given the greatest possible amount of information to the largest number of men and then had given them a chance to express that knowledge in the performance of the day's work. By means of our progress records, that great dynamic creative force which we call the 'will of man' was working with us instead of against us.

"We had not said 'The thing must be done absolutely in this way,' but had given the workman knowledge of what he was accomplishing and let him do some first hand experimenting for himself. I do not mean that we simply told the workman to go ahead and run the job in his own way. We gave him all the information we had available and then measured his progress for him. We did not give him specific instructions as to how he should do every little detail of his work. There is a vast difference in the two methods. One is democracy, the other is autocracy.

"Furthermore, through the graphical chart department, which related all the different operations in the plant to each other, we enabled the man to become conscious of what we learned to recognize as the third field, or the field of 'plant unity,' that thing that has to do with the development of *esprit de corps* in the organization. Each workman could know the effect of his own actions upon the raw materials and also upon the finished product. The plant was so delicately adjusted, that the man in the burner room, operating the sulphur burners, if he opened the slide of his door a little too wide and admitted an excess of air, would know the effect of that action all the way through the process until it came out in the finished pulp. I won't tell you in detail how this was done, but you can see what a sensitive plant nervous system we had developed. . . .

"The conclusion we came to was this: Man does not create matter and he does not create force, . . . but he *does create*. . . . In the plant I have described we had changed the whole physical structure of the plant so that there was not a single process in it which was operating the same as it did when we started. . . .

"What caused this transformation? It was the release of . . . power. . . .

"We increased the yield from a cord of wood seventeen per cent, by creating in our mill new conditions for the more highly specialized operation of the laws which govern the disintegration of wood into pulp. We saved $340,000 a year in raw materials. . . .

"This was not accomplished because a certain group of individuals had extraordinary intelligence, but because all through that plant the individual workman had knowledge of what he was accomplishing and was consciously controlling the process. He worked from 'within out,' and when he knew himself to be limited by the physical equipment he insisted upon the removal of limitations.

"We discovered that there is no such thing as the efficiency of a man. There is such a thing of course as the efficiency of a machine, because the machine is inorganic and cannot change unless it is changed from outside; the man, however, is constantly changing. He has in him that spiritual something which is constantly modifying the structure of his body, and consequently his capacity for accomplishment. When the man gets up against a limiting physical condition in the plant he simply insists upon that thing being changed.

"What we learned to do was to put at the disposal of our workmen our technically trained experts, who were able to help them to modify equipment which they knew should be changed because of their intimate association with it, and thereby released enormous creative forces.

"It is impossible to release these forces effectively unless the man who actually handles the materials desires to change the existing conditions. In one department where I had been urging the department head for two or three years to modify and change a certain equipment, we started progress records of work performed and in less than six months the constant urging of our men forced us to make a change which saved us thousands of dollars. . . .

"You have perhaps heard the story of the man who applied for a mechanic's position in a New England city, claiming that he was a mechanic and had been working at the trade for five years. Upon being questioned he said he had worked in Detroit, in an automobile factory—his job he said had been screwing on nut No. 57, three turns to the right.

"Unfortunately this story is not exaggerated. Such conditions, however, are degrading to any workman for they violate the very reason for his existence. No matter how much welfare work an organization of this kind does, it can never compensate for the crime of treating its human units like animals. As long as we insist upon an operating environment in which the workman uses his brain merely to direct his muscles and has no opportunity to participate in the planning end of the manufacturing process we must inevitably have resistance to production. The truth of this statement we have demonstrated over and over again.

"The minute you interest a man in his job, you create a condition in which joy in work becomes a reality and the workman becomes a constructive individuality. Many violate the moral law because, when a day's monotonous labor is over, they know of no other way to find self-expression except by stimulation of the physical senses. I have seen many men cease immoral practices when given an opportunity to exercise their creative faculties in constructive work—and this applies to men of low as well as high intelligence. . . .

"No real progress in production can be made unless, stationed at the points where raw materials are converted, we have workmen who are not mere connecting links controlled, by the machines, but men who are masters of the machines. Industry at last is going to assist men to become the conscious creators of their own environment."

Wolf, *The Human Relations in Industry* (a pamphlet issued by the Associated Industries of Massachusetts, Boston, 1919).

233. THE SURPLUS FOR THE COMMON GOOD

"We have allowed the riches of our mines, the rental value of the lands superior to the margin of cultivation, the extra profits of the fortunate capitalists, even the material outcome of scientific discoveries—which ought by now to have made this Britain of ours immune from class poverty or from any widespread destitution—to be absorbed by individual proprietors; and then devoted very largely to the senseless luxury of an idle rich class. Against this misappropriation of the wealth of the community, the Labor party . . . emphatically protests. One main pillar of the house that the Labor party intends to build is the future appropriation of the surplus, not to the enlargement of any individual fortune, but to the common good. It is from this constantly arising surplus . . . that has to be defrayed the public provision for the sick and infirm of all kinds (including that for maternity and infancy) which is still so scandalously insufficient; for the aged and those prematurely incapacitated by accident or disease, now in many ways so imperfectly cared for; for the education alike of children, of adolescents and of adults, in which the Labor party demands a genuine equality of opportunity overcoming all differences of material circumstances; and for the organization of public improvements of all kinds, including the brightening of the lives of those now condemned to almost ceaseless toil, and a great development of the means of recreation. From the same source must come the greatly increased public provision that the Labor party will insist on being made for scientific investigation and original research, in every branch of knowledge, not to say also for the promotion of music, literature and fine art, which have been under capitalism so greatly neglected, and upon which, so the Labor party holds, any real development of civilization fundamentally depends. Society, like the individual, does not live by bread alone—does not exist only for perpetual wealth production. . . .

"The Labor party has no belief in any of the problems of the world being solved by good will alone. Good will without knowledge is warmth without light. Especially in all the complexities of politics, in the still undeveloped science of society, the Labor party stands for increased study, for the scientific investigation of each succeeding problem, for the deliberate organization of research, and for a much more rapid dissemination among the whole people of all the science that exists. And it is perhaps specially the Labor party that has the duty of placing this advancement of science in the forefront of its political program. What the Labor party stands for in all fields of life is, essentially, democratic coöperation; and coöperation involves a common purpose which can be agreed to; a common plan which can be explained and discussed, and such a measure of success in the adaptation of means to ends as will ensure a common satisfaction. An autocratic sultan may govern without science if his whim is law. A plutocratic party may choose to ignore science, if it is heedless whether its pretended solutions of social problems that may win political triumphs ultimately succeed or fail. But no Labor party can hope to maintain its position unless its proposals are, in fact, the outcome of the best political science of its time; or to fulfil its purpose unless that science is continually wresting new fields from human ignorance."

Report of the British Labor Party, 1918 (quoted in Edie, *Current Social and Industrial Forces,* New York, Boni Liveright, 1920, p. 183 ff.).

234. Property

"Property is the sole and despotic dominion which one man claims and exercises over the external things of the world in total exclusion of the right of any other individual in the universe."
Blackstone.

235. Limitation upon Rights

"No man has a right to all of his rights."
Phillips Brooks.

236. A Limitation upon the Application of Principles

The right to equality of educational opportunity would, in a democratic society, be generally admitted. To say, however, that the right is absolute and should be enforced at every cost would commit us to a program that most will reject as soon as it is understood. For one thing, our children could no longer remain in their present homes; since homes are necessarily educative, and as educating agencies they are vastly unequal. Absolute equality of educational opportunity, being thus incompatible with separate homes, could be had, under present conditions, only at the cost of giving up, at least for several generations, the home as a place for children. W. Jethro Brown, in his *Underlying Principles of Modern Legislation* (New York, 1915, p. 270) in recognition of this difficulty has proposed to use the term *equity* of opportunity to represent the highest degree of equality feasible under the conditions of contemporary life.

The important bearing of this discussion is that even so admirable and desirable a principle as equality of educational opportunity cannot be applied absolutely, but only in such way as shall take due account of other principles and factors necessarily involved. The considerations here brought forward hold in general: Under any given set of conditions the optimum application of any principle—even of a principle in itself wholly admirable—may well not be the absolute (or maximum) application of that principle. In each particular case the choice of conduct must be decided in the light of the total effect of all the factors involved. We cannot afford to be doctrinaire in the application of even the most important principles.

237. THE MEANING OF CONSTITUTIONS

"A Constitution embodies . . . the principle of Self-Restraint. The people have resolved to put certain rules out of the reach of temporary impulses springing from passion or caprice, and to make these rules the permanent expression of their calm thought and deliberate purpose. It is a recognition of the truth that majorities are not always right, and need to be protected against themselves by being obliged to recur, at moments of haste or excitement, to maxims they had adopted at times of cool reflection."

Bryce, *Modern Democracies* * (New York, Macmillan, 1921), Vol. II, p. 11.

238. INTERNAL PROGRESS AND INTERNATIONAL RELATIONSHIPS

"More and more, as means of communication multiply, the fate of each state is bound up with that of others, and the attitude of hostility still characteristic of the modern world threatens the healthy internal development of each member of the community of nations. If a nation may sometimes be consolidated by fear of an aggressor, it is consolidated as an armed camp, and its military organization tends to bring it back to the authoritarian form; the taxable resources of the community are expended on the means of defense or aggression; and the interests of the public are diverted from the improvement of social relations, not by wars, but by ever-renewed rumors of war. On this side, then, the development of the civic principle seems bound up with internationalism, and with a readjustment in the great empires of the relation of governing state and dependencies."

Hobhouse, *Social Evolution and Political Theory* * (New York, Columbia University, 1911), p. 145.

239. NATIONAL EGOISM

"Egoism, when it is the egoism of a nation, becomes a duty and a virtue. It becomes purified. Does it not affect the fate of millions of living creatures, millions of millions of men yet to be born? Those governments which have not this sense of egoism are guilty; they are dangerously mischievous."

Bainville, *Italy and the War* (English trans., London, 1916).

240. INTERNATIONAL SELFISHNESS

"The old predatory instinct that he should take who has the power survives in industry and commerce as well as war. . . . It is vain to expect nations to act consistently from any motive other than that of interest."

Admiral Mahan, *The Interest of America in International Conditions* * (Boston, Little Brown, 1910), pp. 42, 80 f.

CHAPTER XI

DEMOCRACY AND EDUCATION

241. THE VIRTUE OF OBEDIENCE IN AN AUTOCRATIC SOCIETY
(Russia, 1819)

"The soul of education and the supreme virtue of a citizen is humility; and therefore obedience is the most important virtue in a student."

Darlington, *Education in Russia* (London, 1909), p. 58.

242. EDUCATION FOR DEMOCRACY

"A society marked off into classes need be specially attentive only to the education of its ruling elements. A society which is mobile, which is full of channels for the distribution of a change occurring anywhere, must see to it that its members are educated to personal initiative and adaptability. Otherwise, they will be overwhelmed by the changes in which they are caught and whose significance or connections they do not perceive."

Dewey, *Democracy and Education* * (New York, Macmillan, 1917), p. 102.

243. KANT ON TRAINING AND EDUCATION

"Man can be either merely trained, taught, mechanically instructed, or really enlightened. Dogs and horses are trained and human beings can be trained also. . . .

"It is not enough that children be trained; the most important thing is that they learn *to think*. This leads to those principles from which all actions arise. Thus it becomes apparent that there is very much to be done in a really worthy education."

Buchner, *Kant's Educational Theory* * (Philadelphia, Lippincott, 1904), p. 123 f.

244. PERSONALITY AND SHARING

"Personality must be educated, and personality cannot be educated by confining its operations to technical and specialized things, or to the less important relationships of life. Full education comes only when there is a responsible share on the part of each person, in proportion to capacity, in shaping the aims and policies of the social groups to which he belongs. This fact fixes the significance of democracy. It cannot be conceived as a sectarian or racial thing nor as a consecration of some form of government which has already attained constitutional sanction. It is but a name for the fact that human nature is developed only when its elements take part in directing things which are common, things for the sake of which men and women form groups—families, industrial companies, governments, churches, scientific associations and so on. The principle holds as much of one form of association, say in industry and commerce, as it does in government."

Dewey, *Reconstruction in Philosophy* * (New York, Holt, 1920), p. 209.

245. ONE WAY OF BELIEVING

"Happily for us, we are not required even in our riper years to *understand* divine *mysteries*, but only to believe in them; and children are as capable of *believing* what they cannot *understand* as persons in advanced life; and better disposed to do so because their minds are free from prejudice."

Guardian of Education (London, 1802), 1:60.

246. ONE IDEA OF RELIGIOUS EDUCATION

"The teaching of children, especially the religious teaching of children, is a different process entirely from the intellectual persuasion of, or imparting of information to, one adult person to another. It is a process as nearly mechanical and physical as anything in the region of psychology can be."

Gardiner, in *Westminster Review,* 158:433 (Oct., 1902).

247. EFFECT OF TRAINING IN PRUSSIA

"By an inordinate amount of *memorization* of the selected facts, by constant *drill* on the achievements and power of the German nation, by 'line upon line and precept upon precept' for eight years, and then by service in the army, the youthful mind is Germanized, is set like adamant and is capable of no change. The work of the *Volksschule* is accomplished, for the masses think alike and respond as a man to the slightest suggestion from authority."

Alexander, *Prussian Elementary Schools* * (New York, Macmillan, 1918), p. 554.

248. ONE KIND OF DOCILITY

"By docility I mean readiness to obey for the sake of obeying, avidity for commands and instructions, reluctance to accept responsibility or exercise initiative, inability to react against the pressure of autocratic authority. Docility, in this sense of the word, when it is a national characteristic, may become a destructive force of extreme violence."

Holmes, *Nemesis of Docility* (New York, Dutton, 1916), p. v.

249. THE TWO MEANINGS OF DOCILITY

"The plasticity of the young presents a temptation to those having greater experience and hence greater power which they rarely resist. It seems putty to be molded according to current designs. That plasticity also means power to change prevailing custom is ignored. Docility is looked upon not as ability to learn whatever the world has to teach, but as subjection to those instructions of others which reflect *their* current habits. To be truly docile is to be eager to learn all the lessons of active, inquiring, expanding experience. The inert, stupid quality of current customs perverts learning into a willingness to follow where others point the way, into conformity, constriction, surrender of scepticism and experiment. When we think of the docility of the young we first think of the stocks of information adults wish to impose and the ways of acting they want to reproduce. Then we think of the insolent coercions, the insinuating briberies, the pedagogic solemnities by which the freshness of youth can be faded and its vivid curiosities dulled. Education becomes the art of taking advantage of the helplessness of the young; the forming of habits becomes a guarantee for the maintenance of hedges of custom."

Dewey, *Human Nature and Conduct* * (New York, Holt, 1922), p. 64.

250. EFFECT OF POVERTY

"The worst of poverty is the docility it creates."
New Republic (editorial), 7:264 (July 15, 1916).

251. MILITARY DISCIPLINE

"A perfect army would be one in which each part would respond to the will of the commander as quickly and certainly as the muscles of the body respond to the impulses of the brain."

Quoted in Ross, *Principles of Sociology* (New York, Century, 1921), p. 254.

252. KAISER WILLIAM II ON MILITARY VIRTUES

"The chief pillars of the army are courage, honor, and unconditional blind obedience."

Quoted in Dawson, *What is Wrong with Germany* (New York, Longmans, 1915), p. 117.

253. WEST POINT DISCIPLINE

"No less marked is the change of mental attitude of the new cadet at the end of 'Beast Barracks' [his first three weeks]. All sense of his importance, if he ever had any, has oozed away . . . and he realizes what a very small fish he is in this new pond. He rapidly acquires a most receptive mood in which he absorbs the most important lesson that a soldier must learn,—OBEDIENCE. The officers and cadets in charge of him demand unhesitating and instant compliance with their orders. To this end the new cadets are made to execute every order at a run, not to harass them as they sometimes think, but to form the habit of immediate obedience."

Richardson, *West Point* * (New York, Putnam, 1917), p. 124 f.

254. MILITARY DISCIPLINE

"The war will be won by disciplined fighting soldiers, not by devices or material things. The history of warfare shows this. What is going on abroad confirms it. The intelligence, loyalty, and individual skill of our men are valuable assets. But they are assets which cannot be effectively used in battle unless they are welded into a harmonious and dependable whole through the solid unifying influence of discipline. And this discipline, to be solid and substantial, must be hard as steel.

"It must produce an obedience so prompt and unquestioned that the act is performed subconsciously. Its quality should be such that the physical response to a command is correct in all details. Every battle in the history of warfare had its mistakes, errors, and neglects which affected the results, and these, in most of instances, were due to failure in discipline.

"Every soldier in the division should understand the importance of discipline. His life will largely hang upon it. The lives of his comrades and the value of his regiment will be dependent upon it."

Major General J. F. O'Ryan, in *New York Times,* December 16, 1917.

255. AMERICAN SELF-RELIANCE AND RESOURCEFULNESS

"The combination of self-reliance and resourceful ingenuity which seems to make the individual American equal to any fortune (p. 67) . . . perhaps the most precious of all the American national assets" (p. 75).

Robinson, *The Twentieth Century American* * (New York, Putnam, 1908).

256. EDUCATION FOR DEMOCRACY

"Children in school must be allowed freedom to develop active qualities of initiative, independence, and resourcefulness, before the abuses and failures of democracy will disappear."

John Dewey.

257. SCIENCE DANGEROUS

"We are not amongst the number of those who would teach *Chemistry* to children; it is a fascinating thing, likely to occupy their thoughts and attention to the exclusion of more important things, and to put them upon more dangerous experiments."

Guardian of Education (London, 1803), 2:310.

258. STRONG PERSONALITIES

"The country which has worked out for itself a truly free government must have done so in virtue of the vigorous individuality of its children. Such an individuality does not soon yield even to the pressure of democratic conditions (p. 265) . . .

"In a free country more especially, ten men who care are worth a hundred who do not" (p. 266).

Bryce, *American Commonwealth* * (New York, Macmillan, 1914), Vol. II.

259. Strong Individualities

"Liberty may not have achieved all that was expected, yet it remains true that nothing is more vital to national progress than the spontaneous development of individual character, and that free play of intellect which is independent of current prejudice, examines everything by the light of reason and history, and fearlessly defends unpopular opinions. Independence of thought was formerly threatened by monarchs who feared the disaffection of their subjects. May it not again be threatened by other forms of intolerance, possible even in a popular government?

"Room should be found in every country for men who, like the prophets in ancient Israel, have along with their wrath at the evils of their own time inspiring visions of a better future and the right to speak their minds. That love of freedom which will bear with opposition because it has faith in the victory of truth is none too common. Many of those who have the word on their lips are despots at heart. Those men in whom that love seemed to glow with the hottest flame may have had an almost excessive faith in its power for good, but if this be an infirmity, it is an infirmity of noble minds, which democracies ought to honour.

"Not less than any other form of government does democracy need to cherish Individual liberty. It is, like oxygen in the air, a life-giving spirit. Political liberty will have seen one of its fairest fruits wither on the bough if that Spirit should decline."

Bryce, *Modern Democracies* * (New York, Macmillan, 1921), Vol. I, p. 59.

260. The Greek Idea of How We Love the Good

"Only if the individual is habituated, exercised, practiced in good ends so as to take delight in them, while he is still so immature as to be incapable of really knowing how and why they are good, will he be capable of knowing the good when he is mature. Pleasure in right ends and pain in wrong must operate as a motive force in order to give experience of the good, before knowledge can be attained and operate as the motive force."

Dewey and Tufts, *Ethics* * (New York, Holt, 1908), p. 216.

261. Rousseau on Habit

"Man's education begins at birth. . . . He must . . . be accustomed from the first to the dark, or he will cry if he misses the light. Food and sleep, too, exactly measured, become necessary at regular intervals, and soon desire is no longer the effect of need, but of habit, or rather habit adds a fresh need to those of nature. You must be on your guard against this.

"The only habit the child should be allowed to contract is that of having no habits; let him be carried on either arm, let him be accustomed to offer either hand, to use one or the other indifferently; let him not want to eat, sleep or do anything at fixed hours."

Emile * (Trans. by Foxley. New York, Dutton, no date), Book I, p. 29-30.

262. KANT ON HABITS

"The more habits a man has the less is he free and independent. It is the same with man as with all other animals. He always retains a certain inclination for that to which he was early accustomed. The child must be prevented from habituating himself to anything, and he must not be allowed to form any habits."

Buchner, *Kant's Educational Theory* * (Philadelphia, Lippincott, 1904), p. 146.

263. THE POWER OF HABIT

"The hell to be endured hereafter, of which theology tells, is no worse than the hell we make for ourselves in this world by habitually fashioning our characters in the wrong way. Could the young but realize how soon they will become mere walking bundles of habits, they would give more heed to their conduct while in the plastic state. We are spinning our own fates, good or evil, and never to be undone. Every smallest stroke of virtue or of vice leaves its never-so-little scar. The drunken Rip Van Winkle, in Jefferson's play, excuses himself for every fresh dereliction by saying, 'I won't count this time!' Well, he may not count it, and a kind Heaven may not count it; but it is being counted none the less. Down among his nerve-cells and fibres the molecules are counting it, registering and storing it up to be used against him when the next temptation comes. Nothing we ever do is, in strict scientific literalness, wiped out.

"Of course this has its good side as well as its bad one. As we become permanent drunkards by so many separate drinks, so we become saints in the moral, and authorities and experts in the practical and scientific spheres, by so many separate acts and hours of work. Let no youth have any anxiety about the upshot of his education, whatever the line of it may be. If he keep faithfully busy each hour of the working day, he may safely leave the final result to itself. He can with perfect certainty count on waking up some fine morning to find himself one of the competent ones of his generation, in whatever pursuit he may have singled out. Silently, between all the details of his business, the *power of judging* in all that class of matter will have built itself up within him as a possession that will never pass away. Young people should know this truth in advance. The ignorance of it has probably engendered more discouragement and faintheartedness in youths embarking on arduous careers than all other causes put together."

James, *Talks to Teachers* * (New York, Holt, 1899), p. 77 f.

264. THE INDIVIDUAL AND RACE EXPERIENCE

"Nobody denies that people should be so taught and trained in youth, as to know and benefit by the ascertained results of human experience. But it is the privilege and proper condition of a human being, arrived at the maturity of his faculties, to use and interpret experience in his own way."

Mill, *Liberty* (London, Parker, 1859), p. 104.

265. PURPOSEFUL ACTIVITY IN THE ADULT AND IN THE CHILD

"No one seriously questions that, with an adult, power and control are obtained through realization of personal ends and problems, through personal selection of means and materials which are relevant, and through personal adaptation and application of what is thus selected, together with whatever of experimentation and of testing is involved in this effort. Practically every one of these three conditions of increase in power for the adult is denied for the child. For him problems and aims are determined by another mind. For him the material that is relevant and irrelevant is selected in advance by another mind. And, upon the whole, there is such an attempt to teach him a readymade method for applying his material to the solution of his problems, or the reaching of his ends, that the factor of experimentation is reduced to the minimum. With the adult we unquestioningly assume that an attitude of personal inquiry, based upon the possession of a problem which interests and absorbs, is a necessary precondition of mental growth. With the child we assume that the precondition is rather the willing disposition which makes him ready to submit to any problem and material presented from without. *Alertness* is our ideal in one case; *docility* in the other. With one we assume that power of attention develops in dealing with problems which make a personal appeal, and through personal responsibility for determining what is relevant. With the other we provide next to no opportunities for the evolution of problems out of immediate experiences and ideas that make for their solution. How profound a revolution in the position and service of text-book and teacher, and in methods of instruction depending therefrom, would be effected by a sincere recognition of the psychological identity of child and adult in these respects can with difficulty be realized."

Dewey, *Psychology and Social Practice* * (Chicago, University of Chicago, 1901), pp. 12-14.

266. THE BIBLE IN ENGLISH UNDER HENRY VIII (1542)

"No Women, nor Artificers nor Prentices, Journeymen, Servingmen of the degrees of Yeomen or under, Husbandmen, nor Labourers shall read within this Realm, or other of the Kings dominion, the Bible or New Testament in English to himself, or to any other privately or openly upon pain of one month's imprisonment."

Statutes of the Realm, 34-35, Henry VIII, cap. I, art. 13.

267. NIETZSCHE ON POPULAR EDUCATION

"The education of the masses cannot . . . be our aim; but rather the education of a few picked men for great and lasting work."

Quoted.

268. FREDERICK WILLIAM III ON GARRISON SCHOOLS

(a) "True *enlightenment*, in so far as it is necessary for his and the general good, is the incontestable right of that person, who in the walk of life in which fate has placed him, knows his relationships and duties and has the ability to satisfy them. Therefore, to this purpose the instruction in all *Volksschulen* should be limited. The time which one applies therein to a superficial study of the sciences for which the ordinary man has little use is for the most part lost. He forgets quickly what he has heard, and there remain in his memory only incomplete conceptions out of which false conclusions arise, and tastes which his social standing does not allow him to satisfy, and which only make him discontented and unhappy" (p. 30).

(b) "The spirit of the age has aroused in all classes of society an unceasing effort to raise one's self above one's own social stratum, or at least to extend its pretensions higher. I very gladly make allowance for that which one must accept as a necessary result of the higher value of things. But the evil lies deeper and must be strenuously combated, if all human relationships are not finally destroyed. I will, therefore, see that in all *Volksschulen* such instruction be introduced that will instill in the younger generation more love and respect for the trade and social position of their parents" (p. 32).

(c) "The soldier must be instructed so carefully concerning the claims which the state has upon his services, and also concerning his duties and obligations, and likewise his rights, that his own judgment will lead him to be contented with his lot and that he will cease as far as possible to look with envy and secret hate upon his superiors."

"Whoever has the ability to write a good text-book with this end in view can render great service to the future happiness of the soldiers and can be assured of my most earnest gratitude. I would desire that the religious instruction be included in this text, and that after the discussion of the Ten Commandments all civil crimes and their punishments be explained briefly and plainly in catechetical form. Such a book would in itself be more useful reading for the soldier than all the devotional books and would fully supply the lack of all popular magazines and newspapers, in which on every page one observes the financial speculations of the publishers more than any real advantage to the public, and through which only a hurtful thirst for reading is spread among the common people" (p. 32).

(d) "I have not yet mentioned history, and only wish to remark that it should limit itself solely to the most important national events, and have no other purpose than to awaken patriotic love and affection, pride in the deeds of our forefathers, and the desire to emulate them. . . ." (p. 32 f.).

Alexander, *Prussian Elementary Schools* * (New York, Macmillan, 1918).

269. What Determines the Individual's Efficiency?

"The total mental efficiency of a man is the resultant of the working together of all his faculties. He is too complex a being for any one of them to have the casting vote. If any one of them do have the casting vote, it is more likely to be the strength of his desire and passion, the strength of the interest he takes in what is proposed. Concentration, memory, reasoning power, inventiveness, excellence of the senses,—all are subsidiary to this. No matter how scatter-brained the type of a man's successive fields of consciousness may be, if he really *care* for a subject, he will return to it incessantly from his incessant wanderings, and first and last do more with it, and get more results from it, than another person whose attention may be more continuous during a given interval, but whose passion for the subject is of a more languid and less permanent sort. Some of the most efficient workers I know are of the ultra-scatterbrained type. . . .

"This preponderance of interest, of passion, in determining the results of a human being's working life, obtains throughout. No elementary measurement, capable of being performed in a laboratory, can throw any light on the actual efficiency of the subject; for the vital thing about him, his emotional and moral energy and doggedness, can be measured by no single experiment, and becomes known only by the total results in the long run. A blind man like Huber, with his passion for bees and ants, can observe them through other people's eyes better than these can through their own. A man born with neither arms nor legs, like the late Kavanagh, M. P.—and what an icy heart his mother must have had about him in his babyhood, and how 'negative' would the laboratory-measurements of his motor functions have been!—can be an adventurous traveller, an equestrian and sportsman, and lead an athletic outdoor life. . . .

"Depend upon it, no one need be too much cast down by the discovery of his deficiency in any elementary faculty of the mind. What tells in life is the whole mind working together, and the deficiencies of any one faculty can be compensated by the efforts of the rest. You can be an artist without visual images, a reader without eyes, a mass of erudition with a bad elementary memory. In almost any subject your passion for the subject will save you. If you only care enough for a result, you will almost certainly attain it. If you wish to be rich, you will be rich; if you wish to be learned, you will be learned; if you wish to be good, you will be good. Only you must, then, *really* wish these things, and wish them with exclusiveness, and not wish at the same time a hundred other incompatible things just as strongly. . . .

"Be patient, then, and sympathetic with the type of mind that cuts a poor figure in examinations. It may, in the long examination which life sets us, come out in the end in better shape than the glib and ready reproducer, its passions being deeper, its purposes more worthy, its combining power less commonplace, and its total mental output consequently more important."

James, *Talks to Teachers* * (New York, Holt, 1899), pp. 114, 134 f., 136 f., 142 f.

270. Compulsory Attendance to the Age of 18

A study of the 245,000 boys from the ages of sixteen to eighteen inclusive employed in New York State during 1918-19 shows in the opinion of the author that these boys "are thoroly averse to further schooling and that compulsory part-time continuation school and night school work will be practically valueless unless we can awaken in these boys an interest in further education."

Burdge, *Our Boys* (Albany, Department of Education, 1921), p. 7.

271. Leisure and Learning

"The wisdom of the scribe cometh by opportunity of leisure; and he that hath little business shall become wise. How shall he become wise that holdeth the plow, that glorieth in the shaft of the goad, that driveth oxen, and is occupied in their labours, and whose discourse is of the stock of bulls? He will set his heart upon turning his furrows; and his wakefulness is to give his heifers their fodder."

Ecclesiasticus (Moulton, editor, Macmillan, 1896), Bk. III, ch. xv.

272. The Immigrant Child and the Conventional School

"There are hundreds of boys of various nationalities who conscientiously remain in school and fulfil all the requirements of the early grades, and at the age of fourteen are found in factories, painstakingly performing their work year after year. These later are the men who form the mass of the population in every industrial neighborhood of every large city; but they carry on the industrial processes year after year without in the least knowing what it is all about. The one fixed habit which the boy carries away with him from the school to the factory is the feeling that his work is merely provisional. In school the next grade was continually held before him as an object of attainment, and it resulted in the conviction that the sole object of present effort is to get ready for something else. This tentative attitude takes the last bit of social stimulus out of his factory work; he pursues it merely as a necessity, and his very mental attitude destroys his chance for a realization of its social value. As the boy in school contracted the habit of doing his work in certain hours and taking his pleasure in certain other hours, so in the factory he earns his money by ten hours of dull work and spends it in three hours of lurid and unprofitable pleasure in the evening. Both in the school and in the factory, in proportion as his work grows dull and monotonous, his recreation must become more exciting and stimulating. The hopelessness of adding evening classes and social entertainments as a mere frill to a day filled with monotonous and deadening drudgery constantly becomes more apparent to those who are endeavoring to bring a fuller life to the industrial members of the community, and who are looking forward to a time when work shall cease to be senseless drudgery with no self-expression on the part of the worker. It sometimes seems that the public schools should contribute much more than they do to the consummation of this time. If the army of school children who enter the factories every year possessed thoroughly vitalized faculties, they might do much to lighten this incubus of dull factory work which presses so heavily upon so large a number of our fellow-citizens. Has our commercialism been so strong that our schools have become insensibly commercialized, whereas we supposed that our industrial life was receiving the broadening and illuminating effects of the schools? The training of these children, so far as it has been vocational at all, has been in the direction of clerical work. It is possible that the business men, whom we in America so tremendously admire, have really been dictating the curriculum of our public schools, in spite of the conventions of educators and the suggestions of university professors. The business man, of course, has not said, 'I will have the public schools train office boys and clerks so that I may have them easily and cheaply,' but he has sometimes said, 'Teach the children to write legibly and to figure accurately and quickly; to acquire habits of punctuality and order; to be prompt to obey; and you will fit them to make their way in the world as I have made mine.' Has the workingman been silent as to what he desires for his children, and allowed the business man to decide for him there, as he has allowed the politician to manage his municipal affairs, or has the workingman so far shared our universal optimism that he has really believed that his children would never need to go into industrial life at all, but that all of his sons would become bankers and merchants?"

Addams, *Democracy and Social Ethics* * (New York, Macmillan, 1916), p. 188-191.

273. VOCATIONAL EDUCATION

"Any scheme for vocational education which takes its point of departure from the industrial régime that now exists, is likely to assume and to perpetuate its divisions and weaknesses, and thus to become an instrument in accomplishing the feudal dogma of social predestination.... An education which acknowledges the full intellectual and social meaning of a vocation would include instruction in the historic background of present conditions; training in science to give intelligence and initiative in dealing with material and agencies of production; and study of economics, civics, and politics, to bring the future worker into touch with the problems of the day and the various methods proposed for its improvement. Above all, it would train power of readaptation to changing conditions so that future workers would not become blindly subject to a fate imposed upon them. This ideal has to contend not only with the inertia of existing educational traditions, but also with the opposition of those who are intrenched in command of the industrial machinery, and who realize that such an educational system if made general would threaten their ability to use others for their own ends."

Dewey, *Democracy and Education* * (New York, Macmillan, 1916), pp. 372-3.

274. ONE VIEW OF VOCATIONAL EDUCATION

(Instructions of a state director of vocational training to the principal of a vocational high school)

"This school should be run in the interest of industry.... So much English, history and mathematics do more harm than good.... By the time your (four year high school) graduates have worked in a shop for three or four years they may want to become foremen or superintendents or something like that.... What we want you to do is to teach a boy to stand up to a lathe for nine hours a day for a dollar and a half a day and be satisfied....

"You should not teach girls to make their own clothes, but for the trade. No girl will do careful accurate work except under the exacting requirements of a customer."

275. EDUCATION FOR EFFICIENCY

"The gravest obstacle to the progress of education is the materialism which would subordinate the cultivation of human faculties to the exigencies, or alleged exigencies, of industry, which two generations ago condemned children of ten to inhuman toil in factories and mines, which still permits many thousand young persons to be stunted in body and mind by excessive and premature toil, and which regards the suggestion of increased educational expenditure as an inroad upon its riches or a menace to its comfort. . . .

"Men are first of all men, not animals, servants or tools. The first aim of education, therefore, must be to make, not more efficient workers, but better men, better citizens, and better Christians. Much emphasis is laid at the present time upon the contribution which education may make to productive efficiency, and we do not underestimate the importance of technical and professional training. But, valuable as such training is in its own sphere, it cannot, however highly it may be developed, relieve the community of the duty of cultivating through education those faculties of initiative, of judgment, and of intelligent sympathy with what is excellent in human achievement, which, because they are the attributes of man, are not distinctive of any class or profession of men. In particular, Christians cannot accept the view sometimes advanced which would regard a humane or liberal education as suitable only for those entering the professions, and which would estimate the success of the education offered to the great majority of the population by its ability to qualify them for more efficient labour in their various occupations. There must be diversity of educational methods because there are diversities of gifts. But the basis of differentiation should be differences of taste or of capacity, not differences of class or of income. The manual worker needs a liberal education for the same reason as the barrister or the doctor—that he may develop his faculties and play a reasonable part in the affairs of the community. . . .

"The only sound basis for technical training is the cultivation of mental alertness, judgment, and a sense of responsibility by means of education of a general and non-utilitarian character. A nation which aims primarily at developing to the fullest possible extent the character and intellect of its citizens may find that material prosperity and commercial success are added to it. A nation which regards education primarily as a means of converting its members into more efficient instruments of production is likely not only to jeopardise its moral standards and educational ideals, but to discover that by such methods it cannot attain even the limited success at which it aims."

Report of the Archbishop's Fifth Committee (London, 1918), pp. 112-114.

276. THE PROBLEM OF VOCATIONAL EDUCATION

"Elementary education, the education of the masses, has been not only 'Learning for Earning,' but a badly conceived learning, an education where the ability of the learner to add to the earnings of others rather than to his own earnings has been the main factor in selecting materials of study and fixing methods (p. 331) . . .

"Reading, writing, figuring, with a little geography and a smattering of other things, are what the great mass of those who leave our schools leave with. A few get something more. These things, when nothing else is added on to them, are pretty nearly pure economic tools. They came into the schools when the better-to-do classes discovered that under the conditions an elementary ability to read, write and figure was practically indispensable for salesmen and shop workers. He who is poorly acquainted with the history of the efforts to improve elementary education in our large cities does not know that the chief protest against progress is likely to come from successful business men. They have clamored for the three R's as the essential and exclusive material of primary education—knowing well enough that their own children would be able to get the things they protest against. Thus they have attacked as fads and frills every enrichment of the curriculum which did not lend itself to narrow economic ends. . . .

"Of late years, the situation has changed somewhat. The more intelligent employers have awakened to the fact that the mere rudiments of the three R's are not a good industrial training, while others of the community have awakened to the fact that it is a dangerously inadequate industrial education from the standpoint of the community. Hence there has arisen a demand for vocational and industrial education as if this were an entirely new thing; while, in fact, it is a demand that the present industrial education be so modified as to be efficient under the conditions of present machine industry, rapid transportation and a competitive market. . . .

DEMOCRACY AND EDUCATION

"The real issue at the present time concerning industrial education in public education ... is what sort of an industrial education there shall be and whose interests shall be primarily considered in its development.... To understand the *educational* issue is to see what difference is made in the schools themselves according as we take the *improving* of economic conditions to be the purpose of vocational training, or take its purpose to be supplying a better grade of labor for the present scheme, or helping on the United States in a competitive struggle for world commerce. I know that those who have the latter ends chiefly in view always make much of the increased happiness of the industrial worker himself as a product to result from better industrial education. But after all, there is a great difference between the happiness which means merely contentment with a station and the happiness which comes from the struggle of a well-equipped person to better his station. Which sort of happiness is to be our aim? I know, also, that stress is laid upon ability which is to proceed from a better industrial education to increase earnings. Well and good. But, does this mean simply that laborers are so to have their skill to add to the profits of employers increased, by avoiding waste, getting more out of their machines and materials, that they will have some share in it as an incidental by-product, or does it mean that increase in the industrial intelligence and power of the worker for his own personal advancement is to be the main factor? ... (p. 332 f.).

"Let me now point out some of the particular educational differences which will be made according as one or other idea of industry in education prevails. In the first place, as to administration, those who wish, whether they wish it knowingly or unknowingly, an education which will enable employees to fit better into the existing economic scheme will strive for a dual or divided system of administration. That is to say, they will attempt to have a separate system of funds, of supervisory authorities, and, as far as possible, of schools to carry on industrial education. If they don't go so far as this, they will at least constantly harp on the difference between a liberal or cultural and a money-earning education, and will endeavor to narrow the latter down to those forms of industrial skill which will enable the future workers to fall docilely into the subordinate ranks of the industrial army.

"In the second place, the conception that the primary object of industrial education is merely to prepare more skilled workers for the present system, instead of developing human beings who are equipped to reconstruct that scheme, will strive to identify it with trade education—that is, with training for certain specific callings. It assumes that the needs of industrial education are met if girls are trained to be skilled in millinery, cooking and garment-making, and boys to be plumbers, electric wirers, etc. . . .

"In the third place, the curriculum on this narrow trade plan will neglect as useless for its ends the topics in history and civics which make future workers aware of their rightful claims as citizens in a democracy, alert to the fact that the present economic struggle is but the present-day phase taken by the age-long battle for human liberties. So far as it takes in civic and social studies at all, it will emphasize duties to the established order and a blind patriotism which accounts it a great privilege to defend things in which the workers themselves have little or no share. The studies which fit the individual for the reasonable enjoyment of leisure time, which develop good taste in reading and appreciation of the arts, will be passed over as good for those who belong by wealth to the leisure class, but quite useless in the training of skilled employees.

"In the fourth place, so far as the method and spirit of its work is concerned, it will emphasize all that is most routine and automatic in our present system. Drill to secure skill in the performance of tasks under the direction of others will be its chief reliance. It will insist that the limits of time and the pressure for immediate results are so great that there is no room for understanding the scientific facts and principles or the social bearings of what is done. Such an enlarged education would develop also an intellectual ambition and initiative which might be fatal to contentment in routine subordinate clerical and shop jobs.

"Finally, so far as such a training concerns itself with what is called vocational guidance, it will conceive guidance as a method of placement—a method of finding jobs. It will measure its achievements by the number of children taking out working papers for whom it succeeds in finding places, instead of by the number whom it succeeds in keeping in school till they become equipped to seek and find their own congenial occupations.

"The other idea of industrial education aims at preparing every individual to render service of a useful sort to the community, while at the same time it equips him to secure by his own initiative whatever place his natural capacities fit him for. It will proceed in an opposite way in every respect. Instead of trying to split schools into two kinds, one of a trade type for children whom it is assumed are to be employees and one of a liberal type for the children of the well-to-do, it will aim at such a reorganization of existing schools as will give all pupils a genuine respect for useful work, an ability to render service, and a contempt for social parasites whether they are called tramps or leaders of 'society.' Instead of assuming that the problem is to add vocational training to an existing cultural elementary education, it will recognize frankly that the traditional elementary education is largely vocational, but that the vocations which it has in mind are too exclusively clerical, and too much of a kind which implies merely ability to take positions in which to carry out the plans of others. It will indeed make much of developing motor and manual skill, but not of a routine or automatic type. It will rather utilize active and manual pursuits as the means of developing constructive, inventive and creative power of mind. It will select the materials and the technique of the trades not for the sake of producing skilled workers for hire in definite trades, but for the sake of securing industrial intelligence—a knowledge of the conditions and processes of present manufacturing, transportation and commerce so that the individual may be able to make his own choices and his own adjustments, and be master, so far as in him lies, of his own economic fate. It will be recognized that, for this purpose, a broad acquaintance with science and skill in the laboratory control of materials and processes is more important than skill in trade operations. It will remember that the future employee is a consumer as well as a producer, that the whole tendency of society, so far as it is intelligent and wholesome, is to an increase of the hours of leisure, and that an education which does nothing to enable individuals to consume wisely and to utilize leisure wisely is a fraud on democracy. So far as method is concerned, such a conception of industrial education will prize freedom more than docility; initiative more than automatic skill; insight and understanding more than capacity to recite lessons or to execute tasks under the direction of others. . . . (p. 333 f.)

"The real issue is not the question whether an industrial education is to be added on to a more or less mythical cultural elementary education, but what sort of an industrial education we are to have. The movement for vocational educations conceals within itself two mighty and opposing forces, one which would utilize the public schools primarily to turn out more efficient laborers in the present economic régime, with certain incidental advantages to themselves, the other which would utilize all the resources of public education to equip individuals to control their own future economic careers, and thus help on such a reorganization of industry as will change it from a feudalistic to a democratic order." (p. 334 f.)

Dewey, in *School and Society,** 5:331 ff. (March 24, 1917.)

277. BERNARD SHAW ON EDUCATION IN THE SCHOOLS

"The usual answer is that we must educate our masters: that is, ourselves. We must teach citizenship and political science at school. But must we? There is no must about it, the hard fact being that we must *not* teach political science or citizenship at school. The schoolmaster who attempted it would soon find himself penniless in the streets without pupils, if not in the dock pleading to a pompously worded indictment for sedition against the exploiters. Our schools teach the morality of feudalism corrupted by commercialism, and hold up the military conqueror, the robber baron, and the profiteer, as models of the illustrious and the successful. In vain do the prophets who see through this imposture preach and teach a better gospel: the individuals whom they convert are doomed to pass away in a few years; and the new generations are dragged back in the schools to the morality of the fifteenth century, and think themselves Liberal when they are defending the ideas of Henry VII, and gentlemanly when they are opposing to them the ideas of Richard III. Thus the educated man is a greater nuisance than the uneducated one: indeed it is the inefficiency and sham of the educational side of our schools (to which, except under compulsion, children would not be sent by their parents at all if they did not act as prisons in which the immature are kept from worrying the mature) that save us from being dashed on the rocks of false doctrine instead of drifting down the midstream of mere ignorance. There is no way out through the schoolmaster.

"In truth, mankind cannot be saved from without, by schoolmasters or any other sort of masters; it can only be lamed and enslaved by them. It is said that if you wash a cat it will never again wash itself. This may or may not be true: what is certain is that if you teach a man anything he will never learn it."

Shaw, *Back to Methuselah** (New York, Brentano, 1921), pp. xii-xiii.

278. Criticism upon Present Education

"Certain mental habits are commonly instilled by those who are engaged in educating: obedience and discipline, ruthlessness in the struggle for worldly success, contempt toward opposing groups, and an unquestioning credulity, a passive acceptance of the teacher's wisdom. All these habits are against life. Instead of obedience and discipline, we ought to aim at preserving independence and impulse. Instead of ruthlessness, education ought to aim at producing justice in thought. Instead of contempt, it ought to instill reverence, the attempt at understanding—not necessarily acquiescence, but only such opposition as is combined with imaginative apprehension and a clear comprehension of the grounds for opposition. Instead of credulity, the object should be to stimulate constructive doubt, the love of mental adventure, the sense of worlds to conquer by enterprise and boldness in thought. Contentment with the *status quo,* subordination of the individual pupil to political aims, indifference to the things of the mind, are the immediate causes of these evils; but beneath these causes there is one more fundamental, the fact that education is treated as a means of acquiring power over the pupil, not as a means of fostering his own growth. . . .

"If we took education seriously, if we thought it as important to keep alive the minds of children as to secure victory in war, we should conduct education quite differently: we should make sure of achieving the end, even if the expense were a hundredfold greater than it is. . . .

"If the object were to make pupils think, rather than to make them accept certain conclusions, education would be conducted quite differently: there would be less rapidity of instruction, more discussion, more occasions when pupils were encouraged to express themselves, more attempt to make education concern itself with matters in which the pupils felt some interest.

"Above all, there would be an endeavor to rouse and stimulate the love of mental adventure. The world in which we live is various and astonishing: some of the things which seem plainest grow more and more difficult the more they are considered; other things, which might have been thought forever undiscoverable, have been laid bare by the genius and industry of the men of science. The power of thought, the vast regions which it can master, the much more vast regions which it can only dimly suggest to imagination, give to those whose minds have traveled beyond the daily round an amazing richness of material, an escape from the triviality and wearisomeness of familiar routine, by which the whole of life is filled with interest, and the prison walls of the commonplace are broken down. . . .

"But if thought is to become the possession of many, not the privilege of the few, we must have done with fear. It is fear that holds men back: fear lest their cherished beliefs should prove delusions, fear lest the institutions by which they live should prove harmful, fear lest they themselves should prove less worthy of respect than they have supposed themselves to be. Should the working man think freely about property? Then what will become of us, the rich? Should young men and young women think freely about sex? Then what will become of morality? Should soldiers think freely about war? Then what will become of military discipline? Away with thought! Back into the shades of prejudice, lest property, morals, and war should be endangered! Better that men should be stupid, slothful, and oppressive than that their thoughts should be free. For if their thoughts were free, they might not think as we do. And at all costs this disaster must be averted. So the opponents of thought argue in the unconscious depths of their souls. And so they act in their churches, their schools, and their universities.

"No institution inspired by fear can further life. Hope, not fear, is the creative principle in human affairs. All that has made man great has sprung from the attempt to secure what is good, not from the struggle to avert what was thought evil. It is because modern education is so seldom inspired by a great hope that it so seldom achieves a great result. The wish to preserve the past, rather than the hope of creating the future, dominates the minds of those who control the teaching of the young. Education should not aim at a dead awareness of static facts, but at an activity directed toward the world that our efforts are to create."

Russell, in *Atlantic Monthly*,* 117:754 ff. (June, 1916.)

279. KANT ON EDUCATION FOR THE FUTURE

"Children should be educated, *not* with reference to their present condition, but rather with regard to a possibly improved future state of the human race. . . . This principle is of great moment. Parents usually educate their children for the present world, corrupt though it be. They should, however, educate them *better*, that an improved future condition be thereby realized."

Buchner, *Kant's Educational Theory* * (Philadelphia, Lippincott, 1904), p. 116 f.

280. EDUCATION AND FREEDOM OF THOUGHT

"Nothing should be left undone to impress upon the young that freedom of thought is an axiom of human progress. It may be feared, however, that this is not likely to be done for a long time to come. For our methods of early education are founded on authority. It is true that children are sometimes exhorted to think for themselves. But the parent or instructor who gives this excellent advice is confident that the results of the child's thinking for himself will agree with the opinions which his elders consider desirable. It is assumed that he will reason from principles which have already been instilled into him by authority. But if his thinking for himself takes the form of questioning these principles, whether moral or religious, his parents and teachers, unless they are very exceptional persons, will be extremely displeased, and will certainly discourage him. It is, of course, only singularly promising children whose freedom of thought will go so far. In this sense it might be said that 'distrust thy father and mother' is the first commandment with promise. It should be a part of education to explain to children, as soon as they are old enough to understand, when it is reasonable, and when it is not, to accept what they are told, on authority."

Bury, *History of Freedom of Thought* * (New York,[1] Holt, 1913), p. 251.

281. THE CIRCLE OF POVERTY AND IGNORANCE

"The [British] Labor Party," says Arthur Henderson, "means to break the vicious circle that binds ignorance to poverty and poverty to ignorance."

Quoted in *Evening Post* (New York), July 6, 1918.

282. EDUCATION AND SOCIAL DIRECTION

"It is not surprising that many persons in the United States who are accustomed to think of themselves as belonging to the 'upper' and therefore rightfully ruling class, and who are impressed by the endurance and resistance of Germany in the war,

[1] Originally published in England.

should look with envious admiration upon the Prussian system of authoritarian education. To suppose however that they desire a direct importation of the German system of autocratic power and willing submissiveness in order to secure the discipline and massive order of Germany, is to make a blunder. They see America retaining its familiar traditions; for the most part they would be sincerely shocked at a suggestion of surrender of democratic habits. What they see in their fancy is an America essentially devoted to democratic ideals and rising to the service of these ideals with a thoroughness, a unanimity, an efficiency and ordered discipline which they imagine would be secured by a judicious adoption of German methods. Since they do not perceive the interdependence of ends and means, or of purposes and methods, their error is intellectual rather than perversely immoral. They are stupid rather than deliberately disloyal.

"It is one of the many merits of Veblen's most enlightening book on Imperial Germany that he makes clear the high human cost of the envied German habit. Under modern conditions social automatism is not automatically self-sustaining. It represents a delicate and complicated piece of machinery which can be kept in proper working order only by immense pains. The obedient mind is not a thing which can be achieved by the segregated means of school discipline alone. All the resources of all social institutions have to be centered upon it without let-up. 'It can be maintained only by unremitting habituation, discipline sagaciously and relentlessly directed to this end.' Successful warfare, the effects of warlike preparation, and indoctrination with warlike arrogance are more necessary than the technique of the class room. Only 'bureaucratic surveillance and unremitting interference in the private life' of subjects can, in the face of the disintegrating tendencies of contemporary industry and trade, develop that 'passionate aspiration for subservience' which is a marked feature of the Prussian diathesis. If we look these facts in the face, we shall quickly see the romanticism of any proposal to secure the German type of disciplined efficiency and of patient and persistent 'industry' by borrowing a few features of the personal relation of teacher and pupil and installing them in the school. Only an occasional pedagogical Dogberry can rise to the level of a New York school administrator who would secure permanent good loyal citizenship by 'teaching (sic) instinctive obedience' in the schools.

"Taken in this crude form, the desire to Prussianize the disciplinary methods of American schools is too incoherent and spasmodic to constitute a serious danger. A serious danger there is, however, and it lies in the confused thinking which such efforts stimulate and strengthen. The danger lies not in any likelihood of success. Save here and there and for a brief period, the attempts run hopelessly counter to the trend of countless social forces. The danger is that the vague desire and confused thought embodied in them will cover up the real problems involved in securing an effectively loyal democratic citizenship, and distract attention from the constructive measures required to develop the kind of social unity and social control required in a democracy. For the whole tendency of current lamentations over the failure of American education to secure social integration and effective cohesion, is to put emphasis upon the futile and irritating relations of personal authority and personal subjection, or else upon the regulative power of blind engrained habits, whose currency presupposes an authoritative *deus ex machina* behind the scenes to supply the ends for which the habits are to work. And anybody who hasn't put his soul to sleep with the apologetics of soporific 'idealism' knows that at the present time the power which would fix the ends to which the masses would be habituated is the economic class which has a selfish interest in the exercise of control. To cater to this class by much talk of the importance of discipline, obedience, habituation, and by depreciation of initiative and creative thought as socially dangerous, may be a quick path to favor. But it represents an ignobility of spirit which is peculiarly out of place in an educator, who above all others is called upon to keep his supreme interest sensitively human.

"Unfortunately there is much in the tradition of what is regarded as scientific sociology which lends itself, unwittingly, to such base uses. Sociological science inherited a basic error from the older political science, and has too often devoted itself to a pompous dressing-out of solutions of a problem resting upon a 'fact' which isn't a fact. It has taken as its chief problem how individuals who are (supposedly) non-social become socialized, how social control becomes effective among individuals who are naturally hostile to it. The basic supposition is, of course, mythological. Docility, desire for direction, love for protective control are stronger original traits of human nature than is insubordination or originality. The scales are always weighted in favor of habituation and against reflective thought. Routine is so easy as to be 'natural,' and initiative is so difficult as to require the severe discipline of art. But the sociological antithesis of the individual and the social has invaded educational thought and is employed by the pedagogue to defend unintelligent convention, unexamined tradition, and to feed the irritable vanity of that petty tyrant, the educational administrator, who learns by study of the new sociological pedagogy that the exercise of his personal authority is in reality an exemplar of the great problem of sociology—the 'social control' of the unregenerate, unsocialized individual.

"This thoughtless sociology does something, however, even more harmful than the rationalization of mere personal authority. It serves to justify the laziness, the intellectual inertia, of the educational routineer. The latter finds it easier, say, to rely upon books than to make himself a well informed man at first hand. He is solemnly told that textbooks socialize the pupil, for they embody the intellectual heritage of the race. He then puts to one side the onerous task of achieving any personal originality in the subjects he teaches, lest he might fire his students with 'individualism' having socially disastrous consequences. An uneasy intellectual conscience tells a teacher that in his methods he is following the lines of least resistance furnished by school customs which he has unreflectively picked up. But he is consoled by being told that thinking merely develops individualism, that custom is the great social balance wheel. And far be it from him to undermine the sanctities of institutionalized habit by a little adventure in personal reflection. He has a sense that his ways of dealing with pupils are external and perfunctory. He feels that if he took pains to acquaint himself with the scientific methods of gaining insight into human nature and applied himself with sympathy to understanding it in its immense diversity, he might be able to work from the inside to release potentialities instead of from the outside to impose conventionalities. But then the solemn guardian of 'social control' comes along and warns him of the 'social' value of respect for authority as such, and the dangers of 'catering' to individuality. A scientific excuse for natural laziness and ignorance can go a long way.

"The worst of all this, I repeat, is that it leaves problems which are pressing untouched and ignores the urgent need for the particular kind of social direction fitted to a democratic society—the direction which comes from heightened emotional appreciation of common interests and from an understanding of social responsibilities, an understanding to be secured only by experimental and personal participation in the conduct of common affairs. At this point the antithesis between individual and social ceases to be merely silly. It becomes dangerous. For the unsolved problem of democracy is the construction of an education which will develop that kind of individuality which is intelligently alive to the common life and sensitively loyal to its common maintenance. It is not an antithesis of social control and individual development which our education requires. We want that type of education which will discover and form the kind of individual who is the intelligent carrier of a social democracy—social indeed, but still a democracy."

Dewey, in *The Dial*,* 64:333-5 (April 11, 1918).

283. Jowett's Advice to Administrators

"Never retract, never explain.
Get it done. Let 'em howl."

284. "The Essentials of an Effective System of Schools"

"In a sense, a system of schools may be regarded as an organism created to produce certain changes in people. The fingers and hands are the teachers; the nerves, the supervisory force; the brain, the central administration. . . .

"a. In order that the system may be effective, therefore, it is necessary that there be at the center some agency which, in careful and detailed fashion, shall determine the purpose of the process. . . .

"The content, arrangement, and order of the curriculum should be worked out, and the materials of instruction necessary to the process should be developed and provided. Then the methods should be determined by which the curriculum may be best presented to and mastered by the pupils. How to make this a part of the teachers' work; how to see that the best results are secured, either by standardising the product or watching the process; how to group pupils for most effective work; how to advance them from stage to stage; how to select, train and promote teachers; how to train character; how to form good habits; how to give culture; how to instill good manners and breeding; how to govern schools most effectively; how to keep records and make such reports as may be needed; how to keep children healthy and how to make schools so hygienic as not to impede progress; how to construct proper buildings and secure such equipment that the educational process may be best carried out; these are some of the problems of the brain of the organism. . . .

Without the solution of these problems, the fingers and hands do not know how to work most effectively, the nerves to give impulses, the brain to direct.

"b. The fingers and hands, the teachers, must be competent to carry out the plans of the central organization. Each must be sensitive to the demands confronting him. Each must be skilled in the processes of his task. Not only must he have an appreciation of skilled work when he sees it, but he must himself be trained to become a skilled technician. . . .

"c. The nerves, the supervisors and administrators, are useful only in so far as they facilitate the work of the teacher or carry messages to and from the central organization. Their task is to keep the work going, free the teacher from petty detail, see that the direction of the work is right, and keep the central organization in touch with the work that is going on. . . .

"d. In addition, there must be present a spiritual quality, a sense of devotion to service, consecration to the noble and exalted task confronting the organisms. . . .

"e. . . . Much of the best work will come when teachers and supervisors themselves, either as individuals or groups, investigate their problems, come to certain results, and communicate their findings to all others.

"f. . . . The principles apply as well to the work of a single school, a regional unit, or to a uniform system of schools, nationwide in extent. The thesis is that no school or system is effective, which does not have some central organisation to determine scientifically and thoroughly the purpose of the work and the means and administrative details necessary to carry it out; teachers so well trained that these ideas may be efficiently carried to the pupils; supervisory forces so skilled as to form an effective means of communication between the two; and a spirit of consecration and devotion to so noble a task that the work will not fail."

Christian Education in China * (New York, Foreign Missions Conference, 1922), pp. 135-138.

285. DEMOCRACY IN EDUCATION

"Modern life means democracy, democracy means freeing intelligence for independent effectiveness—the emancipation of mind as an individual organ to do its own work. We naturally associate democracy, to be sure, with freedom of action, but freedom of action without freed capacity of thought behind it is only chaos. If external authority in action is given up, it must be because internal authority of truth, discovered and known to reason, is substituted.

"How does the school stand with reference to this matter? Does the school as an accredited representative exhibit this trait of democracy as a spiritual force? Does it lead and direct the movement? Does it lag behind the work at cross-purposes? I find the fundamental need of the school today dependent upon its limited recognition of the principle of freedom of intelligence. This limitation appears to me to affect both of the elements of school life: teacher and pupil. As to both, the school has lagged behind the general contemporary social movement; and much that is unsatisfactory, much of conflict and of defect, comes from the discrepancy between the relatively undemocratic organization of the school, as it affects the mind of both teacher and pupil, and the growth and extension of the democratic principle in life beyond school doors.

"The effort of the last two-thirds of a century has been successful in building up the machinery of a democracy of mind. It has provided the ways and means for housing and equipping intelligence. . . . But when we turn to the aim and method which this magnificent institution serves, we find that our democracy is not yet conscious of the ethical principle upon which it rests—the responsibility and freedom of mind in discovery and proof—and consequently we find confusion where there should be order, darkness where there should be light. The teacher has not the power of initiation and constructive endeavor which is necessary to the fulfilment of the function of teaching. The learner finds conditions antagonistic (or at least lacking) to the development of individual mental power and to adequate responsibility for its use.

"1. *As to the teacher.*—If there is a single public-school system in the United States where there is official and constitutional provision made for submitting questions of methods of discipline and teaching, and the questions of the curriculum, text-books, etc., to the discussion and decision of those actually engaged in the work of teaching, that fact has escaped my notice. Indeed, the opposite situation is so common that it seems, as a rule, to be absolutely taken for granted as the normal and final condition of affairs. The number of persons to whom any other course has occurred as desirable, or even possible—to say nothing of necessary—is apparently very limited. But until the public-school system is organized in such a way that every teacher has some regular and representative way in which he or she can register judgment upon matters of educational importance, with the assurance that this judgment will somehow affect the school system, the assertion that the present system is not, from the internal standpoint, democratic seems to be justified. Either we come here upon some fixed and inherent limitation of the democratic principle, or else we find in this fact an obvious discrepancy between the conduct of the school and the conduct of social life— a discrepancy so great as to demand immediate and persistent effort at reform.

"The more enlightened portions of the public have, indeed, become aware of one aspect of this discrepancy. Many reformers are contending against the conditions which place the direction of school affairs, including the selection of text-books, etc., in the hands of a body of men who are outside the school system itself, who have not necessarily any expert knowledge of education and who are moved by non-educational motives. Unfortunately, those who have noted this undemocratic condition of affairs, and who have striven to change it, have, as a rule, conceived of but one remedy, namely the transfer of authority to the school superintendent. In their zeal to place the center of gravity inside the school system, in their zeal to decrease the prerogatives of a non-expert school board, and to lessen the opportunities for corruption and private pull which go with that, they have tried to remedy one of the evils of democracy by adopting the principle of autocracy. For no matter how wise, expert, or benevolent the head of the school system, the one-man principle is autocracy.

"The logic of the argument goes farther, very much farther, than the reformer of this type sees. The logic which commits him to the idea that the management of the school system must be in the hands of an expert commits him also to the idea that every member of the school system, from the first-grade teacher to the principal of the high school, must have some share in the exercise of educational power. The remedy is not to have one expert dictating educational methods and subject-matter to a body of passive, recipient teachers, but the adoption of intellectual initiative, discussion, and decision throughout the entire school corps. The remedy of the partial evils of democracy, the implication of the school system in municipal politics, is an appeal to a more thoroughgoing democracy.

"The dictation, in theory at least, of the subject-matter to be taught, to the teacher who is to engage in the actual work of instruction, and frequently under the name of close supervision, the attempt to determine the methods which are to be used in teaching, mean nothing more or less than the deliberate restriction of intelligence, the imprisoning of the spirit. Every well graded system of schools in this country rejoices in a course of study. It is no uncommon thing to find methods of teaching such subjects as reading, writing, spelling, and arithmetic officially laid down; outline topics in history and geography are provided ready-made for the teacher; gems of literature are fitted to the successive ages of boys and girls. Even the domain of art, songs and methods of singing, subject-matter and technique of drawing and painting, come within the region on which an outside authority lays its sacrilegious hands.

"I have stated the theory, which is also true of the practice to a certain extent and in certain places. We may thank our heavens, however, that the practice is rarely as bad as the theory would require. Superintendents and principals often encourage individuality and thoughtfulness in the invention and adoption of methods of teaching; and they wink at departures from the printed manual of study. It remains true, however, that this great advance is personal and informal. It depends upon the wisdom and tact of the individual supervisory official; he may withdraw his concession at any moment; or it may be ruthlessly thrown aside by his successor who has formed a high ideal of 'system.'

"I know it will be said that this state of things, while an evil, is a necessary one; that without it confusion and chaos would reign; that such regulations are the inevitable accompaniments of any graded system. It is said that the average teacher is incompetent to take any part in laying out the course of study or in initiating methods of instruction or discipline. Is not this the type of argument which has been used from time immemorial, and in every department of life, against the advance of democracy? What does democracy mean save that the individual is to have a share in determining the conditions and the aims of his own work; and that, upon the whole, through the free and mutual harmonizing of different individuals, the work of the world is better done than when planned, arranged, and directed by a few, no matter how wise or of how good intent that few? How can we justify our belief in the democratic principle elsewhere, and then go back entirely upon it when we come to education?

"Moreover, the argument proves too much. The more it is

asserted that the existing corps of teachers is unfit to have voice in the settlement of important educational matters, and their unfitness to exercise intellectual initiative and to assume the responsibility for constructive work is emphasized, the more their unfitness to attempt the much more difficult and delicate task of guiding souls appears. If this body is so unfit, how can it be trusted to carry out the recommendations or the dictations of the wisest body of experts? If teachers are incapable of the intellectual reponsibility which goes with the determination of the methods they are to use in teaching, how can they employ methods when dictated by others, in other than a mechanical, capricious, and clumsy manner? The argument, I say, proves too much.

"Moreover, if the teaching force is as inept and unintelligent and irresponsible as the argument assumes, surely the primary problem is that of their improvement. Only by sharing in some responsible task does there come a fitness to share in it. The argument that we must wait until men and women are fully ready to assume intellectual and social responsibilities would have defeated every step in the democratic direction that has ever been taken. The prevalence of methods of authority and of external dictation and direction tends automatically to perpetuate the very conditions of inefficiency, lack of interest, inability to assume positions of self-determination, which constitute the reasons that are depended upon to justify the régime of authority.

"The system which makes no great demands upon originality, upon invention, upon the continuous expression of individuality, works automatically to put and to keep the more incompetent teachers in the school. It puts them there because by a natural law of spiritual gravitation, the best minds are drawn to the places where they can work most effectively. The best minds are not especially like to be drawn where there is danger that they may have to submit to conditions which no self-respecting intelligence likes to put up with; and where their time and energy are likely to be so occupied with details of external conformity that they have no opportunity for free and full play of their own vigor.

"I have dwelt at length upon the problem of the recognition of the intellectual and spiritual individuality of the teacher. I have but one excuse. All other reforms are conditioned upon reform in the quality and character of those who engage in the teaching profession. The doctrine of the man behind the gun has become familiar enough, in recent discussion, in every sphere of life. Just because education is the most personal, the most intimate, of all human affairs, there, more than anywhere else, the sole ultimate reliance and final source of power are in the training, character, and intelligence of the individual. If any scheme could be devised which would draw to the calling of teaching persons of force of character, of sympathy with children, and consequent interest in the problems of teaching and of scholarship, no one need be troubled for a moment about other educational reforms, or the solution of other educational problems. But as long as a school organization which is undemocratic in principle tends to repel from all but the higher portions of the school system those of independent force, of intellectual initiative, and of inventive ability, or tends to hamper them in their work after they find their way into the schoolroom, so long all other reforms are compromised at their source and postponed indefinitely for fruition.

"2. *As to the learner.* The undemocratic suppression of the individuality of the teacher goes naturally with the improper restriction of the intelligence of the mind of the child. The mind, to be sure, is that of a child, and yet, after all, it is mind. To subject mind to an outside and ready-made material is a denial of the ideal of democracy, which roots itself ultimately in the principle of moral, self-directing individuality. Misunderstanding regarding the nature of the freedom that is demanded for the child is so common that it may be necessary to emphasize the fact that it is primarily intellectual freedom, free play of mental attitude, and operation which are sought. If individuality were simply a matter of feelings, impulses, and outward acts independent of intelligence, it would be more than a dubious matter to urge a greater degree of freedom for the child in the school. In that case much, and almost exclusive, force would attach to the objections that the principle of individuality is realized in the more exaggerated parts of Rousseau's doctrines: sentimental idealization of the child's immaturity, irrational denial of superior worth in the knowledge and mature experience of the adult, deliberate denial of the worth of the ends and instruments embodied in social organization. Deification of childish whim, unripened fancy, and arbitrary emotion is certainly a piece of pure romanticism. The would-be reformers who emphasize out of due proportion and perspective these aspects of the principle of individualism betray their own cause. But the heart of the matter lies not there. Reform of education in the direction of greater play for the individuality of the child means the securing of conditions which will give outlet, and hence direction, to a growing intelligence. It is true that this freed power of mind with reference to its own further growth cannot be obtained without a certain leeway, a certain flexibility, in the expression of even immature feelings and fancies. But it is equally true that it is not a riotous loosening of these traits which is needed, but just that kind and degree of freedom from repression which are found to be necessary to secure the full operation of intelligence.

"Now, no one need doubt as to what mental activity or the freed expression of intelligence means. No one need doubt as to the conditions which are conducive to it. We do not have to fall back upon what some regard as the uncertain, distracting, and even distressing voice of psychology. Scientific methods, the methods pursued by the scientific inquirer, give us an exact and concrete exhibition of the path which intelligence takes when working most efficiently, under most favorable conditions.

"What is primarily required for that direct inquiry which constitutes the essence of science is first-hand experience; an active and vital participation through the medium of all the bodily organs with the means and materials of building up first-hand experience. Contrast this first and most fundamental of all the demands for an effective use of mind with what we find in so many of our elementary and high schools. There first-hand experience is at a discount; in its stead are summaries and formulas of the results of other people. Only very recently has any positive provision been made within the schoolroom for any of the modes of activity and for any of the equipment and arrangement which permit and require the extension of original experiences on the part of the child. The school has literally been dressed out with hand-me-down garments—with intellectual suits which other people have worn.

"Secondly, in that freed activity of mind which we term 'science' there is always a certain problem which focusses effort, which controls the collecting of facts that bear upon the question, the use of observation to get further data, the employing of memory to supply relevant facts, the calling into play of imagination, to yield fertile suggestion and construct possible solutions of the difficulty.

"Turning to the school, we find too largely no counterpart to this mental activity. Just because a second-handed material has been supplied wholesale and retail, but anyway ready-made, the tendency is to reduce the activity of mind to a docile or passive taking in of the material presented—in short, to memorizing, with simply incidental use of judgment and of active research. As is frequently stated, acquiring takes the place of inquiring. It is hardly an exaggeration to say that the sort of mind-activity which is encouraged in the school is a survival from the days in which science had not made much headway; when education was mainly concerned with learning, that is to say, the preservation and handing down of the acquisitions of the past. It is true that more and more appeal is made every day in schools to judgment, reasoning, personal efficiency, and the calling up of personal, as distinct from merely book, experiences. But we have not yet got to the point of reversing the total method. The burden and the stress still fall upon learning in the sense of becoming possessed of the second-hand and ready-made material referred to. . . . The prevailing ideal is a perfect recitation, an exhibition without mistake, of a lesson learned. Until the emphasis changes to the conditions which make it necessary for the child to take an active share in the personal building up of his own problems and to participate in methods of solving them (even at the expense of experimentation and error), mind is not really freed.

"In our schools we have freed individuality in many modes of outer expression without freeing intelligence, which is the vital spring and guarantee of all of these expressions. Consequently we give opportunity to the unconverted to point the finger of scorn, and to clamor for a return to the good old days when the teacher, the representative of social and moral authority, was securely seated in the high places of the school. But the remedy here, as in other phases of our social democracy, is not to turn back, but to go farther—to carry the evolution of the school to a point where it becomes a place for getting and testing experience, as real and adequate to the child upon his existing level as all the resources of laboratory and library afford to the scientific man upon his level. What is needed is not any radical revolution, but rather an organization of agencies already found in the schools. It is hardly too much to say that not a single subject or instrumentality is required which is not already found in many schools of the country. All that is required is to gather these materials and forces together and unify their operation. Too often they are used for a multitude of diverse and often conflicting aims. If a single purpose is provided, that of freeing the processes of mental growth, these agencies will at once fall into their proper classes and reinforce each other.

"A catalogue of the agencies already available would include at least all of the following: Taking the child out of doors, widening and organizing his experience with reference to the world in which he lives; nature study when pursued as a vital observation of forces working under their natural conditions, plants and animals growing in their own homes, instead of mere discussion of dead specimens. We have also school gardens, the introduction of elementary agriculture, and more especially of horticulture—a movement that is already making great headway in many of the western states. We have also means for the sake of studying physiographic conditions, such as may be found by rivers, ponds or lakes, beaches, quarries, gulleys, hills, etc.

"As similar agencies within the school walls, we find a very great variety of instruments for constructive work, . . . Under this head come cooking, which can be begun in its simpler form in the kindergarten; sewing, and what is of even greater educational value, weaving, including designing and the construction of simple apparatus for carrying on various processes of spinning, etc. Then there are also the various forms of tool-work directed upon cardboard, wood, and iron; in addition there are clay-modeling and a variety of ways of manipulating plastic material to gain power and larger experience.

"Such matters pass readily over into the simpler forms of scientific experimentation. Every schoolroom from the lowest primary grade up should be supplied with gas, water, certain chemical substances and reagents. To experiment in the sense of trying things or to see what will happen is the most natural business of the child; it is, indeed, his chief concern. It is one which the school has largely either ignored or actually suppressed, so that it has been forced to find outlet in mischief or even in actually destructive ways. This tendency could find outlet in the construction of simple apparatus and the making of simple tests, leading constantly into more and more controlled experimentation, with greater insistence upon definiteness of intellectual result and control of logical process.

"Add to these three typical modes of active experimenting, various forms of art expression, beginning with music, clay-modeling, and story-telling as foundation elements, and passing on to drawing, painting, designing in various mediums, we have a range of forces and materials which connect at every point with the child's natural needs and powers, and which supply the requisites for building up his experience upon all sides. As fast as these various agencies find their way into the schools, the center of gravity shifts, the régime changes from one of subjection of mind to an external and ready-made material, into the activity of mind directed upon the control of the subject-matter and thereby its own upbuilding.

"Politically we have found that this country could not endure half free and half slave. We shall find equally great difficulty in encouraging freedom, independence, and initiative in every sphere of social life, while perpetuating in the school dependence upon external authority. The forces of social life are already encroaching upon the school institutions which we have inherited from the past, so that many of its mainstays are crumbling. Unless the outcome is to be chaotic, we must take hold of the organic, positive principle involved in democracy, and put that in entire possession of the spirit and work of the school.

"In education meet the three most powerful motives of human activity. Here are found sympathy and affection, the going out of the emotions to the most appealing and the most rewarding object of love—a little child. Here is found also the flowering of the social and institutional motive, interest in the welfare of society and in its progress and reform by the surest and shortest means. Here, too, is found the intellectual and scientific motive, the interest in knowledge, in scholarship, in truth for its own sake, unhampered and unmixed with any alien ideal. Copartnership of these three motives—of affection, of social growth, and of scientific inquiry—must prove as nearly irresistible as anything human when they are once united. And, above all else, recognition of the spiritual basis of democracy, the efficacy and responsibility of freed intelligence, is necessary to secure this union."

Dewey, in *Elementary School Teacher*,* 4:193-204 (Dec. 1903).

CHAPTER XII

SOCIAL CONTROL

286. Encroachment upon Individuality

"There is . . . in the world at large an increasing inclination to stretch unduly the powers of society over the individual, both by the force of opinion and even by that of legislation; and as the tendency of all the changes taking place in the world is to strengthen society, and diminish the power of the individual, this encroachment is not one of the evils which tend spontaneously to disappear, but, on the contrary, to grow more and more formidable. The disposition of mankind, whether as rulers or as fellow-citizens, to impose their own opinions and inclinations as a rule of conduct on others, is so energetically supported by some of the best and by some of the worst feelings incident to human nature, that it is hardly ever kept under restraint by anything but want of power: and as the power is not declining, but growing, unless a strong barrier of moral conviction can be raised against the mischief, we must expect, in the present circumstances of the world to see it increase."

Mill, *Liberty* (London, Parker, 1859), p. 29 f.

287. My Opponent's Case

"Paradoxical as it may seem, if I am a sincere seeker for truth, I shall help my antagonist to put his case in the most favorable light and coöperate with him in securing an opportunity for putting his theory to the test. I shall do this because I am convinced that his theory will not work, and that the sooner it is demonstrated that it will not work, under conditions which he himself chooses as being especially favorable for success, the better for my own position."

McCrea, in *Columbia University Quarterly*, 19:27 (Dec. 1916).

288. Tyranny of the Majority

"When society is itself the tyrant—society collectively, over the separate individuals who compose it—its means of tyrannizing are not restricted to the acts which it may do by the hands of its political functionaries. Society can and does execute its own mandates: and if it issues wrong mandates instead of right, or any mandates at all in things with which it ought not to meddle, it practises a social tyranny more formidable than many kinds of political oppression, since, though not usually upheld by such extreme penalties, it leaves fewer means of escape, penetrating much more deeply into the details of life, and enslaving the soul itself. Protection, therefore, against the tyranny of the magistrate is not enough; there needs protection also against the tyranny of the prevailing opinion and feeling; against the tendency of society to impose, by other means than civil penalties, its own ideas and practices as rules of conduct on those who dissent from them; to fetter the development, and, if possible prevent the formation, of any individuality not in harmony with its ways, and compel all characters to fashion themselves upon the model of its own. There is a limit to the legitimate interference of collective opinion with individual independence; and to find that limit, and maintain it against encroachment, is as indispensable to a good condition of human affairs, as protection against political despotism."

Mill, *On Liberty* (London, Parker, 1859), p. 13 f.

289. Decision by Majority

"Decision by majorities is as much an expedient as lighting by gas."

Gladstone, Speech in House of Commons, 1858.

290. Conditions Affecting Majority Rule

"Generally speaking, majority rule is a practicable device for determining the will of the people only under two essential conditions. The first of these conditions is that the matter about which the decision is to be binding on all should be one which it is generally agreed should be decided in one way for all. Few people believe in majority rule in respect to religious practices, and no one believes in majority rule in respect to the color of neckties. Other things equal, majority rule works well in respect to any line of conduct in proportion as the people concerned are agreed that it is a matter calling for a common decision. The second condition, closely connected with the first, is that the group or community within which the rule of the majority is to be applied should possess a high degree of solidarity. In a group in which all have much the same possessions, standards of life, and moral prepossessions, majority rule works well enough precisely because the ideas and interests of the minority are not so radically different from those of the majority that they cannot readily submit to the decision of the majority. The will of the people is sufficiently expressed by the will of the majority only when the minority 'wills' to let it go at that. But when the minority is a more or less fixed group, whose ideas and interests are radically different from those of the majority, or are thought to be so, then majority rule ceases to be 'government by the people' and becomes the oppression of one group by another."

Becker, *United States: an Experiment in Democracy* * (New York, Harper, 1920), p. 325.

291. The Right of the Minority to Speak

"If all mankind minus one, were of one opinion, and only one person were of the contrary opinion, mankind would be no more justified in silencing that one person, than he, if he had the power, would be justified in silencing mankind."

Mill, *Liberty* (London, Parker, 1859), p. 33.

292. Irreconcilable Sub-Groups

"In several nations at the present day there are large bodies of irreconcilables who are unwilling for other reasons to abide by the decision of the majority on the most fundamental of all political questions, the form of government and the right of the existing authorities to rule. They submit, for the moment, because there is no immediate prospect of successful resistance, but so far as they are concerned no general or public opinion can be said to exist in the land.

"In his recent book on *The France of Today*, Professor Barrett Wendell has portrayed one aspect of this state of things. Not only is the monarchial minority irreconcilable, refusing to consider itself under any obligation to accept as final the verdict of the mass of the French people on the form of government, but, as he points out, the dominant majority is disinclined to conciliate that minority on any question or to take its views into account. Its attitude is rather one of repressive hostility. The majority, therefore, is not making an effort to create a true public opinion, in the sense in which we are using the term; and so long as both parties maintain such a relation no opinion of that kind is possible.

"Examples of irreconcilables, always more or less bitter, may be found in the cases of the Irish Nationalists, of the Clericals in Italy, of the Poles, Danes, and Alsatians in Germany, and of the many struggling races in the conglomerate of Austria-Hungary—to speak only of countries that have enjoyed for some time representative institutions. We have had in America also our own painful experience during the period of Reconstruction after the Civil War, when the white people of the states under carpet-bag rule may be fairly said to have been irreconcilable."

Lowell, *Public Opinion and Popular Government* * (New York, Longmans, 1914), p. 32 f.

293. Man's Life Without Law

"Hereby it is manifest, that during the time when men live without a common power to keep them all in awe, they are in that condition which is called war; and such a war, as is of every man, against every man (*bellum omnium contra omnes*). . . . In such a condition, there is no place for industry; because the fruit thereof is uncertain; and consequently no culture of the earth; no navigation, nor use of the commodities that may be imported by sea; no commodious building; no instruments of moving and removing, such things as require much force; no knowledge of the face of the earth; no account of time; no arts; no letters; no society; and which is worst of all, continual fear, and danger of violent death; and the life of man, solitary, poor, nasty, brutish, and short."

Hobbes, *Leviathan* (London, Routledge, 1887 [1]), p. 64.

294. The Function of Force

"The mission of armed force is to give moral ideas time to take root."
Mahan.

295. Function of State Coercion

Coercion "has its value in the action that it sets free. . . . The function of State coercion is to override individual coercion, and, of course, coercion exercised by any association of

[1] First ed., 1651.

individuals within the State. It is by this means that it maintains liberty of expression, security of person and property, genuine freedom of contract, the rights of public meeting and association, and finally its own power to carry out common objects undefeated by the recalcitrance of individual members."

Hobhouse, *Liberalism* (New York, Holt, no date), p. 145 ff.

296. Social Coercion Not Democratic

"Even when the objective consideration leads to the conclusion that the minority is in the wrong and must not be permitted to continue a certain activity, suppression by means of force should be avoided wherever possible. Coercion is the antithesis of everything democratic; it imposes an external will upon the subject; it acts always by limiting the alternative possibilities; it leaves no room for the development of that feeling of responsibility which is the *sine qua non* of a moral life. Democracy's method is the word, not the whip. The means of social control in a free state is education—the bringing of people together into communication, a free press, free speech, free schools, the dissemination of knowledge,—these are the means of influence that a democracy should use in an endeavor to convince of what is reasonable. Whenever it is necessary to substitute some kind of physical force for mental persuasion, some element of democracy has somewhere been left unfulfilled either on the part of the subject (who may not be reasonable enough) against whom it is exercised, or, more often, on the part of the agent exercising it. Whenever it is possible to use any other method, the use of force becomes reprehensible in a democracy. It can only be justified as a lesser evil. 'Force without stint' is the last resort when every other method has proved unavailing. Democracy exists in any situation to the extent that force is unnecessary. When we speak of the recent war as a democratic war, and the incidental activities, such as the draft, the limitation of free speech and free press, the curtailment of freedom for those who happened technically to be enemy aliens, as being democratic in their nature, we are in reality not saying what we mean. These activities had to be carried on, not because they were democratic but because external conditions made democracy impossible within; i.e., because the world is not yet safe for democracy."

Berkson, *Theories of Americanization* * (New York, Teachers' College, 1920), p. 43-4.

297. Puritanism

"Resistance to something was the law of New England nature; ... for numberless generations his [Henry Adams's] predecessors had viewed the world chiefly as a thing to be reformed, filled with evil forces to be abolished."
Education of Henry Adams: an Autobiography * (Boston, Houghton Mifflin, 1922), p. 7.

298. Bernhardi: Might is Right

"Might is at once the supreme right, and the dispute as to what is right is decided by the arbitrament of war. War gives a biologically just decision, since its decisions rest on the very nature of things. ...

"Since the hostility of France once for all cannot be removed by peaceful overtures, the matter must be settled by force of arms. France must be so completely crushed that she can never again come across our path."
Bernhardi, *Germany and the Next War* * (New York, Longmans, 1912), pp. 15, 104.

299. Might Makes Right

"The rule 'might is right' ... has never been defended by any reputable German. Only the enthusiastic perversion that Might ought to be nothing but a servant of Right has been rejected, and rightly, as an ideological soap-bubble."
Quoted from the *Deutsche Tagezeitung* (August 11, 1915), by Dickinson in *The Choice Before Us* (New York, Dodd Mead, 1917), p. 33 f.

300. The Decline of Authoritarianism

"Authoritarianism in the affairs of men wanes to its death. The time was when kings held sway by a 'divine right,' about which their subjects were held to have no choice. Governmental control and its authentication were alike external. In recent times government increasingly derives its powers from the consent of the governed. External authority yields to internal authority. So with learning and knowledge; the time was when the *ipse dixit* of some master, the decree of some council or ecclesiastical potentate, the letter of the biblical text, sufficed to fix the doctrine. It is yet so with many. It is being more and more observed, however, that authority, formerly external and superimposed, is becoming internal and is deriving its just power from the internal process of its efficient working. Criticism and democracy allow no resting place for authoritarianism as such. The internal authority derived from efficient working is the authority which alone can stand the test. It is the realm of morals that is now being called upon to yield its external authoritarian sway. To many of us the prospect is dismaying. But whether we like it or not the time is fast passing when an external authoritarianism of morals can be relied upon to give effective guidance or control to those who stand most in need of it. Already a new generation that came to maturity during the war is asking why and why not, and will not be silenced by the traditional answers. What is worse, they are in large numbers answering their questions by denying any sort of authority, internal as well as external. The external authority of church or book has been in the past the reliance of many in questions of morals. But these external authorities have, for the many, passed beyond recall. For these, if morals are not to descend to a mere temporary expediency, some other basis must be found and found quickly."

Kilpatrick, in *Teachers College Record*,* 22:131 f. (March 1921.)

301. THE FREEDOM OF ANARCHY

"The anarchy which precedes law gives freedom only to the strong; the condition to be aimed at will give freedom as nearly as possible to every one."

Russell, *Why Men Fight* * (New York, Century, 1917), p. 44 f.

302. A THEORY OF PUNISHMENT

"As the essential and irresolvable characteristic of virtue is oughtness and of sin is its opposite oughtnotness, so it is an intrinsic and immutable attribute of sin that it ought to be punished. This obligation to punishment is an ultimate fact of moral consciousness; it cannot be resolved into any other principle whatever; it is intrinsic in sin without reference to any other principle. . . .

"All men thus judge of the sins of others. The consciences of all men are grateful when the just penalty of the law is executed upon the offender, and outraged when he escapes."

Hodge, *The Atonement* (Philadelphia, 1867), p. 55-6.

303. Penalty Theologically Considered

"By penalty, we mean that pain or loss which is directly or indirectly inflicted by the Lawgiver, in vindication of his justice outraged by the violation of the law. . . .

"The object of penalty is not the reformation of the offender or the ensuring of social or governmental safety. These ends may be incidentally secured through its infliction, but the great end of penalty is the vindication of the character of the Lawgiver."

Strong, *Systematic Theology* * (Rochester, American Baptist Publication Society, 1886), pp. 350-1.

304. Vindictive Punishment

"There is a kind of justice which aims neither at the amendment of the criminal, nor at furnishing an example to others, nor at the reparation of the injury. This justice is founded in pure fitness, which finds a certain satisfaction in the expiation of a wicked deed. The Socinians and Hobbes objected to this punitive justice, which is properly vindictive justice, and which God has reserved for himself at many junctures. . . . It is always founded in the fitness of things, and satisfies not only the offended party, but all wise lookers-on, even as beautiful music or a fine piece of architecture satisfies a well-constituted mind. It is thus that the torments of the damned continue, even tho they serve no longer to turn any one away from sin, and that the rewards of the blest continue, even tho they confirm no one in good ways."

Leibnitz, *Théodicée* (quoted in James, *Pragmatism*, New York, Longmans, 1907, p. 26 f.).

305. Treatment of Criminals

" Our legal procedure . . . wobbles between a too tender treatment of criminality and a viciously drastic treatment of it. The vacillation can be remedied only as we can analyze an act in the light of habits, and analyze habits in the light of education, environment and prior acts. The dawn of truly scientific criminal law will come when each individual case is approached with something corresponding to the complete clinical record which every competent physician attempts to procure as a matter of course in dealing with his subjects."

Dewey, *Human Nature and Conduct* * (New York, Holt, 1922), p. 46.

306. The State and Ethics

"The author seems to be quite unaware that he is guilty of an unpardonable confusion of thought. All ethical considerations are completely alien to the state, and the state must therefore resolutely keep them at arm's length."

Prof. Eulenberg of Leipzig, in *Archiv für Sozialwissenschaft u. Sozialpolitik,* July 1916, p. 317.

307. Treitschke on the State's Assertion of Power

"The state is a collective personality. Every personality must be treated as an end, not as means only. Man and every personality 'attains the highest perfection possible when he has developed the most essential part of himself. When we apply this standard to the state and remember that its very personality is power . . . the injunction to assert itself remains always absolute. Weakness must always be condemned as the most disastrous and despicable of crimes, the unforgivable sin of politics.'"

Treitschke, *Politics,* Vol. I, p. 94 f. (Quoted by Tufts in the *International Journal of Ethics,* 28:304, Apr. 1918.)

308. Unselfishness and the State

"Some good men seem inclined to maintain that the action of a state towards other states ought to be the same as the action of an individual towards other individuals. But this contains a fallacy which one might think it should not be difficult to discern. We personify a state, but a state is not a person. It contains a vast number of persons, and those who speak in its name and determine its policy act, not for themselves, but for others. It follows that all that department of morality which requires an individual to sacrifice himself to others, everything which falls under the heading of unselfishness, is inappropriate to the action of a state. No one has a right to be unselfish with other people's interests. It is the business of every ruler to exact to the utmost every claim which can both justly and wisely be made on behalf of his country. He is in the position of a trustee of the interests of others and must be just and not generous."

Cecil, *Conservatism* (London, Willams Norgate, no date), p. 202.

309. NATIONALISM

"The strongest democratic passion in the modern world is nationalism, and it is nationalism that is bringing the nations to ruin. With the progress of methods of destruction, it is to be expected that the next great war will kill about half the civilian population on each side. The intellectuals in every country, ever since 1914, have been doing their best to accelerate and intensify this disaster, by exacerbating national hatreds, spreading untruthful propaganda, and selling their brains to the War Offices and Navy Departments of their respective governments. From this madness all who wish to save the world must stand emphatically aside. War, righteous or unrighteous, defensive or offensive, means, thanks to modern science, the death of all that has value on both sides."
Russell, in *The New Student*, Oct. 7, 1922.

310. NATIONALITY A MODERN RELIGION

"Devotion to the nation is perhaps the deepest and most widespread religion of the present age."
Russell, *Why Men Fight* * (New York, Century, 1917), p. 116.

311. ABSOLUTE NATIONAL SOVEREIGNTY

"The notion of a final absolute and exclusive national sovereignty is unworkable, manifesting itself in fact as truly a nuisance in the world of practical affairs as it is vicious in the moral world. Is a nation subject to the moral law? Surely none among us would dare say no; this denial was our chief complaint against Prussia. If the nation is morally bound to order its affairs so as to respect the rights of other nations, then the notion of absolute sovereignty has already been given up. Mere will backed by power no longer suffices. The individual nation as truly as the individual man, if there be disregard of the rights of others, may—nay, must on moral grounds,—be forced to respect those rights. It is the duty of all to enforce a respect for the rights of each. The efficient means of enforcement may well be debated, but the right and duty only the anarchist can logically deny. When the practical recognition of the properly limited character of national sovereignty has come, we may then hope at last to see the end of the selfish exploitation of undeveloped nations, so provocative hitherto of the injustices within and of wars without."

Kilpatrick, in *Educational Review*,* 61:207 f. (March, 1921.)

CHAPTER XIII

THE MOBILIZATION OF THOUGHT POWER

312. THE VALUE OF DISCUSSION

"Discussion is the mould of measures."
Thucydides.

313. MOBILIZATION OF THOUGHT POWER

"The output of Thought . . . is not only slow to begin, but also, like the revolutions of a heavy fly-wheel, slow to cease. A man, who is reading in order to stimulate his thinking, finds it useful to remain passive for a short time at the end of each chapter, and still more at the end of each book, in order to allow his thoughts to continue of themselves. The householder who works at home finds that it pays to stop writing twenty minutes before lunch, so as to harvest the last gleanings of his Thought, instead of allowing them to present themselves during the meal, and then, having injured both his digestion and his manners, be finally (like 95 per cent of most men's intellectual output) lost through forgetfulness. Hobbes, the father of modern social psychology, took his own intellectual processes in this matter with scientific seriousness. 'He walked much,' says his friend Aubrey, 'and contemplated, and he had in the head of his staffe a pen and inke horne, carried always a note-book in his pocket, and as soon as a thought darted, he presently entered it into his book, or otherwise he might perhaps have lost it.'"

Wallas, *The Great Society* * (New York, Macmillan, 1914), pp. 190-1.

314. FOLLOW THE ARGUMENT

"Whither the argument may blow, thither we go."
Plato, *Republic* * (Trans. by Jowett. Oxford, Clarendon Press, 1888), III 394 d.

315. OUR AVAILABLE THOUGHT POWER

"If the majority of influential persons held the opinions and occupied the point of view that a few rather uninfluential people now do, there would, for instance, be no likelihood of another great war; the whole problem of 'labor and capital' would be transformed and attenuated; national arrogance, race animosity, political corruption, and inefficiency would all be reduced below the danger point. As an old Stoic proverb has it, men are tormented by the opinions they have of things, rather than by the things themselves. This is eminently true of many of our worst problems to-day. We have available knowledge and ingenuity and material resources to make a far fairer world than that in which we find ourselves. . . .

"If certain seemingly indisputable historical facts were generally known and accepted and permitted to play a daily part in our thought, the world would forthwith become a very different place from what it now is. We could then neither delude ourselves in the simple-minded way we now do, nor could we take advantage of the primitive ignorance of others. All our discussions of social, industrial, and political reform would be raised to a higher plane of insight and fruitfulness. . . .

"When we compare the discussions in the United States Senate in regard to the League of Nations with the consideration of a broken-down car in a roadside garage the contrast is shocking. The rural mechanic thinks scientifically; his only aim is to avail himself of his knowledge of the nature and workings of the car, with a view to making it run once more. The Senator, on the other hand, appears too often to have little idea of the nature and workings of nations, and he relies on rhetoric and appeals to vague fears and hopes or mere partisan animosity. . . . The Senator will . . . unblushingly appeal to policies of a century back, suitable, mayhap, in their day, but now become a warning rather than a guide. The garage man, on the contrary, takes his mechanism as he finds it, and does not allow any mystic respect for the earlier forms of the gas engine to interfere with the needed adjustments."

Robinson, *The Mind in the Making* * (New York, Harper, 1921), pp. 3-4, 6, 8 f.

316. POSSIBILITIES OF INTELLIGENT MANAGEMENT

"So I went to the biggest production engineer I could find in the United States, Mr. H. L. Gantt, former Vice-President of the American Society of Mechanical Engineers, and consulting expert for many of America's greatest industrial organizations. . . .

THE MOBILIZATION OF THOUGHT POWER

" 'On the whole,' he said (this was in June, 1918), 'only about 50 per cent of our industrial machines are actually operating during the time they are expected to operate; and on the whole these machines, during the time they are being operated, are producing only about 50 per cent of what they are expected to produce. This brings our productive result down to about one fourth of what it might be if the machines were run all the time at their highest capacity.

" 'This conclusion is not a guess, but is based on reliable data. Unfortunately there are many other elements of unnecessary waste in our productive process which cannot be so accurately calculated, but which reduce our effectiveness certainly to 20, and very probably to 15 per cent.' (p. 41 f.) . . .

" 'There are two main reasons why we have such a low percentage of production. The first is that industry is not managed by men who have learned industrial management but by business men whose specialty has been the study of market conditions. The second is that the autocratic owners of our industries have not always wanted 100 per cent production. They have been gunning for something else—for profits.' (p. 45.) . . .

" 'Henry Ford,' he explained, 'discovered that he could bring automobiles within reach of his people simply by securing maximum production. If industry were controlled generally by production specialists instead of by market specialists, the same result would be more often attained. Everybody would be busy producing things the people want at prices which they can afford to pay.' (p. 110.) . . .

" 'However,' the engineer concluded, 'if America seriously sets out to eliminate ALL the friction in her industrial system, we may expect a four, or perhaps a two-hour day. With production simplified and power utilized to its fullest capacity, we could probably produce all we want in much less than six hours; and with distribution simplified, we would have no trouble in securing the product for our own enjoyment.'

" 'Socialism?' I asked.

" 'Engineering,' he corrected." (p. 111.)

Wood, *The Great Change* * (New York, Boni Liveright, 1918).

317. War not Inevitable

"If a large majority of the Great Powers had a firm determination that peace should be preserved, there would be no difficulty in devising diplomatic machinery for the settlements of disputes, and in establishing educational systems which would implant in the minds of the young an ineradicable horror of the slaughter which they are now taught to admire."

Russell, *Why Men Fight* * (New York, Century, 1917), p. 91.

318. Spread of Ideas

"Still, as we are considering how American democracy works, it may be observed that they are an impressionable people, among whom excitement rises suddenly and spreads fast, quickened by the contagion of numbers. Communication is so easy and swift over the Continent that the same impulse seems to possess every one at the same moment, as if all were assembled, like the Athenians, in one huge public meeting. It is then that the cunningly devised divisions of power and other constitutional checks are found serviceable, for at such moments opinion is apt to be intolerant of opposition, and may even resort to extra-legal methods of suppressing in. But this seldom happens. In ordinary times that tyranny of the majority which Tocqueville described and feared as an evil inherent in democracies no longer exists. Independence of mind is respected. Even cranks are borne with, nor does any country produce a richer crop."

Bryce, *Modern Democracies* * (New York, Macmillan, 1921), Vol. II, p. 121.

319. One View of Public Opinion

"The idea of what the public will think prevents the public from ever thinking at all, and acts as a spell on the exercise of private judgment, so that in short the public ear is at the mercy of the first impudent pretender who chooses to fill it with noisy assertions, or false surmises or secret whispers. What is said by one is heard by all; the supposition that a thing is known to all the world makes all the world believe it, and the hollow repetition of a vague report drowns the still, small voice of reason."

Hazlitt, Essay on Living to One's-self, in *Table Talk* (London, Bell, 1911), p. 131 f.

320. American Politics

"In politics Americans are a little prone to rely on righteous indignation as a substitute for scientific study."

Lowell, *Public Opinion and Popular Government* * (New York, Longmans, 1914), p. 100.

321. FORMATION OF PUBLIC OPINION

"A business man reads in his newspaper at breakfast the events of the preceding day. He reads that Prince Bismarck has announced a policy of protection for German industry, or that Mr. Henry George has been nominated for the mayorality of New York. These statements arouse in his mind sentiments of approval or disapproval, which may be strong or weak according to his previous predilection for or against protection or Mr. Henry George, and of course according to his personal interest in the matter. They rouse also an expectation of certain consequences likely to follow. Neither the sentiment nor the expectation is based on processes of conscious reasoning—our business man has not time to reason at breakfast—they are merely impressions formed on the spur of the moment. He turns to the leading article in the newspaper, and his sentiments and expectations are confirmed or weakened according as he finds that they are or are not shared by the newspaper writer. He goes down to his office in the train, talks there to two or three acquaintances, and perceives that they agree or do not agree with his own still faint impressions. In his counting-house he finds his partner and a bundle of other newspapers which he glances at; their words further affect him, and thus by the end of the day his mind is beginning to settle down into a definite view, which approves or condemns Prince Bismarck's declaration or the nomination of Mr. George. Meawhile a similar process has been going on in the minds of others, and particularly of the journalists, whose business it is to discover what people are thinking. The evening paper has collected the opinions of the morning papers, and is rather more positive in its forecast of results. Next morning the leading party journals have articles still more definite and positive in approval or condemnation and in prediction of consequences to follow; and the opinion of ordinary minds, which in most of such minds has been hitherto fluid and undetermined, has begun to crystallize into a solid mass. . . . In examining the process by which opinion is formed, we cannot fail to note how small a part of the view which an average man entertains when he goes to vote is really of his own making."

Bryce, *American Commonwealth* * (New York, Macmillan, 1914), Vol. II, p. 251 f.

322. Cobden on the Unreason which War Brings

"From the moment the first shot is fired, or the first blow is struck in a dispute, then farewell to all reason and argument; you might as well reason with mad dogs as with men when they have begun to spill each other's blood in mortal combat. I was so convinced of the fact during the Crimean War; I was so convinced of the utter uselessness of raising one's voice in opposition to war when it has once begun, that I made up my mind that so long as I was in political life, should a war again break out between England and a Great Power, I would never open my mouth upon the subject from the time the first gun was fired until the peace was made."

Morley, *Life of Richard Cobden* * (New York, Macmillan, 1908), Vol. II, p. 159.

323. The Myth-Making Tendency of Strong Collective Emotion

"Every powerful passion brings with it an impulse to an attendant system of false beliefs. A man in love will attribute innumerable non-existent perfections to the object of his devotion; a jealous man will attribute equally non-existent crimes to the object of his jealousy. But in ordinary life, this tendency is continually held in check by intercourse with people who do not share our private passions, and who therefore are critical of our irrational beliefs. In national questions, this corrective is absent. Most men meet few foreigners, especially in time of war, and beliefs inspired by passion can be communicated to others without fear of an unsympathetic response. The supposed facts intensify the passion which they embody, and are magnified still further by those to whom they are told. Individual passions, except in lunatics, produce only the germs of myths, perpetually neutralized by the indifference of others; but collective passions escape this corrective, and generate in time what appears like overwhelming evidence for wholly false beliefs.

"Men of learning, who are acquainted with the part played by collective error in the history of religion, ought to have been on their guard against assaults upon their credulity. They ought to have realised, from the obvious falsehood of the correlative opposite beliefs in enemy countries, that the myth-making impulse was unusually active, and could only be repelled by an unusual intellectual vigor. But I do not find that they were appreciably less credulous than the multitude. In the early days of last September (1914), when the Germans were carrying all before them in France, the need for some source of hope produced in England an all but universal belief that a large Russian army had travelled from Archangel, through England, to Belgium. The evidence was very much better than the evidence for most facts of history: most men knew many eyewitnesses of their transit, and at last a newspaper published a telegram from its correspondent saying that he had discovered them in Belgium. Only then was the story officially denied, but for a long time many continued to believe it."

Russell, *Justice in War-Time* * (Chicago, Open Court, 1916), p. 4-6.

324. Danger from Propagandism

"Propaganda is the most terrible weapon so far developed by the war. It is worse than poison gas. If the wind is in the right direction, gas may kill a few and injure others; but the possibilities of manipulating the public mind, by withholding or discoloring the facts, are appalling. One is so helpless in face of it. No one can think intelligently without knowing the facts; and if the facts are controlled by interested men, the very idea of democracy is destroyed and becomes a farce."

Newton, in *Atlantic Monthly,* * 128:158 (August, 1921).

325. The Critical Habit of Thought

"The critical habit of thought, if usual in a society, will pervade all its mores because it is a way of taking up the problems of life. Men educated in it cannot be stampeded by stump orators and are never deceived by dithyrambic oratory."

Sumner, *Folkways* * (Boston, Ginn, 1913), p. 633.

326. Suspended Judgment

"Doubt is not a pleasant condition, but certainty is an absurd one."

Voltaire.

327. Function of the School

"The school should reflect civilization, not attempt to be one of the moving factors of civilization. It should not be a social center or life itself. The school is an institution of instruction, not of construction."

Anonymous.

328. THE POWER OF THE PRESS

"Let me make the newspaper, and I care not who makes religion or the laws."

Wendell Phillips.

329. THE PRESS IN A DEMOCRACY

"It is the newspaper press that has made democracy possible in large countries. The political thinkers of antiquity assumed that a community of self-governing citizens could not be larger than one voice could reach, because only by the voice could discussion be carried on. . . . Within the last hundred years the development of the press has enabled news to be diffused and public discussion to be conducted over wide areas; and still more recently the electric telegraph has enabled news and the opinions of men regarding it to be so quickly spread over a vast and populous country that all the citizens can receive both news and comments thereon at practically the same moment, so that arguments or appeals addressed to the people work simultaneously upon their minds almost as effectively as did the voice of the orator in the popular assembly. . . .

"Universal suffrage has immensely increased the proportion of electors who derive their political views chiefly or wholly from newspapers.

"The causes which enable newspapers well managed, and commanding large capital, to drive weaker papers out of the field, have in all countries reduced the number of influential journals, and left power in comparatively few hands.

"The influence upon opinion exercised by a great newspaper as compared with a prominent statesman or even with the debates in legislative bodies, has grown.

"Newspapers have become more and more commercial undertakings, devoted primarily to their business interests.

"The temptations to use the influence of a newspaper for the promotion of pecuniary interests, whether of its proprietors or of others, have also increased. Newspapers have become one of the most available instruments by which the Money Power can make itself felt in politics.

"The power of the press is a practically irresponsible power, for the only thing it need fear (apart from libel suits) is the reduction of circulation, and the great majority of its readers, interested only in business and sports, know little of and care little for the political errors or tergiversations it may commit.

"Press power is wielded more effectively through the manipulation and suppression of news than by the avowed advocacy of any political views. It is more dangerous in the sphere of foreign than in that of domestic policy, and is one of the chief hindrances to international goodwill.

"Democratic government rests upon and requires the exercise of a well-informed and sensible opinion by the great bulk of the citizens. Where the materials for the formation of such an opinion are so artfully supplied as to prevent the citizens from judging fairly the merits of a question, opinion is artificially made instead of being let grow in a natural way, and a wrong is done to democracy."

Bryce, *Modern Democracies* * (New York, Macmillan, 1921), Vol. I, pp. 92, 108 f.

330. READING NOT SUFFICIENT

"In these days of ours reading has become a substitute for thinking. The man who reads only the newspaper of his own party, and reads its political intelligence in a medley of other stuff, narratives of crimes and descriptions of football matches, need not know that there is more than one side to a question, and seldom asks if there is one, nor what is the evidence for what the paper tells him. . . . On the printed page Truth has no better chance than Falsehood, except with those who read widely and have the capacity of discernment. A party organ, suppressing some facts, misrepresenting others, is the worst of all guides, because it can by incessantly reiterating untruth produce a greater impression than any man or body of men, save only ecclesiastics clothed with a spiritual authority, could produce before printing was invented. A modern voter so guided by his party newspapers is no better off than his grandfather who eighty years ago voted at the bidding of his landlord or his employer or (in Ireland) of his priest. The grandfather at least knew whom he was following, while the grandson, who reads only what is printed on one side of a controversy, may be the victim of selfish interests who own the organs which his simplicity assumes to express public opinion or to have the public good at heart. So a democracy that has been taught only to read, and not also to reflect and judge, will not be the better for the ability to read."

Bryce, *Modern Democracies* * (New York, Macmillan, 1921), Vol. I, p. 72 f.

331. THE INFLUENCE OF THE ADVERTISER

During the infantile paralysis epidemic in New York City in 1916 the New York *Sun* on a page devoted to "Preparatory Schools, Colleges, . . ." gave (August 27, 1916) first space to an article from which the following excerpts are taken. In an adjacent column were advertisements of "New York's Private Schools."

"Any person who has visited the public schools to any extent knows that the saying 'the poor are always with us' applies particularly to the public schools. The writer has no desire to be snobbish, but facts are facts. He defies anyone to point out a single public school in Manhattan, for example, that has not its quota of the children of the poor. . . .

"For safety's sake send your boy or girl not to the public, but to the private school. In the private school the danger of catching the dread disease is reduced to such a minimum as to be practically non-existent.

"The past year, thanks chiefly to the inflation of trade caused by the European war, has been one of the most prosperous in the history of the United States. This is the time, then, when parents of this plague infested city should form the good habit of sending their boys and girls not to the public but to the private school. This is a matter over which there should be no hesitation, a matter concerning which no sacrifice can be too great for its accomplishment. . . .

"Safety first—have your children avoid the public schools if possible. Send them to New York's private schools. There are no finer in the country. Send them there, parents, and have no fear."

332. NEWSPAPER INFLUENCE FOR BAD

"The writer's treatment (Seligmann, *The Negro Faces America*) of city mob outrages at Chicago, East St. Louis, Washington, Omaha, and other places does fix, by downright line and verse, much responsibility for those nightmares of brutality upon certain named newspapers which whipped up race prejudice for their own immediate advantage."

The New Republic (book review by L. B. W.), 24:151 (Oct. 6, 1920).

333. THE PRESS AND THE I. W. W.

"Though nowadays well aware of the existence of the I. W. W., the public still knows little about the organization and its members. Moreover, a great deal of what it does know is false. For thirteen years the I. W. W. has been rather consistently misrepresented—not to say vilified—to the American people. The public has not been told the truth about the things the I. W. W. has done or the doctrines in which it believes. The papers have printed so much fiction about this organization, maintained such a nation-wide conspiracy of silence as to its real philosophy—especially as to the constructive items of this philosophy—that the popular conception of this labor group is weird unreality."

Brissenden, *The I. W. W.: A Study of American Syndicalism* * (New York, Longmans, 1919), p. 8.

334. WHAT "NEWS" IS

A would-be reporter on probation under the famous Charles A. Dana of the New York *Sun* brought in an account of a man bitten by a mad dog. "A man bitten by a mad dog!" exclaimed Mr. Dana, "That's no news. Go out and find a mad dog bitten by a man, and we will give you plenty of space for the story."

Anonymous.

335. HEAD LINES

"WOMEN SOLD VOTES IN SCHOOL ELECTION FOR DOLLAR, IS CHARGE

"Pikeville, . . . Feb. 6. Three women indicted on charges of selling votes in the last school election will be tried with the 1100 men accused of having committed fraud at the August primary. It was alleged in indictments that the women sold their votes for a dollar each."

Atlanta (Georgia) *Semi-Weekly Journal*, February 9, 1915.

336. CERTAIN PRACTICAL MEN AND THOUGHT

"There are certain 'practical' men who combine thought and habit and who are effectual. Their thought is about their own advantage; and their habits correspond. They dominate the actual situation. They encourage routine in others, and they also subsidize such thought and learning as are kept remote from affairs. This they call sustaining the standard of the ideal. Subjection they praise as team-spirit, loyalty, devotion, obedience, industry, law-and-order. But they temper respect for law—by which they mean the order of the existing status—on the part of others with most skilful and thoughtful manipulation of it in behalf of their own ends. While they denounce as subversive anarchy signs of independent thought, of thinking for themselves, on the part of others lest such thought disturb the conditions by which they profit, they think quite literally *for* themselves, that is, *of* themselves. This is the eternal game of the practical men. Hence it is only by accident that the separate and endowed 'thought' of professional thinkers leaks out into action and affects custom."

Dewey, *Human Nature and Conduct* * (New York, Holt, 1922), p. 68 f.

337. Voltaire on Freedom of Speech

"I wholly disapprove of what you say—and will defend to the death your right to say it." (Letter to Helvetius).

Tallentyre, *Voltaire in his Letters* (London, Murray, 1919), p. 65.

338. The Need for Freedom of Speech

"We have now recognized the necessity to the mental well-being of mankind (on which all their other well-being depends) of freedom of opinion, and freedom of the expression of opinion, on four distinct grounds; which we will now briefly recapitulate."

"First, if any opinion is compelled to silence, that opinion may, for aught we can certainly know, be true. To deny this is to assume our own infallibility.

"Secondly, though the silenced opinion be an error, it may, and very commonly does, contain a portion of truth; and since the general or prevailing opinion on any subject is rarely or never the whole truth, it is only by the collision of adverse opinions that the remainder of the truth has any chance of being supplied."

"Thirdly, even if the received opinion be not only true, but the whole truth; unless it is suffered to be, and actually is, vigorously and earnestly contested, it will, by most of those who receive it, be held in the manner of a prejudice, with little comprehension or feeling of its rational grounds. And not only this, but, fourthly, the meaning of the doctrine itself will be in danger of being lost, or enfeebled, and deprived of its vital effect on the character and conduct: the dogma becoming a mere formal profession, inefficacious for good, but cumbering the ground, and preventing the growth of any real and heartfelt conviction, from reason or personal experience."

Mill, *Liberty* (London, Parker, 1859), p. 94 f.

339. THE POWER OF TRUTH

"Let truth and falsehood grapple; who ever knew truth to be put to the worse in a free and open encounter?"

John Milton.

340. WHY NOT FORBID THE TEACHING OF PERNICIOUS DOCTRINES?

Some will say that governments are under the same obligation and have the same rights to suppress pernicious doctrines that they have to suppress vicious acts. "Men, and governments," these men say, "must act to the best of their ability. There is no such thing as absolute certainty, but there is assurance sufficient for the purposes of human life. We may, and must, assume our opinion to be true for the guidance of our own conduct: and it is assuming no more when we forbid bad men to pervert society by the propagation of opinions which we regard as false and pernicious.

"I answer, that it is assuming very much more. There is the greatest difference between presuming an opinion to be true, because, with every opportunity for contesting it, it has not been refuted, and assuming its truth for the purpose of not permitting its refutation. Complete liberty of contradicting and disproving our opinion, is the very condition which justifies us in assuming its truth for purposes of action; and on no other terms can a being with human faculties have any rational assurance of being right."

Mill, *Liberty* (London, Parker, 1859), p. 37 f.

341. SUPPRESSION OF DISCUSSION

"We went into Homestead and held the first open mass-meeting that had ever been held in that city in twenty-seven years. After that meeting was held, other arrangements we had made to organize there were stopped; halls we had rented, arrangements we had made to organize were denied us; the owners who had accepted our money for rent of the halls had to return it, and when they could not use excuses of that kind the health departments at these various towns were used to prevent the committee from holding meetings."

John Fitzpatrick, Union Organizer of Steel Trades (quoted in Edie, *Current Social and Industrial Forces*, New York, Boni Liveright, 1920, p. 221).

342. UNWARRANTED RESTRICTION ON DISCUSSION

"Harry Aurin, who was arrested for disorderly conduct because he distributed extracts from the Constitution and the Declaration of Independence, in which undue emphasis was placed on certain passages, and was sentenced to ninety days in the workhouse by Magistrate Murphy, was freed yesterday by Supreme Court Justice Hendrick in habeas corpus proceedings. The District Attorney of Bronx County, who prosecuted the case, will appeal to the Appellate Division. Justice Hendrick, commenting on the charge against Aurin, said in his opinion:

"'I do not see under what possible circumstances that could be a breach of the peace or an act tending to a breach of the peace. Every one in this country has the right to criticise the Government and the laws that exist, and has the right to agitate for the repeal of a law so long as those acts are not accompanied by violence or statements which might be interpreted as inciting other people to break the law.'"

New York Times, July 18, 1917.

343. EVILS OF SUPPRESSING INQUIRY

"It is not the minds of heretics that are deteriorated most, by the ban placed on all inquiry which does not end in the orthodox conclusions. The greatest harm done is to those who are not heretics, and whose whole mental development is cramped, and their reason cowed, by fear of heresy. Who can compute what the world loses in the multitude of promising intellects combined with timid characters, who dare not follow out any bold, vigorous, independent train of thought, lest it should land them in something which would admit of being considered irreligious or immoral.

". . . Truth gains more even by the errors of one who, with due study and preparation, thinks for himself, than by the true opinions of those who only hold them because they do not suffer themselves to think. Not that it is solely, or chiefly, to form great thinkers, that freedom of thinking is required. On the contrary, it is as much, and even more indispensable, to enable average human beings to attain the mental stature which they are capable of."

Mill, *Liberty* (London, Parker, 1859), p. 61 f.

344. FREEDOM OF DISCUSSION

"The Liberal does not meet opinions which he conceives to be false with toleration, as though they did not matter. He meets them with justice, and exacts for them a fair hearing as though they mattered just as much as his own. He is always ready to put his own convictions to the proof, not because he doubts them, but because he believes in them. For, both as to that which he holds for true and as to that which he holds for false, he believes that one final test applies. Let error have free play, and one of two things will happen. Either as it develops, as its implications and consequences become clear, some elements of truth will appear within it. They will separate themselves out; they will go to enrich the stock of human ideas; they will add something to the truth which he himself mistakenly took as final; they will serve to explain the root of the error; for error itself is generally a truth misconceived, and it is only when it is explained that it is finally and satisfactorily confuted. Or, in the alternative, no element of truth will appear. In that case the more fully the error is understood, the more patiently it is followed up in all the windings of its implications and consequences, the more thoroughly will it refute itself. . . . The more the truth is developed in all its implications, the greater is the opportunity of detecting any element of error that it may contain; and, conversely, if no error appears, the more completely does it establish itself as the whole truth and nothing but the truth."

Hobhouse, *Liberalism* (New York, Holt, no date), pp. 116-118.

345. LIBERTY OF THOUGHT

"If, however, by 'independence of mind' is understood unrestrained liberty of thought in religious matters, it must be admitted that the *Ratio Studiorum* and the whole Institute of the Society are uncompromisingly opposed to it, and that the Jesuits have always endeavored to suppress it."

Schwicherath, Jesuits, Educational Work of, in Monroe, *Cyclopedia of Education* * (New York, Macmillan, 1912), Vol. III, p. 539.

346. Freedom of Thought in America

Ruffini in his *Religious Liberty* points out that "in Germany, England, and Italy, where the most powerful Church or Churches are under the control of the State, there is more freedom, more tolerance of opinion, than in many of the American States where Separation prevails. A hundred years ago the Americans showed appalling ingratitude to Thomas Paine, who had done them eminent service in the War of Independence, simply because he published a very unorthodox book. It is notorious that free thought is still a serious hindrance and handicap to an American, even in most of the Universities. This proves that Separation is not an infallible receipt for producing tolerance. But I see no reason to suppose that public opinion in America would be different, if either the Federal Republic or the particular States had adopted Jurisdiction. Given legal liberty under either system, I should say that the tolerance of public opinion depends on social conditions and especially on the degree of culture among the educated classes."

Bury, *History of Freedom of Thought* * (New York,[1] Holt, 1913), p. 125 f.

347. Limitations upon Freedom of Discussion

"If there is a direct instigation to particular acts of violence, there may be a legitimate case for interference. But the incitement must be deliberate and direct. If I write a book condemning existing societies and defending a theory of anarchy, and a man who reads it presently commits an outrage, it may clearly be established that my book made the man an anarchist and induced him to commit the crime, but it would be illegitimate to punish me or suppress the book unless it contained a direct incitement to the specific crime which he committed."

Bury, *History of Freedom of Thought* * (New York,[1] Holt, 1913), p. 241 f.

[1] Originally published in England.

348. Limits to the Freedom of Speech

"There ought to exist the fullest liberty of professing and discussing, as a matter of ethical conviction, any doctrine, however immoral it may be considered. . . . Instigation . . . in a specific case, may be a proper subject of punishment, but only if an overt act has followed, and at least a probable connection can be established between the act and the instigation."

Mill, *Liberty* (London, Parker, 1859), p. 32 n.

349. Freedom of Discussion a Sign of Civilization

"The struggle of reason against authority has ended in what appears now to be a decisive and permanent victory for liberty. In the most civilized and progressive countries, freedom of discussion is recognized as a fundamental principle. In fact, we may say it is accepted as a test of enlightenment, and the man in the street is forward in acknowledging that countries like Russia and Spain, where opinion is more or less fettered, must on that account be considered less civilized than their neighbors."

Bury, *History of Freedom of Thought* * (New York,[1] Holt, 1913), p. 247.

350. No Respect for the Expert

"The duties of any public office are so simple or admit of being made so simple that any man can in a short time become master of them."

Andrew Jackson.

351. America's Attitude Towards Excellence

"The ordinary American voter does not object to mediocrity. He has a lower conception of the qualities requisite to make a statesman than those who direct public opinion in Europe have. He likes his candidate to be sensible, vigorous, and, above all, what he calls 'magnetic,' and does not value, because he sees no need for, originality or profundity, a fine culture or a wide knowledge."

Bryce, *American Commonwealth* * (New York, Macmillan, 1914), Vol. I, p. 79.

---

[1] Originally published in England.

352. THE PUBLIC DECREASINGLY ABLE TO JUDGE PUBLIC AFFAIRS

"It is not improbable . . . that the amount of knowledge needed for the administration of public affairs is increasing more rapidly than the diffusion of such knowledge, and that this is lessening the capacity of the ordinary citizen to form an opinion of his own on the various matters that arise in conducting the government. If so, the range of questions about which the public cannot form a real opinion tends to enlarge, or at least does not diminish. This is particularly true where the special knowledge of experts is involved, because it is not easy for the community at large to weigh expert opinion. Few things are, in fact, more difficult, or require greater experience; and yet the number of questions on which the advice of experts is indispensable grows with every advance in technical knowledge and mechanical invention."

Lowell, *Public Opinion and Popular Government* * (New York, Longmans, 1914), p. 49 f.

353. DEMOCRACY AND THE EXPERT

"That . . . a quarrel exists [between democracy and the expert] is sufficiently recognized. Unwillingness to trust and adequately reward the expert is one of the standing reproaches against democracy. It is more than a mere shortcoming; it seems often to amount to a positive enmity, to a dislike of fitness as such, to a perverse preference for the incompetent. We sometimes seem to delight in humiliating true accomplishment, and in entrusting our business to quacks.

"Especially is this the case in public affairs, as to which democracy has its fullest swing. If a man has devoted years to special study of a matter that comes before a legislative committee, that very fact goes far to disqualify him as a witness. Successful appeal will be very apt to be made from him to 'common sense,' or to 'the judgment of business men,' which phrases are among the ordinary pet names for ignorant prejudice and incompetence. . . . We have made ourselves the laughing-stock of the world by our easy credulity toward any political quack who will take the trouble to flatter our conceit. We are more easily, and more contentedly, fleeced by sharpers, poisoned by quacks, and ruined by shyster lawyers, than any people on earth. We allow ourselves to be governed by dishonest and impudent pretenders, . . . Our unwillingness to pay our judges such salaries as will command the highest legal ability costs us millions of dollars every month. . . .

"And the worst of it all is that our fault is not merely a mental one: it has a moral quality in it, and the loss accordingly is not merely a material but a moral one. Our easy victimizing results not wholly from mental incapacity to distinguish between the true and the counterfeit. It arises partly from a certain meanness in which democracy is seen at its very worst; from jealousy, from the sneaking envy of the incapable or uneducated man toward those of better training or greater ability than himself. That a mountebank like General Butler came to be chosen representative of a Massachusetts district in Congress, in preference to a citizen of the known worth and capacity of Judge Hoar, was not because anybody was deceived as to the comparative merits of the men, but partly because Hoar was no flatterer, and partly because of the very fact that every voter felt in his bones that he was the superior man. No man felt uneasy in the presence of Butler's virtue. . . .

"The need of such enlightenment has, as I have said, been long and clearly recognized. What has not been recognized is the fact that the fault has not been altogether upon one side, that for the making up of the quarrel it is necessary, not only that democracy should experience a change of heart, but that the expert should recognize that he also has something to learn and to amend. Indeed the bottom fact of all, and one which has hitherto received no recognition whatever, is that the fault of the expert has been the deeper and the more responsible of the two. If democracy has sinned against the expert, the expert has sinned more deeply against democracy; and his sin has been of such a nature as to constitute an offense not only against democracy, but also against good manners and good sense, and against the eternal principles of truth. It is primarily from this fault on the part of the expert that the whole quarrel has arisen, and no fundamental and lasting reconciliation can take place until this fault is cured.

"What has been through all the ages the expert's attitude toward the common people? What has been the customary answer of the lawyer, the doctor, the man of science, when asked for proofs or explanations, when questioned as to the sources of his knowledge or the basis of his claim to public confidence? What is at the present time, or at least what has been until very recently, the answer of our railroad presidents when the surviving members of the public have inquired as to the reasons for the slaughter of their friends and relatives, or the ruin of their business through illegal favoritism? Has not the expert's answer in all ages been practically the same? 'Keep off, ye profane.' 'Seek not to penetrate mysteries too high for you.' 'Meddle not with matters above your sphere.' . . .

"The common people have seen with interest the country gentleman, Oliver Cromwell, largely self-taught so far as military knowledge was concerned, give the professionals some lessons in the art of war. They have seen legal procedure remodeled by the layman Bentham, and medicine revolutionized by the biologist Pasteur. And they have seen the experts in these two latter instances kicking and struggling in a very panic of professional resentment against any acceptance of the newer light. . . .

"The expert himself . . . has placed certain obstacles in the way of the faith which he demands. And then, supposing us possessed of such faith, to whom does it attach? How can we tell the true expert from the counterfeit? . . .

"It is not because of perversity, but by necessity, that democracy refuses to be blindfolded, that it objects to the notice, 'Leave your brains in the umbrella stand when you come in.'—'Excuse me, sir, but they are the only brains I have. If I am not to use my mind, whose shall I use, and by the use of whose judgment shall I decide to use it?'

"But the practical difficulties in the way of the blind faith that the expert requires of us are as nothing compared to those raised by the terms in which the demand itself is put. In the last analysis, the expert's claim is a claim to the exemption of himself, and the subjects with which he deals, from the ordinary jurisdiction of the human mind. His attitude toward the common people has been not merely that they do not understand because they have not had time to give to his particular subject, but that they are constitutionally incapable of understanding it. . . .

"In fact, the essence of the expert's position, in the final analysis, is that expert knowledge is of a different kind from other knowledge; that it is peculiar, esoteric; that it partakes, in short, of the miraculous. It is regarded, not as the product of the purely human faculties, but as revealed, conferred by some sort of initiation or laying on of hands which has raised the acolyte into a sphere which the outsider can never hope to penetrate. The plea is a plea to the jurisdiction. It is a denial of the catholicity and sovereignty of the human mind.

"This attitude, indeed, is not deliberately assumed. It is unconsciously accepted by the expert of to-day as he finds it embodied in time-honoured tradition. . . .

"The dissent on the part of democracy from the traditional expert attitude is, as I have indicated, deeper than a question of manners, or even than one of common sense. The issue is not superficial; it is not the result of misunderstanding; nor does it arise from practical considerations alone. It is radical, fundamental, and inevitable.

"The cardinal doctrine of democracy—the thing for which it stands, on its intellectual side—is faith in the human mind. Democracy believes that the thing to be forever trusted and followed in this world is the human reason; that guidance in human affairs is to be sought not primarily in tradition, in special revelation, or in any mysteries, or from any sources whatsoever, that are not germane to the human intellect, and that do not hold their credentials from it. This is the democratic principle of equality, the fundamental article of the democratic faith. . . . Not equality in any outward or measurable respect; not an arithmetical equality at all, not quantitative; not a question of amount, but of kind.

"The democratic belief in equality is the belief that all men alike are subject to the moral law of obedience to their own best thought, that the supreme authority declares itself, not from the outside but from within. . . .

"Democracy cannot recognize limits to the jurisdiction of the human mind not prescribed by the nature of the mind itself. It believes in the authority, and in the obligation, of the human intellect to read the universe unexpurgated, as it stands. . . .

"And the thing to be forever recognized in this matter is, that democracy is eternally in the right and the expert in the wrong. The attitude of the expert is essentially a false attitude. It is false with the most irreconcilable kind of falseness. It is contrary not only to particular truths but to the nature of truth itself. There are not two kinds of knowledge in this world, but only one; and there is, correspondingly, but one way in which knowledge can be attained. One man may have more mind than another or a better mind, or he may put his mind to a better use. But no man has a different kind of mind. There is in human acquirement no jumping-off place where the jurisdiction of the human intellect comes to an end and some other jurisdiction takes its place. . . .

"This democratic creed of ours does not preclude trust in the expert. On the contrary, it is the only creed that makes truly possible that or any other kind of trust. What it does prescribe is the basis of our faith. It requires that whatever trust we place in the expert, or in any other source, shall result from our trust in our own reason and shall derive whatever strength it has from that. . . . If the expert is to have a standing in the world as it really is, it must be through discarding all pretensions to esoteric knowledge and appealing solely to that common human intelligence which he has hitherto despised.

"And with the making of such appeal the expert's ancient quarrel with democracy will disappear. Democracy has no antipathy to specialization as such, no inherent unwillingness to accept the fact that, as we cannot all do everything, we must recognize the superiority of each in his own domain; . . .

"It is true that the function of the expert will always be a subordinate function; that, though he can help you to carry out your purpose, the purpose must be forever, intimately and concretely, your own. His employment must always be to specific ends which you have prescribed, and not for general purposes; and even within the specific end the trust is always revocable. The one act of sovereignty that the mind cannot perform is to abdicate. . . .

"We of the democratic faith hold ourselves responsible, and utterly responsible, not only for the ends we seek, but for our choice of means. Not that we shall choose right, but that we shall choose in accordance with the only guide we have; that we shall trust, and utterly trust, the judgment of the one supreme tribunal, and shall permit no divided jurisdiction. It may be difficult for me to understand the matter, but except so far as I do understand I cannot judge, and therefore am not at liberty to follow.

"And in all this question of when and how to trust, and whom to follow, though judging may in any given case be difficult, there is one comparatively simple test, and one that democracy very generally applies. . . . Does he appeal to your intelligence or against it? Does he say, 'Use your mind, enter, examine, test, and draw your own conclusions'? or does he say, 'This is a great mystery; keep out. Seek not to understand'? According to this test the expert has been tried, and has been found wanting."

Joseph Lee, in *Atlantic Monthly*,* 102:611-619 (Nov., 1908).

354. Present Status of the Doctrine of Evolution

"Since Huxley and Sully wrote their masterly essays in the 9th edition (1875-1889) of this encyclopædia, the doctrine of evolution has outgrown the trammels of controversy and has been accepted as a fundamental principle. Writers on biological subjects no longer have to waste space in weighing evolution against this or that philosophical theory or religious tradition; philosophical writers have frankly accepted it, and the supporters of religious tradition have made broad their phylacteries to write on them the new words. (p. 34 d) . . .

"The vast bulk of botanical and zoological work on living and extinct forms published during the last quarter of the 19th century increased almost beyond all expectation the evidence for the fact of evolution. The discovery of a single fossil creature in a geological stratum of a wrong period, the detection of a single anatomical or physiological fact irreconcilable with origin by descent with modification, would have been destructive of the theory and would have made the reputation of the observer. But in the prodigious number of supporting discoveries that have been made no single negative factor has appeared, and the evolution from their predecessors of forms of life existing now or at any other period must be taken as proved." (p. 35 a)

Encyclopædia Britannica * (11th ed., 1910-11), article *Evolution*, 10:34-35.

355. A Suggestion to Discussion Groups

"Dialectic is slow and inexact, but in many sciences, and particularly in those whose subject-matter is human action and feeling, it has magnificent possibilities of fertility. . . .

"A dialectical group will . . . be generally wise to read some agreed book before meeting, or to deal with some subject with the facts of which they are familiar in their individual work. They will find that the real advantages of group-dialectic are those which books cannot give. One of them is a great extension of the range of immediate mental 'association.' In individual Thought the thinker waits (in the Problem-Attitude) till some promising idea comes into his mind and then dwells on it till further ideas spring from it. A group of people, however, engaged in dialectic can, like a pack of hounds, follow up the most promising idea which occurs to any one of them. This means that a rule, for instance, requiring the members of such a group to speak in regular order is wrong, as it prevents ideas being brought forward at the moment of their greatest relevance. But if free interjection is allowed, it must be so managed as to prevent any member of the group causing what Socrates, in *The Clouds*, called the 'miscarriage' of ideas amongst the rest. Here the art of dialectic can learn from the introspective evidence of individual thinking. Students who write down their conscious experiences while answering problems in psychological laboratories describe the verbal form of the idea which successively presents themselves and are rejected before the most relevant one is chosen for prolonged consideration, as being curiously bare and curt. A member of an arguing group should generally put his first claim on the attention of his fellows into the same curt form, which takes the minimum of time, can be forgotten in an instant, and if rejected does not interfere with the subconscious process of association with the rest.

"But the relevance of an idea is not always immediately apparent, and therefore, in a well-chosen group of joint thinkers, if any one is impelled, as was Thrasymachus in Plato's *Republic*, to 'leap like a wild beast' into the discussion, he should be allowed to do so, and to indicate the intensity of his impulse by the heightening of his voice. If his conviction of the supreme, though unapparent, relevance of his ideas proves generally to be unfounded, the group can be reorganized without him. We are none of us, indeed, 'unbribed judges' of our own thoughts, and a man who really tries to make use of oral discussion would do well to aim at taking, in a series of evenings, not much more than his equal arithmetical fraction of the common time."

Wallas, *The Great Society* * (New York, Macmillan, 1914), pp. 245-7.

CHAPTER XIV

PROGRESS

356. Progress

"Progress, man's distinctive mark alone,
Not God's and not the beasts': God is, they are;
Man partly is, and wholly hopes to be."
Browning, *A Death in the Desert*.

357. A Chinese Mandarin on Invention

"There is nothing extraordinary in the motorcar. There is nothing extraordinary in anything. Men invented it yesterday. They will invent something else to-morrow. Still the world goes around, and we are not an atom the happier."
New York Times, Sept. 28, 1908.

358. Opposition to Innovation

"The Endeavour Society ... was instituted a few years ago for the laudable purpose of contributing to the propagation of the principles of the Church of England, in opposition to *Infidelity, Depravity,* and *Innovation*."
Guardian of Education (London, 1803), 2:245.

359. Democracy and the Idea of Progress

"The earthly Progress of humanity is the general test to which social aims and theories are submitted as a matter of course. The phrase *civilisation and progress* has become stereotyped, and illustrates how we have come to judge a civilisation good or bad according as it is or is not progressive. The ideals of liberty and democracy, which have their own ancient and independent justifications, have sought a new strength by attaching themselves to Progress. The conjunctions of 'liberty and progress,' 'democracy and progress,' meet us at every turn. Socialism, at an early stage of its modern development, sought the same aid. The friends of Mars, who cannot bear the prospect of perpetual peace, maintain that war is an indispensable instrument of Progress. It is in the name of Progress that the doctrinaires who established the present reign of terror in Russia profess to act. All this shows the prevalent feeling that a social or political theory or programme is hardly tenable if it cannot claim that it harmonises with this controlling idea.

"In the Middle Ages Europeans followed a different guiding star. The idea of a life beyond the grave was in control, and the great things of this life were conducted with reference to the next. When men's deepest feelings reacted more steadily and powerfully to the idea of saving their souls than to any other, harmony with this idea was the test by which the opportuneness of social theories and institutions was judged. Monasticism, for instance, throve under its ægis, while liberty of conscience had no chance. With a new idea in control, this has been reversed. Religious freedom has thriven under the ægis of Progress; monasticism can make no appeal to it.

"For the hope of an ultimate happy state on this planet to be enjoyed by future generations—or of some state, at least, that may relatively be considered happy—has replaced, as a social power, the hope of felicity in another world. Belief in personal immortality is still very widely entertained, but may we not fairly say that it has ceased to be a central and guiding idea of collective life, a criterion by which social values are measured? Many people do not believe in it; many more regard it as so uncertain that they could not reasonably permit it to affect their lives or opinions. Those who believe in it are doubtless the majority, but belief has many degrees; and one can hardly be wrong in saying that, as a general rule, this belief does not possess the imaginations of those who hold it, that their emotions react to it feebly, that it is felt to be remote and unreal, and has comparatively seldom a more direct influence on conduct than the abstract arguments to be found in treatises on morals.

"Under the control of the idea of Progress the ethical code recognized in the Western world has been reformed in modern times by a new principle of far-reaching importance which has emanated from that idea. When Isocrates formulated the rule of life, 'Do unto others,' he probably did not mean to include among 'others' slaves or savages. The Stoics and the Christians extended its applications to the whole of living humanity. But in late years the rule has received a vastly greater extension by the inclusion of the unborn generations of the future. This principle of duty to posterity is a direct corollary of the idea of Progress. In the recent war that idea, involving the moral obligation of making sacrifices for the sake of future ages, was constantly appealed to; just as in the Crusades, the most characteristic wars of our medieval ancestors, the idea of human destinies then in the ascendant lured thousands to hardship and death."

Bury, *The Idea of Progress* * (London, Macmillan, 1920), p. vii ff.

360. Progress

"Progress was conceived [by the general run of my students and associates] as a kind of fatalism, independent of the knowledge and good will of men, subject to vacillations and accidents in which the conscience and energy of man had no part."

Ferrer, *Origin and Ideals of the Modern School* * (New York, Putnam, 1913), p. 4-5.

361. Social Progress *versus* Social Evolution

"I have used the term 'evolution' in regard to human society and also the term 'progress.' This should imply that there is some difference between them, and in point of fact, to grasp this difference is in my view the beginning of understanding in these matters. By evolution I mean any sort of growth; by social progress, the growth of social life in respect of those qualities to which human beings attach or can rationally attach value. Social progress, then, is only one among many possibilities of social evolution. At least it is not to be assumed that any and every form of social evolution is also a form or a stage in social progress. For example, a caste system is a product of social evolution, and the more rigid and narrow the caste, the more complex the hierarchy, the more completely has the caste system evolved. In proportion, that is, as a loose and incipient caste system hardens into an extreme and rigid caste system, there is a distinct process of social evolution going forward; but most of us would question very strongly whether it could be considered in any sense as a phase of social progress. Judged from the standpoint of human values, it looks more like retrogression, or perhaps still more like divergence into a side track, from which there is no exit save by going back over a good deal of the ground travelled. So again there is at the present day a vigorous evolution of cartels, monopolies, rings, and trusts; there is an evolution of imperialism, of socialism, of nationalism, of militarism, in a word, of a hundred tendencies as to the good or evil of which people differ. The fact that a thing is evolving is no proof that it is good, the fact that society has evolved is no proof that it has progressed."

Hobhouse, *Social Evolution and Political Theory* * (New York, Columbia University, 1911), pp. 7-8.

362. Ill Effects of Belief in Inevitable Progress

"To think of progress as a certainty is superstitious—the most splendid and animated of all superstitions, if you like, yet a superstition still. It is a kind of fatalism—radiant, confident and infinitely hopeful, yet fatalism still, and like fatalism in all its other forms, inevitably dangerous to the effective sense of individual responsibility."

Morley, in *Educational Review*,* 29:7-8 (Jan., 1905).

363. Progress No Longer Inevitable

"The doctrine of evolution has been popularly used to give a kind of cosmic sanction to the notion of an automatic and wholesale progress in human affairs. Our part, the human part, was simply to enjoy the usufruct. Evolution inherited all the goods of Divine Providence and had the advantages of being in fashion. Even a great and devastating war is not too great a price to pay for an awakening from such an infantile and selfish dream. Progress is not automatic; it depends upon human intent and aim and upon acceptance of responsibility for its production. It is not a wholesale matter, but a retail job, to be contracted for and executed in sections. I doubt if the whole history of mankind shows any more vicious and demoralizing ethic than the recent widespread belief that each of us, as individuals and as classes, might safely and complacently devote ourselves to increasing our own possessions, material, intellectual, and artistic, because progress was inevitable anyhow."

Dewey, in *International Journal of Ethics*,* 26:315 f. (Apr., 1916.)

364. The Present State of Affairs

"Taking account of various groups of undoubted facts, many of which are so gross, so terrible that they cannot be overstated, it is not too much to say that our whole system of Society is rotten from top to bottom and the social environment as a whole, in relation to our possibilities and our claims, is the worst the world has ever seen."

Wallace, *Social Environment and Moral Progress* * (New York, Funk and Wagnalls, 1914), p. 169.

365. ONE EFFECT OF "AMERICANIZATION"

"Mr. Granville Barker, the British playwright, tells a story which he will forgive me for borrowing. He was taking a walk in spring on Staten Island. It was Sunday. Behind a hedge sat an Italian laborer with all the grime of the week on him, munching dark bread and garlic and reading with great intensity. Mr. Barker caught a glimpse of the book. It was a cheap, well thumbed edition of the Divine Comedy. 'The children of this man,' said Mr. Barker, 'will probably be Americanized. They will be cleaner and have better wages and eat daintier food and perhaps have electric light in their houses. But will they sit behind a hedge on Sunday reading an American Divine Comedy of the future?'"

Lewisohn, *Up Stream* * (New York, Boni Liveright, 1922), pp. 239-240.

366. LUDWIG LEWISOHN ON THE AMERICAN SITUATION

"Among the masses of our countrymen I see no stirring, no desire to penetrate beyond fixed names to living things, no awakening from the spectral delusions amid which they pursue their aimless business and their sapless pleasures. But the critical spirit which is also the creative spirit has arisen among us and it has arisen, naturally and inevitably, in the form of a protest and a rebellion against the life and the ethos which is also described here. . . . The substance of our new literature, of poems and novels and books of criticism, is clearly this: Life among us is ugly and mean and, above all things, false in its assumptions and measures. Somehow we must break these shackles and flee and emerge into some beyond of sanity, of a closer contact with reality, of nature and of truth. . . .

"Shall I now say, in order to end agreeably: It is always darkest before dawn? No; for that kind of professional optimism is precisely one of our national vices. The hour is dark. But that shall not prevent us from working and striving for a better one that may come hereafter."

Lewisohn, *Up Stream* * (New York, Boni Liveright, 1922), pp. 247-8.

367. Democracy and Progress

"The universal prejudice of modern humanity that *progress is constant* and that therefore whatever is of yesterday is *ex hypothesi* inferior to that which is of to-day. . . . (p. 143) Democracy . . . no longer believes in tradition and believes too much in progress." (p. 151.)

Faguet, *Cult of Incompetence* (Trans. by Barstow. London, Murray, 1911).

368. Has Material Progress Outrun Man's Moral Capacity?

"There is, first, the body of new information just being brought to general public attention, which appears to indicate that during the past hundred years and more the material progress of man and his power to control and apply the forces of nature have far outrun both his intellectual and his moral capacity and competence. One of the most distinguished of American scientists recently said in my hearing that he had about come to the conclusion that all his discoveries and advances were harmful rather than helpful to mankind because of the base and destructive uses to which they were likely to be put. He insisted that, in the present state of public intelligence, if there was a lofty use and a lower use of his discoveries and inventions, evidence multiplied that the lower use would be the first chosen. He pointed, among other things, to the fact that the Great War, with all its destructiveness and appalling loss of life and treasure, could never have been fought except by the use of two of the most beneficent and striking of modern inventions, namely, the telephone and typhoid prophylaxis. What, he added, is the use of inventing and improving the telephone or of discovering and applying typhoid prophylaxis, if the killing of millions of men is the best use that can be made of them?"

Nicholas Murray Butler, *Law and Lawlessness* (An Address before Ohio State Bar Association, Jan. 26, 1923).

369. Varying Progress in Nursing

"If we consider the long period of nursing history as a whole, we see how uneven and halting the line of advancement was, rising by slow stages for many centuries, reaching a fairly high crest of enthusiasm and activity from about the twelfth to the fourteenth centuries, only to fall back again into the long dark period of disorganization and decay, which extended from the sixteenth century right up to the threshold of modern times. The reforms of the seventeenth and early nineteenth century in England and Germany start the line upward again, but progress is exceedingly slow till we pass the middle of the last century when we begin to get the sharply ascending curve marking the influence of Florence Nightingale and the discoveries of modern medical science.

"It is a significant picture and one which we need to hold in our memory, not only to show us the long and difficult path by which we have come, but to remind us that continuous progress is by no means an invariable rule in nursing any more than in other human institutions, and that there is always the danger of reaction when the nursing spirit grows dim and the forces which make for progress weaken and fail."

Dock and Stewart, *Short History of Nursing* * (New York, Putnam, 1920), pp. 330-1.

370. EACH GAIN HAS ITS LOSS

"You may remember a certain simile employed by Mr. Herbert Spencer in his 'Study on Sociology.' Give a man a sheet of metal with a dint in it, he says, and ask him to flatten it out. What does he do? If he knows nothing of metal work, he takes a hammer and knocks the dint flat, only to find that it has reappeared elsewhere. He applies the hammer again at the new point with the same result, and so he goes on till he convinces himself that dints are not to be levelled out by this direct and easy method. So it is, urges Mr. Spencer, with society. We find some evil or evils which we seek to prevent by direct and forcible means, only to find, says this critic of social effort, that a corresponding evil appears somewhere else. We put down overt crime only to find that some form of secret vice is increasing. A temperance crusade suppresses drunkenness, and it is discovered that those who used to drink now find an outlet for excitement in gambling. Compensation for accidents is secured by law to workmen, and in consequence it is alleged that elderly workmen are refused situations. Workmen form trade unions to maintain and improve the conditions of their work, and no sooner do they succeed than their employers imitate them and form federations by which the unions are overpowered. Strikes are replaced by mutual agreements which are to initiate an era of industrial peace, and it is found that the wider the agreement the less it meets the local difficulties of mine and workshop, and we see workmen striking substantially against their own leaders. I need not here inquire whether in all these instances the allegation is correct, nor whether even if that be so there may not be some net gain. I am concerned only with the simple and preliminary point, to which Mr. Spencer did well to call attention, that every change, however good in itself, provokes unforeseen reactions, and that if we are to achieve permanent and assured good we must as far as possible keep in view the life of society as a whole."

Hobhouse, *Social Evolution and Political Theory* * (New York, Columbia University, 1911), pp. 5-6.

371. Progress not Necessary but Contingent

"Far from being necessary and universal, progress has been in an eminent degree contingent and partial. Its career has been frequently interrupted by periods of stagnation or declension, and wherever it has gone on, it has been forwarded, not by an inexplicable tendency of *nisus*, but by a concurrence of favourable conditions, external and internal. We must remember moreover as Sir Henry Maine reminds us (*Ancient Law*, p. 24), that the communities which have attained to a conspicuous degree of civilization constitute a numerical minority of mankind. Contemporaneous with the rapidly advancing nations of Europe exist the sluggish nations of Asia, and the almost stationary tribes of Africa and Polynesia."

Fiske, *Outlines of Cosmic Philosophy* * (Boston, Houghton Mifflin, 1891 [1]), Vol. II, p. 195.

372. "The Absurd Effort to Make the World Over"

"If this poor old world is as bad as they say, one more reflection may check the zeal of the headlong reformer. It is at any rate a tough old world. It has taken its trend and curvature and all its twists and tangles from a long course of formation. All its wry and crooked gnarls and knobs are therefore stiff and stubborn. If we puny men by our arts can do anything at all to straighten them, it will only be by modifying the tendencies of some of the forces at work, so that, after a sufficient time, their

[1] 1st ed., 1874.

action may be changed a little and slowly the lines of movement may be modified. This effort, however, can at most be only slight, and it will take a long time. In the meantime spontaneous forces will be at work, compared with which our efforts are like those of a man trying to deflect a river, and these forces will have changed the whole problem before our interferences have time to make themselves felt. The great stream of time and earthly things will sweep on just the same in spite of us. It bears with it now all the errors and follies of the past, the wreckage of all the philosophies, the fragments of all the civilizations, the wisdom of all the abandoned ethical systems, the debris of all the institutions, and the penalties of all the mistakes. It is only in imagination that we stand by and look at and criticize it and plan to change it. Everyone of us is a child of his age and cannot get out of it. Therefore the tide will not be changed by us. It will swallow up both us and our experiments. It will absorb the efforts at change and take them into itself as new but trivial components, and the great movement of tradition and work will go on unchanged by our fads and schemes. The things which will change it are the great discoveries and inventions, the new reactions inside the social organism, and the changes in the earth itself on account of changes in the cosmical forces. These causes will make of it just what, in fidelity to them, it ought to be. The men will be carried along with it and be made by it. The utmost they can do by their cleverness will be to note and record their course as they are carried along, which is what we do now, and it is that which leads us to the vain fancy that we can make or guide the movement. That is why it is the greatest folly of which a man can be capable, to sit down with a slate and pencil to plan out a new social world."

Sumner, in *The Forum,** 17:101-2 (March, 1894).

373. THE ILLUSION OF PROGRESS

"There is the illusion of 'increased command over Nature, meaning that cotton is cheap and that ten miles of country road on a bicycle have replaced four on foot. But even if man's increased command over Nature included any increased command over himself (the only sort of command relevant to his evolution into a higher being), the fact remains that it is only by running away from the increased command over Nature to country places where Nature is still in primitive command over Man that he can recover from the effects of the smoke, the ugliness, the dirt which the cheap cotton costs us. If manufacturing activity means Progress, the town must be more advanced than the country; and the field laborers and village artizans of to-day must be much less changed from the servants of Job than the proletariat of modern London from the proletariat of Cæsar's Rome. Yet the cockney proletarian is so inferior to the village laborer that it is only by steady recruiting from the country that London is kept alive. This does not seem as if the change since Job's time were Progress in the popular sense: quite the reverse. The common stock of discoveries in physics has accumulated a little: that is all."

Shaw, *Three Plays for Puritans* * (New York, Brentano, 1914), p. 201 f.

374. Lost Opportunities

"The saddest memories of political life are of moments at which one had to stand by when golden opportunities were being lost, to see the wrong thing done when it would have been easy to do the right thing."

Bryce, *Modern Democracies* * (New York, Macmillan, 1921), Vol. I, p. ix.

375. Rate of Progress in Science

"The rate of progress in the arts and sciences proceeds in a geometrical ratio as knowledge increases."

Sir Charles Lyell, *Antiquity of Man* (Philadelphia, Childs, 1863), p. 377.

376. Present Sensitivity to Social Ailment

"There was probably never a time at which among civilized peoples there was so much diffused sensitiveness to any form of social ailment."

Hobhouse, *Social Evolution and Political Theory* * (New York, Columbia University, 1911), p. 2.

377. The Gain from Ptolemy to Copernicus

"On the Ptolemic system it was not incongruous or absurd that man, lord of the central domain in the universe, should regard himself as the most important cosmic creature. . . . When the true place of the earth was shown and man found himself in a tiny planet attached to one of the innumerable solar worlds, his cosmic importance could no longer be maintained. . . . But man is resourceful . . . Displaced, along with his home, from the center of things, he discovers a new means of restoring his self-importance; he interprets his humiliation as a deliverance. Finding himself in an insignificant island floating in the immensity of space, he decides that he is at last master of his own destinies; he can fling away the old equipment of final causes, original sin, and the rest; he can construct his own chart and, bound by no cosmic scheme, he need take the universe into account only in so far as he judges it to be to his own profit."

Bury, *The Idea of Progress* * (London, Macmillan, 1920), pp. 160-1.

378. Opposition to Early Missionary Endeavor

(a) Presiding officer to William Carey (c. 1792): "Sit down, young man; when it pleases God to convert the heathen, He will do it without your help."

(b) East India Company (c. 1759): "The sending out of missionaries into our Eastern possessions [we consider] to be the maddest, most extravagant, most costly, most indefensible project which has ever been suggested by a moonstruck religious fanatic. Such a scheme is pernicious, imprudent, useless, harmful, dangerous, profitless, fantastic. It strikes against all reason and sound policy, it brings the peace and safety of our possessions into peril."

(c) General Assembly of the Church of Scotland (1796): "To spread abroad the knowledge of the gospel amongst barbarous and heathen nations seems to be highly preposterous—whilst there remains at home a single individual without the means of religious knowledge, to propagate it abroad would be improper and absurd."

World's Work, 26:641-2 (Oct., 1913).

379. No Continuous Automatic Inevitable Progress

"Social progress . . . is not . . . continuous . . . . It comes in occasional spurts, succeeded by epochs of stagnation and decay. . . .

"It is impossible to shut our eyes to the long periods of stagnation and retrogression that make up a great part of recorded history. The optimism which sees in the declining ages of the Lower Empire and amid the barbaric anarchy of the Merovingian period nothing but the birth of a higher order does not represent the balanced mood of science. . . . The theory of continuous automatic inevitable progress is impossible. Assuming that progress means an advance towards an ideal that would commend itself to a rational judgment of value, it is impossible to maintain that the successive steps which lead from savagery to the civilization of our own day involve point by point a corresponding betterment in the actual life of the people as a whole. The slave or the serf of the middle civilization compares unfavorably with the free savage, and even the low-grade worker of our own days does not in all respects come happily out of the comparison. Without any trace of rhetorical exaggeration or of sentimental idealization of so-called natural conditions, we must admit a real and grave loss in certain elements of value when we compare the relative concreteness and human interest of the primitive hunter's life with the mechanical drudgery of the routine of unskilled modern labor. Moreover, even if it were true that every onward step in civilization taken by itself were net gain, it would still be untrue to suppose that humanity as a whole had always gone forward in civilization. The advance has been greater than the retrogression, but there has been true retrogression as well. Free Athens did not perish without leaving the world the poorer. Much was saved from the wreck, but the loss was real, not to be ignored."

Hobhouse, *Social Evolution and Political Theory* * (New York, Columbia University, 1911), pp. 157, 159, 160 f.

380. Progress not Inevitable

"So far there is not the slightest evidence to warrant the belief in continuous, automatic, inevitable progress; still less the belief that it is a blessing conferred by some mysterious Power from without. Progress is rare, evolution and change universal. Just as the dead far outnumber the living so the abortive civilizations exceed the successful. The past counts far more savages and barbarians than truly civilized. Balfour says, and rightly, progressive civilization 'is not a form of indestructible energy which, if repressed here must needs break out there, if refused embodiment in one shape must needs show itself in another. It is a plant of tender habit, difficult to propagate, not difficult to destroy, that refuses to flourish except in a soil which is not to be found everywhere, nor at all times, nor even, so far as we can see, necessarily to be found at all.' (*Essays and Addresses,* p 243 f.)

"Too often belief in progress is sentimentalism rather than science; or it is pious dogma whose purpose, like that of religious dogma, may be to serve as an anodyne to real thinking. Or again it appears as a baleful kind of complacent egotism which mistakes certain gains in the means to physical comfort and ease for signs that cosmic forces are working irresistibly to improve the whole state of human affairs. Mr. P. E. More accuses some evolutionists of this perfectionism, a romantic belief in some ameliorative drift; for it is just that and nothing more, he declares, 'a faith in drifting; a belief that things of themselves, by a kind of natural gravity of goodness in them, move always on and on in the right direction; a confiding trust in human nature as needing no restraint and compression, but rather full liberty to follow its own impulsive desires to expand. . . .' (*Aristocracy and Justice,* p. viii f.) He is quite justified in denying to such soft thinking the name science or even proper philosophy of progress. Race egotism, the ethnocentric belief that we are the Chosen People, the Sword of God, the Divine Scourge, and that we must hack our way through to demonstrate this Destiny, is bad enough; but even more fatal the comfortable belief that we can drift along on the river of events and wake up each morning to find ourselves still nearer the great ocean of God's Providence. Such beliefs are worse than fatuous: they are paralyzing fatalism. Says John Morley: 'To think of progress as a certainty is superstitious—the most splendid and animated of all superstitions, if you like, yet a superstition still. It is a kind of fatalism—radiant, confident, and infinitely hopeful, yet fatalism still, and like fatalism in all its other forms, inevitably dangerous to the effective sense of individual responsibility.' (*Educational Review,* 29:7-8.) Science, philosophy, history and common sense unite in testifying that progress is not a free gift of the gods but something to be earned by clear vision and hard work; that is, a human contingency based upon human effort, foresight, and constructive utilization of human powers."

Todd, *Theories of Social Progress* * (New York, Macmillan, 1918), p. 103-5.

381. The Principle of Historic Continuity

"The doctrine of the continuity of history is based upon the observed fact that every human institution, every generally accepted idea, every important invention, is but the summation of long lines of progress, reaching back as far as we have the patience or means to follow them. The jury, the drama, the Gatling gun, the papacy, the letter S, the doctrine of *stare decisis,* each owes its present form to antecedents which can be scientifically traced."

Robinson, *The New History* * (New York, Macmillan, 1913), p. 64.

382. THE TERM "STRUGGLE FOR EXISTENCE"

"I use this term in a large and metaphorical sense including dependence of one being on another, and including (which is more important) not only the life of the individual, but success in leaving progeny. Two canine animals, in a time of dearth, may be truly said to struggle with each other which shall get food and live. But a plant on the edge of a desert is said to struggle for life against the drought, though more properly it should be said to be dependent on the moisture. A plant which annually produces a thousand seeds, of which only one on an average comes to maturity, may be more truly said to struggle with the plants of the same and other kinds which already clothe the ground. The misletoe is dependent on the apple and a few other trees, but can only in a far-fetched sense be said to struggle with these trees, for, if too many of these parasites grow on the same tree, it languishes and dies. But several seedling misletoes, growing close together on the same branch, may more truly be said to struggle with each other. As the misletoe is disseminated by birds, its existence depends on them; and it may metaphorically be said to struggle with other fruit-bearing plants, in tempting the birds to devour and thus disseminate its seeds. In these several senses, which pass into each other, I use for convenience' sake the general term of Struggle for Existence."

Darwin, *Origin of Species* (New York, Appleton, 1883 [1]), p. 50.

383. MUST OLD PEOPLES STAGNATE?

"It is often supposed that as old persons die, so must old peoples. There are many facts in history to support the belief. Decadence and degeneration seems to be the rule as age increases. An irruption of some uncivilized horde has then provided new blood and fresh life—so much so that history has been defined as a process of rebarbarization. In truth the analogy between a person and a nation with respect to senescence and death is

[1] 1st ed., 1859.

defective. A nation is always renewed by the death of its old constituents and the birth of those who are as young and fresh as ever were any individuals in the hey-day of the nation's glory. Not the nation but its customs get old. Its institutions petrify into rigidity; there is social arterial sclerosis. Then some people not overburdened with elaborate and stiff habits take up and carry on the moving process of life. The stock of fresh peoples is, however, approaching exhaustion. It is not safe to rely upon this expensive method of renewing civilization. We need to discover how to rejuvenate it from within. A normal perpetuation becomes a fact in the degree in which impulse is released and habit is plastic to the transforming touch of impulse. When customs are flexible and youth is educated as youth and not as premature adulthood, no nation grows old."

Dewey, *Human Nature and Conduct* * (New York, Holt, 1922), p. 101 f.

384. THE POWER OF PURPOSE

" 'To reshape reality by means of ideas is the business of man, his proper earthly task; and nothing can be impossible to a will confident of itself and of its aim' [quoted in original]. . . . To realize in the actual world [ideas of] a new, a higher civilization, and thus to inaugurate a new great epoch of human history, is a matter that lies with ourselves and depends solely on our own earnestness of purpose."

Paulsen, *German Education* * (Trans. by Lorenz. New York, Scribners, 1908), p. 184.

385. THE WILL TO WIN

"Consider the attitude of a soldier going into battle against a foe whom he knows to be nearly his match in force and arms. He possesses, if he is a brave man, some sort of confidence that he will win. . . . In what is this confidence founded? . . . His belief that he will win is identical with his active, manly resolve that he is minded to win, that his teeth are set to win, that this sword is sharpened, that this bayonet has been pointed, that this bullet will soon be winged, with the determination of victory. Each army knows that, other things equal, the force which is thus *most* minded to win is the force destined to conquer, that here is a case where faith can *create* its own object, that the unseen victory will be fashioned precisely by and for the side

which most fully takes hold of that unseen, and which actively creates what it believes in. Well, then, there is in active life this way of vindicating your faith. It is by creating the very . . . world wherein your faith is to come true."
Royce, *Spirit of Modern Philosophy* * (Boston, Houghton Mifflin, 1892), p. 115 f.

386. Our Doubts are Traitors

"Our doubts are traitors,
And make us lose the good we oft might win,
By fearing to attempt."
Shakespeare, *Measure for Measure,* Act I, sc. 5.

387. Pessimism, Optimism, Meliorism

"Pessimism is a paralyzing doctrine. In declaring that the world is evil wholesale, it makes futile all efforts to discover the remediable causes of specific evils and thereby destroys at the root every attempt to make the world better and happier. Wholesale optimism, which has been the consequence of the attempt to explain evil away, is, however, equally an incubus. . . .

"The optimism that says that the world is already the best possible of all worlds might be regarded as the most cynical of pessimisms. If this is the best possible, what would a world which was fundamentally bad be like? Meliorism is the belief that the specific conditions which exist at one moment, be they comparatively bad or comparatively good, in any event may be bettered. It encourages intelligence to study the positive means of good and the obstructions to their realization, and to put forth endeavor for the improvement of conditions. It arouses confidence and a reasonable hopefulness as optimism does not. For the latter in declaring that good is already realized in ultimate reality tends to make us gloss over the evils that concretely exist. It becomes too readily the creed of those who live at ease, in comfort, of those who have been successful in obtaining this world's rewards. Too readily optimism makes the men who hold it callous and blind to the sufferings of the less fortunate, or ready to find the cause of troubles of others in their personal viciousness. It thus coöperates with pessimism, in spite of the extreme nominal difference between the two, benumbing sympathetic insight and intelligent effort in reform. It beckons men away from the world of relativity and change into the calm of the absolute and external."

Dewey, *Reconstruction in Philosophy* * (New York, Holt, 1920), pp. 178-9.

388. THE HISTORIC EFFECT OF MARATHON AND SALAMIS

"If little Greece had . . . been swallowed up by giant Persia, and the nascent political and intellectual freedom extinguished in Athens as it was in the Ionic cities of Asia Minor, the entire future history of Macedonia, of Rome, and of Europe, would have been altered in a way that is not pleasant to contemplate. When we reflect upon the enormous place in human history which is filled by the products of Athenian intellectual activity during the two centuries succeeding the victory of Marathon; when we remember that the foundations of philosophy, of exact science, of æsthetic art in all its branches, of historic and literary criticism, and of free political discussion, were then and there for ever securely laid; when we consider the widely ramifying influences, now obvious and now more subtle, of all this intense productivity upon Roman ethics and jurisprudence, upon the genesis of Christianity, upon the lesser Renaissance of the thirteenth century, and the greater Renaissance of the fifteenth; when we see how inseparably the life of Athens runs as a woof through the entire web of European life down to our own times;—when we come to realize all this, we shall begin to realize how frightful was the danger from which we were rescued at Marathon and at Salamis."

Fiske, *Outlines of Cosmic Philosophy* * (Boston, Houghton Mifflin, 1891 [1]), Vol. II, pp. 261-2.

389. THE INDIVIDUAL IN A LARGE GROUP

"The modern great state is harmful from its vastness and the resulting sense of individual helplessness. The citizen who is out of sympathy with the aims of the State, unless he is a man of very rare gifts, cannot hope to persuade the State to adopt purposes which seem to him better. Even in a democracy, all questions except a very few are decided by a small number of officials and eminent men; and even the few questions which are left to the popular vote are decided by a diffused mass-psychology, not by individual initiative. This is especially noticeable in a

[1] First edition, 1874.

country like the United States, where, in spite of democracy most men have a sense of almost complete impotence in regard to all large issues. In so vast a country the popular will is like one of the forces of Nature, and seems nearly as much outside the control of any one man. This state of things leads, not only in America but in all large States, to something of the weariness and discouragement that we associate with the Roman Empire."

Russell, *Why Men Fight* * (New York, Century, 1917), p. 60 f.

390. The Uncertain Future of Civilization

"Throughout the politics and literature of the twentieth century one traces this fear, conscious or half-conscious, lest the civilisation which we have adopted so rapidly and with so little forethought may prove unable to secure either a harmonious life for its members or even its own stability. The old delight in the 'manifest finger of destiny' and 'the tide of progress,' even the newer belief in the effortless 'evolution' of social institutions are gone. We are afraid of the blind forces to which we used so willingly to surrender ourselves. We feel that we must reconsider the basis of our organised life because, without reconsideration, we have no chance of controlling it. And so behind the momentary ingenuities and party phrases of our statesmen we can detect the straining effort to comprehend while there is yet time. . . .

"We are forced . . . to recognise that a society whose intellectual direction consists only of unrelated specialisms must drift, and that we dare not drift any longer. We stand, as the Greek thinkers stood, in a new world. And because that world is new, we feel that neither the sectional observations of the special student, nor the ever-accumulating records of the past, nor the narrow experience of the practical man can suffice us. We must let our minds play freely over all the conditions of life till we can either justify our civilisation or change it.

"The Greek thinkers, with all their magnificent courage and comprehensiveness, failed in the end either to understand or to guide the actual social forces of their time. Our own brains are less acute, our memories less retentive than those of the Greeks, while the body of relevant fact which we must survey has been increased ten-thousand-fold. How are we to have any chance of success?"

Wallas, *The Great Society* * (New York, Macmillan, 1914), pp. 14-16.

391. Truth and Persecution

"The dictum that truth always triumphs over persecution, is one of those pleasant falsehoods which men repeat after one another till they pass into commonplaces, but which all experience refutes. History teems with instances of truth put down by persecution. If not suppressed forever, it may be thrown back for centuries. To speak only of religious opinions: the Reformation broke out at least twenty times before Luther, and was put down. . . . Persecution has always succeeded, save where the heretics were too strong a party to be effectually persecuted. . . . It is a piece of idle sentimentality that truth, merely as truth, has any inherent power denied to error, of prevailing against the dungeon and the stake. Men are not more zealous for truth than they often are for error, and a sufficient application of legal or even of social penalties will generally succeed in stopping the propagation of either. The real advantage which truth has, consists in this, that when an opinion is true, it may be extinguished once, twice, or many times, but in the course of ages there will generally be found persons to rediscover it, until some one of its reappearances falls on a time when from favorable circumstances it escapes persecution until it has made such head as to withstand all subsequent attempts to suppress it."

Mill, *Liberty* (London, Parker, 1859), p. 52 ff.

392. Freedom of Discussion and Progress

"The progress of civilization, if it is partly conditioned by circumstances beyond man's control, depends more, and in an increasing measure, on things which are within his own power. Prominent among these are the advancement of knowledge and the deliberate adaptation of his habits and institutions to new conditions. To advance knowledge and to correct errors, unrestricted freedom of discussion is required. History shows that knowledge grew when speculation was perfectly free in Greece, and that in modern times, since restrictions on inquiry have been entirely removed, it has advanced with a velocity which would seem diabolical to the slaves of the mediæval Church. Then, it is obvious that in order to readjust social customs, institutions, and methods to new needs and circumstances, there must be unlimited freedom of canvassing and criticising them, of expressing the most unpopular opinions, no matter how offensive to prevailing sentiment they may be. If the history of civilization has any lesson to teach it is this: there is one supreme condition of mental and moral progress which it is completely within the power of man himself to secure, and that is perfect liberty of thought and discussion. The establishment of this liberty may be considered the most valuable achievement of modern civilization, and as a condition of social progress it should be deemed fundamental. The considerations of permanent utility on which it rests must outweigh any calculations of present advantage which from time to time might be thought to demand its violation."

Bury, *History of Freedom of Thought* * (New York,[1] Holt, 1913), p. 239 f.

393. The End of Human Progress

"As nearly as I can state what to me is the end of human progress, it would be somewhat in this form: that the final goal of all things, if they have or can be made to have a goal, is not some merely static perfection for God, society, or the individual; it is *the identification of personal interest with social interest* TO AN INCREASING DEGREE."

Todd, *Theories of Social Progress* * (New York, Macmillan, 1918), p. 547.

394. The Meaning of Progress

"Progress means increase of present meaning, which involves multiplication of sensed distinctions as well as harmony, unification. This statement may, perhaps, be made generally, in application to the experience of humanity. If history shows progress it can hardly be found elsewhere than in this complication and extension of the significance found within experience. It is clear that such progress brings no surcease, no immunity from perplexity and trouble. If we wished to transmute this generalization into a categorical imperative we should say: 'So act as to increase the meaning of present experience.' But even then in order to get instruction about the concrete quality of such increased meaning we should have to run away from the law and study the needs and alternative possibilities lying within a unique and localized situation. The imperative, like everything abso-

---

[1] Originally published in England.

lute, is sterile. Till men give up the search for a general formula of progress they will not know where to look to find it."

Dewey, *Human Nature and Conduct* * (New York, Holt, 1922), p. 283.

395. Progress

There can be no blinking the fact that much of our faith in progress has been "childish and irresponsible. We confused rapidity of change with advance, and we took certain gains in our own comfort and ease as signs that cosmic forces were working inevitably to improve the whole state of human affairs. Having reaped where we had not sown, our undisciplined imaginations installed in the heart of history forces which were to carry on progress whether or no, and whose advantages we were progressively to enjoy. It is easy to understand why our minds were taken captive by the spectacle of change, and why we should have confused progress with change. It is not necessary to rehearse an account of the barriers which for thousands of years kept human society static. Nor is it necessary to do more than allude to the various inventions which by facilitating migration and travel, communication and circulation of ideas and reciprocal criticism, and the production and distribution of goods in a world-wide market, have broken down those barriers. The release of energies has gone on for a century and a half to a degree which we are still impotent to realize. Persons and things have been endlessly redistributed and mingled. The fixed has given way to the mobile; the settled to the free. It was doubtless inevitable that, in its contrast with static conditions and ideals, this mobility and freedom should be taken for progress. Such it doubtless is in some respects. But the present crisis is in vain, so far as our intelligence is concerned, if it does not make us see that in the main this rapid change of conditions affords an opportunity for progress, but is not itself progress. . . .

"Two things are apparent. First, progress depends not on the existence of social change but on the direction which human beings deliberately give that change. Secondly, ease of social change is a condition of progress. Side by side with the fact that the mere substitution of a dynamic or readily changing social structure for a static society does not accomplish progress, stands the fact that this substitution furnishes the opportunity for progress. We cannot too much insist upon the fact that until men got control of natural forces civilization was a local accident. It depended upon the ability of a small number of men to command, with assurance, the labor and services of other men. Any civilization based mainly upon ability to exploit the energies of men is precarious; it is at the mercy of internal revolt and external overflow. By exploring the heaps of rubbish scattered over the face of the earth, we are just beginning to learn how many civilizations have arisen in the past only to sink into rubbish heaps. The dominion of man over the labor of other men is a shaky basis for civilization. And civilization never attained stability upon such a basis. The scientific conquest of nature has at least given us another basis. We have now a sure method. Wholesale permanent decays of civilization are impossible. As long as there exists a group of men who understand the methods of physical science and are expert in their use, recovery, under the worst of circumstances, of the material basis of culture is sure and relatively speedy. While the modern man was deceived about the amount of progress he had made, and especially deceived about the automatic certainty of progress, he was right in thinking that for the first time in history mankind is in command of the possibility of progress. The rest is for us to say. . . .

"We are in possession of a method which enables us to forecast desirable physical changes and to set about securing them. So much is the secure result of the scientific revolution of the last three hundred years. We also know that it is now possible to bring about these physical changes. The men who invented the stationary and locomotive steam engine, and the men who have since then harnessed both steam and electricity to all sorts of ends, have produced social changes by the side of which those produced by Alexander, Cæsar and Napoleon are insignificant. And the same process is going on as long as applied science goes on, whatever we may think about its worth. But, I repeat, while social change, thus brought about, represents an indispensable condition of progress, it does not present a guarantee for progress. The latter depends upon deliberate human foresight and socially constructive work. Hence we have first of all to change our attitude. Instead of congratulating ourselves upon its presence and certainty as a gift of the gods, as we have been wont to do, we have to recognize that it is a human and intentional product—as much so in principle as a telephone or irrigation or a self-binding reaper, and as much more so in fact as the factors upon which it depends are more complex and more elusive."

Dewey, in *International Journal of Ethics*,* 26:312, 313 f., 315 (Apr., 1916).

396. FLUX, PROCESS, AND PROGRESS, AND THEIR RELATIVITY TO MAN

If we think of a succession of changes following each other without actually coöperating to produce any describable result, without leaving anything that could be dignified by the term effect, we may call such a succession of changes a mere *flux*. The movement of the wind and sand in the desert may at times approximate such a state of affairs. If, however, as is more usual, the succession of changes coöperate to produce what we think of as a result or effect, we call the succession of conjoined changes a *process*. If the action of the wind upon the sand is at length to produce a dune, we may correctly say that the dune is the result of a long process, that is, of a long succession of related changes. It is at once clear that the distinction between flux and process as here presented is relative to man and his conceptions. We do not use the term process unless we think of (i) a succession of movements and (ii) a "resulting" state of affairs that appeals to us as having conceivable "character." Man, man's wants, things that affect man's wants, man's conceptions of things that seem to affect his wants,—these lie at the bottom of man's ideas and distinctions. These give or withhold "character" in nature about us. So far relativity clearly holds.

In still clearer fashion is the term *progress* relative to man. In time of war the "advancing" battle front is evidently progress. Not so with the "retreating" line; one cannot call that progress which to him means destruction and defeat. The same battle line is then differently named according as it is differently viewed. Progress is thus a term applied by anyone to a process when he approves the result. For unwelcome results, such terms as retrogression, degeneration, and the like, are deemed appropriate. Progress then being an approved process has all the relativity that belongs to process and more besides; for no man uses the term progress unless he himself approves the end toward which the process is judged to be tending.

Even more inextricably relative to man is that inclusive kind of progress called *social progress*. That progress along certain specific lines is in the sense defined above attested by common observation need not be disputed, but social progress is quite a different matter. By it is meant the net aggregate result of all socially conditioned processes. In addition to the successive relativities of process and progress we have in social progress so defined the complicated factor of humanly judging the process.

Original temperament wrestles with knowledge and judgment in a vain effort to appraise what is in truth infinitely complex, with the result that differently disposed observers single out different elements as significant and determinative. Thus optimist and pessimist each persuades himself and rails at the other, and both wonder at him of suspended judgment, while all three in fact confront the same gross situation. To ask then whether progress, net social progress is a fact, that is, whether such progress is objectively and absolutely demonstrable, is a meaningless inquiry. The social process is infinitely complex; what shall or shall not be included is, as we saw, relative to man, more precisely to the particular man who may chance to be judging. The end or ends of the social process—more exactly the ends within the social process—are again relative to man's wants, man's nature. The ends then that must differentiate progress from decay are relative to man's nature. There can thus be no finally objective or absolute meaning to the term social progress. Absolutely, that is without reference to man, the term progress is meaningless. But, absolutism apart, even within the range of human relativity the determination of the problem of all inclusive progress is impossible: the infinite character of the complex social process renders impossible the solution of the problem. We do not know and apparently can never know whether "human progress" in any all inclusive sense as a net affair is or is not a fact.

CHAPTER XV

EDUCATION AND SOCIAL PROGRESS

397. EDUCATION AND PROGRESS

"The purpose of education is to train children, not with reference to their success in the present state of society, but to a better possible state, in accordance with an ideal conception of humanity."

Kant, quoted in Ruediger, *Principles of Education* (Boston, Houghton Mifflin, 1910), p. 89.

398. DYNAMIC EDUCATION

"So long as conformity to the mores is the prime demand, very little teaching, and that quite uninspired, is needed. Fourth rate men are good enough to pass on superstition, tradition, and colorless orthodoxy. But let education become dynamic, let it thrill with a vision of becoming the chariot horses and the chariot in which society shall urge itself forward to a better day, and men and women of the first rank will arise and consecrate themselves to making the vision full reality. Without that vision educational measurements, movements to increase school efficiency, reforms of curricula, child study, and all the rest of them are but the clattering of machinery grinding chaff; with it they become the tools for generating the self-criticism and creative energies essential to the process of producing an environment in which social man can flourish and rise higher and higher above man the clod."

Todd, *Theories of Social Progress* * (New York, Macmillan, 1918), p. 534.

399. HOW CUSTOMS FORM HABITS

"An individual usually acquires the morality as he inherits the speech of his social group. The activities of the group are already there, and some assimilation of his own acts to their pattern is a prerequisite of a share therein, and hence of having any part in what is going on. Each person is born an infant, and every infant is subject from the first breath he draws and the first cry he utters to the attention and demands of others. These others are not just persons in general with minds in general. They are beings with habits, and beings who upon the whole esteem the habits they have, if for no other reason than that, having them, their imagination is thereby limited. The nature of habit is to be assertive, insistent, self-perpetuating. There is no miracle in the fact that if a child learns any language he learns the language that those about him speak and teach, especially since his ability to speak that language is a pre-condition of his entering into effective connection with them, making wants known and getting them satisfied. Fond parents and relatives frequently pick up a few of the child's spontaneous modes of speech and for a time at least they are portions of the speech of the group. But the ratio which such words bear to the total vocabulary in use gives a fair measure of the part played by purely individual habit in forming custom in comparison with the part played by custom in forming individual habits. Few persons have either the energy or the wealth to build private roads to travel upon. They find it convenient, 'natural,' to use the roads that are already there; while unless their private roads connect at some point with the high-way they cannot build them even if they would. . . ."

Dewey, *Human Nature and Conduct* * (New York, Holt, 1922), p. 58 f.

400. HABIT NOT NECESSARILY CONSERVATIVE

"Only in a society dominated by modes of belief and admiration fixed by past custom is habit any more conservative than it is progressive. It all depends upon its quality. Habit is an ability, an art, formed through past experience. But whether an ability is limited to repetition of past acts adapted to past conditions or is available for new emergencies depends wholly upon what kind of habit exists. The tendency to think that only 'bad' habits are disserviceable and that bad habits are conventionally enumerable, conduces to make all habits more or less bad. For what makes a habit bad is enslavement to old ruts."

Dewey, *Human Nature and Conduct* * (New York, Holt, 1922), p. 66.

401. Freedom

"It is hard to free fools from the chains they revere."
Voltaire.

402. Education for a Better State of Society

"There are possibilities resident in the education of the young which have never yet been taken advantage of. The idea of universal education is as yet hardly a century old, and it is still much more of an idea than a fact, when we take into account the early age at which it terminates for the mass. Also, thus far schooling has been largely utilized as a convenient tool of the existing nationalistic and economic régimes. Hence it is easy to point out defects and perversions in every existing school system. It is easy for a critic to ridicule the religious devotion to education which has characterized for example the American republic. It is easy to represent it as zeal without knowledge, fanatical faith apart from understanding. And yet the cold fact of the situation is that the chief means of continuous, graded, economical improvement and social rectification lies in utilizing the opportunities of educating the young to modify prevailing types of thought and desire.

"The young are not as yet as subject to the full impact of established customs. Their life of impulsive activity is vivid, flexible, experimenting, curious. Adults have their habits formed, fixed, at least comparatively. They are the subjects, not to say victims, of an environment which they can change only by a maximum of effort and disturbance. They may not be able to perceive clearly the needed changes, or be willing to pay the price of effecting them. Yet they wish a different life for the generation to come. In order to realize that wish they may create a special environment whose main function is education. In order that education of the young be efficacious in inducing an improved society, it is not necessary for adults to have a formulated definite ideal of some better state. An educational enterprise conducted in this spirit would probably end merely in substituting one rigidity for another. What is necessary is that habits be formed which are more intelligent, more sensitively percipient, more informed with foresight, more aware of what they are about, more direct and sincere, more flexibly responsive than those now current. Then they will meet their own problems and propose their own improvements."

Dewey, *Human Nature and Conduct* * (New York, Holt, 1922), p. 127 f.

403. Are Acquired Characters Hereditary?

"If acquired characters were really inherited we should expect to find many positive evidences of this instead of a few sporadic and doubtful cases. In particular why do we not find in plant or animal grafting that the influence of the stock changes the hereditary potencies of the graft? Why do we not find that transplanted ovaries show the influence of the foster mother as Guthrie supposed—a thing which has been disproved by Castle? Why do dominant and recessive characters remain pure, even after their intimate union in a hybrid, so that pure dominants and pure recessives may be obtained in subsequent generations from this mixture? Why does every child have to learn anew what his parents learned so laboriously before him? Even the strongest defenders of the inheritance of acquired characters are constrained to admit that it occurs only sporadically and exceptionally."

Conklin, *Heredity and Environment* * (Princeton, Princeton University, 1922), p. 243.

404. Innate Racial Differences

"It may be well to state here once more with some emphasis that it would be erroneous to assume that there are no differences in the mental make-up of the negro race and of other races, and that their activities should run in the same lines. On the contrary, if there is any meaning in correlation of anatomical structure and physiological function, we must expect that differences exist. There is, however, no evidence whatever that would stigmatize the negro as of weaker build, or as subject to inclinations and powers that are opposed to our social organization. An unbiassed estimate of the anthropological evidence so far brought forward does not permit us to countenance the belief in a racial inferiority which would unfit an individual of the negro race to take his part in modern civilization. We do not know of any demand made on the human body or mind in modern life that anatomical or ethnological evidence would prove to be beyond the powers of the negro.

"The traits of the American negro are adequately explained on the basis of his history and social status. The tearing-away from the African soil and the consequent complete loss of the old standards of life, which were replaced by the dependency of slavery and by all it entailed, followed by a period of disorganization and by a severe economic struggle against heavy odds, are sufficient to explain the inferiority of the status of the race, without falling back upon the theory of hereditary inferiority."

Boas, *The Mind of Primitive Man* * (New York, Macmillan, 1911), p. 271 f.

405. KANT ON THE EXPERT IN EDUCATION

"The management of the schools should be left entirely to the judgment of the most intelligent experts. All culture begins with the individual and thence extends itself. The gradual approach of human nature to its true end is possible only through the efforts of liberally inclined propagandists who take an interest in the world's welfare and who are capable of conceiving the idea of a future improved state."

Buchner, *Kant's Educational Theory* * (Philadelphia, Lippincott, 1904), p. 120.

406. ROUSSEAU ON PUBLIC EDUCATION

"As there are laws for maturity, so also should there be laws for childhood, to teach the children obedience. If the reason of each individual is not allowed to be the sole judge of his duties, still less should the education of children be left to the ignorance and prejudices of their fathers. . . . Public education, according to regulations prescribed by the government, and under magistrates appointed by the supreme authority, is therefore one of the fundamental requirements of popular government. If children are educated together on a footing of equality, if they are imbued with the laws of the state and the maxims of the general will, and taught to respect them above all else, if they are surrounded by examples and by objects that unceasingly remind them of the tender mother that fosters them, of the love she bears them, of the inestimable benefits they received from her, and of the return they owe her, it cannot be doubted that they will learn in this way to cherish each other as brothers and wish only what the community wishes, and that one day they will become the defenders and the fathers of the country of which they have so long been the children."

Jean Jacques Rousseau, article on Political Economy written

for the Encyclopedia (Boyd, *The Minor Educational Writings of J. J. Rousseau,* London, Blackie, 1911, p. 44-5).

407. HIGHER EDUCATION FOR CITIZENSHIP

"The living voice of the teacher who can treat of large principles and answer questions out of his stores of knowledge, can warn against the fallacies that lurk in words, can explain the value of critical methods, and, above all, can try to form the open and truth-loving mind, is of inestimable value. In times when class strife is threatened there is a special need for thinkers and speakers able to rise above class interests and class prejudices. Men can best acquire wide and impartial views in the years of youth, before they become entangled in party affiliations or business connections. The place fittest to form such views is a place dedicated to the higher learning and to the pursuit of truth. Universities render a real service to popular government by giving to men whose gifts fit them for leadership that power of distinguishing the essential from the accidental and of being the master instead of the servant of formulas which it is the business of philosophy to form."

Bryce, *Modern Democracies* * (New York, Macmillan, 1921), Vol. I, p. 77.

408. ADVANTAGES OF VARIATION

"As it is useful that while mankind are imperfect there should be different opinions, so is it that there should be different experiments of living; that free scope should be given to varieties of character, short of injury to others; and that the worth of different modes of life should be proved practically, when any one thinks fit to try them. It is desirable, in short, that in things which do not primarily concern others, individuality should assert itself. Where, not the person's own character, but the traditions or customs of other people are the rule of conduct, there is wanting one of the principal ingredients of human happiness, and quite the chief ingredient of individual and social progress."

Mill, *Liberty* (London, Parker, 1859), p. 101 f.

409. THE UNIVERSITY AND DEMOCRACY

"At bottom and forever, the question of academic freedom is the question of intellectual and spiritual leadership in American democracy. Those who lead and teach, are they free, fearless, and worthy of trust? If they fain would lead the people, do they lead under the eye of eternity or under the eye of the trustees' committee on salaries, pensions, and promotions? If they find through research and mature thought that a popular movement is full of peril can they say so and command, as known freemen, the respect of the masses? When they face the questioning multitude, whose whimsies and fallacies they would overbear, do they encounter distrust and contempt or high esteem and confidence?

"Everywhere the tide of democracy comes in. Ancient China struggles for a republic. The crown of the Romanoffs is in the dust. Labor rises higher and higher in the scale of power . . . but who knows what trials or what disasters await? The wrath of man may praise God, but it cannot manage an industry or conduct a government. It may pull down such pillars of order and justice as we have now erected, and leave—dust and ashes. Every student of democracy, every enlightened socialist familiar with history, knows that popular uprisings may lead to ruin as well as to higher things. The fate of republics, democracies, and empires teaches us this. The wise Aristotle learned it centuries ago.

"When the fierce light of popular inquiry beats upon our institutions of government and property after the great war is over, where is to be found the trusted leadership that can guide and mould the forces that may upbuild—or destroy—civilization? What can wisdom accomplish if it is regarded with suspicion and distrust? How can the calm voice of reason prevail if it is known to be modulated to suit the whims of paymasters who come once a month to see that their servants have obeyed orders? . . .

"Intimately related to this greater question of spiritual leadership is the effect of trustee guardianship upon the class of men who will seek academic positions. President Lowell has called our attention sharply to this point. Men who love the smooth and easy will turn to teaching. As long as they keep silent on living issues, their salaries will be secure. It will not be important that they should arouse and inspire students in the class room. They need not be teachers. They are asked to be only purveyors of the safe and insignificant. Afraid of taking risks, they will shrink into timid pusillanimity. Risking nothing, they will make no mistakes; risking nothing, they will accomplish nothing. Perfunctory performance of statutory duties will bring the pay check. They may sit in the chimney corner and curse the trustees and president and even laugh at capitalists, providing they laugh softly. Men of will, initiative, and inventiveness, not afraid of falling into error in search for truth, will shun such a life of futile lubricity, as the free woman avoids the harem. Undoubtedly it will be possible to fill all vacant chairs and keep the number of 'learned' publications up-to-date; but to what purpose? That the belly may be full, the mind slothful with paid and pensioned ease? Those who have the great passion to create, to mould, to lead, to find new paths will look upon the university professorship as an unclean thing, or at best no thing to challenge their hope and courage."

Beard, in *The Dial*,* 64:335-6 (Apr. 11, 1918).

410. ACADEMIC FREEDOM

"Academic freedom . . . the inalienable right of every college instructor to make a fool of himself and his college by vealy, intemperate, sensational prattle about every subject under Heaven, to his classes and to the public, and still to keep on the payroll or be reft therefrom only by elaborate process . . ."

New York Times (editorial), Jan. 21, 1916.

411. PRESIDENT LOWELL ON ACADEMIC FREEDOM

"Experience has proved, and probably no one would now deny, that knowledge can advance, or at least can advance most rapidly, only by means of an unfettered search for truth on the part of those who devote their lives to seeking it in their respective fields, and by complete freedom in imparting to their pupils the truth that they have found. This has become an axiom in higher education, in spite of the fact that a searcher may discover error instead of truth, and be misled, and mislead others, thereby. We believe that if light enough is let in, the real relations of things will soon be seen, and that they can be seen in no other way. . . . One must distinguish between the matters that fall within and those that lie outside of the professor's field of study; then there is a difference in the professor's position in his class room and beyond it. These two cross divisions raise four distinct problems that may profitably be discussed in succession.

"The teaching by the professor in his class room on the subjects within the scope of his chair ought to be absolutely free. He must teach the truth as he has found it and sees it. This is the primary condition of academic freedom, and any violation of it endangers intellectual progress. . . .

"The freedom of the professor within his field of study, but outside of his class room. . . . The object of institutions of learning is not only the acquisition but also the diffusion of knowledge. Every professor must, therefore, be wholly unrestrained in publishing the results of his study in the field of his professorship. . . .

"The other half of our subject, the right of a professor to express his views without restraint on matters lying outside the sphere of his professorship. This is not a question of academic freedom in its true sense, but of the personal liberty of the citizen. . . .

"The argument in favor of a restraining power on the part of the governing boards of universities and colleges is based upon the fact that by extreme, or injudicious, remarks that shock public sentiment a professor can do great harm to the institution with which he is connected. . . .

"In spite, however, of the risk of injury to the institution, the objections to restraint upon what professors may say as citizens seem to me far greater than the harm done by leaving them free. In the first place, to impose upon the teacher in a university restrictions to which the members of other professions, lawyers, physicians, engineers and so forth, are not subjected, would produce a sense of irritation and humiliation. . . .

"There is another [objection], not less weighty, from [the standpoint] . . . of the institution itself. If a university or college censors what its professors may say, if it restrains them from uttering something that it does not approve, it thereby assumes responsibility for that which it permits them to say. This is logical and inevitable, but it is a responsibility which an institution of learning would be very unwise in assuming."

Annual Report, 1916-17, pp. 17-20. Cambridge, Mass.

412. Metternich's Carlsbad Resolutions, 1819

"1. A special representative of the ruler of each state shall be appointed for each university, with appropriate instructions and extended powers, and shall reside in the place where the university is situated. . . . The function of this agent shall be to see to the strictest enforcement of existing laws and disciplinary regulations; to observe carefully the spirit which is shown by the instructors in the university in their public lectures and regular courses, and, without directly interfering in scientific matters or in the methods of teaching, to give a salutary direction to the instruction, having in view the future attitude of the students. . . .

"2. The confederated governments mutually pledge themselves to remove from the universities or other public educational institutions all teachers who, by obvious deviation from their duty, or by exceeding the limits of their functions, or by the abuse of their legitimate influence over the youthful minds, or by propagating harmful doctrines hostile to public order or subversive of existing governmental institutions, shall have unmistakably proved their unfitness for the important office intrusted to them. . . . No teacher who shall have been removed in this manner shall be again appointed to a position in any public institution of learning in another state of the union.

"3. Those laws which have for a long period been directed against secret and unauthorized societies in the universities shall be strictly enforced. These laws apply especially to that association established some years since under the name Universal Students' Union (Allgemeine Burschenschaft), since the very conception of the society implies the utterly unallowable plan of permanent fellowship and constant communication between the various universities. . . . The governments mutually agree that such persons as shall hereafter be shown to have remained in secret or unauthorized associations, or shall have entered such associations, shall not be admitted to any public office.

"4. No student who shall be expelled from a university by a decision of the university senate which was ratified or prompted by the agent of the government, or who shall have left the institution in order to escape expulsion, shall be received in any other university. . . .

"So long as this decree shall remain in force no publication which appears in the form of daily issues, or as a serial . . . shall go to press in any state of the union without the previous knowledge and approval of the state officials. . . . Each state of the union is responsible . . . for every publication appearing under its supervision in which the honor or security of other states is infringed or their constitution or administration attacked. . . .

"The Diet shall have the right, moreover, to suppress on its own authority . . . such writings . . . as, in the opinion of a commission appointed by it, are inimical to the honor of the union, the safety of individual states, or the maintenance of peace and quiet in Germany. There shall be no appeal from such decisions, and the governments involved are bound to see that they are put into execution. . . . When a newspaper or periodical is suppressed by a decision of the Diet, the editor thereof may not within a period of five years edit a similar publication in any state of the union.

"Within a fortnight . . . from the passage of this decree, there shall convene . . . an extraordinary commission of investigation. . . . The object of the commission shall be a joint investigation, as thorough and extensive as possible, of the facts relating to the origin and manifold ramifications of the revolutionary plots and demagogical associations directed against the existing constitution and the internal peace both of the union and of the individual states."

Robinson, *Readings in European History* * (Boston, Ginn, 1906), Vol. II, pp. 547-550.

CHAPTER XVI

SOCIAL STABILITY IN A DYNAMIC SOCIETY

413. A Characteristic Attitude towards Change

"The two master-spirits of society—the Demon of Progress and the Angel of Conservatism. . . ."
Goodrich (Peter Parley), *Recollections of a Life Time* (New York, Miller Orton, 1856), p. 134.

414. An Older Attitude toward Change

"All change is error, and all error leads to hell fire."
Mohammedan doctrine.

415. Stability and Progress

" 'The beginning of civilisation is marked by an intense legality; that legality is the very condition of its existence, the bond which ties it together; but that legality—that tendency to impose a settled customary yoke upon all men and all actions—if it goes on, kills out the variability implanted by nature, and makes different men and different ages facsimiles of other men and other ages, as we see them so often. Progress is only possible in those happy cases where the force of legality has gone far enough to bind the nation together, but not far enough to kill out all varieties and destroy nature's perpetual tendency to change.' (p. 64.)

"The greatest living contrast is between the old Eastern and customary civilisations and the new Western and changeable civilisations. . . . These customary civilisations were the only ones which suited an early society. . . . But now . . . if fixity is an invariable ingredient in early civilisations, how then did any civilisation become unfixed? . . .

"To this question history gives a very clear and very remarkable answer. It is that the change from the age of status to the age of choice was first made in states where the government was to a great and growing extent a government by discussion, and where the subjects of that discussion were in some degree abstract, or, as we should say, matters of principle. . . .

"A government by discussion, if it can be borne, at once breaks down the yoke of fixed custom. The idea of the two is inconsistent. As far as it goes, the mere putting up of a subject to discussion, with the object of being guided by that discussion, is a clear admission that that subject is in no degree settled by established rule, and that men are free to choose in it. It is an admission too that there is no sacred authority—no one transcendent and divinely appointed man whom in that matter the community is bound to obey. And if a single subject or group of subjects be once admitted to discussion, ere long the habit of discussion comes to be established, the sacred charm of use and wont to be dissolved. 'Democracy,' it has been said in modern times, 'is like the grave; it takes but it does not give.' The same is true of 'discussion.' Once effectually submit a subject to that ordeal, and you can never withdraw it again; you can never again clothe it with mystery, or fence it by consecration; it remains for ever open to free choice, and exposed to profane deliberation. . . .

"If a nation has in any considerable degree gained the habit, and exhibited the capacity, to discuss these questions with freedom, and to decide them with discretion, to argue much on politics and not to argue ruinously, an enormous advance in other kinds of civilisation may confidently be predicted for it. . . . The first pre-historic men were passionate savages, with the greatest difficulty coerced into order and compressed into a state. . . . The only sufficient and effectual agent in so doing was consecrated custom; but then that custom gathered over everything, arrested all onward progress, and stayed the originality of mankind. If, therefore, a nation is able to gain the benefit of custom without the evil—if after ages of waiting it can have order and choice together—at once the fatal clog is removed, and the ordinary springs of progress, as in a modern community we conceive them, begin their elastic action. . . .

"Tolerance . . . is learned in discussion, and, as history shows, is only so learned. In all customary societies bigotry is the ruling principle. In rude places to this day any one who says anything new is looked on with suspicion, and is persecuted by opinion if not injured by penalty. One of the greatest pains to human nature is the pain of a new idea. It is, as common people say, so 'upsetting'; it makes you think that, after all, your favorite notions may be wrong, your firmest beliefs ill-founded. . . . Naturally, therefore, common men hate a new idea, and are disposed more or less to ill-treat the original man who brings it. Even nations with long habits of discussion are intolerant enough. . . . But discussion, to be successful, requires tolerance. It fails wherever, as in a French political assembly, any one who hears anything which he dislikes tries to howl it down." . . . (p. 156 ff.)

Bagehot, *Physics and Politics* (New York, Appleton, 1887).

416. THE CHANGE FROM EXTERNAL TO INTERNAL AUTHORITY

"Society is dissolving every moment, and the question is, How shall the reconstruction of authority in the minds and lives of men be made? In the past largely by the authoritarian process, by taboo, superstition, ignorance, and force. In our day this is still largely true, perhaps, but there is also an increasing process in which authority is maintained by recreating appreciation of and agreement with the values that are transmitted, with allowance for shifting values and attitudes and interests. That order of things, whether social, economic, or political, is now most secure which constantly recreates the loyalty and obedience of its members, which constantly redevelops the sources of its interest and power from interest and reflection. That order is weakest which must largely depend upon authority and force with suppression of discussion and reason and criticism."

Merriam, in *American Journal of Sociology,** 27:98 (July, 1921).

417. NATURAL CONSERVATISM

"Natural conservatism is a tendency of the human mind. It is a disposition averse from change; and it springs partly from a distrust of the unknown and a corresponding reliance on experience rather than on theoretic reasoning; partly from a faculty in men to adapt themselves to their surroundings so that what is familiar merely because of its familiarity becomes more acceptable or more tolerable than what is unfamiliar. . . . Novelties, at the first sight, are regarded as new-fangled and either futile or dangerous by the great majority of men. They frighten and irritate, they fatigue and perplex those who for the first time seek to understand them. Human nature shrinks from them and is wearied by them. Men feel that they live in the midst of mysteries; they dwell in the world like children in a dark room. Dangers from the unseen spiritual world, dangers from the unfathomed passions of other men, dangers from the forces of nature:—these all haunt the minds of men and make them fear to change from whatever experience has proved to be at least safe and endurable. And change is not only fearful, it is tiring. As men try to perceive and judge a new plan, the effort tires and overtasks their powers. The faculties of judgment and discernment ache within them. Why depart from the known which is safe to the unknown which may be dangerous?"

Cecil, *Conservatism* (London, Williams Norgate, no date), p. 9 f.

418. CONSERVATISM AND PROGRESS

"Desire to move forward and try what is new must be harmonised with distrust of the untried and fear of the dangers that may be lurking in the unknown. Wisdom is not so anxious for progress as not to be afraid of novelty; not so afraid of novelty as to be contented without progress. The two sentiments of desire to advance and fear of the dangers of moving, apparently contradictory, are in fact complementary and mutually necessary. The restraints of conservatism are the indispensable condition of the security and efficiency of progress in all regions of human activity from Parliament to a motorcar. In both a brake is necessary to safety. And restraint is not only essential to hinder what is foolish, but also to guide and control what is wisely intended and save movement from becoming vague, wild and mischievous. Progress depends on conservatism to make it intelligent, efficient and appropriate to circumstance. Without conservatism progress may be if not destructive at least futile. The expansiveness of steam and the explosiveness of petrol are only useful when they are boxed up. A cartridge without a gun is a futility. And it is only when a man is controlling his wish to get forward with a strong sense of the risk of entering the unknown that he is likely to make wise and effectual progress."

Cecil, *Conservatism* (London, Williams Norgate, no date), p. 13 f.

419. CONSERVATISM

"One of the strongest factors of social stability is the inertness, nay rather the active hostility with which human societies receive all new ideas."

Karl Pearson, quoted in *School and Society*, 12:511 (Nov. 27, 1920).

420. Opposition to Freedom of Speech

"At present, in the most civilized countries, freedom of speech is taken as a matter of course and seems a perfectly simple thing. We are so accustomed to it that we look on it as a natural right. But this right has been acquired only in quite recent times, and the way to its attainment has lain through lakes of blood. It has taken centuries to persuade the most enlightened peoples that liberty to publish one's opinions and to discuss all questions is a good and not a bad thing. Human societies (there are some brilliant exceptions) have been generally opposed to freedom of thought, or, in other words, to new ideas, and it is easy to see why.

"The average brain is naturally lazy and tends to take the line of least resistance. The mental world of the ordinary man consists of beliefs which he has accepted without questioning and to which he is firmly attached; he is instinctively hostile to anything which would upset the established order of this familiar world. . . .

"The repugnance due to mere mental laziness is increased by a positive feeling of fear. The conservative instinct hardens into the conservative doctrine that the foundations of society are endangered by any alterations in the structure. . . . Wherever that belief prevails, novel opinions are felt to be dangerous as well as annoying, and any one who asks inconvenient questions about the why and the wherefore of accepted principles is considered a pestilent person. . . . (p. 8. f.)

"The psychological motives which produce a conservative spirit hostile to new ideas are reinforced by the active opposition of certain powerful sections of the community, such as a class, a caste, or a priesthood, whose interests are bound up with the maintenance of the established order and the ideas on which it rests. . . . (p. 10.)

"A long time was needed to arrive at the conclusion that coercion of opinion is a mistake, and only a part of the world is yet convinced. That conclusion, so far as I can judge, is the most important ever reached by men." (p. 14.)

Bury, *History of Freedom of Thought* * (New York,[1] Holt, 1913).

421. Conservatism

"No one will ever comprehend the arrested civilisations unless he sees the strict dilemma of early society. Either men had no

[1] Originally published in England.

law at all, and lived in confused tribes, hardly hanging together, or they had to obtain a fixed law by processes of incredible difficulty. Those who surmounted that difficulty soon destroyed all those that lay in their own yoke. The customary discipline, which could only be imposed on any early men by terrible sanctions, continued with those sanctions, and killed out of the whole society the propensities to variation which are the principle of progress.

"Experience shows how incredibly difficult it is to get men really to encourage the principle of originality. They will admit it in theory, but in practice the old error—the error which arrested a hundred civilisations—returns again. Men are too fond of their own life, too credulous of the completeness of their own ideas, too angry at the pain of new thoughts, to be able to bear easily with a changing existence; or else, *having* new ideas, they want to enforce them on mankind—to make them heard, and admitted, and obeyed before, in simple competition with other ideas, they would ever be so naturally. (p. 57 f.)

"We can only comprehend why so many nations have not varied, when we see how hateful variation is; how everybody turns against it; how not only the conservatives of speculation try to root it out, but the very innovators invent most rigid machines for crushing the 'monstrosities and anomalies'—the new forms, out of which, by competition and trial, the best is to be selected for the future. The point I am bringing out is simple:— one most important pre-requisite of a prevailing nation is that it should have passed out of the first state of civilization into the second stage—out of the stage where permanence is most wanted into that where variability is most wanted; and you cannot comprehend why progress is so slow till you see how hard the most obstinate tendencies of human nature make that step to mankind. (p. 60-61.)

"The persecuting tendency of all savages, and, indeed, of all ignorant people, is even more striking than their imitative tendency. No barbarian can bear to see one of his nation deviate from the old barbarous customs and usages of their tribe. Very commonly all the tribe would expect a punishment from the gods if any one of them refrained from what was old, or began what was new. In modern times and in cultivated countries we regard each person as responsible only for his own actions, and do not believe, or think of believing, that the misconduct of others can bring guilt on them. Guilt to us is an individual taint consequent on choice and cleaving to the chooser. But in early ages the act of one member of the tribe is conceived to make all the tribe impious, to offend its peculiar god, to expose all the tribe to penalties from heaven. There is no 'limited liability' in the political notions of that time. The early tribe or nation is a religious partnership, on which a rash member by a sudden impiety may bring utter ruin. If the state is conceived thus, toleration becomes wicked. A permitted deviation from the transmitted ordinances becomes a simple folly. It is a sacrifice of the happiness of the greatest number. It is allowing one individual, for a moment's pleasure or a stupid whim, to bring terrible and irretrievable calamity upon all." (p. 102 f.)

Bagehot, *Physics and Politics* (New York, Appleton, 1887).

422. SCIENCE DANGEROUS FOR WOMEN

"But books of Chemistry or Electricity, and all that might lead them [females] prematurely to making philosophical experiments we would still keep from them."

Guardian of Education (London, 1803), 2:408.

423. HUXLEY ON THE REJECTION OF AUTHORITY

"Among the moral convictions most fondly held by barbarous and semi-barbarous people . . . are the convictions that authority is the soundest basis of belief; that merit attaches to a readiness to believe; that the doubting disposition is a bad one, and scepticism a sin; that when good authority has pronounced what is to be believed, and faith has accepted it, reason has no further duty. There are many excellent persons who yet hold by these principles, and it is not my present business, or intention, to discuss their views. All I wish to bring clearly before your minds is the unquestionable fact, that the improvement of natural knowledge is effected by methods which directly give the lie to all these convictions, and assume the exact reverse of each to be true.

"The improver of natural knowledge absolutely refuses to acknowledge authority, as such. For him, Scepticism is the highest of duties; blind faith the one unpardonable sin. And it cannot be otherwise, for every great advance in natural knowledge has involved the absolute rejection of authority, the cherishing of the keenest scepticism, the annihilation of the spirit of blind faith; and the most ardent votary of science holds his firmest convictions, not because the men he most venerates hold them;

not because their verity is testified by portents and wonders; but because his experience teaches him that whenever he chooses to bring these convictions into contact with their primary source, Nature—whenever he thinks fit to test them by appealing to experiment and to observation—Nature will confirm them."

Huxley, *Method and Results* (New York, Appleton, 1896 [1]), p. 40-41.

424. HERD OPINIONS

"When, therefore, we find ourselves entertaining an opinion about the basis of which there is a quality of feeling which tells us that to inquire into it would be absurd, obviously unnecessary, unprofitable, undesirable, bad form, or wicked, we may know that the opinion is a non-rational one, and probably, therefore, founded upon inadequate evidence."

Trotter, *Instincts of the Herd in Peace and War* * (New York, Macmillan, 1917), p. 44.

425. DECLINE OF AUTHORITY

"Along with . . . increasing intercourse and interaction, with all its dangers and opportunities, there has come a relaxation of the bonds of social discipline and control. I suppose none of us would be willing to believe that the movement away from dogmatism and fixed authority is anything but a movement in the right direction. But no one can view the loosening of the power of the older religious and social authorities without deep concern. We may feel sure that in time independent judgment, with the individual freedom and responsibility that go with it, will more than make good the temporary losses. But meantime there is a temporary loss. Parental authority has much less influence in controlling the conduct of children. Reverence seems to decay on every side, and boisterousness and hoodlumism to increase. Flippancy toward parental and other forms of constituted authority waxes, while obedient orderliness wanes. The domestic ties between husband and wife themselves, as well as to their children, lose something of their permanence and sanctity. The church, with its supernatural sanctions, its means of shaping the daily life of its adherents, finds its grasp slowly slipping away. We might as well frankly recognize that many of the old agencies for moralizing mankind, that kept men living decent, respectable, and orderly lives, are losing in efficiency—particularly those

[1] First edition, 1866.

agencies whose force rested in custom, tradition, and unquestioning acceptance. It is impossible for society to remain purely a passive spectator in the midst of such a scene. It must search for other agencies with which it may repair the loss, and which may produce the results the former methods are failing to secure."

Dewey, in *Elementary School Teacher*,* 3:79 (Oct., 1902).

426. Declining Stability of Character

"The 'moral unrest' so deeply penetrating all western societies, the growing vagueness and indecision of personalities, the almost complete disappearance of the 'strong and steady character' of old times, in short, the rapid and general increase of Bohemianism and Bolshevism in all societies, is an effect of the fact that not only the early primary group controlling all interests of its members on the general social basis, not only the occupational group of the mediæval type controlling most of the interests of its members on a professional basis, but even the special modern group dividing with many others the task of organizing permanently the attitudes of each of its members, is more and more losing ground. The pace of social evolution has become so rapid that special groups are ceasing to be permanent and stable enough to organize and maintain organized complexes of attitudes of their members which correspond to their common pursuits. In other words, society is gradually losing all its old machinery for the determination and stabilization of individual characters."

Thomas and Znaniecki, *The Polish Peasant in Europe and America* * (Boston, Badger, 1918), Vol. III, pp. 63-64.

427. Lessening Confidence

"There is a dangerously narrowing limit now to the confidence of the common man in the intelligence and good faith of those who direct his affairs."

Wells (and others), in *Atlantic Monthly*,* 123:111 (Jan., 1919).

428. Conservatism of the Educated

"Education ought, no doubt, to enlighten a man; but the educated classes, speaking generally, are the property-holding classes, and the possession of property does more to make a man timid than education does to make him hopeful. He is apt to underrate the power as well as the worth of sentiment; he overvalues the restraints which existing institutions impose, he has [only] a faint appreciation of the curative value of freedom, and of the tendency which brings things right when men have been left to their own devices, and have learnt from failure how to attain success."

Bryce, *American Commonwealth* * (New York, Macmillan, 1914), Vol. II, p. 256 f.

429. THE CONSERVATIVE AND HOW TO FREE HIM

"The hard and fast conservative is the man who cannot conceive that existing constitutions, institutions, and social arrangements are mechanisms for achieving social results. To him they *are* the results, they are final. If he could once cure himself of this illusion, he would be willing to admit that they grew up at haphazard and cross purposes, and mainly at periods quite unlike the present. Admitting this, he would be ready to conceive the possibility that they are as poor mechanisms for accomplishing needed social results as were the physical tools which preceded the mastery of nature by mind. He would then be free . . . to consider what improved social mechanisms or contrivances are demanded at the present day."

Dewey, in *International Journal of Ethics*,* 26:319 (April, 1916).

430. A 1914 PROPHESY

"The blindness and ultra-conservatism of many of our privileged classes on the one hand, the fanatical radicalism and one-sidedness of many of the leaders of the non-privileged on the other, would breed trouble in any social order. Unless plasticity of mind and a sense of social obligation can be instilled into our socially fortunate classes and broadminded and constructive views shall dominate the leaders of our masses, western civilization is indeed brewing for the world something worse than a French Revolution."

Ellwood, *The Social Problem* * (New York, Macmillan, 1914), p. 2.

431. THE PURPOSE OF AMELIORATIVE LEGISLATION

"The deeper if unconscious purpose of recent ameliorative legislation is, not to establish freedom, but to supply such palliatives as will make the continuance of a parasitic class possible."

Hilaire Belloc, *The Servile State* (Edinburgh, Foulis, 1913).

432. The Two Fundamentally Opposed Views of our Times

The one:

"The present social system must and shall be preserved. It rests on the sovereign will of God and the inviolable order of nature. It is like the atmosphere or the seasons—not to be challenged by human wisdom, nor reconstructed by man's craft. It came into being by operation of laws which cannot be controlled, and it will persist in spite of impudent spasms of revolt. To question this social order is intellectual stupidity and social treason. Every sign of disposition to treat these self-evident truths as legitimate subjects for debate should be disapproved, discouraged, and, if need be, suppressed."

The other:

"The existing social system must and shall be destroyed. It is a crazy mixture of accident, and design, and compromise, with a negligible unknown modicum of necessity. It is, like our tools and our amusements, the creature of our knowledge and our choice and our contrivance, to be cast aside the moment we know better or acquire more skill, or to be exchanged to suit variations of our taste. It was constructed to meet particular occasions, and, in spite of impotent opposition to the march of human progress, it will be reconstructed to fit changed conditions. To question these self-evident truths is intellectual stupidity and social treason. Every refusal to accept these positions without qualification should be taken as conclusive evidence of treachery against the general welfare. It should be denounced, discredited, and defeated."

Small, *General Sociology* * (Chicago, University of Chicago, 1905), p. 383 f.

433. How Thinking Enhanced Athenian Life

"For we have a peculiar power of thinking before we act and of acting too, whereas others are courageous from ignorance but hesitate upon reflection. And they surely are to be esteemed the bravest spirits who having the clearest sense both of the pains and pleasures of life do not on that account shrink from danger."

Pericles, in *Thucydides* (Trans. by Jowett. Oxford, Clarendon Press, 1900), Book II, par. 40.

SOCIAL STABILITY IN A DYNAMIC SOCIETY

434. Jefferson and Lincoln on Revolution

"The spirit of resistance to government is so valuable on certain occasions that I wish it always to be kept alive. It will often be exercised when wrong, but better so than not to be exercised at all."
The Writings of Thomas Jefferson (Ford editor. New York, Putnam, 1894), Vol. IV, p. 370.

"Whenever they [the American people] grow weary of their existing government they can exercise their constitutional right of amending it, or their revolutionary right to dismember or overthrow it."
Letters and Addresses of Abraham Lincoln (New York, Bell, 1903), p. 197.

435. Who are to Blame for Revolutions?

"The rebel is not self-generated. In the beginning no one is a revolutionist simply for the fun of it, however it may be after the furor of destructive power gets under way. The rebel is the product of extreme fixation and unintelligent immobilities. Life is perpetuated only by renewal. If conditions do not permit renewal to take place continuously it will take place explosively. The cost of revolutions must be charged up to those who have taken for their aim arrest of custom instead of its readjustment. The only ones who have the right to criticize 'radicals'—adopting for the moment that perversion of language which identifies the radical with the destructive rebel—are those who put as much effort into reconstruction as the rebels are putting into destruction. The primary accusation against the revolutionary must be directed against those who having power refuse to use it for ameliorations. They are the ones who accumulate the wrath that sweeps away customs and institutions in an undiscriminating avalanche. Too often the man who should be criticizing institutions expends his energy in criticizing those who would re-form them. What he really objects to is any disturbance of his own vested securities, comforts and privileged powers."
Dewey, *Human Nature and Conduct* * (New York, Holt, 1922), p. 167-8.

436. Moderation not always the True Position

"Let us not say to ourselves that the best truth always lies in moderation, in the decent average. This would perhaps be so if the majority did not think on a much lower plane than is needful. That is why it behooves others to think and hope on a higher plane than seems reasonable. The average, the decent moderation of to-day, will be the least human of things to-morrow. At the time of the Spanish Inquisition, the opinion of good sense and of the just medium was certainly that people ought not to burn too large a number of heretics; extreme and unreasonable opinions obviously demanded that they should burn none at all."

Maeterlinck, *The Measure of the Hours* * (New York, Dodd Mead, 1907), p. 99 f.

437. Freedom not yet Permanently Won

"One hears commonly the expression, 'There is no fear that this, that or the other measure—of militarism, state control of opinion, censorship, or what not—will ever be permanent because the people here have control and they will never tolerate it.' But the tyrannies do not come because the people have lost their power to resist them; they come because they have lost their desire to do so. The problem of freedom is at the bottom the problem of preserving the desire for freedom; preserving the capacity to know what it is even, to 'know it when we see it.'"

Angell, *The British Revolution and the American Democracy* * (New York, Huebsch, 1919), p. 269.

438. Need of Habits

"The teacher's prime concern should be to ingrain into the pupil that assortment of habits that shall be most useful to him throughout life. Education is for behavior, and habits are the stuff of which behavior consists.... The great thing in all education is *to make our nervous system our ally instead of our enemy*. It is to fund and capitalize our acquisitions, and live at ease upon the interest of the fund. *For this we must make automatic and habitual, as early as possible, as many useful actions as we can,* and as carefully guard against the growing into ways that are likely to be disadvantageous. The more of the details of our daily life we can hand over to the effortless custody of automatism, the more our higher powers of mind will be set free for their own proper work. There is no more miserable human being than one in whom nothing is habitual but indecision, and for whom the lighting of every cigar, the drinking of every cup, the time of rising and going to bed every day, and the beginning of every bit of work are subjects of express volitional deliberation. Full half the time of such a man goes to the deciding or regretting of matters which ought to be so ingrained in him as practically not to exist for his consciousness at all. If there be such daily duties not yet ingrained in any one of my hearers, let him begin this very hour to set the matter right."

James, *Talks to Teachers* * (New York, Holt, 1899), p. 66 f.

439. Permanent Progressiveness

"Permanent progressiveness is found where the social aggregate is characterized by a cohesion among its parts which is neither too little nor too great. An excess and a deficiency of individual mobility have been shown to be alike incompatible with that persistent tendency toward internal rearrangement which we call progressiveness."

Fiske, *Outlines of Cosmic Philosophy* * (Boston, Houghton Mifflin, 1891 [1]), Vol. II, p. 282.

440. The Intellectual Interest

Every modern minded person is supposed to assume that growing is the world's destiny and should be its policy. However, with respect to the vested interests of their own class most men repudiate this premise and resist the policy. Instead of welcoming the enquiry, "How do the claims of my interest comport with the development of welfare on the whole?" most men refuse to see or admit that their interest is ever questionable. We may flatter ourselves that civilisation has passed from a regime of force to a regime of reason, but in this pretended regime of reason each vested interest continues to assert the special privilege of unreason, the maintenance of itself by force.

The intellectual interest is in such matters unique. It alone asks no favors. It alone abhors status. It alone rejects force. Science if true to itself wishes no support for its position other than a fair hearing. The only thing it fears is a denial of scrutiny. The intellectual interest is at all times ready to stake

[1] First edition, 1874.

all on a re-examination. All that it holds, it holds tentatively—subject to change upon further light.

Such a position of supreme allegiance to the new truth whatever it may prove to be is abhorrent to the satisfied holders of vested privilege. On such a basis they are never safe. Their wealth or their social position or their creed might not stand the test. Scrutiny might destroy. Impartial scrutiny is thus not yet a welcome co-partner in the world of affairs. So long as science consents to be hand-maiden, so long as she will invent and exploit in the service of other interests, for that long she is most welcome. But so soon as the intellectual interest proposes to project into real life the idea that the *status quo* is debatable, that its continuance may be only provisional, that the true social welfare may demand something else; then the intellectual interest becomes a disturber of the peace. So long as it remains "academic"—that is keeps out of the actual world—or is merely gymnastic, so long the world patronizes and approves. But when the intellectual interest with its impartial scrutiny demands a hearing in the directors' meeting, or in the legislative committee room, or in the counsels of campaign managers, or as umpire between laborers and employers, or in reconciling ecclesiastical differences, then it is jeered or sneered or browbeaten out of court.

Adapted with modifications from Small, *General Sociology* (Chicago, Univ. of Chicago Press, 1905), pp. 389 ff.

441. Change Inherent and Inevitable

"Change is inherent in the very process of civilization, and, so far as it concerns human institutions, practically all embracing. It is only too true that many among us have been hoping and praying that affairs will at last quiet down and let civilization catch its breath. It is not improbable that the war has acted temporarily to hasten the process of change; but, taking centuries together, change will never cease. On the contrary it will almost certainly become increasingly rapid. What, do you ask, can be the justification for so disquieting a prophecy? Consider the facts. Civilization takes its character from, or better finds its character in, the fabric of human achievement known to us as tools, machines, and the like, and the correlative customs, institutions, and systems of thought. See what the single invention of the steam engine has done to change the affairs of men, or the telegraph, or the germ theory of disease. Every first class invention makes far-reaching demands for changes in human behavior and relationships. The increasing aggregation of human affairs hastens the spread of change. More first-class inventions have been made in the past two hundred years than in the two thousand years before. We have every reason to expect, unless civilization goes to pieces, that the next two hundred years will show even more invention, because thought begets thought, and tested thought begets fruitful thought. If this be so, more change will come, and so *ad infinitum*. As inevitably as civilization continues to exist and thought continues to be itself, just so inevitably will changes come. We face, then, a world of inherent and unending change. What the changes will be, whither they will carry us, we know not. The only thing we can assert with certainty is that we face rapidly changing forces which are shaping an unknown future."

Kilpatrick, in *Teachers College Record,** 22:132 f. (March, 1921).

CHAPTER XVII

THE STATE AND EDUCATION

442. The New Road to Equality

"This newer tendency, through legislation, to give special advantages in order to maintain a balance of equality has had some unfortunate results. But the solution of the problem of class-conflict will not come through returning to the older attitude, even if that were possible. A continuation of the *laissez-faire* individualism of the nineteenth century would have resulted in the creation of a new aristocracy based on wealth rather than on birth,—in the beginning, at least,—which, if unrestrained, would have developed all the objectionable features of feudalism. A return to this older attitude, the reincorporation into our legal and political practice of the older interpretation of equality before the law, would mean, not the saving of democracy, but its destruction."

Clark, in *Atlantic Monthly*,* 128:78 (July, 1921).

443. The Present Outlook

"The supreme problem of the future will be, not how to thwart the movement towards State control, but how to direct it in such a way as to achieve legitimate ends without sacrificing the individuality of the citizen. He who clings blindly to the *status quo* in legislation, while economic, political, and moral conditions are rapidly changing, is a menace to the very social order he affects to defend. If I were asked to name the worst enemy of the existing social order, I should point to the man who opposes any and every proposal for social amelioration. There are, I fear, many men to-day, men often of great ability and even of exemplary private character, whose political opinions are based upon an unalterable conviction that every new idea or proposal in politics is impracticable. These very men may be quite open-minded when it is a question of applying new machinery or new discoveries within the sphere of the particular form of industry with which they are themselves associated. But they dismiss any new idea in politics as impracticable if it does not square with preconceptions which they have never submitted to the test of serious examination. Such men are unassailable by argument; and, by their attitude of uncompromising opposition to reform, they are the unconscious instruments of social catastrophe. By combining with other forces, they may succeed in delaying reforms; but the ultimate result of their effort, if successful for a time, must be to give a plausibility and an irresistible power to the demand for revolutionary change in the near future. . . .

"When I reflect upon the power of the forces that to-day impel toward legislative action; upon the peril that the action thus taken may be injudicious and harmful; upon the need of the co-operation of all classes, of mutual sympathy, of comprehensive views, and of wise statesmanship—when I reflect upon these things, I cannot but feel that we are on the eve of a great crisis in the nation's history. We have reached a stage when the ignorance of the citizen is a menace and his apathy a crime. Among the many disturbing facts with which we have to reckon, one stands out pre-eminently. Each of us has gone too much his own way. Education, for example, has never become with us a really national question; and the subject has only awakened a general interest under the stimulus of sectarian conflict or of the loss of foreign markets. Our employers, as a class, have gone too much their own way, lacking even the generosity that is based on sound policy. The employed have borrowed from their masters the ruthless principle of getting as much as possible by giving as little as possible, and threaten to pass under the leadership of the fanatical reformers who hope for social salvation through the propagation of a class war. The air is full of remedies more or less deserving of attention. But the one supreme need is that, as a nation we pull together."

W. Jethro Brown, *Underlying Principles of Modern Legislation* (New York, Dutton, 1915), pp. 316-8.

444. ANARCHISM, SOCIALISM, AND LAISSEZ-FAIRE

(a) In the popular mind, an Anarchist is a person who throws bombs and commits other outrages, either because he is more or less insane, or because he uses the pretense of extreme political opinions as a cloak for criminal proclivities. This view is, of course, in every way inadequate. Some Anarchists believe in throwing bombs; many do not. Men of almost every other shade of opinion believe in throwing bombs in suitable circumstances. ... And those Anarchists who are in favor of bomb-throwing do not in this respect differ on any vital principle from the majority of the community. ... Anarchists, like Socialists, usually believe in the doctrine of the class war, and if they use bombs, it is as Governments use bombs, for purposes of war: but for every bomb manufactured by an Anarchist, many millions are manufactured by Governments, and for every man killed by Anarchist violence, many millions are killed by the violence of States. We may, therefore, dismiss from our minds the whole question of violence, which plays so large a part in the popular imagination, since it is neither essential nor peculiar to those who adopt the Anarchist position.

Anarchism, as its derivation indicates, is the theory which is opposed to every kind of forcible government. It is opposed to the State as the embodiment of the force employed in the government of the community. Such government as Anarchism can tolerate must be free government, not merely in the sense that it is that of a majority, but in the sense that it is that assented to by all. Anarchists object to such institutions as the police and the criminal law, by means of which the will of one part of the community is forced upon another part. In their view, the democratic form of government is not very enormously preferable to other forms so long as minorities are compelled by force or its potentiality to submit to the will of majorities. Liberty is the supreme good in the Anarchist creed, and liberty is sought by the direct road of abolishing all forcible control over the individual by the community. (Taken with minor changes from Russell, *Proposed Roads to Freedom*,* New York, Holt, 1919, p. 32 f.)

(b) By Socialism is meant any theory or system of social organization which would abolish, either entirely or in great part, the individual effort and competition on which modern society in great measure rests, and substitute for it coöperative action. It would at the same time introduce a more perfect and equal distribution of the products of labor, and would make land and capital, as the instruments and means of production, the joint possession of the members of the community.

The term Socialism is in point of fact rather a tendency than a strictly definable body of doctrine. Any definition of Socialism is sure either to include some views which certain would regard as not Socialistic or to exclude others which would claim to be included. The central tendency of meanings, however, would seem to be that given above. (Adapted mainly from the Century Dictionary, under Socialism.)

(c) The principle of Laissez-faire is suggested by the meaning of the term, Let-alone. It stands for a policy of non-interference with the free play of social forces. In economics it would advocate free-trade as opposed to protection. In general it would reduce the sphere of governmental action to lowest terms, and is accordingly often spoken of as the police power theory, because it would limit the function of government to the bare protection of the citizens from violence directed either against themselves or their property. The most thoroughgoing advocate of this policy is Herbert Spencer. "In his *Social Statics,* published in 1850, he holds it to be the essential duty of government to *protect*—to maintain men's rights to life, to personal liberty and to property; and the theory that the government ought to undertake other offices besides that of protector he regards as an untenable theory. Each man has a right to the fullest exercise of all his faculties, compatible with the same right in others. This is the fundamental law of equal freedom, which it is the duty and the only duty of the state to enforce. If the state goes beyond this duty, it becomes, not a protector, but an aggressor. Thus all state regulations of commerce, all religious establishments, all government relief of the poor, all state systems of education and of sanitary superintendence, even the state currency and the post-office, stand condemned, not only as ineffective for their respective purposes, but as involving violations of man's natural liberty." (Adapted from the *Encyclopædia Britannica* * article on *Government,* XII, p. 298.)

445. Universal Public Education an Evil

"That the whole or any large part of the education of the people should be in State hands, I go as far as any one in deprecating. All that has been said of the importance of individuality of character, and diversity in opinions and modes of conduct, involves, as of the same unspeakable importance, diversity of education. A general State education is a mere contrivance for moulding people to be exactly like one another: and as the mould in which it cases them is that which pleases the predominant power in the government, whether this be a monarch, a priesthood, an aristocracy, or the majority of the existing generation, in proportion as it is efficient and successful, it establishes a despotism over the mind, leading by natural tendency to one over the body. An education established and controlled by the State, should only exist, if at all, as one among many competing experiments, carried on for the purpose of example and stimulus, to keep the others up to a certain standard of excellence."

Mill, *Liberty* (London Parker, 1859), p. 190 f.

446. THE MICHIGAN PRIVATE AND PAROCHIAL SCHOOL LAW OF 1921

"*Section 1.* The superintendent of public instruction is hereby given supervision of all the private, denominational and parochial schools of this state in such manner as is hereinafter provided. . . . It is the intent of this act that the sanitary conditions of such schools, the courses of study therein, and the qualifications of the teachers thereof shall be of the same standard as provided by the general school laws of the state. . . .

"*Section 3.* No person shall teach or give instruction in any of the regular or elementary grade studies in any private, denominational or parochial school within this state who does not hold a certificate such as would qualify him or her to teach in like grades of the public schools of the state. . . .

"*Section 5.* The superintendent of public instruction by himself, his assistants, or any duly authorized agent, shall have authority at any time to investigate and examine into the conditions of any school operating under this act as to the matters hereinbefore set forth and it shall be the duty of such school to admit such superintendent, his assistants or authorized agents and to submit for examination its sanitary condition, the record of enrollment of pupils, its courses of study as set forth in Section 1 of this act and the qualifications of its teachers."

School and Society, 14:23 f. (July 9, 1921).

447. ROMAN CATHOLIC SCHOOLS

"They [Roman Catholic schools of the United States] have all sprung from Catholic impulse and they all share in the common aim of the preservation of the Catholic faith of our children and the salvation of their souls."

Shields, *Philosophy of Education* * (Washington, Catholic Education Press, 1917), p. 7.

THE STATE AND EDUCATION

448. Obligation to Patronize Parochial Schools

"All Catholic parents are bound to send their children to the parochial schools, unless either at home or in other Catholic schools they may sufficiently and evidently provide for the Christian education of their children, or unless it be lawful to send them to other schools on account of a sufficient cause approved by the bishop, and with opportune cautions and remedies. As to what is a Catholic school, it is left to the judgment of the Ordinary to define." (3rd Plenary Council, Baltimore, 1884.)

Burn, *Catholic School System in the United States* * (New York, Benziger, 1912), p. 195.

449. The Roman Catholic Position

"If, upon examination, it should be found that the Catholic school is incapable of educating for citizenship or that it neglects its obvious duty in the attainment of this aim, it would become the duty of the state to interfere. On the other hand, if the Catholic school should prove itself capable and show that it does, in fact, attain the ultimate aim of state education as well or even better than the state system, then it is obvious that the state system should not only tolerate the Catholic school, but it should, as far as possible, free the portion of the population who support and attend the Catholic school from the burden of supporting public schools, which while less efficient in attaining the aim of the State, prove themselves wholly inadequate for the attainment of the higher aims maintained by the Church and cherished by the Catholic population."

Shields, in *Catholic Education Association*, Vol. 13, No. 1, p. 55, Nov., 1916.

450. Foreign Language Schools

"The almost universal rule in the schools is to teach in English for half a day, and in Polish, Italian, Portuguese, French or Greek for half a day. These bilingual schools, of which there are over 90 in Massachusetts . . . Many of these teachers have but a limited knowledge of the English language; comparatively few speak it fluently, some do not speak it at all. Such lay teachers as are employed are, generally speaking, wholly unqualified. . . ." (p. 148.)

"The atmosphere of any one of these schools depends mainly

upon the attitude of the pastor of the church with which it is connected. While some of these pastors are thoroughly imbued with American ideals, the majority are of foreign birth, education and training, so intensely devoted to their native land that their patriotism permits no divided allegiance; hence any special emphasis upon the study of English or upon American traditions and ideals, which often the Superior in charge would gladly undertake, does not enlist their sympathy or meet with their approval." (p. 149.)

For compulsory attendance purposes, the Massachusetts law requires the local school committee to approve private schools, "when the instruction in all the studies required by law is in the English language, and when they are satisfied that such instruction equals in thoroughness and efficiency, and in progress made therein, the public schools in the same city or town." (Rev. Laws of Mass., ch. 44, sec. 2.) (p. 151.)

Massachusetts Report of the Committee on Immigration, 1914.

451. THE OREGON SCHOOL LAW OF 1922

(Adopted Nov. 7, 1922, at a referendum by a vote of 106,996 to 93,349.)

Purpose: "Requiring any parent, guardian or other person having control, charge or custody of a child over eight and under sixteen years of age, from and after September 1, 1926, to send such child to a public school during the entire school year, excepting: (a) children physically unable; (b) children who have completed the eighth grade; (c) children between the ages of eight and ten living more than one and one-half miles, and children over ten years of age living more than three miles from a public school, except when transportation is furnished; (d) children taught by parent or private teacher."

Arguments (selections from those given in the official election pamphlet):

(a) Affirmative (by certain ones speaking for various Masonic bodies):

. . . .

"The assimilation and education of our foreign-born citizens in the principles of our government, the hopes and inspiration of our people, are best secured by and through attendance of all children in our public schools.

"We must now halt those coming to our country from forming groups, establishing schools, and thereby bringing up their chil-

THE STATE AND EDUCATION

dren in an environment often antagonistic to the principles of our government.

"Mix the children of the foreign born with the native born, and the rich with the poor. Mix those with prejudices in the public school melting pot for a few years while their minds are plastic, and finally bring out the finished product—a true American.

. . . . . .

"When every parent in our land has a child in our public school, then and only then will there be united interest in the growth and higher efficiency of our public schools.

"Our children must not under any pretext, be it based upon money, creed or social status, be divided into antagonistic groups, there to absorb the narrow views of life as they are taught. If they are so divided, we will find our citizenship composed and made up of cliques, cults and factions each striving, not for the good of the whole, but for the supremacy of themselves. A divided school can no more succeed than a divided nation."

(b) Negative (by a committee of Lutherans):

"This bill if enacted into law would be

A Terrific Blow to Personal Liberty

"Who owns your child? The state? Do not you? Who feeds and clothes your child? The state? Not while you are living and able to care for your own. *Why* do you feed and clothe your child? Because it is *your child*. If you don't own your own child, what in the wide world do you own?

"Now if you own your child and are in duty bound to feed and clothe it, you certainly have 'some say' about your child's education and its teacher. The state has a right to compel you to educate your child, just as it has a right to compel you to feed and clothe your child. But the state has no more right to choose the teacher for your child and the school it shall attend than it has to tell you where to buy your child's clothing and what style of clothing it must wear. This bill, if enacted into law, will deal *a terrific blow to your constitutional rights, confiscate your parental authority, and undermine your personal liberty.*

"It will also

Seriously Curtail Your Religious Liberty

"Under the constitution of the United States and of the State of Oregon you enjoy religious liberty; that is, the liberty to worship God according to the dictates of your conscience and to rear your child according to your religion. If you see fit to send your child to a school in which the religion of your choice is taught, not one day in the week, but every day, and the whole training of the child is permeated by such religion, the state, under the constitution, *must not prohibit you from doing so.* . . .

(c) Negative (by certain citizens of Portland):

"This measure imitates the method of public education which brought Prussia to her deserved destruction—giving the state dictatorial powers over the training of children and destroying independence of character and freedom of thought.

Method of Bolshevist Russia

"In present day Russia the Bolshevist government treats the child as the ward of the state. This measure proposes to adopt this method and to substitute state control for the authority and guidance of the parents and is destructive of American independence.

Overcrowding of Schools and Increased Taxes

"We, in Oregon, are justly proud of our school system but we have already felt the burden of taxes necessary for its support. If the number of children now attending the public schools is to be increased by adding those now taught in private schools it is inevitable that overcrowding must result, and it is also certain that taxes must be materially increased or that the present standards of instruction must be materially lowered."

(d) Negative (by certain principals of non-sectarian private schools):

" . . . The public schools necessarily and properly educate the vast majority, but by methods exacted by large numbers. The private schools educate comparatively few but with more attention to the individual. The ordinary branches of learning are acquired in both systems. The public schools by their independent position offer varied opportunities and individual development impossible or unsuitable in the public schools. . . .

"We object to the proposed law as it directly affects us in the following respects:

"1. It will destroy the capital invested in our schools. . . .

"2. It will deprive us and our teachers of the right to earn a living in a lawful occupation. . . .

"3. This law will destroy schools which provide desirable methods and courses of study, which the public schools have not adopted and probably never can adopt."

(e) Negative (by the Catholic Civic Rights Association):

"The right of the parent to select the mental and moral training of the child is fundamental and inalienable. It is the most primary right recognized by enlightened countries. That right cannot be invaded without violating the constitutional guarantees. . . . For more than 140 years these private schools have been maintained and they exist in every state in the Union. They are thoroughly efficient in every department of instruction. They carry the same course of study as the public schools, and these courses are supervised by the superintendent of public instruction. . . .

"All of the private schools give instruction in civics and American history, and patriotic exercises, at least equal in amount to such courses in the public schools, and with text books approved by the department of public instruction. No foreign language is used as a medium of instruction; all use English. Few of the students attending private schools are children of foreign born parents. The vast majority of the children of foreign born parentage in Oregon attend the public schools. . . .

"The proposers are the aggressors, and have forced this issue upon the public. Persons who arouse racial or religious prejudices as a means of securing place or power will not be convinced by any showing, but the broad, liberal-minded American wants to know the facts. He will realize that this measure will create a tremendous burden of taxation, and that it is an invasion of fundamental rights guaranteed in terms by the Constitution of Oregon."

Official State Election Pamphlet, 1922, pp. 21-32.

CHAPTER XVIII

HOW SHALL WE CONCEIVE EDUCATION

452. EDUCATION IN THE WIDEST SENSE

"In the widest sense of the word a man is *educated,* either for good or evil, by everything that he experiences from the cradle to the grave. But in the more limited and usual sense, the term education is confined to the efforts made of set purpose to train men in a particular way—the efforts of the grown up part of the community to inform the intellect and mould the character of the young; and more especially to the labors of professional educators or schoolmasters."

Chambers' *Encyclopædia* (London, Chambers, 1884), Vol. III, p. 771.

453. ONE CONCEPTION OF EDUCATION

"What is the business of a *teacher?* . . . His position is strictly that of a conveyor of knowledge—moral and intellectual—to a yet unoccupied and growing mind. To do this successfully, requires that his instruction should carry to that waiting mind a conviction of its *truth,* and that he should also *connect* that truth with the *duties* of life."

Mansfield, *American Education* (New York, Barnes, 1851), p. 65.

454. STEIN'S EDUCATION AS HARMONIOUS UNFOLDING

"Education is the harmonious and equable evolution of the human faculties by a method based upon the nature of the mind for developing all the faculties of the soul, for stirring up and nourishing all the principles of life, while shunning all one-sided culture and taking account of the sentiments upon which the strength and worth of men depend."

Quoted in Ruediger, *Principles of Education* (Boston, Houghton Mifflin, 1910), p. 74.

455. Pestalozzi's Education as Unfolding from Within

"Sound education stands before me symbolized by a tree planted near fertilizing waters. A little seed, which contains the design of the tree, its form and proportions, is placed in the soil. See how it germinates and expands into trunk, branches, leaves, flowers, and fruit! The whole tree is an uninterrupted chain of organic parts, the plan of which existed in its seed and root. Man is similar to the tree. In the new-born child are hidden those faculties which are to unfold during life. The individual and separate organs of his being form themselves gradually into unison and build up humanity in the image of God.... It is not the educator who puts new powers and faculties into man, and imparts to him breadth and life. He only takes care that no untoward influence shall disturb nature's march of developments."

Krüsi, *Pestalozzi* (Cincinnati, Wilson Hinkle, 1875), pp. 159-160.

456. The Meaning of Development

"Is the child the germ of the man in the preformation sense? As regards the body in its principal outward and visible characteristics, we may answer yes, and accept, in a sense, the corollary of liberty. We can do little if anything with the body besides giving it freedom to grow. The food, sunshine, fresh air, sleep, rest, and exercise, demanded by it (as interpreted, however, by our best study of it, not by its immediate inclination), furnish the best regimen for its growth. In the main, the final and good result was contained with a certain uniqueness in the original germ. Our part is to furnish the favorable conditions for its realization.

"But when we come to the psychological, the situation is quite otherwise. Here conscious, intentional human guidance and redirection are necessary in far greater degree in order to reach a result fitted to meet the inevitable demands of life. We may take two cases as typical of all others, to show the part necessarily played by society in 'developing' the child. A baby's prattle contains many varied sounds: some one of these will by chance approximate '*ma-ma*.' This sound will be noted by the mother, and the child will receive approval accordingly. The repetition of this satisfaction with the accompanying disregard of the 'mere prattle' will fix the word as one of the child's accomplishments. Now this word evidently came from the child's original stock of tendencies; in this sense it has been 'developed.' But it was not uniquely contained in that stock. It survived from among very many possibilities; all of which were equally contained in the original stock. In a true sense, there was a struggle for existence among these many babbling sounds. The word *ma-ma* survived through no intrinsic worth or merit in it, but solely by reason of outside selection. This is what 'development' means in this case. Nature furnished a variety of possibilities; society selected the one suited to its purpose. In this way any language, as English or French, is 'developed' from the child's native stock of responses; but clearly we cannot say that either language or any language was present in that original stock.

"The second instance shows the action of social disapproval, the psychology, however, being much the same in both cases. A child has, among other reactions to an annoying situation, that of anger. The careful parent sees to it that this reaction is left unsatisfied, at the same time satisfying other more approved forms of reaction. By the law of habit formation, this rejected reaction tends to be called into play less often, until in the 'well-bred' person, anger has small place. Here anger was contained in the original stock—probably as a very strong natural predisposition—but was not allowed to reach its maximum possible strength, because in existing social conditions the child was counted to be better off without it. These two instances may be taken as typical of all learning, and consequently of all 'development' in the mental and moral realm.

"To sum up the whole discussion, the word 'development' as applied to the child, covers a wide range, the extremes of which can still be easily differentiated. At the one extreme, the bodily, are certain elements so fixed in the original germ that they will, if permitted by passively favorable conditions, unfold with a minimum of guidance into their full and proper realization. Such, for example, are all those things that distinguish man as an animal from other animals. So far as these are functional, they are concerned, largely at any rate, with our survival on the animal plane. According to biological evolution, the elements at this extreme represent our oldest inheritance. At the other extreme are those elements, and their arrangement in our psychical make up, which have to do with adaptation to the most recent part of our social inheritance. The latter elements have been fixed in our several individual characters by the action of our social environment in selecting from among our native reactions those which best fit us to utilize and control this environment."

Kilpatrick, *Froebel's Kindergarten Principles* * (New York, Macmillan, 1916), pp. 86-90.

457. A Definition of Education

Education is such an ordering of individual experience in the light of past experiences that through the resulting character modifications richer experience accrues to all concerned.

458. A Definition of Education

Education is the process by which the individual comes into continually increasing possession of himself and his powers through continually increased participation in the race achievement.

459. The Task of Early Education

"The peculiar problem of the early grades is, of course, to get hold of the child's natural impulses and instincts, and to utilize them so that the child is carried on to a higher plane of perception and judgment, and equipped with more efficient habits; so that he has an enlarged and deepened consciousness and increased control of powers of action. Wherever this result is not reached, play results in mere amusement and not in educative growth."

Dewey, *School and Society* * (Chicago, University of Chicago, 1915), p. 123.

460. The Happiness of Childhood

"Childhood . . . with all its extravagancies and uncertainties, its effusions and reticences, . . . remains a standing proof of a life wherein growth is normal not an anomaly, activity a delight not a task, and where habit-forming is an expansion of power not its shrinkage. Habit and impulse may war with each other, but it is a combat between the habits of adults and the impulses of the young, and not, as with the adult, a civil warfare whereby personality is rent asunder."

Dewey, *Human Nature and Conduct* * (New York, Holt, 1922), p. 99.

461. Deferred Values

"Education . . . as traditionally conducted, . . . strikingly exhibits a subordination of the living present to a remote and precarious future. To prepare, to get ready, is its key-note. The actual outcome is lack of adequate preparation, of intelligent adaptation. The professed exaltation of the future turns out in practice a blind following of tradition, a rule of thumb muddling along from day to day; or, as in some of the projects called industrial education, a determined effort on the part of one class of the community to secure *its* future at the expense of another class. If education were conducted as a process of fullest utilization of present resources, liberating and guiding capacities that are now urgent, it goes without saying that the lives of the young would be much richer in meaning than they are now. It also follows that intelligence would be kept busy in studying all indications of power, all obstacles and perversions, all products of the past that throw light upon present capacity, and in forecasting the future career of impulse and habit now active—not for the sake of subordinating the latter but in order to treat them intelligently. As a consequence whatever fortification and expansion of the future that is possible will be achieved—as it is now dismally unattained."

Dewey, *Human Nature and Conduct* * (New York, Holt, 1922), p. 269 f.

462. Growth as an Aim and Ideal

"Does not . . . the conception of growth imply something final and remote toward which growth is directed? Must we not conceive of growth as approximation to a far-away goal? If so, growth cannot be an aim and ideal except in a secondary sense. This question raises some of the deepest issues of philosophy. Is the universe static or dynamic? Is rest superior to movement as a sign of true reality? Is change merely a falling away from or an approach to something fixed, changeless? Is evolution a positive thing, a reflex of power; or is it negative, due to defect and the effort to pass beyond it? An adequate discussion of such questions would take us far beyond the limits of this article. In addition to noting that the philosophy of education—here as elsewhere—finally leads into general philosophy, we must content ourselves with two remarks.

"In the first place, the conception of growth as merely a

means of reaching something which is superior to growth and beyond it, is a survival of theories of the universe as being essentially static. These theories have been expelled by the progress of science from our notions of Nature. Motion, change, process, are fundamental. In the last half century these same ideas have been successfully applied to the life and structure of living things, plants and animals. The moral sciences, to which education belongs, have become the last refuge of ideas which have lost their intellectual repute elsewhere. The scientific presumption is working against them everywhere.

"In the second place, even if our ultimate philosophy accepts a static conception of reality to which growth is relative (a position not here accepted), yet the educator, if his aims are to be at once definite and capable of support upon the basis of ascertained fact, must start from the process of growth. He must obtain from it clues and hints as to the nature of the final end, instead of trying to decide what is and what is not growth on the basis of a conception of an ultimate end. Opinions as to the latter differ widely. To start from that end is to involve education in disputes that cannot be decided except by personal taste or the acceptance of external authority. The physical growth of a child can, however, be decided by tests applied to present conditions—observable and recorded changes in height, weight, and other phenomena. These things, and not an ideal of an ultimate physical perfection, guide the wise physician and parent in estimating whether a child is growing, standing still, or retrograding. The problem of the educator is, likewise, to devise means of studying and discovering changes actually going on in the mental and moral disposition of pupils, and to construct criteria for determining what these changes signify with respect to growth. Only as the philosophy of education recognizes that for *its* purposes, at all events, growth is the chief aim and ideal, can philosophy be applied intelligently to the specific facts of education, instead of remaining a body of remote and inapplicable—even though lofty—conceptions."

Dewey, article on Aims and Ideals of Education in Foster Watson (Editor), *Encyclopædia and Dictionary of Education* (London, Pitman, 1921).

463. INTEREST IN THE ROUTINE

"*It is possible for the mind to develop interest in a routine or mechanical procedure, if conditions are continually supplied which demand that mode of operation and preclude any other sort.* I frequently hear dulling devices and empty exercises defended and extolled because 'the children take such an "interest" in them.' Yes, that is the worst of it; the mind, shut out from worthy employ and missing the taste of adequate performance, comes down to the level of that which is left to it to know and do."

Dewey, *Child and Curriculum* * (Chicago, University of Chicago, 1902), p. 35 f.

464. A Former Attitude towards Childhood

(The "infant school" of a century ago included children from about two to seven years of age. The following excerpts from a manual in actual use then will give some indication of the prevailing ideas.)

The song to be sung as the children marched in each morning:

"We'll all take our places, and shew no wry faces,
We'll say all our lessons distinctly and slow:
For if we don't do it, our teacher will know it,
And into that corner we surely must go." (p. 35.)

A hymn sung by the children:

"My thoughts are vain, my heart is hard,
My temper apt to rise,
And when I would be on my guard
It takes me by surprise.

"Often, when I begin to pray,
And lift my feeble cry,
Some thought of folly or of play,
Draws off my heart from thee.

"O look with pity in thine eye,
Soften a heart so hard;
O do not slight my feeble cry,
My Saviour and my God." (p. 20.)

Total depravity was explicitly taught:

"Yes, I was even born in sin,
And all my heart is bad within." (p. 66.)

The days of "swat the fly" had not then come:

> "I must not touch a little fly,
> For if I pinch it, it will die." (p. 47.)

A formal intellectualism pervaded all:

> "What is the kind of animals called which have wings and fly?
> Volatiles.
> Does the Cock belong to this race?
> He does.
> Where does he live?
> He is a tame fowl and lives in farmers' yards.
> For what is he remarkable?
> He is very bold.
> What bad use is made of these fowls?
> Men set them to fight each other merely to see which will conquer.
> How do they fight?
> By biting and scratching, and they will continue to fight till one kills the other.
> Which are wicked, the cocks for fighting, or the men for setting them to fight?
> The cocks are not wicked; they do not know what is right, but the men are wicked and cruel." (p. 260.)

> "Can you tell, dear children, what kind of spirit God is?
> God is an infinite spirit, Omnipotent, Omnipresent, Omniscient, Eternal, Holy, Wise, Just, Good, True, Merciful, Unchangeable." (p. 43.)

> "What is a spirit?
> That which thinks, knows and loves, without a body.
> Have you a spirit?
> I have; my soul is a spirit and can think when my eyes are shut and when my body is asleep." (p. 42.)

Information and admonition were combined in "attractive" verses:

> "To make one pint it takes four gills,
> Which tipplers drink for pleasure:

Two pints it takes to make one quart
  And all should give good measure.

Four quarts it takes to make one gallon,
  All those who cheat, must fare ill;
Thirty-one gallons and one half
  Will fill a common barrel.

Two pipes it takes to make one tun
  Of brandy, wine or rum,
These, if men drink, 'twill lead them on,
  Until they are undone." (p. 191.)

Infant School Manual (Worcester, Mass., 1830).

CHAPTER XIX

THE EDUCATIVE PROCESS: SUBJECT MATTER AND CURRICULUM

465. "Mr. Dooley" on the Curriculum

"It makes no difference what you teach a boy so long as he doesn't like it."
Quoted in *School and Society*, 1:625.

466. Wisdom and Knowledge

"Knowledge comes, but wisdom lingers."
Tennyson, *Locksley Hall*, Line 141.

467. Valuation of Subject Matter

"If we start from the standpoint of the active powers of the children concerned, we shall measure the utility of the new subject matter and new modes of skill by the way in which they promote the growth of these powers. We shall not insist upon tangible material products, nor upon what is learned being put to further use at once in some visible way, nor even demand evidence that the children have become morally improved in some respect: save as the growth of powers is itself a moral gain."
Dewey, *Interest and Effort* * (Boston, Houghton Mifflin, 1913), pp. 63-4.

468. The Child and the Curriculum

"The fundamental factors in the educative process are an immature, undeveloped being; and certain social aims, meanings, values incarnate in the matured experience of the adult. The educative process is the due interaction of these forces. Such a conception of each in relation to the other as facilitates completest and freest interaction is the essence of educational theory.

"But here comes the effort of thought. It is easier to see the conditions in their separateness, to insist upon one at the expense of the other, to make antagonists of them, than to discover a reality to which each belongs. (p. 7 f). . . . When this happens a really serious practical problem—that of interaction—is transformed into an unreal, and hence insoluble, theoretic problem. Instead of seeing the educative process steadily and as a whole, we see conflicting terms. We get the case of the child *vs.* the curriculum; of the individual nature *vs.* social culture. (p. 8.) . . .

"What, then, is the problem? It is just to get rid of the prejudicial notion that there is some gap in kind (as distinct from degree) between the child's experience and the various forms of subject matter that make up the course of study. From the side of the child, it is a question of seeing how his experience already contains within itself elements—facts and truths—of just the same sort as those entering into the formulated study; and, what is of more importance, of how it contains within itself the attitudes, the motives, and the interests which have operated in developing and organizing the subject-matter to the plane which it now occupies. From the side of the studies, it is a question of interpreting them as outgrowths of forces operating in the child's life, and of discovering the steps that intervene between the child's present experience and their richer maturity.

"Abandon the notion of subject-matter as something fixed and ready-made in itself, outside the child's experience; cease thinking of the child's experience as also something hard and fast; see it as something fluent, embryonic, vital; and we realize that the child and the curriculum are simply two limits which define a single process. Just as two points define a straight line, so the present standpoint of the child and the facts and truths of studies define instruction. It is a continuous reconstruction, moving from the child's present experience out into that represented by the organized bodies of truth that we call studies." (p. 15 f.)

Dewey, *The Child and the Curriculum* * (Chicago, University of Chicago, 1902).

469. TECHNIQUE AS AN END

"The interest in technique, in acquiring skill, demands, in order not to lead to arrested development, a sufficient background of actual experience. Even if children of six and seven were psychologically ready for analysis, for attention to form and symbols and rules, very few of them have had the range of vital experience which would make it profitable for them to devote themselves very exclusively to the former at the expense of the latter. Hence, once more, attention must still be directed to positive subject-matter that enlarges and deepens their world of imagination and thought, rather than to analysing an experience they have not yet got, or learning rules for doing things that make no personal appeal to them.

"And, . . . the *introduction* to technique must come in connection *with ends that arise within the children's own experience, that are present to them as desired ends, and hence as motives to effort.* The too frequent assumption is that it is enough for the teacher to see the end; and that because, as matter of fact, a child is going to need a certain power, this is sufficient basis upon which to engage him in its acquisition. But the prime psychological necessity is that the child see and feel the end as *his own end*, the need as his own need, and thus have a motive for making the analysis and mastering the 'rules,' i.e. methods of procedure. This is possible only as the formal work is kept in connection with active, with constructive, and expressive work, which, presenting difficulties, suggests the need of acquiring an effective method of coping with them."

Dewey, in *Elementary School Record* * 1:51-52 (March, 1900).

470. KANT ON THE EFFECT OF PLAYS

"His interest being absorbed in . . . plays, the boy denies himself other needs, and thus learns gradually to impose other and greater privations upon himself. At the same time he becomes accustomed to continuous occupation; but for this very reason, his plays must not be merely plays; they must be plays having a purpose and an end; for the more his body is strengthened and hardened in this manner the safer is he from the disastrous consequences of pampering."

Buchner, *Kant's Educational Theory* * (Philadelphia, Lippincott, 1904), p. 162.

471. THE EDUCATIONAL VALUE OF SOCIAL PLAY

"The second kind of play is the playing of children with children . . . On the play-place [play-ground] they first issue from the speaking and audience hall into the true sphere of action, and begin their human praxis . . . Where then can the child show and mature his governing power, his resistance, his generosity, his gentleness, in short every root and blossom of society, except in freedom among his equals? Teach children by children! The entrance into their playroom is for them an entrance into the great world, and their mental school of industry is in the child's playroom and nursery."

Richter, *Levana* (1807 Bohn ed.), p. 157.

472. Value of Play

"For years play was looked upon merely as a sort of inevitable waste of time among children, but scientific study of the cultivation of these organisms has shown that play is in most respects the best, the ideal form of the exercise of the powers. Particularly is this true for the younger children, but it is in large measure true as they grow older. Play is the activity which their own natures suggest and guide; it is varied as their diverse budding capabilities require; and when free it is not carried beyond the point where one activity interferes with the development of others. The young child perhaps learns more and develops better through its play than through any other form of activity. Opportunity for varied play under healthful outward conditions is beyond doubt the chief need of children; comparative study of the mental and physical development of children to whom full opportunity for such play is given shows striking superiority, as compared with children to whom such opportunities are denied."

Jennings, in *Suggestions of Modern Science Concerning Education* * (New York, Macmillan, 1917), p. 46 f.

473. Criteria for Judging Games and Play

The teacher must ask "two questions: Will the proposed mode of play appeal to the child as his own? Is it something of which he has the instinctive roots in himself, and which will mature the capacities that are struggling for manifestation in him? And again: Will the proposed activity give that sort of expression to these impulses that will carry the child on to a higher plane of consciousness and action, instead of merely exciting him, and then leaving him just where he was before, plus a certain amount of nervous exhaustion and appetite for more excitation in the future? . . .

"The peculiar problem of the early grades is, of course, to get hold of the child's natural impulses and instincts, and to utilize them so that the child is carried on to a higher plane of perception and judgment, and equipped with more efficient habits; so that he has an enlarged and deepened consciousness, and increased control of powers of action. Wherever this result is not reached, play results in mere amusement and not in educative growth.

"Upon the whole, constructive, or 'built up' work (with, of course, the proper alternation of story, song, and game which may be connected, so far as is desirable, with the ideas involved in the construction) seems better fitted than anything else to secure these two factors—initiation in the child's own impulse, and determination upon a higher plane. It brings the child in contact with a great variety of material: wood, tin, leather, yarn, etc.; it supplies a motive for using these materials in real ways instead of going through exercises having no meaning except a remote symbolic one; it calls into play alertness of the senses and acuteness of observation; it demands clear-cut imagery of the ends to be accomplished, and requires ingenuity and invention in planning; it makes necessary concentrated attention and personal responsibility in execution, while the results are in such tangible form that the child may be led to judge his own work and improve his standards."

Dewey, in *Elementary School Record,** 1:145-149 (June, 1900).

474. THE SERVICE OF ART AND PLAY

"Relief from continuous moral activity—in the conventional sense of moral—is itself a moral necessity. The service of art and play is to engage and release impulses in ways quite different from those in which they are occupied and employed in ordinary activities. Their function is to forestall and remedy the usual exaggerations and deficits of activity, even of 'moral' activity and to prevent a stereotyping of attention. To say that society is altogether too careless about the moral worth of art is not to say that carelessness about useful occupations is not a necessity for art. On the contrary, whatever deprives play and art of their own careless rapture thereby deprives them of their moral function. Art then becomes poorer as art as a matter of course, but it also becomes in the same measure less effectual in its pertinent moral office. It tries to do what other things can do better, and it fails to do what nothing but itself can do for human nature, softening rigidities, relaxing strains, allaying bitterness, dispelling moroseness, and breaking down the narrowness consequent upon specialized tasks."

"Art releases energy and focuses and tranquilizes it. It releases energy in constructive forms. Castles in the air like art have their source in a turning of impulse away from useful production. Both are due to the failure in some part of man's constitution to secure fulfilment in ordinary ways. But in one case the conversion of direct energy into imagination is the starting point of an activity which *shapes* material; fancy is fed upon a stuff of life which assumes under its influence a rejuvenated, composed and enhanced form. In the other case, fancy remains an end in itself. It becomes an indulging in fantasies which bring about withdrawal from all realities, while wishes impotent in action build a world which yields temporary excitement. Any imagination is a sign that impulse is impeded and is groping for utterance. Sometimes the outcome is a refreshed useful habit; sometimes it is an articulation in creative art; and sometimes it is a futile romancing which for some natures does what self-pity does for others. The amount of potential energy of reconstruction that is dissipated in unexpressed fantasy supplies us with a fair measure of the extent to which the current organization of occupation balks and twists impulse, and, by the same sign, with a measure of the function of art which is not yet utilized."

Dewey, *Human Nature and Conduct* * (New York, Holt, 1922), p. 161-2, 163-4.

475. Habit and Expression

"Mechanization is not . . . *all* there is to habit. Consider the conditions under which the first serviceable abilities of life are formed. When a child begins to walk he acutely observes, he intently and intensely experiments. He looks to see what is going to happen and he keeps curious watch on every incident. What others do, the assistance they give, the models they set, operate not as limitations but as encouragements to his own acts, reinforcements of personal perception and endeavor. The first toddling is a romantic adventuring into the unknown; and every gained power is a delightful discovery of one's own powers and of the wonders of the world. We may not be able to retain in adult habits this zest of intelligence and this freshness of satisfaction in newly discovered powers. But there is surely a middle term between a normal exercise of power which includes some excursions into the unknown, and a mechanical activity hedged within a drab world. . . .

"All life operates through a mechanism, and the higher the form of life the more complex, sure and flexible the mechanism. This fact alone should save us from opposing life and mechanism, thereby reducing the latter to unintelligent automatism and the former to an aimless splurge. How delicate, prompt, sure and varied are the movements of a violin player or an engraver! How unerringly they phrase every shade of emotion and every turn of idea! Mechanism is indispensable. If each act has to be consciously searched for at the moment and intentionally performed, execution is painful and the product is clumsy and halting. Nevertheless the difference between the artist and the mere technician is unmistakeable. The artist is a masterful technician. The technique or mechanism is fused with thought and feeling. The 'mechanical' performer permits the mechanism to dictate the performance. It is absurd to say that the latter exhibits habit and the former not. We are confronted with two kinds of habit, intelligent and routine. . . .

"The current dualism of mind and body, thought and action, is so rooted that we are taught (and science is said to support the teaching) that the art, the habit, of the artist is acquired by previous mechanical exercises of repetition in which skill apart from thought is the aim, until suddenly, magically, this soulless mechanism is taken possession of by sentiment and imagination and it becomes a flexible instrument of mind. The fact, the scientific fact, is that even in his exercises, his practice *for* skill, an artist uses an art he already has. He acquires greater skill because practice of skill is more important to him than practice *for* skill. . . . A flexible, sensitive habit grows more varied, more adaptable by practice and use. We do not as yet fully understand the physiological factors concerned in mechanical routine on one hand and artistic skill on the other, but we do know that the latter is just as much habit as is the former. Whether it concerns the cook, musician, carpenter, citizen, or statesman, the intelligent or artistic habit is the desirable thing, and the routine the undesirable thing."

Dewey, *Human Nature and Conduct* * (New York, Holt, 1922), p. 70-2.

476. CERTAIN BAD EFFECTS OF SCHOOL LIFE

"Entrance to school stops or slows the growth of the child. Its sedentary life, bad air and mental strain, destroys or weakens the appetite, and decreases the respiration. Actual counts show a decrease in the number of red blood corpuscles, on which respiration depends. Hence the chemical processes of the body become disarranged; malnutrition with all its attendant evils comes into view. Resistance shows that all sorts of morbid states increase greatly as the children progress further in school; headaches, nose bleed, eye troubles, insomnia and other nervous disorders become commoner; tuberculosis increases. Further, by continued repression of many of the powers, and by forcing activity in powers not yet ready, strain is brought about; spontaneity is done away with; interest in work is destroyed; the instinct of workmanship rooted out, hate for work cultivated in place of love for it.

"No one maintains that these things happen to all children, but that there is a tendency toward such results no one will deny. . . . But the pertinent question is—Is there any necessity for these evil effects? . . .

"The question must be answered—No! The good can be done without the evil. Schools already exist in which most or all of the evils have been done away with. . . . Schools are now carried on where individuality and spontaneity are cultivated, not repressed; where strain is not allowed to play its fearful part; where love for work, not hatred of it, is developed. The movement for increased activity in schools; for greater opportunity for play; for shortening of the hours of sedentary labor, is tremendously improving schools in the more advanced communities."

Jennings, in *Suggestions of Modern Science Concerning Education* * (New York, Macmillan, 1917), p. 48 f.

477. Adaptation of Education to Individual Interests

"The natural avenue to the minds of a large number of children lies not through books, but through some kind of creative work, and . . . they learn most when they are engaged in some activity which so absorbs them that they forget they are learning. If this view is a sound one, then the encouragement of forms of education which are practical, in the sense, not of aiming at results other than the development of the child, but of awakening his mind and forming his character through the use of the hand, the eye, and the ear, is at least as important as formal instruction of a literary or scientific character. It is important for all classes alike, for the children of the well-to-do as well as for the children of poorer parents. The object of manual work in the elementary schools, to give one example of our meaning, is no more to make children efficient workers in industry than the object of singing is to enable them to earn their living as musicians. . . .

"To starve the appeal of form and colour is to empty life of beauty and to provoke a reaction which seeks not beauty, but excitement. We believe that the natural culture of many children is some form of artistic or creative work, as the natural culture of others is science or literature. To divorce education from the natural tastes of a considerable proportion of the children is to sterilise the former and brutalise the latter. . . . It is only in so far as it is intimately related with the ordinary interests of mankind that education will become the expression which it ought to be, of popular ideals, or give the inspiration to a better social life which, rightly used, it is able to convey. . . .

"An increasing number of rural schools have school gardens attached to them, and there is a growing habit of taking parties of children on visits to picture galleries, and to other places of interest. . . . The children in certain schools have been encouraged by their teachers to undertake co-operative enterprises, and to take a large share in the maintenance of discipline and good order in school. We cannot doubt that if our national system of education is to realise its full potentialities of good for the community, far more attention must be given in the future than has been given hitherto to the discovery of the ways in which children may not merely acquire knowledge, but may develop a capacity for employing their leisure in reasonable and humanising pursuits, which will remain with them when their school days are over, and above all may train themselves through the corporate life of their school in the art of self-government."

Report of the Archbishop's Fifth Committee (London, 1918), pp. 117-118.

478. CHILDREN'S TALKING

". . . Normal children from three to five years of age utter, under ordinary circumstances, from 1000 to 1400 words per hour during the entire day. . . . The child of four and a half years, if allowed perfect freedom in talking, was not linguistically inactive for a period exceeding three minutes at one time during the entire day. . . . The author spent 70 hours observing . . . in the various grades. In a fourth grade where 15 hours were spent the highest number of words spoken per hour by pupils was 992, the lowest 416, and the average 705. The average number of children . . . was 25 . . . including words in oral reading although . . . little of this . . . In all grades . . . the rate . . . seemed . . . about the same. . . .

"Average for each pupil is, at most, not over 40 words per hour."

Brandenburg, in *Journal of Educational Psychology,** 9:330 f. (June, 1918).

479. BUILDING INTERESTS

(a) "We act as we have learned to act, see what we have learned to see, are interested in what we have learned to be interested in, enjoy what we have learned to enjoy, and dislike what or whom we have learned to dislike. (p. 77.) . . .

(b) "It is a general principle of human activity that we are interested in overcoming difficulties and interested, on the other hand, in what we can do successfully—in a word, we are interested in successfully overcoming difficulties. The difficulty may lie on the side of motor execution of an act or on the side of perceiving and grasping a state of affairs, or on both sides at once. Action that is too easy because all the difficulties have been smoothed away or already subjugated by well-formed habits is automatic rather than interesting, and action that meets with unsurmountable obstacles is distinctly annoying; but action that encounters resistance but overcomes it without resorting to the last ounce of effort is distinctly interesting. . . .

(c) "To sum up—almost any object, almost any act, and particularly almost any process or change in objects that can be directed by one's own activity towards some definite end, is interesting on its own account, and furnishes its own drive, once it is fairly initiated. To be interesting, the process must present some difficulty and yet some prospect of a successful issue. . . . The truth is that, having native capacity for performing certain acts and dealing with certain classes of material, we are interested in performing these acts and handling this material; and that, once these activities are aroused, they furnish their own drive. This applies to abilities developed through training as well as to strictly native capacities. Almost anything may be made play and furnish its own motive." (p. 202.)

Woodworth, *Dynamic Psychology* * (New York, Columbia University, 1918).

480. MANY SIMULTANEOUS LEARNINGS INEVITABLE

In considering educational outcomes the usual view has been in the case of any one activity to fix almost exclusive attention upon one primary outcome, the knowledge or skill immediately sought, for instance, a given list of spelling words, a given lesson in grammar, or a given event described in history. It has been assumed that one thing and one only could be learned at a time; that the proper business of the school was to fix such a list of things in a desirable order and to see that they were learned. Children have usually been promoted or not according as they have or have not learned the quota prescribed for the term or year; and teachers are often judged upon the success of their classes in this respect.

The advocates of the point of view here under consideration challenge the assumption that one thing and only one can be learned at a time. They believe contrariwise that no child can learn just one thing at once. Whether we like it or not, whether we know it or not, a child learning the multiplication combinations is also at the same time learning something about dawdling or not dawdling. The way he studies his multiplication fixes or tends to fix him somewhere on the dawdling-alert-manner-of-learning scale; and his position on this scale is sometimes just as important as the thing which he and the teacher, both with a curious narrowness of vision, thought he was learning singly and alone. There are, moreover, many other scales on which he is simultaneously registering himself: the scale of liking or disliking arithmetic; the scale of liking or disliking school and teacher (how many of our children leave school as soon as the law allows?); the scale of self-respect; the scale of a just or unjust estimate of one's powers; the scale of believing that it does or does not pay to try; the scale of believing that books and schools have nothing or something to do with life as I and my family know it and believe in it; the scale of believing that I have succeeded in the degree that I have "put it over" the teacher; the scale of believing that teachers, principals and the whole tribe of law-givers and law-enforcers wherever found do or do not represent a tyrannical effort to suppress real living.

There are, to be sure, many questions regarding these various scales and the transfer of the attitudes so built to other situations. But who can question that there are many such learnings going on in each child all the time, and that the sum of the concomitant, incidental, or by-product learnings may and often does vastly overshadow the specific school learnings, and may in the end determine whether the child shall continue in school?

Kilpatrick, Adapted from *Teachers College Record*, 22:313-314 (Sept., 1921).

481. Psychological and Logical

"It may be of use to distinguish and to relate to each other the logical and the psychological aspects of experience—the former standing for subject-matter in itself, the latter for it in relation to the child. A psychological statement of experience follows its actual growth; it is historic; it notes steps actually taken, the uncertain and tortuous, as well as the efficient and successful. The logical point of view, on the other hand, assumes that the development has reached a certain positive stage of fulfilment. It neglects the process and considers the outcome. It summarizes and arranges, and thus separates the achieved results from the actual steps by which they were forthcoming in the first instance. . . . (p. 25.)

"Every study or subject thus has two aspects: one for the scientist as a scientist; the other for the teacher as a teacher. These two aspects are in no sense opposed or conflicting. But neither are they immediately identical. For the scientist, the subject-matter represents simply a given body of truth to be employed in locating new problems, instituting new researches, and carrying them through to a verified outcome. To him the subject-matter or the science is self-contained. He refers various portions of it to each other; he connects new facts with it. He is not, as a scientist, called upon to travel outside its particular bounds; if he does, it is only to get more facts of the same general sort. The problem of the teacher is a different one. As a teacher he is not concerned with adding new facts to the science he teaches; in propounding new hypotheses or in verifying them. He is concerned with the subject-matter of the science *as representing a given stage and phase of the development of experience.* His problem is that of inducing a vital and personal experiencing. Hence, what concerns him, as teacher, is the ways in which that subject may become a part of experience; what there is in the child's present that is usable with reference to it; how such elements are to be used; how his own knowledge of the subject-matter may assist in interpreting the child's needs and doings, and determine the medium in which the child should be placed in order that his growth may be properly directed. He is concerned, not with the subject-matter as such, but with the subject-matter as a related factor in a total and growing experience. Thus to see it is to psychologize it." (p. 29 f.)

Dewey, *The Child and the Curriculum* * (Chicago, University of Chicago, 1902).

482. Psychological and Logical

"What is conventionally termed logical (namely, the logical from the standpoint of subject-matter) represents in truth the logic of the trained adult mind. Ability to divide a subject, to define its elements, and to group them into classes according to general principles represents logical capacity at its best point reached *after* thorough training. The mind that habitually exhibits skill in divisions, definitions, generalizations, and systematic recapitulations no longer needs training in logical methods. But it is absurd to suppose that a mind which needs training because it cannot perform these operations can begin where the expert mind stops. *The logical from the standpoint* of subject-matter represents the goal, the last term of training, *not the point of departure*.

"In truth, the mind at every stage of development has its own logic.... Any teacher who is alive to the modes of thought naturally operative in the experience of the normal child will have no difficulty in avoiding the identification of the logical with a ready-made organization of subject-matter, as well as the notion that the only way to escape this error is to pay no attention to logical considerations. Such a teacher will have no difficulty in seeing that the real problem of intellectual education is the transformation of natural powers into expert, tested powers: the transformation of more or less casual curiosity and sporadic suggestion into attitudes of alert, cautious, and thorough inquiry. He will see that the *psychological* and the *logical*, instead of being opposed to each other, or even independent of each other), are connected *as the earlier and the later stages in one continuous process of normal growth*. The natural or psychological activities, even when not consciously controlled by logical considerations, have their own intellectual function and integrity; conscious and deliberate skill in thinking, when it is achieved, makes habitual or second nature. The first is already logical in spirit; the last, in presenting an ingrained disposition and attitude, is then as *psychological* (as personal) as any caprice or chance impulse could be."

Dewey, *How We Think** (New York, Heath, 1910), pp. 61-63.

483. Psychological and Logical

"Logical order is not a form imposed upon what is known; it is the proper form of knowledge as perfected. For it means that the statement of subject matter is of a nature to exhibit to one who understands it the premises from which it follows and the conclusions to which it points. . . . As from a few bones the competent zoologist reconstructs an animal; so from the form of a statement in mathematics or physics the specialists in the subject can form an idea of the system of truths in which it has its place.

"To the non-expert, however, this perfected form is a stumbling block. Just because the material is stated with reference to the furtherance of knowledge as an end in itself, its connections with the material of everyday life are hidden. To the layman the bones are a mere curiosity. Until he has mastered the principles of zoology, his efforts to make anything out of them would be random and blind. From the standpoint of the learner scientific form is an ideal to be achieved, not a starting point from which to set out. It is, nevertheless, a frequent practice to start in instruction with the rudiments of science somewhat simplified. The necessary consequence is an isolation of science from significant experience. The pupil learns symbols without the key to their meaning. He acquires a technical body of information without ability to trace its connections with the objects and operations with which he is familiar—often he acquires simply a peculiar vocabulary.

"There is a strong temptation to assume that presenting subject matter in its perfected form provides a royal road to learning. What more natural than to suppose that the immature can be saved time and energy, and be protected from needless error by commencing where competent inquirers have left off? The outcome is written large in the history of education. Pupils begin their study of science with texts in which the subject is organized into topics according to the order of the specialist. Technical concepts, with their definitions, are introduced at the outset. Laws are introduced at a very early stage, with at best a few indications of the way in which they were arrived at. The pupils learn a 'science' instead of learning the scientific way of treating the familiar material of ordinary experience. The method of the advanced student dominates college teaching; the approach of the college is transferred into the high school, and so down the line, with such omissions as may make the subject easier.

"The chronological method which begins with the experience of the learner and develops from that the proper modes of scientific treatment is often called the 'psychological' method in distinction from the logical method of the expert or specialist. The apparent loss of time involved is more than made up for by the superior understanding and vital interest secured. What the pupil learns he at least understands. Moreover by following, in connection with problems selected from the material of ordinary acquaintance, the methods by which scientific men have reached their perfected knowledge, he gains independent power to deal with material within his range, and avoids the mental confusion and intellecual distaste attendant upon studying matter whose meaning is only symbolic. Since the mass of pupils are never going to become scientific specialists, it is much more important that they should get some insight into what scientific method means than that they should copy at long range and second hand the results which scientific men have reached. Students will not go so far, perhaps, in the 'ground covered,' but they will be sure and intelligent as far as they do go. And it is safe to say that the few who go on to be scientific experts will have a better preparation than if they had been swamped with a large mass of purely technical and symbolically stated information."

Dewey, *Democracy and Education* * (New York, Macmillan, 1916), pp. 256-8.

484. Principles of Curriculum Making

"The purpose of elementary education should be: *To help boys and girls do better in all those wholesome activities in which they normally engage.*"

"Principle One. The curriculum should contribute primarily to enabling boys and girls to be efficient in what they are now doing, only secondarily to preparing them to be efficient later." (p. 137.) . . .

"Principle Two. The curriculum should be selected directly from real life and should be expressed in terms of the activities and the environments of people." (p. 171.) . . .

"Principle Three. The curriculum should provide for great scope and flexibility to meet individual differences in interests and abilities." (p. 207.) . . .

"Principle Four. The curriculum should be so organized that it will admit of easy rearrangement of the schedule for any day, of the work for any grade, and even of the transfer of work from grade to grade." (p. 237.) . . .

"Principle Five. The curriculum should lead the pupil to appreciate both work and leisure and to develop a habit of engaging in both." (p. 255.)

Meriam, *Child Life and the Curriculum* * (Yonkers-on-Hudson, World Book Company, 1920).

485. Curriculum Making

"The word *curriculum* is Latin for a *race-course,* or the *race* itself,—a place of deeds, or a series of deeds. As applied to education, it is that *series of things which children and youth must do and experience* by way of developing abilities to do the things well that make up the affairs of adult life; and to be in all respects what adults should be. (p. 42.) . . .

"The curriculum may, therefore, be defined in two ways: (1) it is the entire range of experiences, both undirected and directed, concerned in unfolding the abilities of the individual; or (2) it is the series of consciously directed training experiences that the schools use for completing and perfecting the unfoldment. Our profession uses the term usually in the latter sense. But as education is coming more and more to be seen as a thing of experiences, and as the work-and-play experiences of the general community life are being more and more utilized, the line of demarcation between directed and undirected training experience is rapidly disappearing. Education must be concerned with both, even though it does not direct both. (p. 43.) . . .

"The curriculum of the schools will aim at those objectives that are not sufficiently attained as a result of the general undirected experience. (p. 44.) . . .

"The curriculum of the directed training is to be discovered in the shortcomings of individuals after they have had all that can be given by the undirected training." (p. 45.)

Bobbitt, *The Curriculum* * (Boston, Houghton Mifflin, 1918).

486. The Curriculum as Method

"It must be insisted that the curriculum consists of both ideals and activities on the one hand and their methods of realization and performance on the other hand. In a very real sense, education has not only to show youth how to control objectives but also how to want to control them. . . .

"The method of instilling ideals is in particular a pedagogical problem. . . .

"In propagating interest in the control of ideals it is evident that the curriculum consists of methods of achieving objectives, but it is not so evident, though equally true, that all the content

SUBJECT MATTER AND CURRICULUM

of the curriculum is methodic. Everything taught or discovered, recorded or achieved, has been a method. Ideals were first formulated and used as means of realizing older desires. In childhood they are first understood as means to other ends. Loyalty, for instance, originally was and still is being developed as a means of attaining group solidarity. The moral ideals, such as honesty, have been accepted by the race only after it was demonstrated that they constitute superior methods for obtaining the satisfaction of a whole range of objectives. . . .

"In like manner facts are methods of control. . . .

"If we consider painting, sculpture, architecture, or literature, the same principle holds. Every product of the brush, the chisel, and the mallet, the draughting board, and the pen is a means of achieving some function. *The Bells* expressed the feelings of Poe about the sounds described. The Venus de Milo, the Parthenon, and *Cymbeline*, each is a medium through which an idea is put into concrete form by its creator.

"Not only are they media for the creator, they are in like manner methods by which the observer can build up in his experience the ideal embodied in them by the artist. They are not raw material to be catalogued by those who encounter them; they were brought into being because they furthered the achieving of an objective. They are retained by the race and imparted to the young because they assist the rising generation to realize the same or similar ends. . . .

"As a matter of common procedure the schools have sought to give information upon the assumption that the mere giving of information will influence conduct. But a different idea is now gaining ground: that in practice as well as in theory, the function of instruction is not fulfilled until the information has actually modified conduct."

Charters, *Curriculum Construction* * (New York, Macmillan, 1923), p. 74-77.

487. Charters' Steps in Curriculum Construction

"The rules for curriculum construction may be stated as follows:

"First, determine the major objectives of education by a study of the life of man in its social setting.

"Second, analyze these objectives into ideals and activities and continue the analysis to the level of working units.

"Third, arrange these in the order of importance.

"Fourth, raise to positions of higher order in this list those ideals and activities which are high in value for children but low in value for adults.

"Fifth, determine the number of the most important items of the resulting list which can be handled in the time allotted to school education, after deducting those which are better learned outside of school.

"Sixth, collect the best practices of the race in handling these ideals and activities.

"Seventh, arrange the material so obtained in proper instructional order, according to the psychological nature of children."

Charters, *Curriculum Construction* * (New York, Macmillan, 1923), p. 102.

488. BONSER ON THE CURRICULUM

"In making the curriculum the measure of the educational value of any experience is the degree in which it makes a desirable difference in conduct. . . .

"Conduct may be helpfully considered as made up of experiences which relate to health, to practical efficiency, to citizenship, and to the use of leisure. . . .

"In form the curriculum should be in three parts:

"a. Suggestive projects which reflect the activities and interests of the life in which the children themselves are participating.

"b. The subject matter available from the results of race experience required for the carrying forward of these projects in the best way.

"c. A briefly summarized organization of essential methods and skills, and of ideals, attitudes, and appreciations to be developed in connection with the projects and subject matter. This organization is to serve as a standard of reference for the teacher.

"The essential elements constituting the third part of the curriculum should be practically the same for all elementary schools. The subject matter representing the second part should be much the same, although in some details and in sequence there may be much difference. The projects may differ very much in response to the environing differences of schools.

"All methods, processes, principles, degrees of skill, or facts, as of manipulation, speaking, reading, writing, design, science, geography, history, or civics, should be introduced in response to specific needs or situations which require them.

"To avoid the dangers of arrested mental development, the interest in drills in number, phonetics, language forms, spelling, oral reading, penmanship, drawing, or manipulation should not be permitted to develop to such an extent that these interests become greater than those in the purposeful uses of these mechanical elements."

Bonser, *The Elementary School Curriculum* * (New York, Macmillan, 1920), pp. 150-152.

489. Practical Thinking

Thinking "does not occur for its own sake, nor end in itself. It arises from the need of meeting some difficulty, in reflecting upon the best way of overcoming it, and thus leads to planning, to projecting mentally the result to be reached, and deciding upon the steps necessary and their serial order. This concrete logic of action long precedes the logic of pure speculation or abstract investigation, and through the mental habits that it forms is the best of preparations for the latter."

Dewey, in *Elementary School Record,* * 1:83 (April, 1900).

490. Goethe on the Education of Taste

"Taste is only to be educated by contemplation, not of the tolerably good, but of the truly excellent. I, therefore, show you only the best works; and when you are grounded in these, you will have a standard for the rest which you will know how to value without over-rating them. And I show you the best in each class, that you may perceive that no class is so despised but that each gives delight when a man of genius attains its highest point."

Conversations of Goethe.

491. English not a Subject of Instruction

"English is not really a subject at all. It is a condition of existence rather than a subject of instruction. It is an inescapable circumstance of life, and concerns every English-speaking person from the cradle to the grave. The lesson in English is not merely one occasion for the inculcation of knowledge; it is a part of the child's initiation into the life of man."

Sampson, *English for the English* * (New York, Macmillan, 1921), p. 125.

CHAPTER XX

THE EDUCATIVE PROCESS: THE PROBLEM OF METHOD

492. A Listening School

The three year old grandson of one of America's best known educators having as a privileged guest enjoyed a modern kindergarten desired when the family moved away to attend similarly the village school. One visit however sufficed. Being asked why he would go no more, he replied with an insight almost uncanny: "It's a *listening* school. I don't like it."

493. Dr. Johnson on Motivation

"My schoolmaster beat me most unmercifully, else I had done nothing."
Quoted in *DeBows Review,* 1: 533.

494. Oliver Goldsmith on Child Nature

"Whatever pains a master may take to make learning agreeable to his pupil, he may depend it will be at first extremely unpleasant . . . and I know of no passion capable of conquering a child's natural laziness but fear."
Quoted in *DeBow's Review,* 1:532-3.

495. Alcuin on Motivation

"It is the scourge that teaches children the ornaments of wisdom and to accustom themselves to good manners."
Dodd, *Early English Social History* (London, Bell, 1913), p. 149.

496. "Letters go in with Blood"

"Sometimes parents came to me with the rank proverb, 'Letters go in with blood,' on their lips and begged me to punish their children."

Ferrer, *The Origin and Ideals of the Modern School* * (New York, Putnam, 1913), p. 77 f.

497. Effect of Severity

"The utmost that severity can do is to make hypocrites; it can never make converts."
Spencer, *Social Statics* (New York, Appleton, 1878 [1]), p. 203.

498. Law of Effect

"Knowledge which is acquired under compulsion has no hold on the mind."
Plato, *Republic* * (Trans. by Jowett. Oxford, Clarendon Press, 1888), VII, 536d.

499. The Law of Effect

"No profit grows where is no pleasure ta'en;
In brief, sir, study what you most affect."
Shakespeare, *Taming of the Shrew,* Act i, Sc. 1.

500. Difficulties of Childhood

". . . We grown people all have . . . the fault of considering every difference of a child from ourselves as a failing, our scoldings as lessons, childish errors as greater than our own; and thence it is that we so thoughtlessly convert our educational rein and leading strings into a hanging rope. . . .

"Even a grown up man whom some one should follow all day long with a movable pulpit and stool of confession, from which to hurl sermons and anathemas, could never attain any real activity and moral freedom; how much less then a weak child, who, at every step in life, must be entangled in a 'stop-run-be quiet-do that.'"
Richter, *Levana* (1807 Bohn ed.), p. 170.

501. Pupil Sabotage

"Looking back on those years which we spent in school, we know that something was wrong. In this respect our adult con-

---
[1] First edition, 1850.

victions find impressive support in our earlier views on the subject. If we will remember, we did not, at the time, exactly approve of the school system. Many of us, in fact, went in for I. W. W. tactics—especially sabotage. Our favourite brand of sabotage was the 'withdrawal of efficiency.'"

Dell, *Were You Ever a Child* * (New York, Knopf, 1919), p. 10.

502. Attention without Interest

"A person condemned to spend his whole life in constantly reiterated efforts to fix his mind on a hopelessly uninteresting topic, would go mad, commit suicide, or sink into a state of coma."

Stout, *Manual of Psychology* * (New York, Hinds Noble, 1899), p. 613.

503. The Spirit Broken by Past Oppression

"The moroseness and surrender to alcoholic excess of the Indians of the Andean uplands from Ecuador to Bolivia probably result from the bafflement of the instincts of self-assertion and liberty. Even to-day Cuzco Indians, women as well as men, doff hat to every white man they pass. In the remoter districts the Indian who sees a white man coming along the trail will make a long detour to avoid him. If you approach an Indian abruptly he will fall on his knees, put up his arm to shield his face, and cry, "Don't hurt me, master!" The old brutalities are gone but fear continues to inhibit self-assertion, so that this broken-hearted race has little of the virtue and happiness it enjoyed before the Spaniards set their heel on its neck."

Ross, *Principles of Sociology* * (New York, Century, 1921), p. 48.

504. Early Habituation

"We at first send children to school, not so much with the intention that they shall learn something here, as with the idea that they may become accustomed to sit still and to observe promptly that which is enjoined upon them, in order that in the future they may not attempt immediately to carry out their every caprice."

Buchner, *Kant's Educational Theory* * (Philadelphia, Lippincott, 1904), p. 104.

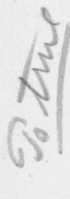

505. Hegel on Youthful Reasoning

"The tendency of youth to independent reflection and reasoning is one-sided. It should be indulged in as little as possible. The pupils of Pythagoras kept silence during their first four years; that is, they were not to have personal ideas and thoughts, or to express them. For the chief end of education is to do away with these personal ideas, thoughts, reflections of youth, and their utterance. If the tendency toward self-reasoning be unchecked, there is no discipline or order in thought, no coherent and consequent knowledge."

Luqueer, *Hegel as Educator* * (New York, Macmillan, 1896), p. 140 f.

506. Kant on Education towards Freedom

"The child should be left perfectly free, from earliest childhood, in everything (except in such instances where he might injure himself; as, for example, when he reaches for an open knife), unless the manner of his freedom interferes with that of others; as, for example, when he screams, or is merry in too noisy a way, he discommodes others.

"The child must be shown that he can attain his aims only as he permits others to reach theirs; as, for example, he will be granted no pleasure if he does not do what others desire, that he must learn, etc.

"It must also be shown to the child that he is under such constraint as will lead him to the use of his own freedom; that he is cultivated, so that one day he may be free,—that is, not dependent upon the foresight of others. That is the child's latest acquisition. For the consideration that each must rely upon himself for his own sustenance comes to the child very late. They fancy it will always be as it is in the parental home; that food and drink will come without any thought on their part. Without such treatment, children, and especially those of rich parents and princes, become like the inhabitants of Tahiti, who remain children their whole life long.

"Here public education has the most evident advantage, since in it one learns to measure his powers and the limitations which the rights of others impose upon him. In this form of education no one has prerogatives, since opposition is felt everywhere, and merit becomes the only standard of preferment. This education produces the best prototype of the future citizen."

Buchner, *Kant's Educational Theory** (Philadelphia, Lippincott, 1904), p. 132 f.

507. PLACE OF PURPOSE

"Purposive behavior is the most important case of the influence of the attitude or set or adjustment of an organism in determining (1) which bonds shall act and (2) which results shall satisfy."

Thorndike, *Educational Psychology** (New York, Teachers College, 1913), Vol. II, p. 51.

508. CONDITIONS OF WORK

"The children of a school class may work with doubled efficiency simply from learning the significance of the work to their wants, and associating the work with sociability, cheerfulness and achievement."

Thorndike, *Educational Psychology** (New York, Teachers College, 1913), Vol. III, p. 128.

509. DAWDLING

"Next to the youth who has no calling, he is most to be pitied who toils without heart, and therefore forever dawdling—loitering and lingering, instead of striking with all his might."

Mathews, *Getting On in the World* (Chicago, Griggs, 1883), p. 165.

510. THE GENUINE PRINCIPLE OF INTEREST

"The genuine principle of interest is the principle of the recognized identity of the fact to be learned or the action proposed with the growing self; that it lies in the direction of the agent's own growth, and is, therefore, imperiously demanded, if the agent is to be himself. Let this condition of identification once be secured, and we have neither to appeal to sheer strength of will, nor to occupy ourselves with making things interesting. . . .

"Genuine interest is the accompaniment of the identification, through action, of the self with some object or idea, because of the necessity of that object or idea for the maintenance of a self-initiated activity. Effort, in the sense in which it may be opposed to interest, implies a separation between the self and the fact to be mastered or task to be performed, and sets up an habitual division of activities. Externally, we have mechanical habits with no mental end or value. Internally, we have random energy or mind-wandering, a sequence of ideas with no end at all, because they are not brought to a focus in action. Interest, in the sense in which it is opposed to effort, means simply an excitation of the sense organ to give pleasure, resulting in strain on one side and listlessness on the other."

Dewey, *Interest and Effort* * (Boston, Houghton Mifflin, 1913), pp. 7, 14.

511. Effort

"True effort consists in reinforcing by additional ideas, desires, and motives the side felt to be the weaker. It may be true that action follows the strongest desire but it is also true that we have the power to call up considerations and feelings that strengthen and that weaken the forces of desire."

Anonymous.

512. Wholehearted Activity

"When activity is at its best, either physical or mental, it has back of it all the individual's powers and resources. The whole being urgently calls out for and demands this activity. The self wills it fully and completely, interest and desire prompt it, the entire organism affirms it and gives itself gladly to it, no part of the self is latent or withheld."

Anonymous.

513. Vigor of Action

In an experiment on animal learning it was found that "the importance of the vigor with which an animal performs an act has been underestimated by some students of behavior. The more nearly the whole active organism is directed towards the accomplishment of the act the more rapidly will the act be perfected. The subjects which chose most quickly and made the greatest effort to reach the food learned in about one half the time that it took for those subjects which did not seem anxious to get to the food."

Dodson, in *Psycho-biology*, 1:272 (Nov., 1918).

514. Inner *versus* Outer Attention

"Children have an inner and an outer attention. The inner attention is the giving of the mind without reserve or qualification to the subject in hand. It is the first-hand and personal play of mental powers. As such, it is a fundamental condition of mental growth. To be able to keep track of this mental play, to recognize the signs of its presence or absence, to know how it is initiated and maintained, how to test it by results attained, and to test *apparent* results by it, is the supreme mark and criterion of a teacher. It means insight into soul-action, ability to discriminate the genuine from the sham, and capacity to further one and discourage the other.

"External attention, on the other hand, is that given to the book or teacher as an independent object. It is manifested in certain conventional postures and physical attitudes rather than in the movement of thought. Children acquire great dexterity in exhibiting in conventional and expected ways the *form* of attention to school work, while reserving the inner play of their own thoughts, images, and emotions for subjects that are more important to them, but quite irrelevant."

Dewey, *Relation of Theory to Practice*,* in Third Yearbook of the National Society for the Scientific Study of Education, pp. 13-14.

515. INTEREST AND CAPACITY

"These facts unanimously witness to the importance of early interests. They are shown to be far from fickle and evanescent. On the contrary, the order of interests at twenty shows six-tenths of perfect resemblance to the order from eleven to fourteen, and has changed therefrom little more than the order of abilities has changed. It would indeed be hard to find any feature of a human being which was a much more permanent fact of his nature than his relative degrees of interest in different lines of thought and action.

"Interests are also shown to be symptomatic, to a very great extent, of present and future capacity or ability. Either because one likes what he can do well, or because one gives zeal and effort to what he likes, or because interest and ability are both symptoms of some fundamental feature of the individual's original nature, or because of the combined action of all three of these factors, interest and ability are bound very closely together. The bond is so close that either may be used as a symptom for the other as well as for itself."

Thorndike, in *Popular Science Monthly*,* 81:456 (Nov., 1912).

516. Three Periods of Child Development

"In the first, there is no anticipation or preliminary consciousness of ends at all. The start is made with the child's instinctive and spontaneous powers, and through the operation of these powers certain results are reached. Ends are attained, but not aimed at.

"In the second stage ends consciously suggest themselves to the child and these ends at once call out the powers or suggest the doing of certain things. This stage differs from the previous one in that there is anticipation or some consciousness of the results which may be brought about in action. But it differs from the stage next to be spoken of, in that there is no reflective examination of these ends, and no special analysis of means.

"The third stage then is conscious control proper, where the individual agent clearly defines to himself what it is that he wants after deliberation, after comparison with other possible ends, and then has at command a definite and orderly series of specially discriminated means with which to work out the proposed aim."

Dewey, Unpublished Lecture.

517. Human Beings Always Active

We are not to think of man as naturally inert, doing nothing until something external stirs him to action. On the contrary mental emptiness, as Thorndike says, is one of man's greatest annoyers. Alive and awake each human being craves occupation. To meet this there are almost innumerable possibilities available. Foremost, perhaps, stand all those instinctive cravings commonly called curiosity, attention to novel objects and to human behavior, reaching and grasping, tasting, biting, general exploration with the eyes and general manipulation with the hands. Such experiences often lead to further activity, but they are in themselves their own sufficient reward. In addition to such more physical actions amid tangible affairs there are countless other activities that go on in the realms of thought and imagination. In this all engage, some more extensively than others. An imaginative child will wear threadbare the patience of his prosaic elders by asking what would happen under this, that and the other impossible contingency. Some unusual children create imaginary companions and spend hours at a time for months in conversation and play with these continuing creatures of their imagination. Even the most prosaic of us if not otherwise occupied indulge in day dreams of some kind or fashion. Of like fabric in origin are our most highly valued creations of artistic imagination and even our scientific hypotheses and moral ideals. Occupation we must have, good or bad, useful or fruitless, something will engage us.

We are thus to think of the human individual as a bundle of neural connections leading on in a thousand different directions of activity, all craving exercise but at any one time differing much among themselves as to readiness. Which of the neural connections shall at any given moment be more "ready" to act, which shall win out and be put in "drive," depends on a variety of factors: on their respective organized connections with the outside world, on their organized connection with other parts of the body and among themselves, on the state of the neurones (mechanisms) themselves due to recent experiences. If I have been running a severe race, certain "tired" neurones are relatively unready to act, while others for hearing pleasing speeches on my effort are particularly fresh and ready to act. Whether this readiness to hear will be satisfied by overt action depends upon the bystanders and what they think and choose to say. If there are no bystanders at hand, my mind may run the race over again in memory and imagination: What did happen? What might have happened? If my knee is sprained, attention may go thitherward. And so on. What shall happen among these many contending neurones is exactly a resultant of all that life itself at that time selects from among all the infinite possibilities. But action there will be. Alive and awake, action and occupation of some sort is inevitable and incessant.

Adapted largely from Thorndike, *Educational Psychology* (New York, Teachers College, 1913), Vol. I, p. 140 ff.

518. THE PSYCHOLOGICAL EFFECT OF RESISTANCE

The general effect of a hindrance or obstacle or rival is to spur to increased effort. More exactly, if one is already moving toward some object or seeking to effect some end, failure to get nearer when one moves forward or failure to grasp when one reaches— in fact any failing movement—provokes annoyance and calls forth more vigorous movements towards attaining the end already set up. If one sees another striving for the same object or busied with it, the tendencies toward possession are strengthened.

To resistance the response is pulling and twisting the object and pushing away whoever or whatever is in touch with it. Failure to get nearer, when one has moved toward such an object of attention, and failure to grasp it when one reaches for it, provoke annoyance, more vigorous responses of the same sort as before and the neural action which produces an emotion which is the primitive form of desire.

Any hindrance then, actual or threatened, to any movement already under way will, if not too great, strengthen the tendency to persist in the movement and evokes increased vigor of action toward the end sought.

Adapted from Thorndike's *Educational Psychology* (New York, Teachers College, 1913), Vol. I, p. 51.

519. Effect of Emotions

"In testing the grasping reflex in infants . . . we found that in very many cases the child could not at first support its full weight, but if by *hampering its movements we could produce rage, the muscular strength suddenly increased and the child would immediately support its whole weight,* and in other cases could sustain its weight for a much longer period of time. A possible explanation of this has been advanced by Dr. Cannon of the physiological laboratory of Harvard University. In the primary emotions certain internal glandular secretions are set free which tend to wash out fatigue products from the muscles and to increase the amount of food for the muscles, etc. Hence, when in the throes of the major emotions, we do actually possess greater muscular strength and endurance than at other times."

Watson, in *Suggestions of Modern Science Concerning Education* * (New York, Macmillan, 1917), p. 68 f.

520. The Emotions

"Closely connected with . . . native or instinctive reactions are the bodily and conscious states called *emotions,* and these also must be included under the head of native equipment. For it is quite evident that fear, anger, grief, mirth, lust, and the other emotions do not arise in the individual as the result of training. He learns to be afraid of certain objects, but he does not learn how to be afraid. . . .

"The close connection of the emotions with certain overt reactions, such as flight, fighting, laughing or crying, and also with certain internal bodily changes, such as quickened heartbeat and breathing, flushing or paling of the skin, has long been a matter of common observation . . . (p. 51.)

"The relation of the bodily changes and the emotion has come into much clearer light through recent physiological studies." . . . Cannon has discovered by the use of the X-rays "that fear or anger is attended by a prompt cessation of the churning movements of the stomach, as it is attended also by stopping of the flow of the gastric juice. In fact, the whole digestive activity is sidetracked during these emotions, and the blood is driven from the digestive organs to the heart, brain, and muscles. Thus, once more, a condition of bodily readiness is produced suitable to the muscular exertions to which the angry or frightened animal or man is impelled.

"The bodily preparation for flight or fighting goes much further than this. Not only is the digestive activity checked, but the heart beats rapidly, the blood pressure rises, and the breathing becomes deeper and more rapid—all suitable preparations for a period of intense muscular activity. Sweat may break out on the skin and thus make an early start towards the elimination of heat from the body that must occur with muscular activity. All of these bodily changes, it is interesting to note, result through the action on the organs of the sympathetic system of nerves, which, though not under voluntary control, is thus shown to be aroused by the brain. But the most curious set of facts recently added by the physiologists to our knowledge of emotional states concerns the participation of two small glands that are adjuncts of the sympathetic system—the adrenal glands. . . . They are glands producing an 'internal secretion,' that is to say, a fluid discharged into the blood stream, and by it carried to all the organs of the body, many of which it takes effect upon, the effect varying with the organ. The heart it stimulates to greater activity, the blood vessels of the internal organs it causes to constrict, the movements of the stomach and intestines it stops, the liver it excites to pour out into the blood its stores of sugar, that best fuel for rapid combustion by the muscles, the muscles, in some obscure but efficient way, it preserves from fatigue, and finally the blood itself it puts in such a condition that it will clog rapidly in any wound that may chance to occur. (p. 53 f.)

"All in all, it appears as if the formula developed from our rather precise knowledge of fear and anger were probably applicable also to a number of other emotions, and possibly to all; so that it is a reasonable theory that the emotion, as a conscious state, represents or is correlative with (1) the drive towards a certain consummatory reaction, and (2) the bodily state of preparedness for that reaction. It is clear also that native equipment provides for the internal preparation as well as for the overt reaction." (p. 58 f.)

Woodworth, *Dynamic Psychology* * (New York, Columbia University, 1918).

521. WE LEARN TO DO BY DOING

"What has to be done must be learned by practice. Artisans do not detail their apprentices with theories, but set them to do practical work at any early stage; thus they learn to forge by forging, to carve by carving, to paint by painting, and to dance by dancing. In schools, therefore, let the students learn to write by writing, to talk by talking, to sing by singing, and to reason by reasoning. In this way schools will become workshops humming with work, and students whose efforts prove successful will experience the truth of the proverb: 'We give form to ourselves and to our materials at the same time.'"

Comenius, *Great Didactic* (Trans. by Keatinge. London, Black, 1910[1]), p. 194 f.

522. THE PSYCHOLOGY OF LEARNING

(The following account is based generally on Thorndike, *Educational Psychology*, Vol. I, ch. 14, Vol. II, ch. 1, Woodworth, *Dynamic Psychology*, pp. 56 ff., and Woodworth, *Psychology*, chs. 2, 16.)

(a) The underlying point of view here is that of behavior and how to change it. Behavior is as broad as life itself and refers especially to our ways of reacting, internally or externally, to the various situations of life. By changing behavior we mean especially changing people so that they can and will behave or react differently. The physiological basis for behavior is to be found in the nervous system, of which the *neurone* is for us the important constituent. A typical neurone has (i) a receiving end usually branching out like a tree, (ii) a thread-like conducting part,

[1] Written in 1632. First published, 1649.

and (iii) a discharging end usually also branching out into many endings. The simplest behavior system ("reflex arc") consists of a sensory neurone and a motor neurone meeting in a kind of junction point (called a synapse). The two neurones meeting thus are in contact but are not grown together. The following diagram (which is very much simplified) will perhaps make this clearer:

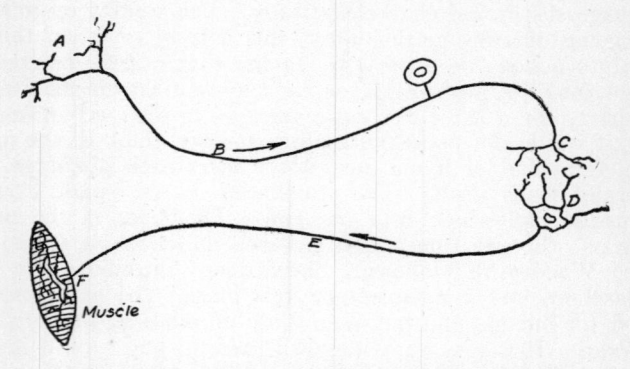

FIG. 1. Two neurones ("reflex arc") with synapse.

Here A will be the receiving end of the sensory neurone ABC, B is its conducting part, C its discharging end. CD forms a junction point or synapse (here a reflex center). DEF is the motor neurone, with D its receiving end, E its conducting part and F its discharging end. In this case the branchings of F will be joined with a muscle (or system of muscles). Suppose we take sneezing as an illustration and arbitrarily let this diagram represent the nervous machinery for sneezing. (The mechanism for sneezing is in fact much more complicated.) We may imagine some pepper attacking the sensory receiving end at A. The disturbance will be conducted along B to its discharging end at C. Here it will pass through the synapse to the receiving end D and thence along E to the motor discharging ends at F, which are appropriately connected with certain muscles. These muscles upon receiving the stimulation from F contract and produce the movements we call sneezing.

The whole piece of organized neural machinery by which sneezing thus takes place we may call the sneezing *mechanism,* and we have as many different mechanisms as there are specific things we can do,—a mechanism for raising the head, another for focusing the eye, another for skipping, another for thinking what Constantinople is, etc., etc. When we were tracing the course of the sneeze a moment ago, it was evident that "life" or vital energy of some sort was in some way stored up in the discharging endings with their connections so that when the disturbance was received from the connecting line the sneezing mechanism "went off," "got busy," "got to work," or, in more dignified language, discharged characteristically. This waking up to action, this going off, this getting busy, this getting to work, this getting into action, we express by saying that a *drive* entered into or got into the mechanism, or we may say the mechanism was "in drive," or, a drive was communicated to the mechanism. We may, if we do not press the analogy too far, think of the mechanism as a kind of living gun, which after each discharge automatically loads itself. The stimulation is the spark from the percussion cap which fires the gun. The drive is the powder going off; the gun (mechanism) is then in action (in drive).

(b) Woodworth (following Sherrington) introduces the terms *preparatory* and *consummatory* reactions. To which may be added for our specific purposes those of *mind-set-to-an-end* and *readiness*. It is easy to distinguish these in any typical instance of animal activity, which may serve, if we are sufficiently careful, to illustrate human activity.

A tiger which has gone an unusually long time without food is (a) lying asleep. He is (b) suddenly awakened by a noise and rustle among the bushes. Raising his head in the direction of the noise he sees a deer. Recognizing the deer as suitable for food (c), he "determines" (d) to catch it and eat it. Thereupon he creeps stealthily forward till, being close enough, he springs through the air, seizes the deer, and (e) devours it. It is at once easy to see that devouring the deer is a *consummatory reaction,* and that all the steps necessary for catching the deer are in fact *preparatory* to this consummation. But in the instance given there are two kinds of preparatory reactions,—first, marked (b) above, when the tiger responded to the noise by raising his head and looking about as if to find out its source; and, second, marked (d) above, when following his "determination" to catch and devour the deer, he began to creep forward, etc. Of all the steps in the described process that marked (d) above is of especial significance for us, namely the "determination" to catch and devour the deer. This determination is an instance of *mind-set-to-an-end*. The tiger's "mind" became at that point "set" by some sort of anticipation upon devouring the deer, and this mind-set furnished the drive for all steps (mechanisms in drive) necessary to catching and devouring the deer. Such a mind-set clearly looks forward to the consummatory reaction as its end; so that we may properly call it a mind-set-to-an-end.†

The state of affairs called *readiness* is equally apparent. The tiger had not dined recently. Though sleeping, he was by reason of his hunger the more sensitive to the noise. His mechanism for hearing was more *ready* to act. Similarly, having perceived a deer "as the cause" of the noise, his hunger had made it easier to arouse the mind-set for devouring the deer. *Readiness,* thus, is that state or condition of a mechanism wherein it is more easily put in drive.

(c) The symbol S → R. Any act of conduct can be conceived as a response (R) to some situation (S), or perhaps more precisely as a response (R) to some situation acting as stimulus (S). We represent this by the symbol S → R. I hear my name (S), I turn and look (R). The simplest instance of this S → R is seen in the diagram of (a) above, where S is represented in the nervous system by the action of the sensory neurone ABC, and R by the action of the motor neurone DEF. The arrow connecting S and R may be thought of as representing the whole path from the initial receiving end A to the final discharging end F. For discussions of the psychology of learning [see (f) below] this arrow path furnishes the significant feature. It is frequently called a "bond" or "connection" with especial attention to the intervening synapse or synapses. For it must be noted here that in the usual S → R bond or connection there are intervening between S and R many connecting neurones with their correlative synapses.

(d) Learning.—We all know that people learn. In the S → R symbolism learning means that the R is joined more surely to the S (or less surely, since we must also include the negative cases). We may take this to mean that learning is located in the synapse (or synapses) which join the R to the S. Exercise under conditions favorable to learning thus "strengthens" (or "weakens") the synapse (or synapses) so that the stimulation will pass more (or less) readily and surely from the sensory

---

† The reader must be cautioned that the story is told in the language of Æsop. "Recognizing," "determines," etc., belong strictly to men, not to tigers. We cannot even be sure that this tiger, when he started for the deer, "expected" (in the human sense of expectation) to eat it. The end is known to us, but certainly not in the same way to the tiger.

neurone to the responding neurone. Woodworth (*Psychology*, p. 415) thus pictures four stages of a synapse as it is "strengthened" by (proper) exercise and a succeeding fifth after it has been "weakened" by disuse:

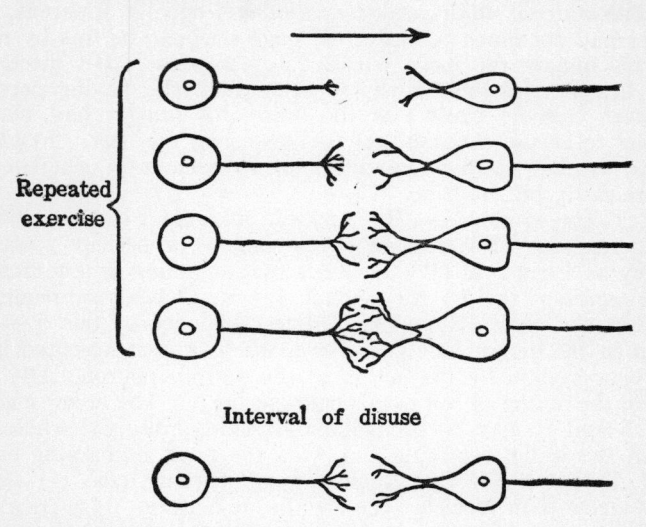

FIG. 2. The law of exercise in terms of synapse. A nerve current is supposed to pass along this pair of neurones in the direction of the arrow. Every time it passes, it exercises the discharging and receiving end branches at the synapse (for the "passage of a nerve current" really means activity on the part of the neurones through which it passes), and the after-effect of this exercise is growth of the exercised parts, and consequent improvement of the synapse as a linkage between one neurone and the other. Repeated exercise may probably bring a synapse from a very loose condition to a state of close interweaving and excellent power of transmitting the nerve current. (Adapted from Woodworth, *Psychology*,* New York, Holt, 1921, p. 415.)

Psychologists have spent much study upon the conditions under which learning takes place. A careful statement of these conditions is to be found in formulations called the Laws of Learning.

(e) Multiple Response.—It often happens that if one response does not succeed, we try another, and if need be a third, and so on until we either succeed or give up the attempt. This is called *Multiple Response* and is very important in discussions of how learning practically takes place. The simplest case of this, almost too simple to happen, may be schematically diagramed as follows:

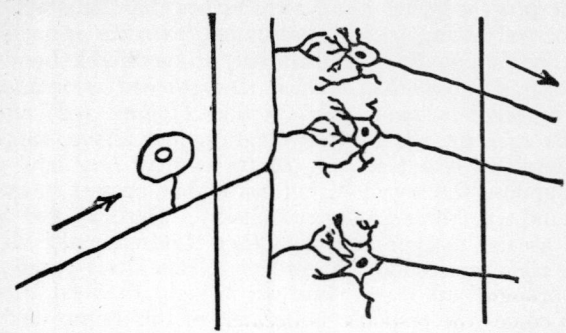

FIG. 3. A branching sensory neurone joined with three distinct motor neurones. (Adapted from Woodworth, *Psychology,** New York, Holt, 1921, p. 38.)

Here the sensory neurone has three branches which form synapses with three different motor responses. We may suppose in a particular case that the stimulation finds its most open outlet along the topmost synapse of the diagram, while the middle synapse would be next open, and the bottom synapse least. If upon trial the response joined with the topmost synapse proves not satisfying, and the stimulation still continues, the middle response will next be tried, and finally if need be the remaining response will be brought into action.

(f) *Laws of Learning.*—Thorndike recognizes three principal laws of learning, namely the laws of Readiness, Exercise, and Effect. Following the discussion on readiness given in (b) above we may say that a "bond" is in a state of readiness when its correlative response is more readily put in drive (brought into action). We may then state the *Law of Readiness* as follows: *When a bond is ready to act, to act gives satisfaction and not to act gives annoyance; when a bond is not ready to act, to be forced to act gives annoyance.* A hungry small boy before an unlimited amount of ice-cream begins with his ice-cream-eating-bonds ready to act. This being so, for them to act (i.e., for him to eat), gives satisfaction. Not to act (e.g., to be compelled to wait till a long line of others are served) gives annoyance. As the boy eats, the readiness of his ice-cream-eating-bonds may for a while be increased, but as he disposes of plateful after plateful this readiness declines. At length he is satisfied, the bonds then are no longer ready to act. If now he be compelled to eat more, the process brings annoyance rather than satisfaction; and if the coerced eating be long continued, extreme annoyance will ensue. The *Law of Effect* applies only to modifiable bonds and is as follows: *A modifiable bond is strengthened or weakened according as (success and) satisfaction or (failure and) annoyance attend its exercise.* Using the diagram just above, suppose the stimulation (S) is a teacher's asking a small boy how much is 7 x 6. Suppose the boy does not know, but guesses in succession 35, 45, and 42 (three motor responses). Here 35 and 45 were failures, as the teacher and the other children make clear, but 42 being right succeeded. According to this law 35 and 45 being failures brought annoyance, and accordingly the next time a call for 7 x 6 comes the response is because of this failure and annoyance less likely than before to be either 35 or 45. Similarly because 42 was successful and brought satisfaction, this response is next time more likely to come than on the former occasion. These changes in the likelihood that a response will come we called learning in (d) above. A single experience, however, is usually not sufficient to fix 42 as an abiding response to the stimulus 7 x 6. The *Law of Exercise* (or *Use and Disuse*) then comes in to say: *When a given stimulus arouses a certain response, the connection between stimulus and that response is strengthened by the exercise so obtained.* This statement covers only the factor of use. Analogously if a connection is not exercised, is not called into play, it is weakened by disuse. There are other things to be said about this law, but these are the most important of its features. The more often the stimulus 7 x 6 brings 42 (with satisfaction), the better is that response fixed. If, however, the boy should after learning 7 x 6 = 42 fail to make use of it, he would gradually "forget" it.

523. Trial and Error (or Trial and Success)

"Place a hungry young cat in a strange cage, with a bit of fish lying just outside, and you are sure to get action. The cat extends his paw between the slats but cannot reach the fish; he pushes his nose between the slats but cannot get through; he bites the slats, claws at anything small, shakes anything loose, and tries every part of the cage. Coming to the button that fastens the door, he attacks that also, and sooner or later turns the button, gets out, and eats the fish. The experimenter, having noted the time occupied in this first trial, replaces the cat, still hungry, in the cage, and another bit of fish outside. Same business, but perhaps somewhat quicker escape. More trials, perhaps on a series of days, give gradually decreasing times of escape. The useless reactions are gradually eliminated, till finally the cat, on being placed in the cage, goes instantly to the door, turns the button, goes out and starts to eat, requiring but a second or two for the whole complex reaction. Perhaps 15 or 20 trials have been required to reach this stage of prompt, unerring response. The course of improvement is rather irregular, with ups and downs, but with no sudden shift from the varied reaction of the first trial to the fixed reaction of the last. The learning process has been gradual.

"This is the typical instance of learning by 'trial and error,' which can be defined as varied reaction with gradual elimination of the unsuccessful responses and fixation of the successful one. . . .

"There is no evidence that the cat reasons his way out of the cage. His behaviour is impulsive, not deliberative. There is not even any evidence that the cat clearly observes how he gets out. If he made a clean-cut observation of the manner of escape, his time for escaping should thereupon take a sudden drop, instead of falling off gradually and irregularly from trial to trial, as it does fall off. Trial and error learning is learning by doing, and not by reasoning or observing. The cat learns to get out by getting out, not by seeing how to get out."

Woodworth, *Psychology* * (New York, Holt, 1921), pp. 308-310.

524. THE EDUCATIONAL SITUATION

"The studies of the symbolic and formal sort represented the aims and material of education for a sufficiently long time to call into existence a machinery of administration and of instruction thoroughly adapted to themselves. This machinery constituted the actual working scheme of administration and instruction. These conditions persist long after the studies to which they are well adapted have lost their theoretical supremacy. . . .

"It is easy to fall into the habit of regarding the mechanics of school organization and administration as something comparatively external and indifferent to educational purposes and ideals (p. 22). . . . We forget that it is precisely such things as those that really control the whole system, even on its distinctively educational side (p. 23). . . . The school environment and machinery almost compel the more mechanical features of school-work to lord it over the more vital aims" (p. 25).

Dewey, *The Educational Situation* * (Chicago, University of Chicago, 1906).

525. THE LOGICAL RESULT

"Eventually our schools will, in certain respects, resemble great manufacturing plants. The achievement tests will become accurate gauges of the educational (manufacturing) processes. In each subject the children will pass through a given number of steps in as definite and sequential an order as the steps in a manufacturing process. The standard tests will measure the accomplishments as the machine products are gauged. Each process within each subject will be mastered before an advance is made. Each process will be taught by an expert, automatic devices and machines being used where possible.

"The achievement tests compel the child to aim each educational effort at one object where we are now aiming at a flock. For a certain definite and limited time, each child will attack his own specific difficulty after the application of the test has shown him what that difficulty is. The children will be grouped in such a manner that all who are overcoming a specific obstacle concentrate their efforts upon it at the same time."

Leonard Power, in *N. E. A. Bulletin of Elementary School Principals*, 2:16 (1923).

526. SUGGESTIONS FROM THE TEACHER

"There is no ground for holding that the teacher should not suggest anything to the child until he has *consciously* expressed a want in that direction. A sympathetic teacher is quite likely to know more clearly than the child himself what his own instincts are and mean. But the suggestion must *fit in* with the dominant mode of growth in the child; it must serve simply as stimulus to bring forth more adequately what the child is already blindly striving to do. Only by watching the child and seeing the attitude that he assumes towards suggestions can we tell whether they are operating as factors in furthering the child's growth, or whether they are external, arbitrary impositions interfering with normal growth.

"The same principle applies even more strongly to so-called dictation work. Nothing is more absurd than to suppose that there is no middle term between leaving a child to his own unguided fancies and likes or controlling his activities by a formal succession of dictated directions. As just intimated, it is the teacher's business to know what powers are striving for utterance at a given period in the child's development, and what sorts of activity will bring these to helpful expression, in order then to supply the requisite stimuli and needed materials. The suggestion, for instance, of a playhouse, the suggestion that comes from seeing objects that have already been made to furnish it, from seeing other children at work, is quite sufficient definitely to direct the activities of a normal child of five. Imitation and suggestion come in naturally and inevitably, but only as instruments to help him carry out his own wishes and ideas. They serve to make him realize, to bring to consciousness, what he already is striving for in a vague, confused, and therefore ineffective way. From the psychological standpoint it may safely be said that when a teacher has to rely upon a series of dictated directions, it is just because the child has no image of his own of what is to be done or why it is to be done. Instead, therefore, of gaining power of control by conforming to directions, he is really losing it—made dependent upon an external source."

Dewey, in *Elementary School Record,** 1:150-151 (June, 1900).

527. PUPIL ATTITUDES

Horace Mann Fifth Grade pupils (1919-20) said of their project work:

"I like being able to use many books and look up work because it makes the recitation more interesting. Before, I was allowed to use only one book, and all the boys and girls had the same one."

"I like being able to help each other. We are more of a unit."

Marie Hennes, in *Teachers College Record,** 22:148 (March, 1921).

528. DEFINITION AND CLASSIFICATION OF PROJECTS

"The particular word, project (as here used), is of small consequence; the idea or point of view back of the word is the important element. We understand the term project to refer to any unit of purposeful experience, any instance of purposeful activity where the dominating purpose, as an inner urge, (1) fixes the aim of the action, (2) guides its process, and (3) furnishes its drive, its inner motivation.

"The project thus may refer to any kind or variety of life

experience which is in fact actuated by a dominating purpose. I myself distinguish four types which in their border cases merge, to be sure, into each other. Moreover an example of any type might conceivably appear as a subordinate purpose under any other of the four types or under another instance of its own type. Let us consider the four types in turn.

"The first type represents those experiences in which the dominating purpose is to do, to make, or to effect; to embody an idea or aspiration in material form. The material of which the thing is made, in which the idea is to be embodied, may vary from clay, wood, cloth, and the like, through marble or pigment, to the words and thoughts and aspirations of a letter, a speech, a poem, a symphony, or a prayer. The finished production may be as insignificant as a child's sand pile on the seashore or as great as Alexander's empire. It may be built in a moment and perish in the building, or it may take as long in the making and remain as enduring as Newton's *Principia*. The criterion for judging is the character of the purpose. Is there an idea to be embodied? Is there an animating purpose to realize the idea? Is there consequent effortful action dominated by this purpose? If 'yes' is the answer to all these questions, then the project is of the first type.

"The second type of project may be defined as one which involves purposeful enjoying or appropriation of an experience. A boy will see and enjoy fireworks, or a circus, or a parade of soldiers. He will watch and enjoy watching a bee-martin drive off a hawk, or a spider spin a web and catch a fly in it. His mother will with a similar true purpose see and enjoy a sunset, or the beauties of the Mona Lisa. At succeeding periods in her life a girl will hear and enjoy a story, read and enjoy a novel, hear and see and enjoy a play of Shakespeare. Experiences of this type are, in comparison with those of the first type, relatively passive. For this reason, I suppose, some have been troubled that this type of experience should be included in the discussion and be called a project. The criterion again is the presence of a purpose. If the experience were in fact an entirely passive one, then purpose would have no place. But in all such experiences there is much activity. So again we ask: Is there a purpose for engaging in, and appropriating, and enjoying the experience? Does the purpose guide the action of seeing or hearing, as the case may be? If there is this purpose, then the experience described is a project of the second type. We may digress to ask whether the presence or absence in the child of the attitude of purpose in such experiences makes any difference to the teacher who would use them educatively? The inevitable affirmative answer is sufficient reason for including this type of purposeful experience in an educational treatment of the subject. Perhaps the school of the future will know better how to exploit the educational possibilities of this second type of project.

"The third kind of project is one in which the dominating purpose is to solve a problem, to unravel and so compose some intellectual entanglement or difficulty. The problem has its natural setting and origin, at least in the race history, in the pursuit of some end. Thus it begins, both for the individual and for the race, as a subordinate part of a project of the first type. Probably for most people thinking is limited largely to such practical situations as arise in ordinary life: a difficulty arises; thinking is necessary to surmount it. If this were all, it would probably have been wise not to set off this purposive problem-solving as a separate type. But with intellectual growth there comes the possibility of relatively separated problems. To the intellectually-minded a problem has a grip of its own. The solution of problems has a technique of its own, varying, to be sure, with the field of enquiry. The essential part which ideas play in effective intelligence affords sufficient justification for encouraging our pupils to work much with problems. In no other way can ideas be better clarified or better organized. So far all are agreed. There are some, however, who profess difficulty in distinguishing a problem from a project. The criterion is as elsewhere, the presence or absence of a dominating purpose. I may be confronted now with an ax, now with a problem. I may recognize both, the one as an ax, the other as a problem; but so far there is no project. If further I decline to wield the one or solve the other, there is still no project. A project for me begins exactly when my purpose arises. You ask me: 'What is one-third of the number whose third is three?' I may say, and many will say, 'I could work it if I tried, but I don't like mathematics.' If I do answer in this way, I recognize it as a problem, but I decline to purpose its solution. There exists then no project for me. A project of the third type implies first a felt difficulty, a problem; and second, a purpose to solve the problem. The use of problems being granted, the part that purpose plays in solving them, especially the more complex ones, is so clear and definite that none will question the proper inclusion of this as a third type of project.

"The fourth type includes experiences in which the purpose is to acquire some item or degree of knowledge or skill, or more generally, experiences in which a person purposes his own education at a specific point. The difference between this and other kinds of drill is again exactly one of attitude. Here the child purposes to learn the thing at hand, an attitude which makes a great difference in the efficiency of learning? A particularly valuable purpose in the realm of school work is one in which the person purposes to organize a point of view already more or less in hand, and to fix it in his memory for effective use later. Whether the making of the organization puts this under Type I, or whether the effort to fix it in memory keeps it here under Type IV is a matter of no moment. It is very important, however, that the teacher who would use the project method shall see the utility of the procedure and seek its use by his pupils. The dominating purpose to learn is the essence of projects of Type IV.

"We may further distinguish group projects from individual projects. In the latter one person alone is considered as feeling the dominating purpose. In the former several unite in a common purpose and pursue coöperatively, by a more or less clearly marked division of labor, the end held jointly in view. The social value of such coöperative pursuit of joint purposes needs no discussion here. . . .

"It may not be out of place by way of negative definition to say emphatically that a project is *not a topic*—large or small. What gave rise to the idea that a large topic constitutes a project is beyond my power to explain. We hold no copyright for the term; but what sense or purpose there can be in introducing this kind of confusion is more than I can see. Projects may arise in connection with topics; but most emphatically a topic as such is not a project."

Kilpatrick, in *Teachers College Record*,[*] 22:283-7 (Sept., 1921).

CHAPTER XXI

THINKING

529. THE PROCESS OF DELIBERATION

"Deliberation is a dramatic rehearsal (in imagination) of various competing possible lines of action. It starts from the blocking of efficient overt action. . . . Then each habit, each impulse, involved in the temporary suspense of overt action takes its turn in being tried out. Deliberation is an experiment in finding out what the various lines of possible action are really like. It is an experiment in making various combinations of selected elements of habits and impulses, to see what the resultant action would be like if it were entered upon. But the trial is in imagination, not in overt fact. The experiment is carried on by tentative rehearsals in thought which do not affect physical facts outside the body. Thought runs ahead and foresees outcomes, and thereby avoids having to await the instructions of actual failure and disaster. An act overtly tried out is irrevocable, its consequences cannot be blotted out. An act tried out in imagination is not final or fatal. It is retrievable.

"Each conflicting habit and impulse takes its turn in projecting itself upon the screen of imagination. It unrolls a picture of its future history, of the career it would have if it were given head. . . .

"We can judge its nature, assign its meaning, only by following it into the situations whither it leads, noting the objects against which it runs and seeing how they rebuff or unexpectedly encourage it. In imagination as in fact we know a road only by what we see as we travel on it. Moreover the objects which prick out the course of a proposed act until we can see its design also serve to direct eventual overt activity. Every object hit upon as the habit traverses its imaginary path has a direct effect upon existing activities. It reinforces, inhibits, redirects habits already working or stirs up others which had not previously actively entered in. In thought as well as in overt action, the objects experienced in following out a course of action attract, repel, satisfy, annoy, promote and retard. Thus deliberation proceeds. To say that at last it ceases is to say that choice, decision, takes place.

"What then is choice? Simply hitting in imagination upon an object which furnishes an adequate stimulus to the recovery of overt action. Choice is made as soon as some habit, or some combination of elements of habits and impulse, finds a way fully open. Then energy is released. The mind is made up, composed, unified. As long as deliberation pictures shoals or rocks or troublesome gales as marking the route of a contemplated voyage, deliberation goes on. But when the various factors in action fit harmoniously together, when imagination finds no annoying hindrance, when there is a picture of open seas, filled sails and favoring winds, the voyage is definitely entered upon. This decisive direction of action constitutes choice."

Dewey, *Human Nature and Conduct* * (New York, Holt, 1922), pp. 190, 192-3.

530. SUCCESSIVE TYPES OF ATTENTION

"Play . . . is typical of what writers call spontaneous attention, or, as some say, non-voluntary attention. The child is simply absorbed in what he is doing; the occupation in which he is engaged lays complete hold upon him. He gives himself without reserve. Hence, while there is much energy spent, there is no *conscious* effort; while the child is intent, to the point of engrossment, there is no *conscious* intention.

"With the development of a sense of more remote ends, and of the need of directing acts so as to make them means for these ends . . . we have the transition to what is termed indirect, or, as some writers prefer to say, voluntary, attention. A result is imaged, and the child attends to what is before him or what he is immediately doing, because it helps to secure the result. Taken by itself, the object or the act might be indifferent or even repulsive. But because it is felt to belong to something desirable or valuable, it borrows the latter's attracting and holding power.

"This is the transition to 'voluntary' attention, but only the transition. The latter comes fully into being only when the child entertains results in the form of problems or questions, the solution of which he is to seek for himself. In the intervening stage (in the child from eight to, say, eleven or twelve), while the child directs a series of intervening activities on the basis of some end he wishes to reach, this end is something to be done or made, or some tangible result to be reached; the problem is a practical difficulty, rather than an intellectual question. But with growing power, the child can conceive of the end as something to be found out, discovered; and can control his acts and images so as to help in the enquiry and solution. This is reflective attention proper. . . .

"In history work there is change from the story and biography form, from discussion of questions that arise, to the formulation of questions. Points about which difference of opinion is possible, matters upon which experience, reflection, etc., can be brought to bear, are always coming up in history. But to use the discussion to develop this matter of doubt and difference into a definite problem, to bring the child to feel just what the difficulty is; and then throw him upon his own resources in looking up material bearing upon the point, and upon his judgment in bringing it to bear, or getting a solution, is a marked intellectual advance. So in the science studies there is a change from the practical attitude of making and using cameras to the consideration of the problems intellectually involved in this—to principles of light, angular measurements, etc., which give the theory or explanation of the practice. . . .

"In general, this growth is a natural psychical process. But the proper recognition and use of it is perhaps the most serious problem in instruction upon the intellectual side. A person who has gained the power of selective attention, the power to hold problems, questions, before the mind, *is* in so far, intellectually speaking, educated. He has mental discipline—power *of* the mind and *for* the mind. Without this the mind remains at the mercy of custom and external suggestions."

Dewey, in *Elementary School Record,** 1:111-112 (May, 1900).

531. MEANING

If I hear a certain familiar and characteristic voice, even though I do not see the speaker I immediately say to myself, "It is my old friend, Tom Jones." To me the sound of that voice is joined surely and uniquely to Tom Jones. To hear that voice makes me think exactly of him. That voice to me means him. This illustration tells us what meaning means: one thing present to sense or thought, another thing (usually more important) so joined in me to it that the thought of the one calls up the thought of the other. This is all exactly an illustration of $S \rightarrow R$. A bond has been built up in me between two things (a "this" and a "that") so that when "this" is present as a

THINKING

stimulus to me I respond by thinking "that." Under such conditions we say "this" means "that."

532. What is a Concept?

Imagine the extraordinary case of a child old enough to play with dogs but practically ignorant of them. One glorious day a playful little white dog, Fido, comes into Hal's life. They have great fun playing together. At the close of day Hal is a different boy from what he was that morning. He has experienced Fido, or more exactly he has had a series of varied experiences with Fido, and—without any special intention or effort on his part—he has organized into his nervous make-up these experiences. He now thinks certain things about Fido, his looks and ways of behaving, what he can do to and with Fido, what Fido can and will do, etc., etc.

All of these things are tied up together in the boy's mind. If he should hear the little bark, he would at once expect Fido and—in greater or less degree—the other parts of the experience, the white coat, the four feet, the sharp little teeth, the way Fido rushes at the robins or fetches a stick. Any one of these things if present to sense will recall with greater or less faithfulness all the others.

Such an organization of experience we call a concept. There are other things that might be said about a concept but this is its essence: an aggregate of experiences or phases of experience so organized in one's mind that the presence to thought of any one of them tends to call up an expectation of the others. It is at once evident that each one of us is continually revising his concepts: Fido may next time bite Hal in earnest or the next dog Hal sees may be black and not playful. Thus it is that concepts are built, whether of the particular dog Fido or of the dog as a class of animals.

The latter type of concept especially, that of a class, has apparently two parts, the first consisting of all our experiences of dogs aggregated as it were into a complex but more or less well organized expectation of what may happen in connection with any dog we might meet; the second consisting of those qualities that we think of as belonging to all dogs and exclusively to dogs, signs, as it were, by which we identify this approaching object as a dog. In earlier times, when formal logic was more to the fore, the second part, which has to do with the definition of the class, received predominant attention and to this day at times tries to claim an exclusive right to the name of concept. But in these more practical days the first—the aggregation of past experiences and therefore the expectation of possible future experiences—is far and away the more important. More strictly still perhaps, the distinction between the two is rather as to the way in which the concept is used than a separation of the concept into two parts: We need to *identify* this approaching thing with its class in order to know what to *expect* from it. Identification and consequent foretelling are specific functions performed by the concept. The concept, then, is an organization of past experiences which serves to identify and foretell and accordingly to direct future experiences along chosen lines.

533. ABSTRACTION

Abstraction is "a term of logic meaning the separation, for *intellectual* purposes only, of a quality from the thing to which it belongs, or a relation from the pair of things between which it subsists. Its possibility rests upon capacity for *selective* attention, in virtue of which some trait not sensuously conspicuous or intense is dwelt upon because of its importance in relation to some conceived end. . . . Since reasoning depends upon the capacity to treat an extracted quality or relation as a sample or typical instance, rational thought is dependent on abstraction or selective attention. The consideration of some quality or relation irrespective of the particular context in which it is found is obviously an indispensable prerequisite for all generalization, so much so that it may be put down as a general principle that abstraction exists for the sake of a resulting generalization."

Dewey, Abstraction, in Monroe, *Cyclopedia of Education* * (New York, Macmillan, 1911).

534. GENERALIZATION

Generalization is "the process by which a principle or law is reached. . . . The term expresses the use or function of induction, which endeavors, beginning with a number of scattered details, to arrive at a general statement. Generalization . . . works a measure of economy and efficiency from the standpoints alike of observation, memory, and thought. The number of particulars that can be obtained is limited. When, however, different cases are brought together,—and this bringing together is expressed in a general principle,—a great variety of cases are practically reduced to one case, and further observation is freed to attack new particular things and qualities not yet systematized. Exactly the same holds good for memory. There are a few prodigies who can carry in mind an indefinite number of unrelated details; but most persons need the help of generalizations in order to retain specific facts and to recall them when needed. Logically, a principle not only sums up and registers the net intellectual outcome of a great many different experiences which have been undergone at diverse times and places, but is an illuminating and clarifying means of interpreting new cases that without it could not be understood. . . .

"Generalization is a continuous, gradual movement away from mere isolated particulars toward a connecting principle. A necessary part of the work of instruction is, therefore, to make the conditions such that the mind will move in the direction of a fruitful generalization as soon as it begins to deal with and to collect particulars. The resulting generalization will, of course, be crude, vague, and inadequate, but, if formed under proper conditions, it will serve at once to direct and vitalize further observations and recollections, and will be built out and tested in the application to new particulars. This suggests the final educational principle: A generalization or law is such not in virtue of its structure or bare content, but because of its use or function. We do not first have a principle and then apply it; an idea becomes general (or a principle) in process of fruitful application to the interpretation, comprehension, and prevision of the particular facts of experience."

Dewey, Generalization, in Monroe, *Cyclopedia of Education* *
(New York, Macmillan, 1912).

535. BUILDING GENERALIZATIONS

"One particular type of idea building fundamental to our needs is that called generalization, in which from a limited number of instances of a class we build up an idea that enables us to recognize a novel instance of the same class. When we consider any individual instance of a class, we find in it many elements or parts. When we compare the individuals of the class with each other, we find that these elements or parts do not all stand on the same footing. Some parts or elements are common to all the instances studied. Among such common elements, some are of especial importance in that they most account for the striking characteristics of the class. The process by which the mind picks out from a limited number of individual cases the fundamental principles or characteristics of the class we call generalization.

"Consider the way by which the child comes to the generalized notion of *fair play*. In playing his childish games he hears the more knowing ones say that such a move is "no fair." He comes thus to learn that certain specific things are "no fair" and accordingly are to be avoided. At this stage he applies the term "fair" or "no fair" only to these specifically learned cases. But almost at the same time he is hearing like expressions applied in the more natural situations of dividing candy, or being taken in or left out of an automobile where there is not room for all, or the distribution of desired privileges in the schoolroom, in which some one receives more or less than he considers "fair." From these varied instances, he is practically compelled to pick out the elements of being "against the rule," bearing unequally or with partiality, and the like, and to generalize these into a partial concept of fairness and unfairness. This process will under favorable conditions continue until the child, now grown older, will have developed his partial concept into one at least fairly adequate.

"Among the conditions favorable for such effective generalization are (i) a wide variety and diversity of instances experienced, (ii) a high degree of interest or concern in the outcome of the situation, and (iii) a wise guidance. This guidance may act either by calling attention to instances not yet considered by the child, or by helping him to single out more consciously and definitely the really significant elements. As has already been indicated, it is exactly in this connection that class discussion is so important. A discussion in which the children freely disclose the adequacy or inadequacy of their own ideas regarding the matter under consideration affords precisely the best opportunity for correcting their inadequacies. It is of course true that the ease and rapidity with which the process of generalization goes forward, and the degree to which it is carried, will vary greatly with original mental differences found among children."

Bagley, Dunn, and Kilpatrick, Unpublished MS.

CHAPTER XXII

MORAL EDUCATION

536. Temptation

"Why comes temptation, but for man to meet
And master and make crouch beneath his foot,
And so be pedestaled in triumph."

Browning, *The Ring and the Book*. The Pope. Lines 1185-7.

537. Discipline

"A person who is trained to consider his actions, to undertake them deliberately, is in so far disciplined. Add to this ability a power to endure in an intelligently chosen course in face of distraction, confusion, and difficulty, and you have the essence of discipline."

Dewey, *Democracy and Education* * (New York, Macmillan, 1916), p. 151.

538. Education for Morals

"Education has for its object the formation of character.... Those, therefore, who advocate the use of authority, and if need be—force in the management of children, must do so because they think these the best means of compassing the desired object —formation of character.... Suppose an amiable little urchin is pursuing his own gratification regardless of the comfort of others—is perhaps annoyingly vociferous in his play.... Paternity, with knit brows, and in a severe tone, commands desistance— ... if need be, hints at a whipping ... —and complacently resumes the newspaper under the impression that all is as it should be: most unfortunate mistake!

"If the thing wanted had been the mere repression of noise, or the mechanical transfer of a plaything, perhaps no better course could have been pursued. Had it been of no consequence under what impulse the child acted, so long as it fulfilled a given mandate, nothing would remain to be said. But something else was needed. Character was the thing to be changed rather than conduct. It was not the deeds, but the feeling from which the deeds sprung that required dealing with. . . . What, then, was the thing wanted? Evidently an alteration in the child's disposition. What was the problem to be solved? Clearly to generate a state of mind which had it previously existed would have prevented the offending actions. What was the final end to be achieved? Unquestionably the formation of a character which should spontaneously produce greater generosity of conduct. Or, speaking definitely, it was necessary to strengthen that sympathy to the weakness of which this ill behavior was traceable.

"But sympathy can be strengthened only by exercise. No faculty whatever will grow, save by the performance of its special function—a muscle by contraction; the intellect by perceiving and thinking; a moral sentiment by feeling. Sympathy, therefore, can be increased only by exciting sympathetic emotions. A selfish child is to be rendered less selfish, only by arousing in it a fellow-feeling with the desires of others. If this is not done, nothing is done."

Spencer, *Social Statics* (New York, Appleton, 1878 [1]), p 201 ff.

539. JAMES ON IDEO-MOTOR ACTION

"There is no sort of consciousness whatever, be it sensation, feeling, or idea, which does not directly and of itself tend to discharge into some motor effect. The motor effect need not always be an outward stroke of behavior. It may be only an alteration of the heart-beats or breathing, or a modification in the distribution of blood, such as blushing or turning pale; or else a secretion of tears, or what not. But, in any case, it is there in some shape when any consciousness is there; and a belief as fundamental as any in modern psychology is the belief at last attained that conscious processes of any sort, conscious processes merely as such, *must* pass over into motion, open or concealed.

"The least complicated case of this tendency is the case of a mind possessed by only a single idea. If that idea be of an object connected with a native impulse, the impulse will immediately proceed to discharge. If it be the idea of a movement, the movement will occur. Such a case of action from a single idea has been distinguished from more complex cases by the name of 'ideo-motor' action, meaning action without express decision or effort. Most of the habitual actions to which we are trained are of this

[1] First edition, 1850.

ideo-motor sort. We perceive, for instance, that the door is open, and we rise and shut it; we perceive some raisins in a dish before us, and extend our hand and carry one of them to our mouth without interrupting the conversation; or, when lying in bed, we suddenly think that we shall be late for breakfast, and instantly we get up with no particular exertion or resolve. All the ingrained procedures by which life is carried on—the manners and customs, dressing and undressing, acts of salutation, etc. —are executed in this semi-automatic way unhesitatingly and efficiently, the very outermost margin or consciousness seeming to be concerned in them, while the focus may be occupied with widely different things."

James, *Talks to Teachers* * (New York, Holt, 1899), pp. 170-172.

540. THORNDIKE ON IDEO-MOTOR ACTION

"Next, and even more orthodox, is the theory of ideo-motor action, that the idea of an act or of the result of an act, or some part of such result, tends, in and of itself, to produce or connect with that act. . . .

"The classic statement of the power to bind acts to situations by so linking ideas of them is given by James (p. 176). . . .

"Against this orthodox opinion, I contend that the idea of a movement (or of any response whatever), is, in and of itself, unable to produce it. I contend that an idea does not tend to provoke the act which it *is an idea of*, but only that which it *connects with as a result of the laws of instinct, exercise and effect*.

"In particular I contend that any idea, image, sensation, percept, or any other mental state whatever, has, apart from use, disuse, satisfaction and discomfort, no stronger tendency to call up any other movement (p. 177). . . .

"Many thinkers about moral education have assumed the truth of the ideo-motor theory and so have trusted that presenting stories of noble acts was such a universal means of ennobling conduct (p. 289). . . .

"This confidence that an idea will be realized in behavior if only we can get it into the mind and keep the opposite ideas out, has as its consequence, in turn, the expectation of vast moral improvement from the study of literary descriptions of virtue, . . . and in the end the deliberate insertion in the curriculum of subject-matter chosen because it gives impressive ideas of good acts and so, supposedly, creates them (p. 291). . . .

"It is, of course, my contention that the theory itself is wrong" (p. 292).

Thorndike, *Educational Psychology* * (New York, Teachers College, 1913), Vol. I.

541. JAMES ON MORAL DELIBERATION

"The hackneyed example of moral deliberation is the case of an habitual drunkard under temptation. He has made a resolve to reform, but he is now solicited again by the bottle. His moral triumph or failure literally consists in his finding the right *name* for the case. If he says that it is a case of not wasting good liquor already poured out, or a case of not being churlish and unsociable when in the midst of friends, or a case of learning something at last about a brand of whiskey which he never met before, or a case of celebrating a public holiday, or a case of stimulating himself to a more energetic resolve in favor of abstinence than any he has ever yet made, then he is lost. His choice of the wrong name seals his doom. But if, in spite of all the plausible good names with which his thirsty fancy so copiously furnishes him, he unwaveringly clings to the truer bad name, and apperceives the case as that of "being a drunkard, being a drunkard, being a drunkard," his feet are planted on the road to salvation. He saves himself by thinking rightly.

"Thus are your pupils to be saved: first, by the stock of ideas with which you furnish them; second, by the amount of voluntary attention that they can exert in holding to the right ones, however unpalatable; and, third, by the several habits of acting definitely on these latter to which they have been successfully trained."

James, *Talks to Teachers* * (New York, Holt, 1899), pp. 187-188.

542. WHAT IS A MORAL SITUATION?

"A moral situation is one in which judgment and choice are required antecedently to overt action. The practical meaning of the situation—that is to say the action needed to satisfy it—is not self-evident. It has to be searched for. There are conflicting desires and alternative apparent goods. What is needed is to find the right course of action, the right good. Hence, inquiry is exacted: observation of the detailed makeup of the situation; analysis into its diverse factors; clarification of what is obscure; discounting of the more insistent and vivid traits; tracing the consequences of the various modes of action that suggest themselves; regarding the decision reached as hypothetical and tentative until the anticipated or supposed consequences which led to its adoption have been squared with actual consequences. This inquiry is intelligence. Our moral failures go back to some weakness of disposition, some absence of sympathy, some onesided bias that makes us perform the judgment of the concrete case carelessly or perversely. Wide sympathy, keen sensitiveness, persistence in the face of the disagreeable, balance of interests enabling us to undertake the work of analysis and decision intelligently are the distinctively moral traits—the virtues or moral excellencies."

Dewey, *Reconstruction in Philosophy* * (New York, Holt, 1920), p. 163-4.

543. KANT ON CHARACTER

"Character means that the person derives his rules of conduct from himself and from the dignity of humanity. Character is the common ruling principle in man in the use of his talents and attributes. Thus it is the nature of his will, and is good or bad. A man who acts without settled principles, with no uniformity, has no character. A man may have a good heart and yet no character, because he is dependent upon impulses and does not act according to maxims. Firmness and unity of principle are essential to character. Character is developed late and supports itself at last."

Buchner, *Kant's Educational Theory* × (Philadelphia, Lippincott, 1904), p. 228.

544. OBEDIENCE

"The obedience of children, in itself alone, without consideration of its motive, can have no other value than that thereby much is made easier to the parents."

Richter, *Levana* (1807, Bohn ed.), p. 172.

545. THE AMERICAN BOY IN GERMAN EYES

"The pert American boy who does just what he pleases may thus get an early training in democratic politics; but while he wastes the best of the home and of the classroom, he gets at the same time the worst possible training for the duties of life, all of which demand that he do later quite other things than those which he likes to do. He will learn too late that it is a great thing to command, but a greater thing to obey, and that no one can too early sign the declaration of dependence."

Münsterberg, *American Traits* * (Boston, Houghton Mifflin, 1901), p. 198 f.

546. John Wesley: Break your Child's Will

"Break your child's will in order that it may not perish. Break its will as soon as it can speak plainly—or even before it can speak at all. It should be forced to do as it is told, even if you have to whip it ten times running. Break its will, in order that its soul may live."

James, *Talks to Teachers* (New York, Holt, 1899), p. 182.

547. Bishop Welles: Duties of Parents to Children

"Endeavor as soon as possible, to break their [your children's] passions; use them to be governed, and to submit patiently their wills to yours . . . a great part of the sins, and most of the troubles we fall into in the course of our lives, come from the want of due care of breaking our passions when we were young."

Guardian of Education (London, 1802), 1:30.

548. The Scylla and Charybdis of Education

"The Principle of all Virtue and Excellency lies in a Power of denying ourselves the Satisfaction of our own Desires, where Reason does not authorize them. This Power is to be got and improv'd by Custom, made easy and familiar by an *early* Practice. If therefore I might be heard, I would advise, that, contrary to the ordinary Way, Children should be us'd to submit their Desires, and go without their Longings, even *from their very Cradles*. The first Thing they should learn to know, should be, that they were not to have any Thing because it pleas'd them, but because it was thought fit for them. . . .

"He that has not a Mastery over his inclinations, he that knows not how to *resist* the Importunity of *present Pleasure or Pain,* for the sake of what Reason tells him is fit to be done, wants the true Principle of Virtue and Industry, and is in danger never to be good for any Thing. . . .

"On the other Side, if the Mind be curb'd, and *humbled* too much in Children; if their *Spirits* be abas'd and *broken* much, by too strict an Hand over them, they lose all their Vigour and Industry, and are in a worse State than the former. For extravagant young Fellows, that have Liveliness and Spirit, come

MORAL EDUCATION

sometimes to be set right, and so make able and great Men; but *dejected Minds,* timorous and tame, and *low Spirits,* are hardly ever to be rais'd, and very seldom attain to any Thing. To avoid the Danger that is on either Hand, is the great Art; and he that has found a Way how to keep up a Child's Spirit easy, active, and free, and yet at the same time to restrain him from many Things he has a Mind to, and to draw him to Things that are uneasy to him; he, I say, that knows how to reconcile these seeming Contradictions, has, in my Opinion, got the true Secret of Education."

Locke, *Education* (Cambridge, 1892 [1]), pp. 25 f., 29 f.

549. THE ILL EFFECT OF PLAY

"Let it then be resolved, whether amusements, free and spontaneous amusements should not be discarded; and in their place employments only admitted, as part of an education uniformly consistent in design. Let these employments be changes or remissions from school business, but not from continued discipline. I propose that the same discipline should still be carried on as much out of school as in school by a course of exercises, active and emulative, sheltered and unsheltered, but subject to strict regulation as much as literary employment. All the difference between school and remission will be this; one is active, and the other sedentary: between this use of remission and the former; one was voluntary and the other is now imposed. Remissions of study reduced to stated rule and subordination will operate much in favour of the internal school discipline; habits of obedience will be deeply because they are continuedly impressed. Study is a hard word and chiefly irksome because exercise is left to be self-directed. Let both be placed on a nearer level as to inducement, and they will both be more equally coveted. . . . Study, like the business of man will be a duty no longer irksome, if you restrain the great antidote play."

Parsons, *Essays on Education* (London, 1794), pp. 107-109.

550. ON THE CHASTISEMENT OF CHILDREN

"He that loveth his son will continue to lay stripes upon him, that he may have joy of him in the end. He that chastiseth his son shall have profit of him, and shall glory of him among his acquaintance. . . . He that maketh too much of his son shall bind up his wounds; and his heart will be troubled at every

[1] First edition, 1693.

cry. An unbroken horse becometh stubborn; and a son left at large becometh headstrong. Cocker thy child, and he shall make thee afraid; play with him, and he will grieve thee. Laugh not with him, lest thou have sorrow with him; and thou shalt gnash thy teeth in the end. Give him no liberty in his youth, and wink not at his follies. Bow down his neck in his youth, and beat him on the sides while he is a child, lest he wax stubborn, and be disobedient unto thee; and there shall be sorrow to thy soul. Chastise thy son, and take pains with him, lest his shameless behaviour be an offence unto thee."

Ecclesiasticus (Moulton ed., Macmillan, 1896), Bk. II, ch. xxi.

551. Plutarch on Incentives

"I affirm that boys should be led on to the performance of noble action by admonitions and arguments—most decidedly not by blows and harsh treatment. I regard such treatment as more suitable to slaves than to free-born citizens. It blunts the sensibilities and engenders a distaste for work. The cause is, in part, the pain produced by the blows inflicted; in part by the feeling of shame arising from the rough usage suffered."

Plutarch, *Education of Boys* * (Trans. by Super. Syracuse, Bardeen, 1910), Ch. XII.

552. The Use of Punishment

"The selection of good responses by associating their connection with appropriate situations with satisfaction is in general preferable to the elimination of bad responses by pain or deprivation.† It is true that if an animal learns to respond correctly from the infliction of pain, it may learn rapidly. But there is a strong tendency for an animal, if punished for a given response, not to avoid it in favor of the right one, but to avoid making any. The more intense the punishment, the more likely this is to be the case. . . .

"To hit a baby's hand every time that it starts to reach for some improper object on a table can be shown to be useful; but to hit a child's hand because a blot is found upon his sheet of writing can be shown to be wasteful as well as cruel."

† "Where the desired response is simply *not to do* a certain thing punishment is very useful. When there are only two alternatives, to do A or to do B, A being wrong, punishment is fairly effective. When there are many possibilities, A, B, C, D . . . N, which are of varying merit, punishment is likely to be very wasteful." (Footnote in original.)

Thorndike, *Education** (New York, Macmillan, 1912), p. 201-2.

553. Some Method Effects

"A thoughtful Chinese woman, a third generation Christian, and an earnest Christian worker, confessed that when she left middle school it was with the resolution never to open her Bible again, so weary was she of the uninteresting required Bible study which she had had throughout her school years. . . .

"Some schools lay emphasis on the creation and development of the mood of worship through the chapel service. It is held in a room built for the purpose, the very lines and coloring of which are conducive to worship. The service is reverent and dignified, given wholly to the things of the spirit. Perhaps some of us do not fully appreciate this means of religious education, yet to many an impressionable student, the atmosphere and spirit of worship may teach more of Christianity than many a talk about it."

Christian Education in China* (New York, Foreign Missions Conference, 1922), p. 289.

554. August Francke on the Attractiveness of Evil

"We may praise the works of God, but we must be very careful in speaking of the works of the devil. For the human heart contains sparks of evil which easily catch fire."

Quoted in Paulsen, *System of Ethics** (Trans. by Thilly. New York, Scribners, 1899), p. 305.

555. Kant on Duty in Moral Education

"It is always said that everything should be presented to children in such a manner that they will do it from *inclination*. Without doubt this is good in many cases; but there is also much that must be prescribed for them as *duty*.† This will be

† "The most ordinary observation shows that when one represents an action of uprightness, free from any idea of an advantage of any sort, in this or another world, performed faithfully amid the greatest temptations of need or enticement, it leaves every similar action which was in the least degree affected by a foreign motive far behind, and overshadows it; it elevates the soul and arouses the wish to be able also to behave thus. Even children of moderate age feel this impression, and duties should never be represented to them in any other way." (Footnote in original.)

of very great value during their whole life; for, in public duties, in the labors of an office, and in many other instances, duty alone, not inclination, can guide us. Even if we suppose that the child does not perceive the duty, it is none the less better if he be given the idea of it. . . .

"To do anything for the sake of duty means to obey reason. It is useless to speak of duty to (young) children. They come to look upon it as something the transgression of which is followed by the rod. The child could be guided by his instincts alone; but as soon as he begins to develop, the idea of duty must be added."

Buchner, *Kant's Educational Theory* * (Philadelphia, Lippincott, 1904), pp. 189-191, 193.

556. Line of Least Resistance

The term" line of least resistance" is seldom or never used in discussions of moral theory unless to apply to a weak or inglorious failure to measure up to a hard duty. The failure to measure up may be a blameworthy failure to see or acknowledge the call of duty through a weak yielding to the call of inclination, or it may—and properly—be a situation of conscious moral stress. It thus implies (i) a moral situation where duty or higher obligation in fact calls to a course of action hard or repellent, while immediate inclination points to an easier and more attractive alternative; and (ii) the weak and blameworthy choice of the easy and alluring prospect. The phrase is thus always one of disparagement implying that particular defect which we call moral weakness.

557. Love of the Good is better than Fear of the Evil

"It is clear that in general we ought, whenever we can, to employ the method of inhibition by substitution. He whose life is based upon the word 'no,' who tells the truth because a lie is wicked, and who has constantly to grapple with his envious and cowardly and mean propensities, is in an inferior situation in every respect to what he would be if the love of truth and magnanimity positively possessed him from the outset, and he felt no inferior temptations. Your born gentleman is certainly, for this world's purposes, a more valuable being than your 'Crump, with his grunting resistance to his native devils,' even though in

MORAL EDUCATION

God's sight the latter may, as the Catholic theologians say, be rolling up great stores of 'merit.'

"Spinoza long ago wrote in his Ethics that anything that a man can avoid under the notion that it is bad he may also avoid under the notion that something else is good. He who habitually acts *sub specie mali,* under the negative notion, the notion of the bad, is called a slave by Spinoza. To him who acts habitually under the notion of good he gives the name of freeman. See to it now, I beg you, that you make freemen of your pupils by habituating them to act, whenever possible, under the notion of a good. Get them habitually to tell the truth, not so much through showing them the wickedness of lying as by arousing their enthusiasm for honor and veracity. Wean them from their native cruelty by imparting to them some of your own positive sympathy with an animal's inner springs of joy. And, in the lessons which you may be legally obliged to conduct upon the bad effects of alcohol, lay less stress than the books do on the drunkard's stomach, kidneys, nerves, and social miseries, and more on the blessings of having an organism kept in lifelong possession of its youthful elasticity by a sweet, sound blood, to which stimulants and narcotics are unknown, and to which the morning sun and air and dew will daily come as sufficiently powerful intoxicants."

James, *Talks to Teachers* * (New York, Holt, 1899), p. 194 f.

INDEX OF SOURCES

Adams, Henry. The Education of Henry Adams. Houghton Mifflin. Boston 1922. 297.
Addams, Jane. Democracy and Social Ethics. Macmillan. New York 1916. 272.
Alexander, Thomas. Prussian Elementary Schools. Macmillan. New York 1918. 247, 268.
Angell, Norman. The British Revolution and the American Democracy. Huebsch. New York 1919. 437.
Anonymous (reference not located). 187, 190, 201, 274, 327, 334, 412, 414, 511.
Archbishop's Fifth Committee. London. 1918. 80, 84, 86, 177, 184, 221, 222, 223, 224, 275, 477.
Aristotle. Nicomachean Ethics (Welldon's translation). Macmillan. London 1906. 140, 191.
Aristotle. Politics (Welldon's translation). Macmillan. London 1908. 98.
Arnold, Matthew. Civilization in the United States. DeWolfe Fiske. Boston 1888. 128.
Arnold, Matthew. Culture and Anarchy. Macmillan. New York 1912. 146, 147.
Arnold, Matthew. Discourses in America. Macmillan. London 1912. 199.
Atlanta Journal. Atlanta. 1915. 335.

Bagehot, Walter, Physics and Politics. Appleton. New York 1887. 49, 159, 204, 415, 421.
Bagley, Dunn and Kilpatrick. Unpublished Ms. 535.

Bainville, Jacques. Italy and the War. London. Hodder 1916. 239.
Bakewell, Charles M. A Source Book in Ancient Philosophy. Scribners. New York 1907. 21, 134, 135, 139, 150, 153.
Baldwin, J. M. Individual and Society. Badger. Boston 1911. 96.
Baldwin, J. M. Social and Ethical Interpretations. Macmillan. New York 1906. 39.
Beard, Charles A., in The Dial. The Dial. New York 1918. 409.
Becker, Carl. United States: An Experiment in Democracy. Harpers. New York 1920. 290.
Belloc, Hillaire. The Servile State. Foulis. Edinburgh 1913. 431.
Bentham, Jeremy. Works. 1882. 148.
Berkson, I. L. Theories of Americanization. Teachers College. New York 1920. 296.
Bernhardi, F. von. Germany and the Next War. Longmans. New York 1912. 298.
Bible. 155, 166, 271, 550.
Bismarck. (Source of quotation not located). 7.
Blackstone. (Source of quotation not located). 234.
Boas, Franz. The Mind of Primitive Man. Macmillan. New York 1911. 404.
Bobbitt, Franklin. The Curriculum. Houghton Mifflin. Boston 1918. 485.
Bodenhafer, W. B., in American Journal of Sociology. Univer-

INDEX OF SOURCES

sity of Chicago Press. Chicago 1921. 99.

Bonser, F. G. The Elementary School Curriculum. Macmillan. New York 1920. 488.

Boyd, William. The Educational Theory of J. J. Rousseau. Longmans. London 1911. 161.

Boyd, William. The Minor Educational Writings of J. J. Rosseau. Blackie. London 1911. 406.

Brandenburg, G. C., in Journal of Educational Psychology. Warwick and York. Baltimore 1918. 478.

Brissenden, P. F. The I. W. W. Longmans. New York 1919. 333.

British Labor Party. Program. 1918. 233.

Brooks, Phillips. (Source of quotation not located). 235.

Brown, W. Jethro. Underlying Principles of Modern Legislation. Dutton. New York 1915. 43, 201, 443.

Browning, Robert. Poetical Works. Macmillan. New York 1894. 356, 536.

Bryce, James. American Commonwealth. Macmillan. New York 1914. 258, 321, 351, 428.

Bryce, James. Modern Democracies. Macmillan. New York 1921. 63, 205, 217, 237, 259, 318, 329, 330, 374, 407.

Buchner, Edward F. Kant's Educational Theory. Lippincott. Philadelphia 1904. 79, 182, 183, 243, 262, 279, 405, 470, 504, 506, 543, 555.

Burdge, Howard G. Our Boys. Department of Education. Albany 1921. 270.

Burke, Edmund. (Quoted in Report of Archbishop's Fifth Committee). 184.

Burn, J. A. The Catholic School System in the United States. Benziger. New York 1912. 448.

Bury, J. H. History of the Freedom of Thought. Holt. New York 1913. 178, 280, 346, 347, 349, 392, 420.

Bury, J. H. The Idea of Progress. Macmillan. London 1920. 38, 359, 377.

Bush, Wendell T., in Journal of Philosophy. Science Press. New York 1911. 23, 28.

Butler, Nicholas Murray. Address before Ohio State Bar Association. 1923. 368.

Caird, John. Philosophy of Religion. Maclehose. Glasgow 1901. 78.

Carver, Thomas N. Principles of Political Economy. Ginn. Boston 1919. 188, 219.

Cecil, Hugh. Conservatism. Holt. New York. No date. 308, 417, 418.

Century Dictionary. Century. New York 1911. 444.

Chambers Encyclopedia. Chambers. London 1884. 452.

Charters, W. W. Curriculum Construction. Macmillan. New York 1923. 486, 487.

Christian Education in China. Foreign Missions Conference of North America. New York 1922. 284, 553.

Clark, Grover, in Atlantic Monthly. Atlantic Monthly Press. Boston 1921. 442.

Colvin, S. S. The Learning Process. Macmillan. New York 1911. 109.

Comenius. Great Didactic (Keatinge's translation). Black. London 1910. 521.

Compte. (Source of quotation not located). 125.

Conklin, E. G. Heredity and Environment. Princeton University Press. Princeton 1922. 403.

Coulton, G. G. A Medieval Garner. Constable. London 1910. 137.

Croly, Herbert. The Promise of American Life. Macmillan. New York 1914. 210.

Darlington, Thomas. Education in Russia. Special Report on

INDEX OF SOURCES

Educational Subjects, Vol. 24. H. M. Stationery Office. London 1909. 16, 17, 241.

Darwin, Charles. Origin of Species. Appleton. New York 1883. 382.

Dawson, Wm. H. What is Wrong with Germany. Longmans. New York 1915. 252.

Dealey, J. Q., and Ward, L. F. Textbook of Sociology. Macmillan. New York 1907. 55.

Dell, Floyd. Were You Ever a Child? Knopf. New York 1919. 501.

Democritus. (Quoted in Bakewell, Source Book in Ancient Philosophy). 150.

Deutsche Tageszeitung. Berlin 1915. 299.

Dewey, John. The Child and the Curriculum. University of Chicago Press. Chicago 1902. 114, 463, 468, 481.

Dewey, John, in Creative Intelligence. Holt. New York 1917. 30.

Dewey, John. Democracy and Education. Macmillan. New York 1916. 242, 273, 483, 537.

Dewey, John. The Educational Situation. University of Chicago Press. Chicago 1906. 524.

Dewey, John. German Philosophy and Politics. Holt. New York 1915. 36, 208.

Dewey, John. How We Think. New York. Heath. 1910. 482.

Dewey, John. Human Nature and Conduct. Holt. New York 1922. 27, 37, 54, 77, 83, 88, 94, 95, 172, 173, 249, 305, 336, 383, 394, 399, 400, 402, 435, 460, 461, 474, 475, 529.

Dewey, John. Interest and Effort. Houghton Mifflin. Boston 1913. 106, 116, 467, 510.

Dewey, John. Influence of Darwin on Philosophy and Other Essays. Holt. New York 1910. 31.

Dewey, John. Moral Principles in Education. Houghton Mifflin. Boston 1909. 5.

Dewey, John. Psychology and Social Practice. University of Chicago Press. Chicago 1901. 265.

Dewey, John. Reconstruction in Philosophy. New York. Holt 1920. 1, 4, 29, 51, 56, 73, 115, 117, 120, 156, 194, 244 387, 542.

Dewey, John, School and Society. University of Chicago Press. Chicago 1915. 459.

Dewey, John. Unpublished lectures. 516.

Dewey, John, in The Dial. The Dial. New York 1918. 282.

Dewey, John, in Elementary School Record. University of Chicago Press. Chicago 1900. 469, 473, 489, 526, 530.

Dewey, John, in Elementary School Teacher. University of Chicago Press. Chicago 1902, 1903. 285, 425.

Dewey, John, in International Journal of Ethics. International Journal of Ethics. Chicago 1916. 363, 395, 429.

Dewey, John, in School and Society. Science Press. Garrison, N. Y., 1917. 276.

Dewey, John, in Third Yearbook of the National Society for the Scientific Study of Education. University of Chicago Press. Chicago 1904. 514.

Dewey, John, in Watson's Encyclopedia and Dictionary of Education. Pitman. London 1921. 462.

Dewey, John, in Monroe's Cyclopedia of Education. Macmillan. New York 1911. 45, 533, 534.

Dewey, John. (Source of quotation not located). 256.

Dewey, John, and Tufts, J. H. Ethics. Holt. New York 1908. 61, 121, 149, 163, 192, 193, 260.

Dickinson, G. Lowes. Justice and Liberty. Doubleday Page. Garden City 1909. 206.

Diogenes Laertius. Bohn Edition. 138.

INDEX OF SOURCES

Diogenes Laertius. (Quoted in Bakewell, Source Book in Ancient Philosophy). 134, 153.
Dock, Lavinia, and Stewart, Isabel M. A Short History of Nursing. Putnam. New York 1920. 369.
Dodd, Agnes F. Early English Social History. Bell. London 1913. 495.
Dodson, J. D., in Psycho-biology. Williams and Wilkins. Baltimore 1917. 513.
"Dooley, Mr." Quoted in School and Society. Science Press. Garrison, N. Y. 465.

Ecclesiasticus. 271, 550.
Eliot, George. Romola. Doubleday Page. Garden City 1901. 130.
Ellwood, C. A. The Social Problem. Macmillan. New York 1915. 430.
Encyclopedia Britannica (11th edition). Encyclopedia Britannica. New York 1911. 202, 354, 444.
Epictetus. Discourses. Bohn edition. 92.
Epicurus. (Quoted in Bakewell. Source Book in Ancient Philosophy). 135.
Erasmus. (Quoted in Morgan, Educational Mosaics). 6.
Ervine, St. John, in the Century Magazine. Century Company. New York 1921. 72.
Eucken, Rudolph. The Meaning and Value of Life (Translation by Gibson). Black. London 1910. 181.
Eulenberg. In Archiv für Socialwissenschaft u. Socialpolitik. 306.

Faguet, Émile. The Cult of Incompetence. (Trans. by Barstow). Murray. London. No date. 197, 207, 367.
Ferrer, Francisco. Origin and Ideals of the Modern School. Putnam. New York 1913. 360, 496.
Fichte. Werke. 24.

Fiske, John. Outlines of Cosmic Philosophy. Houghton Mifflin. Boston 1891. 371, 388, 439.
Fitzpatrick, John. (Quoted in Edie, Current Social and Industrial Forces). 341.
Fouillée, Alfred. Education from a National Standpoint. Appleton. New York 1892. 62.

Gandhi, Mohandas K. (Quoted in Current History Magazine. New York Times. New York 1922). 126.
Gardiner, Thomas, in the Westminster Review. Baldwin, Craddock and Joy. London 1902. 246.
Gladstone, Wm. E. (Source of reference not located). 289.
Goddard, H. H. Feeblemindedness. Macmillan. New York 1914. 212.
Goethe. (Source of quotation not located). 93, 490.
Goldsmith, Oliver. (Quoted in DeBows Review). 494.
Goodrich, S. G. Recollections of a Lifetime. Miller Orton. New York 1856. 413.
Guardian of Education. London. 1802. 218, 358, 422.

Harada, Tasuku. The Faith of Japan. Macmillan. New York 1914. 124
Hayes, Carlton J. H. History of Modern Europe. Macmillan. New York 1916. 11, 12.
Hayes, E. C. Introduction to the Study of Sociology. Appleton. New York 1915. 102.
Hazlitt, William. Table Talk. Bell. London 1911. 319.
Hegel. (Source of quotation not located). 200.
Helvetic Confession. 1566. 144.
Henderson, E. N. Principles of Education. Macmillan. New York 1910. 90.
Herbart, John F. A B C of Sense Perception (Trans. by Eckoff). Appleton. New York 1903. 154.

INDEX OF SOURCES

Hennes, Marie, in Teachers College Record. Teachers College. New York 1921. 527.
Hobbes. Leviathan. Routledge. London 1887. 293.
Holmes, Edmond G. The Nemesis of Docility. Dutton. New York 1916. 248.
Hobhouse, L. T. Liberalism. Holt. New York. No date. 214, 295, 344.
Hobhouse, L. T. Social Evolution and Political Theory. Columbia University Press. New York 1911. 40, 52, 58, 67, 151, 162, 180, 185, 238, 361, 370, 376, 379.
Hodge, A. A. The Atonement. Presbyterian Board of Publication. Philadelphia 1867. 302.
Hutcheson, Francis. Inquiry: Concerning Moral Good and Evil. 1720. 175.
Huxley, T. H. Method and Results. Appleton. New York 1896. 423.
Huxley. (Source of quotation not located). 196.

Infant School Manual. Worcester, Mass., 1830. 464.
Inge, Dean W. R., in Atlantic Monthly. Atlantic Monthly Press. Boston 1922. 198, 216.

Jackson, Andrew. (Source of quotation not located). 350.
James, William. Principles of Psychology. Holt. New York 1890. 74, 75.
James, William. Pragmatism. Longmans Green. New York 1907. 2, 304.
James, William. Talks to Teachers. Holt. New York 1899. 263, 269, 438, 539, 541, 546, 557.
Jefferson, Thomas. Writings. Putnam. New York 1894. 14, 434.
Jefferson, Thomas, and Cabell, J. C. Early History of University of Virginia. Randolph. Richmond 1856. 13, 15.
Jennings, Herbert, in Suggestions of Modern Science Concerning Education. Macmillan. New York 1917. 472, 476.
St. Jerome. Letters and Select Works. Scribners. New York 1912. 136.
Jesus, in Gospel of Mark. 155.
Johnson, Samuel. (Quoted in DeBow's Review). 493.
Jouin, L. Logic and Metaphysics. St. Johns College. Fordham, N. Y., no date. 174.
Jowett, Benjamin. (Source of quotation not located). 283.

Kant, Emanuel. Fundamental Principles of the Metaphysics of Ethics. (Trans. by Abbott). Longmans. London 1895. 81.
Kant, Emanuel. (Source of quotation not located). 103, 397.
Kant, Emanuel. über Pädagogik. (See Buchner, Kant's Educational Theory).
Kidd, Benjamin. Social Evolution. Macmillan. New York 1894. 164.
Kilpatrick. Wm. H. Froebel's Kindergarten Principles Critically Examined. Macmillan. New York 1916. 456.
Kilpatrick, Wm. H., in Educational Review. Doubleday Page. Garden City 1921. 70, 311.
Kilpatrick, Wm. H., in Teachers College Record. Teachers College. New York 1921. 300, 441, 480, 528.
Kipling, Rudyard. The Second Jungle Book. Doubleday Page. Garden City 1922. 48.
Koran. 167.

Laski, Harold J. Authority in the Modern State. Yale University Press. New Haven 1919. 220.
Lecky, Wm. E. H. Democracy and Liberty. Longmans. New York 1896. 213.
Lee, Joseph, in Atlantic Monthly. Atlantic Monthly Press. Boston 1908. 353.
Leibnitz. (Quoted in James, Pragmatism). 304.

INDEX OF SOURCES

Lessing, Gotthold E. The Laocoon (Ronnfeldt ed.). Scott. London. No date. 108.

Lewisohn, Ludwig. Up Stream. Boni Liveright. New York 1922. 365, 366.

Liebknecht, in New York Evening Post. Evening Post. New York 1914. 66.

Lincoln, Abraham. Letters and Addresses. Bell. New York 1903. 434.

Locke, John. Education. Cambridge 1892. 548.

Lowell, A. L. Public Opinion and Popular Government. Longmans. New York 1914. 292, 320, 352.

Lowell, A. L. President's Report, Harvard University, 1916-17. Harvard University Press. Cambridge 1918. 411.

Lubbock, Sir John. Origin of Civilization and Primitive Condition of Man. Appleton. New York 1882. 158.

Luqueer, F. J. Hegel as Educator. Macmillan. New York 1896. 505.

Luther, Martin. (Source of quotation not located). 82.

Lyell, Sir Charles. Antiquity of Man. Childs. Philadelphia 1863. 375.

Macdonald, J. (Quoted in Todd, Theories of Social Progress). 157.

McCrea, N. G., in Columbia University Quarterly. Columbia University Press. New York 1916. 287.

MacIver, R. M. Community. Macmillan. New York 1917. 41, 46, 53, 60, 76, 97.

Mackenzie, J. S. Manual of Ethics. Hinds Noble. New York 1901. 176.

Maeterlink, Maurice. The Measure of the Hours. Dodd Mead. New York 1907. 436.

Mahan, Admiral. The Interest of America in International Conditions. Little Brown. Boston 1910. 240.

Mahan, Admiral. (Source of quotation not located), 294.

Manderville, B. Essay on Charity and Charity Schools. (Bound in the Fable of the Bees. Edinburgh 1772). 20.

Mansfield, Edward D. American Education. Barnes. New York 1851. 453.

Massachusetts (State) Report of the Committee on Immigration. 1914. 450.

Mathews, Wm. Getting on in the World. Griggs. Chicago 1883. 509.

Menander. (Source of quotation not located). 215.

Methodist Episcopal Church Discipline. 1792. 8.

Meriam, J. L. Child Life and the Curriculum. World Book Company. Yonkers-on-Hudson 1920. 484.

Merriman, Charles E., in American Journal of Sociology. University of Chicago. Chicago Press 1921. 416.

Metternich. (Quoted in Robinson, Readings in European History). 1819. 412.

Michigan (State) Private and Parochial School Law. 1921. 446.

Mills, J. S. Liberty. Parker. London 1859. 209, 264, 286, 288, 291, 338, 340, 343, 348, 391, 408, 445.

Mills, J. S. Principles of Political Economy. Appleton. New York 1890. 186.

Milton, John. (Source of quotation not located). 339.

Mohammedan proverb. 414.

Monroe, Paul. Cyclopedia of Education. Macmillan. New York 1912. 45, 345, 533, 534.

Monypenny, W. F. Life of Disraeli. Macmillan. New York 1910. 59.

Moore, E. C. What is Education. Ginn. Boston 1915. 112, 118.

INDEX OF SOURCES

Morley, John. Life of Richard Cobden. Macmillan. New York 1908. 322.
Morley, John. On Compromise. Macmillan. London 1910. 179.
Morley, John. Voltaire. Macmillan. London 1906. 9.
Morley, John, in Educational Review. Doubleday Page. Garden City 1905. 362.
Morley, John. (Source of quotation not located). 171.
Münsterberg, Hugo. American Traits. Houghton Mifflin. Boston 1902. 89, 545.

Napoleon Bonaparte. (Sundry sources). 10.
Newton, J. H., in Atlantic Monthly. Atlantic Monthly Press. Boston 1921. 324.
Nietzschke. (Source of quotation not located). 267.
Novicow, Jacques, in American Journal of Sociology. University of Chicago Press. Chicago 1917. 57.

Omar Khayyam. Rubaiyat (Trans. by Fitzgerald). Quaritch. London 1872. 131.
Oregon School Law of 1922. State Election Pamphlet. 451.
O'Ryan, J. F., in New York Times. The Times. New York 1917. 254.

Parker, G. H., in Science. Science Press. Garrison, N. Y., 1917. 33.
Parsons, J. W. Essays on Education. London. 1794. 549.
Pasteur. (Source of quotation not known). 195.
Paulsen, Friedrich. Ethics. (Trans. by Thilly). Scribners. New York 1899. 26, 133, 168, 169, 554.
Paulsen, Friedrich. German Education (Trans. by Lorenz). Scribners. New York 1912. 384.

Paulsen, Friedrich. Introduction to Philosophy (Trans. by Thilly). Holt. New York 1895. 3, 119.
Pearson, Karl. Grammar of Science. Macmillan. London 1911. 34.
Pearson, Karl. (Quoted in School and Society, 1920). 419.
Pericles, in Thucydides (Trans. by Jowett). Clarendon Press. Oxford 1900. 433.
Pestalozzi. (Source of quotation not located. Quoted in Krusi, Pestalozzi). 455.
Phillips, Wendell. (Source of quotation not located). 328.
Plato. Republic (Trans. by Jowett). Clarendon Press. Oxford 1888. 22, 314, 498.
Plato. Symposium (Trans. by Jowett). Clarendon Press. Ox- 1875. 152.
Plutarch. Education of Boys (Trans. by Super). Bardeen. Syracuse 1910. 551.
Pope, Alexander. Works. 87.
Power, Leonard, in Natural Education Association Bulletin of Elementary School Principals. 1923. 525.

Reisner, E. H. Nationalism and Education. Macmillan. New York 1922. 19.
Richardson, R. C. West Point. Putnam. New York 1917. 253.
Richter, Jean Paul. Levana. Bohn edition. 107, 471, 500, 544.
Robinson, H. P. The Twentieth Century American. Putnam. New York 1908. 255.
Robinson, J. H. The Mind in the Making. Harpers. New York 1921. 315.
Robinson, J. H. The New History. Macmillan. New York 1913. 381.
Robinson, J. H. Readings in European History. Ginn. Boston 1906. 412.
Roosevelt, Theodore, in New York Tribune. The Tribune. New York 1918. 85.

INDEX OF SOURCES

Ross, E. A. Principles of Sociology. Century. New York 1921. 44, 225, 251, 503.

Rousseau, J. J. Emile (Trans. by Foxley). Dutton. New York. No date. 160, 261.

Rousseau, J. J. Article on Political Economy. (Quoted in Boyd, Minor Educational Writings of J. J. Rosseau, q. v.). 406.

Rousseau, J. J. (Source of quotation not located. Quoted in Boyd, Educational Theory of J. J. Rosseau, q. v.). 161.

Royce, Josiah. The Spirit of Modern Philosophy. Houghton Mifflin. Boston 1892. 385.

Ruediger, W. C. Principles of Education. Houghton Mifflin. Boston 1910. 397, 454, 511.

Ruskin, John. (Source of quotation not located). 123.

Russell, Bertrand. Proposed Roads to Freedom. Holt. New York 1919. 444.

Russell, Bertrand. Justice in War Time. Open Court. London 1916. 323.

Russell, Bertrand. Why Men Fight. Century. New York 1917. 122, 127, 141, 301, 310, 317, 389.

Russell, Bertrand, in Atlantic Monthly. Atlantic Monthly Press. Boston. 142 (1916), 278 (1910).

Russell, Bertrand, in The New Student. National Student Forum. New York 1922. 309.

Sampson, George. English for the English. Macmillan. New York 1921. 491.

Schwickerath, R., in Monroe's Cyclopedia of Education. 345.

Shakespeare. Works. 25, 105, 386, 499.

Shaw, G. Bernard. Back to Methuselah. Brentano. New York 1921. 277.

Shaw, G. Bernard. Three Plays for Puritans. Brentano. New York 1914. 373.

Shields, Thomas C. Philosophy of Education. Catholic University Press. Washington 1917. 447.

Shields, Thomas C., in Catholic Education Association Bulletins. Catholic Education Association. Columbus, Ohio, 1916. 449.

Small, A. W. General Sociology. University of Chicago Press. Chicago 1905. 50, 432, 440.

Smith, Adam. Wealth of Nations. Clarendon Press. Oxford 1869. 211.

Socrates, in Xenophon's Memorabilia. Bohn ed. 129.

Spencer, Herbert. Social Statics. Appleton. New York 1878. 143, 497, 538.

Spinoza. Ethics. 91.

Statutes of the Realm. London. 266.

Stein. (Quoted in Ruediger, Principles of Education). 454.

Stout. G. F. Manual of Psychology. Hinds Noble. New York 1899. 502.

Strong, H. H. Systematic Theology. American Baptist Publishing Society. Philadelphia 1908. 303.

Sumner, Wm. G. Folkways. Ginn. New York 1913. 42, 325.

Sumner, Wm. G., in The Forum. The Forum. New York 1894. 372.

Tallentyre, S. G. Voltaire in his letters. Murray. London 1919. 337.

Tennyson. Poetical Works. Houghton Mifflin. Boston 1892. 170, 466.

Thackeray, Wm. M. Pendennis. Crowell. New York. No date. 101.

Thomas, W. I., and Znaniecki, Florian. The Polish Peasant in Europe and America. Badger. Boston 1918. 426.

Thorndike, E. L. Education. Macmillan. New York 1912. 552.

INDEX OF SOURCES

Thorndike, E. L. Education Psychology. Teachers College. New York 1913-4. 110, 189, 507, 508, 517, 518, 522, 540.

Thorndike, E. L., in Educational Review. Doubleday Page. Garden City 1914. 64.

Thorndike, E. L., in Popular Science Monthly. Science Press. Garrison, N. Y., 1912. 515.

Thucydides. (Source of quotation not located). 312.

Todd, A. J. Theories of Social Progress. Macmillan. New York 1918. 380, 393, 398.

Trietschke. Politics. (Quoted by Tufts, in International Journal of Ethics, 1918). 307.

Trotter, W. Instincts of the Herd. Macmillan. New York 1917. 47, 71, 104, 424.

Voltaire. (Source of quotation not located). 326, 337, 401.

Wallace, Alfred R. Social Environment and Moral Progress. Funk and Wagnalls. New York 1914. 364.

Wallas, Graham. The Great Society. Macmillan. New York 1914. 69, 313, 355, 390.

Watson, Foster. Encyclopedia and Dictionary of Education. Pitnam. London 1921. 462.

Watson, John B., in Suggestions of Modern Science Concerning Education. Macmillan. New York 1917. 111, 519.

Welles, Bishop, in Guardian of Education. London 1802. 547.

Wells, H. G., and others, in Atlantic Monthly. Atlantic Monthly Press. Boston 1919. 65, 427.

William II. Quoted in Dawson, What is Wrong with Germany. 252.

Wilson, Woodrow. The New Freedom. Doubleday Page. Garden City 1914. 68.

Wolf, R. B. Human Relations in Industry. Associated Industries of Massachusetts. Boston 1919. 232.

Wood, Charles W. The Great Change. Boni Liveright. New York 1918. 316.

Woodworth, R. S. Dynamic Psychology. Columbia University Press. New York 1918. 165, 479, 520, 522.

Woodworth, R. S. Psychology. Holt. New York 1921. 522, 523.

Wordsworth. William. Poetical Works. Oxford Press. London 1911. 113.

Xenophon. Memorabilia. Bohn ed. 120.

Zimmern, A. E. Nationality and Government. McBride. New York 1919. 229, 231.

INDEX OF SUBJECTS

Abstraction, defined, 533.†
Academic freedom, in higher schools, 409, 410, 411; in lower schools (Bernard Shaw), 277; President Lowell on, 411; New York Times on, 410; Metternich's Carlsbad resolutions, 412.
Acquired characters, not inherited, 403.
Activity leading to further activity (Chapter VII, 105-122): secondary neurone action, 110; humans always active, 517; differs with individual, 109; meaning of indulgence, 95, 114, 116, 459, 510; ethical conduct "leads on," 119; basis for criticizing institutions, 194; basis for judging men, 117; brings happiness, 106, 127, 460; effort and happiness, 26, 105; growing as the aim, 462; proper interest "leads on," 116; interest in the routine, 463; helped by play, 472; playthings should "lead on," 107; "deferred values," 461; Lessing's search for truth, 108; "a primrose by a river's brim," 113. *See also* Growing as the good; Education as growing; Indulgence.
Adaptability, significance of, 242.
Administration of schools: democratic respect for personality, 284; the expert in, 405; Jowett's advice, 283.
Age, effect of, on learning, 111; effect of, on "leading on," 109.
Aims, discussed, 27.
Alcuin, on motivation, 495.

America (United States): individual resourcefulness, 255; freedom for children, 545; adversely criticized, 145, 226, 366; attitude toward excellence, 351; disregards the expert, 320; opposed to free speech, 341, 342, 346; neglects politics, 187; overstandardized, 72; materialistic, 145; excitement spreads fast, 318; bigness overwhelms, 389. *See also* Americanization.
Americanization, adverse effect of, 365; foreign language schools, 450.
Amusement, mere, 459. *See also* Indulgence.
Anarchy, defined and contrasted, 444; the freedom of, 301.
Animals, how man differs from, 73.
A priori categories, disadvantages of, 36; favor conservatism, 4; *a priori* justice, 181.
Aristocracy, value of natural, 211; should govern, 213.
Aristotle: the good life, 140; moral character, 191; man a political animal, 98.
Arnold, Matthew, on the good, 146, 147.
Art, function of, 474.
Asceticism, 136, 137.
Argument, "follow the argument," 314.
Association, defined, 46; result of perceived advantage, 55; the unit element of society, 51, 52.
Attention, how secured, 265; growth in, 530; inner *vs.* outer, 514; without interest, 502.

†Numbers refer to quotations, not to pages.

INDEX OF SUBJECTS

Authority, social necessity for, 293; in science, 423; the basis of ordinary education, 280; education against, 280; Prussianized, sought in our schools, 282; change from external to internal, 416; decline of authoritarianism, 300, 349, 416, 423, 425. *See also* Autocracy; Social control.

Autocracy, education for, 7, 17, 18, 241, 247, 268; Napoleon on education, 10, 11; public opinion in, 200; America an autocracy, 72; the method of contemporary industry, 229, 230, 231.

Automatic inheritance of allegiance, defined, 44; why bad, 44, 424; education against, 280.

Bernhardi: might is right, 298.
Bismarck, on training children, 7.
Brain, to further action, 33.
Browning, service of temptation, 536; progress man's alone, 356.
Capacity, influence on interest, 479, 515.

Caste system, education for, 16, 17, 20, 201, 242, 247, 268.
Catholicism. *See* Roman Catholicism.
Causality, man's reliance on, 28; use of, 27; does not bring fatalism, 31.
Centralization in school administration. *See* Administration of schools.
Change, opposition to, 413, 414; inevitable, 441; controlled by knowledge, 31.
Character: moral character, 149, 191, 260; Goethe on, 93; Kant on, 543. *See also* Individuality; Self; Moral education.
Childhood, why happy, 460; humans always active, 517; children's talking, 478; made difficult by adults, 500; naturally lazy (Goldsmith), 494; three periods in, 516; credulous, 245; some schools hurtful to, 476; repression needed, 504; youthful reasoning to be checked, 505; not ready for duty, 555; "good" children, 83; pupil sabotage, 501; a "listening school," 492; a former infant school attitude, 464; Münsterberg on the American boy, 545. *See also* Obedience; Play.

Choice, defined, 529; necessary to personality, 76; equality of opportunity at, 209.

Citizenship: strong personalities needed, 63, 258, 259; "education for, 406, 407, 477; higher education for, 407; reading not sufficient, 63, 330; Kant on 506. *See also* Democracy and education.

Civilization, product of cooperation, 49; materialistic only, 145; should be satisfying, 128; as culture, 147; Gandhi's idea of western, 126.

Cobden, on unreason in war, 322.
Coercion, retards learning, 498; by society not democratic, 296; function of state coercion, 295; should regulate all play, 549.

Communication, necessary to social relationship, 65; in international affairs, 238; easy in America, 318; German censorship of, in 1914, 66.

Communism, *vs.* private property, 186.

Compte, on the good, 125.
Compulsory attendance, in secondary period, 270; interest necessary, 270.

Concept, how built, 532; use of ideas, 29. *See also* Abstraction; Generalization.

Concomitant learnings, 480, 527, 551.

Conscience, herd theory of, 104; Kant on, 182.

Conservatism, arrests civilizations, 421; provocative of revolution, 430, 435; opposition to free discussion, 420; opposition to change, 358, 378, 413, 414, 415, 421; two opposed views on, 413, 432; not inherent in habit, 400; influence on progress, 418; nat-

INDEX OF SUBJECTS

ural conservatism, 417; a factor in social stability, 419; leans on *a priori* philosophy, 4; how to free the conservative, 429; herd conduct, 71; must old peoples stagnate, 383; of the educated, 428; extreme Toryism, 202, 203; science dangerous for children and females, 257, 422; "horrid principles" of democracy, 218.

Constitutions, function of, 237.

Constructive work, children's, how good, 473.

Control, discussed, 30; by means of causalities, 28; ideas make for, 29; assisted by laws of nature, 31; attitude a factor in, 386, 387; man's control limited, 363, 372, 378; growing in childhood, 516; signs, superstitions, magic, and science, 32; men masters of their fate, 25. *See also* Effort; Causality; Experience; Interest; Purpose.

Cooperation, foundation of civilization, 49; maintenance of social life, 43; the one supreme need, 443; herd conduct, 71; of the wolf pack, 47.

Crime, social responsibility for, 88.

Criminals, treatment of, 88, 305.

Critical attitude, social value of, 325.

Culture, M. Arnold on, 146, 147.

Curriculum: subject matter and curriculum, 465-491 (Chapter XIX); child and curriculum, 468. *See also* Curriculum making; Subject matter; Technique.

Curriculum making: democratic procedure, 284, 285; deferred values, 461; the curriculum as method, 486; Bobbitt on, 485; Charters on, 487; Meriam on, 484; Bonser on, 488; "Mr. Dooley" on, 465.

Custom, vs. institution, 60; forms habits, 54, 399; waning power of, 425; power of the mores, 42; stagnating peoples bound by, 157, 158, 383, 415; status in primitive life, 204. *See also* Institutions; Automatic inheritance of allegiance; Savage life.

Cynic idea of the good, 134.

Dawdling, 509.

Deferred values, discussed, 272, 461.

Deliberation, process of, 27, 529, 541; moral deliberation, 541. *See also* Thinking.

Democracy (Chapter X, 195-240): defined, 195, 205, 244; arguments for, 217; equality of opportunity, 209; popular participation, 200, 244; individual choice in, 264, 286; individual differences in, 210, 211; discrimination in, 210, 214; coercion in, 296; constitutions, 237; contrasted with autocracy, 199; better a good master than poverty, 215; contrasted with aristocracy, 207, 213; depends on public opinion, 329; attitude towards the expert, 285, 350, 353; needs strong individualities, 258, 259; dangers from, 62, 187, 198, 207, 213; city unfavorable to, 219; affected by foreign affairs, 238; in industry, 84, 86, 221, 229, 230, 231; surplus for the common good, 233; a living wage and adequate leisure, 224; justification of profits, 223; how related to war, 296; freedom not yet permanent, 437; influence on, of idea of progress, 359; Hegel on subordination of the individual, 193; Faguet on, 207; politeness in, 207; power to go wrong, 196. *See also* Social control; Autocracy; Caste system.

Democracy and education, (Chapter XI, 241-285): the two inherently connected, 120; democracy in education, 285; education for democracy, 80, 256, 275, 282; place of university, 409; reading not sufficient, 330; present education wrong, 270, 272; docility, 248, 249; public education an evil, 445; compulsory attendance to age of 18, 270; Nietzschke on popular education, 267. *See also*

Democracy; Autocracy; Caste system.

Democritus, on the good life, 150.

Development, meaning of, 454, 455, 456; power of habit in, 263; three periods of, 516.

Difficulty. *See* Hindrance.

Discipline, defined, 537; repression necessary, 505; severity a failure, 497; Prussianized, in our schools, 282; military discipline, 251, 254; at West Point, 253; breaking the will, 546, 547; when to use punishment, 552; often cruel, 496; pupil sabotage, 501; "Mr. Dooley" on, 465; should include play, 549. *See also* Method; Motivation; Moral education.

Discussion, the mould of measures, 312; means of progress, 392, 415; reading not sufficient, 330; suppression of, 341; limitations upon, 347; my opponent's case, 287. *See also* Freedom of speech and press.

Discussion groups, a suggestion for, 355.

Disraeli, on institutions, 59.

Divided self: ill effects of suppression, 94; inner vs. outer attention, 514.

Division of labor, how useful, 43.

Docility, meaning of, 248, 249; only too natural, 282; result of bad teaching, 265, 278; created by poverty, 250; early schooling to inculcate, 504.

"Dooley, Mr.," on the curriculum, 465.

Double personality, 75.

Doubt: a duty, 278, 423, 424; education for doubt, 278, 280; better than certainty, 326; "our doubts are traitors," 386.

Duty, meaning of, 121; Kant on, 183.

Dynamic education, 398. *See also* Education and social progress.

Dynamic society: stability and progress, 415; education in, 398; how to free the conservative, 429; available thought power, 315. *See also* Social stability in a dynamic society; Conservatism.

Education, definitions of, 45, 452, 453, 454, 455, 457, 458; how conceived, 452-464 (Chapter XVIII), 45, 80, 243, 438, 452, 453, 454, 455, 457, 458, 505, 525; power of, 6, 7, 38, 79; criticisms upon present education, 272, 276, 277, 278, 285; early education, 459; influence on docility, 249; simultaneous learnings, 480; adaptation to the individual, 477; for real efficiency, 275; self-denial vs. repression, 548. *See also* Democracy and education; Education and social progress; State and education; Education as growing; Educative process; Training; Religious education; Vocational education; Esthetic education; Autocracy; Caste system; Play; Jefferson; Napoleon.

Education and social progress (Chapter XV, 397-412): education as an agency of progress, 5, 6, 38, 256, 279, 280, 281, 397, 398, 402; inefficiency of present schools, 277, 278; conservatism of the educated, 428; must old peoples stagnate, 383; the university and progress, 409; against war, 317; education for freedom of thought, 278, 280; use of the expert, 285, 320, 350, 353, 405. *See also* Training; Conservatism; Academic freedom.

Education as growing: reconstruction of experience, 45; task of early education, 459; related to interest, 510; acquiring meanings, 394; when interest is proper, 116; growing as the aim of life, 462; bad effect of mere preparation, 120, 272, 285 (2), 461; successive types of attention, 530; criteria for play, 473; selfhood essentially growing, 194; choice of subject matter, 467. *See also* Activity leading to further activity; Objectives in education; Growing.

Educational situation, relation of school method and organization, 524.

Educative process, fundamental factors in, 468; subject matter and curriculum, 465-491 (Chapter XIX); problem of method 492-528 (Chapter XX); calls for freedom, 256, 285 (2); mechanizing the process, 525; understanding not always necessary, 245, 246; reconstruction of experience, 45; pupil sabotage, 501; simultaneous learnings, 480; school method and machinery correlatives, 524. *See also* Method; Purpose; Discipline; Moral education; Concomitant learnings.

Effect, Law of, stated, 449, 498, 522 f.

Efficiency, enhanced by the emotions, 520; real education for, 275; not determined by intelligence, 269.

Effort, defined, 511; necessary to happiness, 26, 105, 127; as opposed to interest, 510; hindered by doubt, pessimism, etc., 386, 387; opportunities lost, 374; will to win, 385; men masters of their fate, 25; effort counts, 25, 31, 374, 385, 386; bad effect of inevitable progress, 362.

Emotions, function of, 519, 520; collective emotion fosters myths, 323.

Ends: nature and function of, 27, 35; man an end in himself (Kant), 81, 82, 84, 86, 221; as seen in childhood, 516; pleasure not the end, 168, 169; ends of human endeavor, 133; Treitschke on state's end, 307.

English, not a subject of instruction, 491; teaching to read, 112.

Epictetus, on freedom, 92; on the good, 139.

Epicurus, on the good life, 135; on philosophy, 21.

Erasmus, on the power of education, 6.

Esthetic education, Goethe on, 490; demanded for children, 477.

Ethics, problem of, 119. *See also* Right and wrong; Morals.

Evil, attractive to man, 554.

Evolution, historic continuity everywhere seen, 381; not same as progress, 361, 395; present status of doctrine, 354.

Experience, concept of (Chapter II, 23-36): discussed, 30; in the educative process, 45, 285 (2), 457; the ultimate universe of discourse, 23; *a priori vs.* experiential reasoning, 36; the basis of everything, 24; education as reconstruction of, 45.

Expert, the, and democracy, 285, 320, 350, 353; Kant on, 405.

Exploitation, 225; in vocational education, 374.

Expression, habit in relation to, 475; *vs.* suppression, 94, 95, 548; character a factor in, 93; through play, 473; thwarted in some schools, 476; children's talking, 478; a "listening school," 492; institution a means to, 163; denied in modern industry, 122; self-expression in industry (Wolf), 232. *See also* Suppression; Childhood; Play.

Fatalism, paralyzing effect of, 362, 380; not imposed by laws of nature, 31; use of ideas to escape, 29.

Flux, defined and contrasted, 396.

Force, function of, 294; when right, when wrong, 295, 296.

Foreign language schools, 450.

Force. *See* Coercion.

Frederick William III, orders to "garrison schools," 268.

Freedom, as self-expression, 90; as inner harmonization, 89; furthered by using ideas, 29; for the pupil learner, 256, 285 (2), 506, 545, 548; hampered by habits, 261 (Rousseau), 262 (Kant); good of political freedom, 217; not yet permanent, 437; advantages of variation, 408; threatened by society, 286; threatened by bigness of organization, 220; not found among savages, 157, 158, 421; of anarchy, 301; better growing in, 196; Kant on education for, 506; for Spinoza, 91; for the Stoics, 153; for Epictetus, 92; Voltaire on freeing fools, 401; slavery better than poverty, 215.

Freedom of speech and press, why needed, 259, 312, 338, 343, 344, 392, 415, 416; power of truth, 339; truth not always triumphant, 391; why not forbid pernicious doctrines, 340, 344; Voltaire on, 337; why opposed, 420; sign of civilization, 349; hampered in America, 341, 342, 346; endangered by public excitement, 318; proper limitations to, 342, 347, 348; independence of thought, 259; right of minority, 291; Napoleon's consorship, 10, 12; my opponent's case, 287; German censorship 1914, 66; Metternich's Carlsbad resolutions, 412; Jesuit attitude, 345; bible reading forbidden by Henry VIII, 266. *See also* Academic freedom; Press; Discussion.

Gandhi, on the good life, 126.
Generalizations, defined, 534; building of, 535.
God, law of, not final, 176.
Goethe, on character, 93; on the education of taste, 490.
Goldsmith, Oliver, on child nature, 494.
"Good" children, 83.
Good life, what constitutes the (Chapter VIII, 123-153): exercise of functions, 133, 143; unselfishness, 61, 130, 149, 192; social development as the good, 151; the good life social, 192; growing as the good, 460; involves effort, 26, 105, 127; B. Russell on happiness, 142; civilization should be satisfying, 128; service of art and play, 474; buying happiness, 141; materialism, 145; man not a consumer of pleasures, 132; psychologic hedonism, 168, 169; M. Arnold, culture as the good, 146, 147; Ruskin, 123; Compte, 125; asceticism, 136, 137; Gandhi, 126; Omar Khayyam, 131; nirvana, 124; Greek love of the good, 260; Socrates, 129; Plato, 152; Aristotle, 140; Democritus, 150; the Cynics, 134; Zeno, 138; Epicurus, 135; the Stoics, 153; Epictetus, 139. *See also* Education as growing; Activity leading to further activity.

"Great society," defined, 69; newly come, 68, 69; integration increasing, 70; bigness overwhelming, 220, 389; founded on exchange, 57; external and internal relationships, 238. *See also* Socialization.

Group, defined, 50.
Growing, psychological basis of, 110, 517; as the good life, discussed, 106, 120, 460, 462; is moral progress, 120; essence of selfhood, 194; basis for judging, 117; sense of duty in relation to, 121; playthings should bring growing, 107. *See also* Activity leading to further activity; Education as growing; Indulgence.

Habit, function of, 77, 263, 438, 475; need for, 438; power of, 263; related to self and will, 77; formed by customs, 399; influence of social inheritance on, 37; not inherently conservative, 400; Plato on habit and thought, 22; Kant opposed to, 262; Rousseau opposed to, 261.
Happiness, of childhood, 460; as gratification, 143; social nature of, 130, 149; the pursuit of happiness, 148; buying happiness, 141; as growing, 106, 460; achieving necessary to, 26, 105, 122, 127, 141; not result of progress, 357; defined by B. Russell, 142; how assured, 151. *See also* Good life, nature of; Hedonism.
Health, hurt in some schools, 476.
Hedonism, 148, 168, 169.
Hegel: relation of individual to institutions, 193; public opinion,

INDEX OF SUBJECTS

200; the state, 208; would suppress youthful reasoning, 505.
Henry VIII, forbids English bible reading, 266.
Herbart, definition of the good character, 154.
Herd opinions, to be suspected, 424.
Hindrance, effect of, 518, 519, 536; overcoming satisfactory, 26, 479.
History: William II on teaching of, 19; Frederich William III on, 268 d.
Hobbes, *bellum omnium contra omnes,* 293.
Human nature, originally sinful, 144, 464. *See also* Individual, nature of.
Huxley, on the rejection of authority, 423.

Ideo-motor action, James on, 539; Thorndike on, 540.
Individual, nature of (Chapter VI, 73-104): original nature, 64; humans always active, 517; selfhood essentially active, 194; very complex, 51; self and socius built together, 100; individuality to be achieved, 79, 156; social nature of, 98, 101, 103, 165; man not naturally social, 55; how man differs from lower animals, 73; capacity and interest, 479, 515; what determines efficiency, 269; effect of age on learning, 111; man an end in himself, 81; meaning of development, 456; economic man a myth, 222; men infinite isolation, 101; originally sinful, 144, 464, 554. *See also* Individual and society; Self; individuality; Individualization.
Individual and society (Chapter IX, 154-194): discussed, 102; relationship of two inherent, 40, 43, 53, 54, 56, 67, 102, 103, 149, 165, 393, 471; "socius" rather than "individual," 99; individualization and socialization, 96, 97, 162, 180, 244; the two mutually antagonistic, 164; personality and sharing, 244; development of each in relation to all, 162; institutions needed, 163, 180; bigness overwhelms, 220, 389; the wolf pack, 47, 48; Kipling's "law of the jungle," 48; democracy disintegrates, 198; Hegel on, 193; men infinite isolations, 101. *See also* Society; Socialization; Individual, nature of.
Individuality, defined, 76; independence of thought, 259; need for strong, 63, 258, 259; relation of, to sociality, 97; institutions means of creating, 156; grows through sharing, 244; threatened by bigness of affairs, 220, 389; to be achieved, 79, 156; intelligence not sole factor, 269; forbids universal public schools, 445; Goethe on character, 93. *See also* Personality; Respect for personality.
Individualization, relation to socialization, 96, 97, 162, 244, 282. *See also* Individual, nature of; Individual and society; Individuality.
Indulgence, *vs.* growth, 114, 115, 116, 459, 510; *vs.* expression, 95; dilemma between spoiling and suppressing, 548. *See also* Expression.
Industrial democracy, discussed, 229, 230, 231; demanded by present conditions, 84, 86; economic man a myth, 222.
Infant school, attitude towards childhood, 464.
Instincts, slavery to, 89; utilization of, in early education, 459.
Institutions, as solutions to problems, 289, 429; subordinate to sharing, 56; must build personality, 194; free individual energies, 122, 163; means of human welfare, 155, 156, 180; preserve rights, 59; vs. customs, 60; opposed views as to existing order, 432; to avert war, 317; history of, pathethic, 216; hurt by inheriting of allegiance, 44; property, 166, 186, 234; power of the mores, 42; binding effect of, in

savagery, 157, 158. *See also* Custom.
Intellectual interest, alone dynamic, 440.
Intelligence, differences of: democracy and individual differences, 210, 211; not sole factor in efficiency, 269; use for the feeble-minded, 212.
Interest, genuine principle of, 510; inner *vs.* outer attention, 514; relation of capacity to, 479, 515; relation of attention to, 502, 509; when proper, 115, 116; a factor in efficiency, 269; school uninteresting, 50, 270, 494; in the routine, 463, 488; intellectual interest, 440; building interests, 463, 479; securing interest in modern industry, 232. *See also* Effort; Expression; Divided self; Emotions.
International relationships, as affecting internal affairs, 238. *See also* Nationality; Great society.
Irreconcilability, defined, 292.
I. W. W., as discussed in the press, 333.

James, William, the meaning of philosophy, 2; moral deliberation, 541; need of habits, 438; ideo-motor action, 539; many potential selves, 74.
Jefferson, Thomas, on revolutions, 434; on elementary *vs.* higher education, 13; school plan for Virginia, 14; on local control, 15.
Johnson, Samuel, on motivation, 493.
Jowett's advice to administrators, 283.
Justice, founded on experience, 178; based on *a priori* considerations, 181; demands punishment, 302, 304.

Kant, Emanuel: man an end in himself, 81, 82, 84, 86, 221; man's unsocial sociableness, 103; training *vs.* education, 243; education for a better state, 279, 397; education for freedom, 506; effect of play, 470; the power of education, 79; duty, 183; habits, 262; conscience, 182; character, 543; moral education, 555.
Kipling, "law of the jungle," 48.

Labor, attitude toward, 227, 228; Roosevelt on, 85; workingmen as means primarily, 84, 86, 221; monotony of, 84, 95, 122; self-expression in industry (Wolf), 232; division of labor, 43; industrial democracy, 229, 230, 231; Labor Party platform, 233; kind of education needed for, 272, 275; a living wage and adequate leisure, 224; limitation on profits, 223.
Laissez-faire, defined and contrasted, 444.
Laws of nature, do not govern, 31.
Learning, effect of age on, 111; influence of vigor of action, 513; laws of, 105, 522, effect of leisure, 271; simultaneous learnings, 480.
Leisure, and learning, 271.
Lessing, on search for truth, 108.
Liberty, a French conception of, 197.
Life, enhanced by thinking, 433.
Lincoln, Abraham, on revolutions, 434.
Line of least resistance, defined, 556.
"Listening school," 492.
Logical and psychological. *See* Psychological and logical.

Magic, contrasted with science, 32.
Majority, decision by, 289; right to rule, 203, 290; tyranny of, 288, 290, 318. *See also* Social control; Minority rights.
Meanings, defined, 531, significance of, 73.
Means, defined, 35; man not to be used as mere means, 81, 82, 84, 86, 221; as used by childhood, 516; relation of causality to, 28.
Method, problem of, 492-528 (Chapter XX): favorable condi-

INDEX OF SUBJECTS

tions for, 508; failure of severity, 497; method and curriculum, 486; place of thinking, 489; problem of broad vs. narrow, 112, 270, 480; simultaneous learnings, 480; concomitant effects, 553; education for democracy, 256; evils of Prussianization, 282; construction desirable, 473; suggestions from the teacher, 526; wholehearted activity, 512; adaptation to the individual, 477; education for progress, 278; determines organization, 524; present schooling repellent, 270; health sometimes hurt, 476; interest in the routine, 463; specific exercise necessary, 538; learn by doing, 302; a "listening school," 492; at West Point, 253; Prussian training, 247; when to use punishment, 552; extreme mechanization, 525; cruel methods, 496; Kant, advocacy of freedom, 506; Kant on plays, 470. *See also* Childhood; Discipline; Educative process; Obedience; Purpose; Purposeful activity; Motivation; Success; Training.

Metternich, Carlsbad resolution, 412.

Might and right: function of force, 294; Bernhardi quoted, 298; might makes right, 299; Treitschke on, 307.

Military, discipline, 251, 253, 254; virtues, 251, 252; censorship, 66; Napoleon's schools, 10 d.

Minority rights, right to speak, 291. *See also* Social control; Freedom of speech and press.

Missionary endeavor, early opposition to, 378.

Mobilization of thought power (Chapter XIII, 312-355): discussed, 313; the social mind, 58; the place of the expert, 285, 320, 350, 353; power of thought, 384; influence of the press, 328, 329, 332, 333; dangers from endowed thought, 336, 440; schools as propagandistic agencies, 19, 317; bad effect of public opinion, 319; collective emotion fosters myths, 323; possibilities of intelligent management, 316; truth may not win, 391; demanded by British Labor, 233. *See also* Propagandism; Public opinion; Press; Freedom of speech.

Moderation, not always best, 436.

Monotony of life, danger of, 95, 122, 272; lessened by Wolf, 232.

Moral education (Chapter XXII, 536-557): the good moral character, 149, 191, 543; analysis of moral character, 541, 542; power of habit, 263; on growth basis, 467; freedom for children, 285 (2), 545; purposeful activity, 527; specific exercise necessary, 538; positive better than negative, 557; when to use punishment, 552; breaking the will, 546, 547; line of least resistance, 556; Greek idea of loving the good, 260; discussed by Kant, 555; Kant on conscience, 182. *See also* Morals; Punishment; Criminals, treatment of; Obedience; Discipline.

Moral unrest, 300, 416, 425, 426.

Morals, nature of, 61, 118, 120, 149, 171, 172, 173, 174, 175, 176, 179, 192; no mundane basis for, 174; criterion for, 154, 163, 174, 236; based on social experience, 61, 149, 162, 179, 192; moral character, 149, 191, 541, 543, 557; analysis of moral character, 541; moral deliberation, 541; conceptions of the moral law, 176; what is a moral situation, 542; problem of ethics, 119; tendency the basis of judging, 177; objective study of, 172; the state in relation to, 238, 239, 306, 311; better positive than negative, 557; herd theory of conscience, 104; Hegel on, 193. *See also* Right and wrong.

Motivation, inherent, 469; Plutarch on, 551; Alcuin on, 495; Dr. Johnson on, 493; Goldsmith on, 494.

Movement prior to brain, 33.

Myth-making fostered by collective emotions, 323.

Napoleon Bonaparte, catechism, 11; on education, 10; press censorship, 12.
Nationalism: sovereignty, 311; a religion, 310; an evil, 309; national selfishness, 238, 239, 308; independent of ethics, 306.
Nature, laws of, do not govern, 31.
Nature, original. *See* Human nature; Individual, nature of.
Nietzschke, on popular education, 267.
Nirvana, 124.
Nursing, varying progress in, 369.

Obedience, in children, 278, 544, 545; waning in modern life, 423; democracy and obedience, 63, 80, 278, 282; Prussianization of, in our schools, 282; in the soldier, 252, 254; a convenience to elders, 544; in an autocratic society, 241, 278; at West Point, 253. *See also* Moral education.
Objectives in education, Bobbitt on, 485; Bonser on, 488; Charters on, 487; in theory of growing, 394, 459, 467, 530.
Office, sacredness of, 167.
Omar Khayyam, on the good life, 131.
Oregon School Law of 1922, 451.

Parochial schools: Oregon (1922) school law, 495; Michigan (1921) law, 446; foreign language schools, 450; Roman Catholics to patronize, 448; inclusive public education an evil, 445. *See also* Roman Catholicism.
Patriotism, education for, 406; civic patriotism and strong individualities, 258.
Personality, built by institutions, 194; built by sharing, 56. *See also* Individuality; Self; Respect for personality.
Pessimism, discussed and contrasted, 387; harm of doubt and pessimism, 386, 387; bigness overwhelming, 389; present state of affairs, 364.
Pestalozzi, education as unfolding, 455.
Philosophy, Dewey on, 1, 4, 36; James on, 2; Paulsen on, 3; experiential *vs. a priori*, 4, 24, 36, 179, 181, 182, 235, 236; Plato on, 22; Epicurus on, 21; "evolution" universal, 381. *See also* Growing as the good life.
Philosophy of education, meaning and bearing of, 1-22 (Chapter I).
Plato, on the good life, 152; on the service of philosophy, 22; on the law of effect, 498.
Play, function of, 470, 471, 472, 474; how educative, 470, 473; criteria for judging, 473; attitude against, 8, 549; should be compelled, 549.
Playthings, should "lead on," 107.
Pleasure not the end of desire, 168, 169.
Plutarch, on incentives, 551.
Pope on teaching adults, 87.
Poverty, creates docility, 250; the circle of poverty and ignorance, 281.
Press, the: power of, 328, 329; makes democracy possible, 329; perversion of, 332, 333; what "news" is, 334; misleading headlines, 335; influence of the advertiser, 331; reading not sufficient, 330; Napoleon's censorship, 10, 12; student press forbidden by Metternich, 412. *See* Freedom of speech and press; Public opinion; Propagandism.
Principles, limitation upon, 235, 236.
Private schools: Oregon (1922) school law, 451; Michigan (1921) law, 446; universal public education an evil, 445; selfish arguments for, 331.
Progress (Chapter XIV, 356-396): meaning of, 394-396; not same as evolution, 361, 395; goal of, 393; loss along with gain, 370; devious and doubtful, 59, 352,

366, 369, 371, 396, 431; superstition of, 362, 367, 380; not inevitable, 363, 371, 379, 380, 390, 395; relative to man, 356, 396; hindered by doubt, pessimism, etc., 386, 387; independent of man, 360, 363, 372, 378; must be earned, 362, 369, 380, 395; an illusion, 373; rate of, 375; relation of, to happiness, 357; demands variation, 408; must old peoples stagnate, 383; lost opportunities, 374; influence of conservatism on, 418; the present bad, 364, 430; gain from Ptolemy to Copernicus, 377; effect of Marathon and Salamis, 388; influence of idea of, on democracy, 359; permanent progressiveness, 439; struggle for existence, 382; cooperation the one supreme need, 443; present sensitivity to suffering, 376. See also Education and social progress; Evolution.

Project. See Purposeful Activity.

Propagandism, danger of, 324; in the press, 332, 333; in the schools, 19, 317.

Property, defined, 234; no limitations upon, 166; communism, 186. See also Institutions.

Prussia (before 1918): training in the Volksschule, 247; William II's (1889) school order, 19; Frederick William III's order on garrison schools, 268.

Psychological and logical, defined and discussed, 481, 482, 483; learn by doing, 521.

Psychology. See Learning; Trial and error; Instinct; Interest; Brain; Secondary neurone action; Social psychology; Ideomotor action.

Public education. See State and education; Democracy and education; Private schools; Parochial schools.

Public opinion, how formed, 321; necessary to democracy, 329; the social mind, 58; dependent on the press, 329, 333; decreasingly adequate, 352; may prevent private opinion, 288, 319; reading not sufficient, 330; the spread of ideas, 318; collective emotion fosters myths, 323; Hegel on, 200. See also Press; Propagandism.

Punishment, problem of, 88, 305; theories of, 302, 303, 304; psychology of, 552; efficacy of, 493, 552; function of penalty, 303; chastising necessary, 550. See also Social control; Criminals, treatment of.

Puritanism, defined, 297.

Purpose, function of, 507, 508; power of, 384; exploits laws of nature, 31; vigor of action and learning in, 513. See also Purposeful activity; Dawdling.

Purposeful activity, how desirable, 265, 512; defined and classified, 528; wholehearted activity, 512; how activities arise, 526; use of, in curriculum, 488; purposes suggested by teacher, 526; growth in attention, 530; thinking in, 473, 489; criteria for play, 473; pupil sabotage, 501; pupil attitude to, 527; Kant on purpose in play, 470. See also Method.

Pythagoras, referred to, 505.

Racial differences, due mainly to social inheritance, 38, 404.

Radicalism, danger from fanatical, 430.

Reconstruction of experience. See Experience.

Relativity, of order, reason, etc., 34; of principles, 235, 236; of flux, process and progress, 396.

Religion, of nationalism, 310; a former attitude against play, 8.

Religious education, unthinking, 245, 246; aim of Roman Catholic schools, 447.

Respect for personality, in school administration, 284, 285; "good" children, 83; broken spirits, 503; exploitation, 225; use for the feeble-minded, 212; breaking the will, 546, 547; Luther on child bearing, 82; education for real efficiency, 275; education for caste system, 271, 274; disregarded in trade training, 274; in industry, 84, 86, 221, 229, 230, 231, 232; Roosevelt on "hands," 85; a living wage and adequate leisure, 224; workingmen in industry, 84, 86, 221; Wolfe's experiment, 232; Pope on teaching adults, 87. *See also* Training; Docility; Suppression; Childhood; Labor; Poverty.

Revolution, Jefferson and Lincoln on, 434; fostered by conservatism, 430, 435.

Right and wrong, nature of, 34, 119, 170, 171, 174, 178, 179, 181; criterion for, 154, 175, 178; relative to situation, 235, 236; no mundane basis for, 174; conceptions of the moral law, 541; problem of ethics, 119; *a priori* justice, 181; alien to the state, 306. *See also* Morals, Might and right.

Roman Catholicism, position on schools, 447, 449; obligation to patronize parochial schools, 448; Jesuits on liberty of thought, 345.

Roosevelt, Theodore, on treatment of labor, 85.

Rosseau: social state unnatural, 160, 161; on public education, 406; opposed to habits, 261.

Routine, interest in, 282, 463.

Ruskin, on the good, 123.

Savage life, characteristics of, 159; bound by custom, 157, 158.

Scepticism, a duty in science, 423.

School, function of, 327; power of, 5, 6, 7; method and machinery of, correlatives, 524; bad effect of, on health, 476; present type repellant, 270; early schooling to repress, 504; a "listening school," 492; *see also* Education; Education and social progress; Democracy and education; Administration of schools.

School administration. *See* Administration of schools.

Science, contrasted with magic, 32; does not foster fatalism, 31; demanded by Labor party, 233; dangerous to females and children, 257, 422.

Secondary neurone connections, 110.

Self, an aggregate of habits and reactions, 57, 77; a center of choices, 76; essentially active, 115, 194; humans always active, 517; dependent on social inheritance, 41; built simultaneously with socius, 100; identification of self in interest, 510; double personality, 75; many potential selves, 74; the broad self, 78 b. *See also* Divided self; Individual, nature of; Individuality.

Selfishness, defined, 188; dangerous to society, 62; not sufficient, 185; works for general good, 184; national selfishness, 238, 239, 308; of vested interests, 199, 225, 336, 431.

Serial transfer, 189, 190.

Severity makes hypocrites, 497.

Shaw, Bernard, education in the schools, 227; the illusion of progress, 373.

Simultaneous learnings, 112, 270, 480, 553.

Smith, Adam, on natural aristocracy, 211.

Social control (Chapter XII, 286-311): society steadily encroaching, 286; coercion not democratic, 296; not a matter of "training," 282; freedom not permanent, 437; government not a success, 216; function of force, 294, 295; tyranny of, 288, 290, 318; public education a means of, 19; influence of endowed thought, 336; free speech in relation to, 291; the place of the expert, 353; lessening public confidence, 427; irreconcilability, 292; anarchy, 301, 444; herd conduct, 71; herd theory of conscience, 104; Napoleon's ideas on, 10, 12; Hobbes on, 293. *See also* Majority; Minority rights; Freedom of speech and press;

INDEX OF SUBJECTS

Revolutions; Puritanism; Might and right; Propagandism; Mobilization of thought power; State; Nationalism.

Social inheritance (Chapter III, 37-45): defined and discussed, 39, 40; value of, 38, 41, 43; more important than biological, 38; foundation of progress, 37; how custom forms habits, 399; as social mind, 58; power of the mores, 42; of savages, 157, 158.

Social mind, discussed, 58.

Social progress. *See* Progress; Education and social progress.

Social solidarity, how secured, 63.

Social psychology, the problem of, 54.

Social stability in a dynamic society (Chapter XVI, 413-441): discussed, 426; how maintained, 59, 163, 416, 419; effect of education, 242, 278, 383, 398, 402; place of institutions, 59; relation of conservatism to, 419, 430, 435; moral unrest, 300, 416, 425, 426; change inevitable, 441; government not a success, 216; lessening public confidence, 427; disintegration from democracy, 62, 198; plasticity of mind needed, 430; fearless thinking needed, 278; discussion and progress, 415; intellectual interest alone dynamic, 440; permanent progressiveness, 439. *See also* Progress; Education and social progress; Revolutions; Conservatism; Freedom of speech and press.

Socialism, defined and contrasted, 444.

Socialization (Chapter V, 61-72): related to individualization, 96, 98, 162, 244, 282; personality and sharing, 244; not an external process, 282; the good life social, 61, 149, 192; increasing integration inevitable, 70; dangers to, 62, 206; democracy disintegrates, 62, 198; foreign language schools, 450; herd conduct, 71.

Society, the nature of (Chapter IV, 46-60): natural, 54, 165; unnatural, 55, 160, 161; a process of sharing, 56; consists of many associations, 51, 52; nature of associations, 46; depends on communication, 65; needs homogeneity, 63; ties that form, 53; founded on exchange, 57; definition of group, 50; not formed of discrete entities, 54, 99; may disintegrate, 62; the social mind, 58; herd conduct, 71; herd theory of conscience, 104. *See also* Individual and society; Socialization; Association; Great society.

Socius, defined, 99; built simultaneously with self, 100.

Socrates, on the good, 129.

Specialization, dangers of excessive, 95.

Spencer, Herbert: on happiness, 143; on the failure of severity, 497; education for morals, 538.

Spinoza, definition of freedom, 91.

Stability of character, declining, 426.

Stability, social. *See* Social stability in a dynamic society.

State, theories of, 208, 443, 444; "prior" to individual, 98; subordinate to sharing, 56; government not yet successful, 216; anarchy, 301, 444; anarchy, socialism, and laissez-faire, 444; failure of laissez-faire, 442; communism, 186; the present emphasis, 443; subordination of individual to, 193; who shall govern, 213; sovereignty, 311; independent of ethics, 306, 308; Hegel on, 193, 208; Treitschke on, 307. *See also* Nationalism, Social control.

State and education (Chapter XVII, 442-451): Jefferson on local control, 15; William II on, 19; Rousseau on, 406; public education on evil, 445; Oregon (1922) school law, 451; Michigan (1921) law, 446. *See also* State; Democracy and education; Roman Catholicism; Private schools; Parochial schools.

INDEX OF SUBJECTS

Status, characteristic of primitive life, 204; change from status to choice, 415.
Stein, education as harmonious unfolding, 454.
Stoics, on the good life, 153.
Stratification, social, 206.
Struggle for existence, defined, 382.
Subject matter: Subject matter and curriculum, 465-491 (Chapter XIX); the race experience, 264; not fixed or outside child, 265, 468; how conceived on growth theory, 467; technique as an end, 469, 475; deferred values, 461, 488; dictated from above, 265, 285; English not a subject, 491. *See also* Educative process; Curriculum; Curriculum making.
Subjects, school: Bonser on, 488; English not a subject, 491.
Success, service of, 508; zeal a main factor in, 269.
Superstitions, 32.
Supervision of schools, democratic respect for personality, 284.
Suppression, of impulses, 95; ill effects of, 94; breaking the will, 546, 547; broken spirit of Andean Indians, 503. *See also* Asceticism; Expression.

Talking, children's, extent of, 478.
Taste, education of, Goethe on, 490.
Teachers, why incompetent, 285 (1); democratic participation of, 285 (1).
Technique, as an end, 469; of the artist, 475.
Temptation, service of, 536.
Thinking: Thinking and education, 529-535 (Chapter XXI); process of deliberation, 27, 529, 541; significance of, 278, 473, 505; place of, in experience, 30, 489; place of, in affairs, 336, 384, 440; aim in, 27; guided by a problem, 265, 473; ideas make for control, 29; reflective attention, 530; involved in construction, 473; moral deliberation, 541; function of doubt, 278, 326, 423, 424; free thinking, 278; why endowed, often futile, 336, 440; possibilities of intelligent management, 316; follow the argument, 314; with the Athenians, 433. *See also* Attention; Control; Critical attitude.
Thought power available, 315. *See also* Mobilization of thought power.
Tiger story, 522 b.
Toryism, 202, 203.
Training, as a rival to true education, 247, 249; effect of, 401; Prussianized, in our schools, 282; in religious education, 245, 246; Kant on, 243; early schooling for, 504. *See also* Education; Method.
Trial and error (success), discussed, 523.
Treitschke, on the power of the state, 307.
Truth, defined, 4.
Uniformity: America overstandardized, 72.

University, place in democracy, 409; education for citizenship, 407; less important than elementary education to Jefferson, 13. *See also* Academic Freedom.

Variation, place of, in development, 456; an advantage to society, 408; repressed in primitive life, 421.
Vocational education, problem of, 273, 276; exploitation in, 274; real efficiency not materialistic, 275.
Voltaire, character and attitude, 9; on freedom of speech, 337; freeing fools, hard, 401.

War, not inevitable, 317; relations with democracy, 296; relations with nationalism, 309; Cobden on the unreason in, 398. *See also* Military.

Wesley, John, breaking the will, 546; against play, 8.

Will, consists of habits, 77; a main factor in success, 269; will to win, 385; "breaking" the will, 546, 547; broken spirit of Andean Indians, 503.

William II, order to schools (1889), 19; on military virtues, 252.

Wisdom, lingers, 466.

Wolf's experiment: self expression in industry, 232.

Zeno the Stoic, on the good, 138.